THE DICTIONARY OF

Developmental and Educational Psychology

THE DICTIONARY OF

Developmental and Educational Psychology

EDITED BY

Rom Harré and Roger Lamb

ADVISORY EDITORS

Peter Bryant
R. Maliphant

BLACKWELL REFERENCE

Based on material from *The encyclopedic dictionary of psychology*, first published 1983.

Copyright © Basil Blackwell Ltd 1986
© Editorial organization Rom Harré and Roger Lamb 1983, 1986

First published 1986

Basil Blackwell Ltd
108 Cowley Road, Oxford OX4 1JF, UK

BRITISH LIBRARY CATALOGUING IN PUBLICATION DATA

The Dictionary of developmental and educational psychology.
1. Developmental psychology — Dictionaries
I. Harré, Rom   II. Lamb, Roger
155'.03'21   BF713

ISBN 0-631-14603-2
ISBN 0-631-14604-0 Pbk

Typeset in 9 on 10pt Linotron Ehrhardt
by Oxford Publishing Services, Oxford
Printed in Great Britain by Page Bros (Norwich), Ltd

CONTENTS

PREFACE

The highly successful and comprehensive *Encyclopedic dictionary of psychology* included a dozen psychological specialities. The editors have selected, updated and supplemented material from the original dictionary to provide in this and similar volumes a compact but compendious coverage of the most widely studied of these specialities. In preparing the independent dictionaries we have had in mind the needs of both students and practitioners in many branches of psychology and allied fields. In addition to this volume which concentrates on developmental and educational psychology, three further volumes cover physiological and clinical psychology, personality and social psychology, and ethology and animal learning.

The selected articles have been brought up to date, and the bibliographies have been revised to include the most recent publications. Many new entries have been added to fill the inevitable gaps of the first edition. The number of biographies of great psychologists has been increased to help to bring the research process and its scientific findings to life.

Psychology has developed within several different conceptual frameworks, often treating the same subject matter with very different assumptions and methods. We have tried, we hope without being uncritically eclectic, to reflect a wide range of approaches to human thought and behavior, including those popular in academic, applied and clinical branches of psychology.

Rom Harré and Roger Lamb

ACKNOWLEDGMENTS

The Editors and Publisher are grateful for permission to reproduce the following illustrations:

development of the nervous system

Blackwell Scientific Publications. (Redrawn from J. G. Beaumont, *Introduction to neuropsychology*, (1983), p. 28.)

CONTRIBUTORS

Jeffrey W. Adams   JWA
Brunel University

Jeffrey R. Alberts   JRAl
Indiana University

John Archer   JA
Preston Polytechnic

James R. Averill   JRAv
University of Massachusetts

Phillip J. Bairstow   PJB
University of London

Jack I. Bardon   JIB
University of North Carolina, Greensboro

Jane Barrett   JBa
Medical Research Council on the Development and Integration of Behaviour, Cambridge

Michael Basseches   MBa
Cornell University

Suzanne Benack   SBe
Union College, Schnectady

Michael Berger   MBe
University of London

Marion Blank   MB
Rutgers University

David E. Bond   DEB
Royal School for the Deaf, Margate

Peter E. Bryant   PEB
University of Oxford

George E. Butterworth   GEB
University of Southampton

Anne Campbell   AC
Temple University, Philadelphia

Joseph J. Campos   JJCa
University of Denver

Janet Caplan   JSC
Williams College, Massachusetts

Karen Stojak Caplovitz   KSC
University of Denver

Neil M. Cheshire   NMC
University College of N. Wales, Bangor

Guy Claxton   GCl
University of London

Tony I. Cline   TIC
Inner London Education Authority

Joel Cooper   JCo
Princeton University

Richard F. Cromer   RFC
Medical Research Council Cognitive Development Unit, London

Gerald C. Cupchick   GCC
University of Toronto

Nancy Datan   ND
West Virginia University

Cliff J. Denton   CJD
University of Oxford

J. A. Edmondson   JAE
University of Texas, Arlington

Roger P. Elbourne   RPE
Brunel University

Robert N. Emde   RNE
University of Denver

Ronald Fletcher   RF
University of Reading (Emeritus Professor)

Gillian C. Forrest GCF
Park Hospital for Children, Oxford

John Forrester JF
University of Cambridge

N. H. Freeman NHF
University of Bristol

Uta Frith UF
Medical Research Council Cognitive Development Unit, London

Adrian Furnham AF
University of London

David M. Galloway DMG
University of Wellington

M. A. G. Garman MAGG
University of Reading

Marianthi Georgoudi MG
Temple University, Philadelphia

Kenneth J. Gergen KJG
Swarthmore College, Pennsylvania

Ronald Gulliford RG
University of Birmingham

Milton D. Hakel MDH
Ohio State University

David Hargreaves DHH
University of Oxford

Rom Harré RHa
University of Oxford

R. W. Hiorns RWH
University of Oxford

Robert Hogan RHo
Johns Hopkins University

Gary P. Horowitz GPH
State University of New York, Binghamton

Charles Hulme ChasH
University of York

Chris M. Hutton CMH
University of Oxford

R. R. Jacobs RRJ
Pennsylvania State University

Joseph M. F. Jaspars JMFJ
Formerly University of Oxford

Carl N. Johnson CNJ
University of Pittsburgh

Gregory V. Jones GVJ
University of Bristol

Shirley J. Kavanagh SJK
London

Hans Kummer HK
University of Zurich

Roger Lamb RL
University of Oxford

D. Legge DL
North Staffordshire Polytechnic

Howard Leventhal HL
University of Wisconsin, Madison

Barbara B. Lloyd BBL
University of Sussex

Edwin A. Locke EAL
University of Maryland

Ingrid Lunt IL
Inner London Education Authority

Robert McHenry RMcH
University of Oxford

N. J. Mackintosh NJM
University of Cambridge

Rodney Maliphant RM
University of London

W. A. Marshall WAM
University of Technology, Loughborough

Richard A. Mayou RAM
University of Oxford

Luciano Mecacci LM
University of Rome

John E. Merritt JEM
Open University

Alexandre Métraux   AM
University of Heidelberg

Janet Milewski   JM
Rutgers University

Susanna Millar   SMi
University of Oxford

Peter J. Mortimore   PJM
Inner London Education Authority

Peter Mühlhäusler   PM
University of Oxford

John R. Nesselroade   JRN
Pennsylvania State University

Stephen Nowicki Jr   SN
University of Emory, Atlanta, Georgia

W. Ll. Parry-Jones   WLlP-J
University of Oxford

Renée B. Paton-Saltzberg   RBP-S
Oxford Polytechnic

Michael Pressley   MP
University of Western Ontario

Patrick Rabbitt   PR
University of Durham

Lindsay T. Sharpe   LTS
University of Freiburg

Mildred L. G. Shaw   MLGS
York University, Ontario

J. M. Shorter   JMS
University of Oxford

John J. Sidtis   JJS
Cornell University

Richard R. Skemp   RRS
University of Warwick

Peter K. Smith   PKS
University of Sheffield

Saradha D. Supramaniam   SDS
Open University

Kathy Sylva   KS
University of Oxford

David C. Taylor   DCT
University of Manchester

Talbot J. Taylor   TJT
University of Oxford

Michael J. Tobin   MJT
University of Birmingham

Richard G. Totman   RGT
University of Sussex

Philip E. Vernon   PEV
University of Calgary

Peter B. Warr   PBW
University of Sheffield

K. Wedell   KW
University of London

H. Weinrich-Haste   HW-H
University of Bath

Andrew Whiten   AW
University of St Andrews

Glayde Whitney   GW
Florida State University

Anna K. Wright   AKW
Surrey County Council

EDITORIAL NOTE

Asterisks against titles in the bibliographies indicate items suitable for further reading. The convention 1920 (1986) indicates a work first published in 1920 but widely accessible only in an edition of 1986, to which the publication details given refer.

Cross references to other entries are printed in small capitals in the text. Leads to further additional information can be found from the index.

A

able children *See* gifted children.

absence from school and truancy
"Absence from school" is failure to attend school irrespective of reason whereas "truancy" is unjustifiable absence from school without parental knowledge or consent. In England parents are required by the 1981 Education Act to ensure that their children receive education 'suitable to their age, ability, and aptitude and special educational needs' between the ages of five and sixteen. In practice, most parents do this by registering their child at a school maintained or aided by the local education authority and ensuring that he or she attends regularly unless prevented by illness or religious observance. Similar laws exist in the United States and most other developed countries although the ages of compulsory schooling vary: children in the United States, for example, are not legally required to attend school before the age of six.

There are remarkable consistencies in rates of school attendance. Cutter and Jones (1971) found a 90 per cent attendance rate in a sample of American elementary schools. Rates in Britain are similar; indeed the proportion of pupils absent has remained stable throughout the twentieth century: 89 per cent attendance at London Board Schools in 1906 (Rubinstein 1969); 89 per cent attendance in the Inner London Education Authority's schools in 1970 (Hill 1971); and a Department of Education and Science survey reported that on a given day in January 1974 90.1 per cent of all pupils aged twelve or over in England and Wales were present. This survey also showed that absence rates were highest in the final year of compulsory education, and similar trends have been found in the United States.

There has been sharp disagreement about the proportion of absent pupils who are absent illegally. Estimates range from 4 per cent (DES 1967) to 75 per cent (Reynolds and Murgatroyd 1974). A study by Galloway (1982) showed that from a sample of British schools 4 per cent of pupils were recorded as absent illegally for at least 50 per cent of their final year. The difficulties in establishing the illegality of a pupil's absence are considerable; it is likely that many published figures have given an over-optimistic view.

Traditionally clinical practice has distinguished between SCHOOL PHOBIA, also known as school refusal, and truancy. Children referred to clinics for school phobia tend to be younger (Tyerman 1958; Hersov 1960). While Hersov and Tyerman both noted poor social adjustment, low average IQ and low educational attainments, Cooper (1966) found no evidence of educational retardation relative to IQ.

Truancy and school phobia together account for a very small proportion of absences from both primary and secondary schools. By far the most common explanations in Galloway's study (1982) were 'absence with parental knowledge, consent and approval', and 'parents unable or unwilling to insist on return'. It is clear that parents are aware of their children's absence in a large majority of cases, and in roughly half these cases the parents withhold their children from school. In the remainder, the child insists on remaining at home, with the parents unable or unwilling to insist on return.

Surprisingly little attention has been directed at reasons for parents condoning their children's absence from school. A high positive correlation has been demonstrated in Belfast and Sheffield between parental poverty and persistent absentee

1

rates (Harbison and Caven 1977; Galloway 1982). Harbison and Caven did not find this association in rural areas of Northern Ireland. It seems probable that absence from school and poverty may both arise from other variables associated with depressed inner city areas. (See also SOCIAL DISADVANTAGE.)

This suggestion received some support in a study of all persistent absentees in one area of Sheffield (Galloway 1982). Parents of absentees were significantly more likely to be unemployed than parents of good attenders selected from the same class in school and living in the same areas. More important, a health questionnaire revealed a high prevalence of probable psychiatric illness in the mothers of absent pupils. The most common symptoms were those associated with depression. Anxiety about parental health was frequently associated with absence, but social, educational and disciplinary problems at school became increasingly important in the secondary school years.

Several studies have reported poor attenders as being less successful on tests of educational attainment and general intelligence than regular attenders (see TESTS: EDUCATIONAL ATTAINMENT). There is disagreement about whether educational retardation is the cause or the result of poor attendance. May (1975) argued that poor attenders were performing badly at school before their irregular attendance started. It has also been demonstrated that poor attenders at the age of seven were not educationally retarded at the age of sixteen, compared with their peers, if they were attending regularly at fifteen. On the other hand, continued poor attendance at fifteen was related to poor attainment. This suggests that absentees who miss a considerable amount of schooling at an early age can catch up through subsequent regular attendance, and hence that the poor attainments of the continued absentees whose teachers did not regard them as truants may be causally related to that absence. Tennent (1971) listed twenty studies of juvenile or adult offenders which reported at least 20 per cent of the sample having a history of truancy. May

(1975) found that truants were more likely to have criminal records than absentees whose teachers did not regard them as truants. Galloway (1982) found that over 20 per cent of boys whose parents condoned their absence from school had criminal records; this also applied to 19 per cent of boys whose absence was attributed mainly to illness. The general picture is one of a consistent association between truancy and DELINQUENCY, and of a slightly less consistent association between absenteeism and delinquency. Nevertheless, it should be emphasized that a majority of poor attenders are not known to offend.

There appears to be a substantial overlap between school drop-out and truancy. Many American studies on individuals who leave school without qualifications show them to end up with low occupational status, higher likelihood of being unemployed, and decreased participation in adult education. Because truancy is associated with early school leaving, it is often difficult to tell whether it is the truancy *per se* or the lack of qualifications that leads directly to the adult outcome.

Robins and Ratcliff (1980) investigated the long-term effects of truancy on the lives of a large sample of black males, all of whom had attended ordinary state schools in St. Louis and had been above average in ability. The men were interviewed at 30–36 years of age while at the same time their records on education, housing, armed forces, police and hospital files were scrutinized. In this large group of men high truancy was found to be associated with school drop-out and later with low earnings and deviant behavior in adulthood. These poor adult outcomes were in part explained by the truants' dropping out of school and by their adolescent deviance, but the authors stress that the 'truancy itself continued to have predictive power even when these intermediary events were taken into account' (p.80). On the basis of their research Robins and Ratcliff urged measures to prevent truancy which, if successful, could be expected not only to affect truancy levels, but 'to forestall a variety of related deviant acts that may otherwise appear later' (p.80).

Greater attention has been paid to family and social variables in poor school attenders than to the school's own contribution in promoting regular attendance. Reynolds and Murgatroyd (1977) reported consistent differences in attendance rates between Welsh secondary modern schools with similar catchment areas (see SCHOOL DIFFERENCES), differences associated with the school's rules and policies rather than with structural variables such as size or age of buildings. More recently Rutter et al. (1979) have reported significant differences in attendance rates between London schools, after controlling for intake variables. Galloway (1982) demonstrated significant changes in persistent absentee rates within individual schools over a period of three years. His evidence suggests that the school's influence on attendance is greatest in disadvantaged areas where the likelihood of absence is highest in the first place.

There have been few systematic studies on either the prognosis or the management of absence from school. Galloway (1985) reported that legal action is taken against only a very small proportion of persistent unauthorized absentees. The prognosis following legal action was extremely poor, but substantial improvement was associated with a change of school when this was arranged for some special reason, rather than as an ordinary age-related transfer (Galloway et al 1982). More recently many local education authorities have established special centers for poor attenders. However, these are only able to cater for a very small minority of the pupils in question, and systematic studies of their effect on subsequent attendance are conspicuously absent.

There is no simple explanation for absence from school. Variables within the individual and within his or her family, home neighborhood and school are all likely to be important. A comprehensive assessment is required in each case, focusing on the school's provision for the pupil as well as on the pupil and his or her background. Successful management requires parental cooperation with assistance from teachers and members of the educational and social work support services.

DMG

Bibliography

Cooper, M.G. 1966: School refusal. *Educational research* 8, 223–9.

Cutter, N.C. and Jones, E.R. 1971: Evaluation of ESEA Title VIII Dropout Prevention Program-Project KAPS' School Year. 1970–71. Mimeo. Quoted in Robins and Ratcliff 1980: op. cit.

Department of Education and Science, 1974: Press Notice: *Results of school absence survey.* London: DES.

Galloway, D. 1982: A study of persistent absentees and their families. *British journal of educational psychology* 52 (3), 317–30.

—— 1985: *Schools and persistent absentees.* Oxford: Pergamon.

——, Ball, C., Blomfield, D. and Seyd, R. 1982: *Schools and disruptive pupils.* London: Longman.

Harbison, J. and Caven, N. 1977: *Persistent school absenteeism in Northern Ireland.* Belfast: Statistics and Economics Unit, Dept. of Finance (Northern Ireland).

Hathaway, S.R., Reynolds, P.C. and Monachesi, E.D. 1969: Follow up of the later careers and lives of 1,000 boys who dropped out of high school. *Journal of consulting clinical psychology* 33, 370–80.

Hersov, L. 1960: Refusal to go to school. *Journal of child psychology and psychiatry* 2, 137–45.

May, D. 1975: Truancy, school absenteeism and delinquency. *Scottish educational studies* 7, 97–107.

Reynolds, D. and Murgatroyd, S. 1974: Being absent from school. *British journal of law and society* 1, 78–80.

—— 1977: The sociology of schooling and the absent pupil: the school as a factor in the generation of truancy. In *Absenteeism in South Wales: studies of pupils, their homes and their secondary schools,* ed. H.C.M. Carroll. Swansea: University College of Swansea, Faculty of Education.

Robins, L.N. and Ratcliff, K.S. 1980: The long-term outcome of truancy. In *Out of school,* eds. L. Hersov and I. Berg. London: Wiley.

Rubinstein, D. 1969: *School attendance in*

London, 1870–1904: A social history. Hull: University of Hull.

Rutter, M. et al. 1979: *Fifteen thousand hours: secondary schools and their effects on pupils*. London: Open Books; Cambridge, Mass.: Harvard University Press.

Tennent, T.G. 1971: School non-attendance and delinquency. *Educational research* 13, 185–90.

Tyerman, M.J. 1958: A research into truancy. *British journal of educational psychology* 28, 217–25.

accommodation In PIAGET's theory of cognitive development accommodation is adaptation as the result of pressures exerted by the environment. In Piaget's words (1936; 1952), 'mental life is accommodation to the environment'. In his view, however, 'adaptation is an equilibrium between assimilation and accommodation' (p. 18). Accommodation 'cannot be dissociated from progressive assimilation' (p. 45), and, in fact, presupposes it (p. 162). Flavell (1963) points out that the assimilation-accommodation model is basic to Piaget's theory, and provides 'the crucial link between biology and intelligence', since it is derived from 'more primitive activities' such as digestion. When digesting food the organism incorporates what it eats and thereby "assimilates" it. But the organism also accommodates to different foods, chewing some more than others and producing different chemical combinations to break different foods down. The accommodation-assimilation model therefore 'permits us to see intelligence in its proper context' as an extension of those activities (Flavell 1963).

Piaget describes the development of sensori-motor and cognitive SCHEMAS out of basic reflex actions. In sucking the nipple, the infant's 'contact with the object and repetitions of the action modify the activity of the reflex' (1936; 1952). After that 'sucking . . . a new object such as the thumb . . . transforms the schema' (sc. of sucking), since the infant has now learnt to apply an established action to a novel object. This produces a gain in control over the world by reducing (assimilating)

extra parts of the world to an established action-schema, and at the same time accommodating the action-schema to novel demands.

A similar process of adaptation occurs in cognitive growth. 'Intelligence is assimilation to the extent that it incorporates all the given data of experience within its framework' (p. 18), but 'assimilation can never be pure because by incorporating new elements into its earlier schemata the intelligence constantly modifies the latter in order to adjust them to new elements'. When an infant is acquiring its first habits, accommodation and assimilation are bound together in an undifferentiated way, since the attempts to assimilate novelty oblige the infant to accommodate to it. When the infant begins to explore its environment physically ("effective groping") and mentally, it develops an interest in novelty for its own sake, and 'accommodation becomes an end in itself'. The deliberate accommodation involved in experimentation and search for new means to solve problems then becomes differentiated from assimilation of novel problems to old solutions. The two processes, however, alternate and remain interdependent. (See also ASSIMILATION.)

RL

Bibliography

Flavell, J.H. 1963: *The developmental psychology of Jean Piaget*. New York: Van Nostrand Reinhold.

Piaget, J. 1936 (1952): *La naissance de l'intelligence chez l'enfant*. Trans. *The origins of intelligence in children*. New York: International Universities Press; London: Routledge and Kegan Paul (1953). Also published by Penguin, 1977.

———— 1983: Piaget's theory. In *Handbook of child psychology*, vol. 1. 4th edn, ed. W. Kessen. New York: Wiley.

achievement motivation This concept was developed by McClelland (see McClelland et al. 1953) and refers to the motive to achieve some standard of accomplishment or proficiency. People with a strong achievement motive (which McClelland calls need for achievement) prefer moderate to easy or hard goals or risks, want concrete feedback regarding task performance, prefer tasks where skill rather than luck determines the outcome, seek personal responsibility, have a future time perspective, and err somewhat on the side of optimism in estimating their chances for success, especially on new tasks. McClelland (1961) claims that the achievement motive is crucial in entrepreneurship and influences success in entrepreneurial occupations (e.g. selling); he has even claimed that cultural differences in achievement motivation account for differences in economic growth rates. It is argued that the need for achievement is fostered by child rearing practices which encourage independence. It is held by McClelland to be a subconscious motive, and therefore it can be measured more accurately by projective techniques, such as the Thematic Apperception Test, than by self reports. Research on achievement motivation has been criticized on numerous grounds, including: unreliability of the Thematic Apperception Test measures; inconsistency of results; excessive use of post hoc explanations when the results failed to turn out as predicted; and ethnocentrism. Heckhausen (1967) and Atkinson and Raynor (1978) have summarized much of the achievement motivation research.   EAL

Bibliography
Atkinson, J.W. and Raynor, J.O. 1978: *Personality, motivation and achievement*. New York: Hemisphere.
Heckhausen, H. 1967: *The anatomy of achievement motivation*. New York: Academic Press.
McClelland, D.C. 1961: *The achieving society*. Princeton: Van Nostrand.
———— et al. 1953: *The achievement motive*. New York: Appleton-Century-Crofts.
Nicholl, J. ed. 1984: *The development of achievement motivation*. Greenwich, Conn.: JAI.

adaptation in infants Those characteristics and processes which, in the course of development, fit the infant to the environment. Some characteristics of the newborn are preadapted to the evolutionarily predictable structures of the physical and social milieu. Behaviors essential for survival, such as sucking, are well organized and may even have been "practiced" *in utero*. Other behavior such as neonatal imitation, reaching for objects or looking in the direction of sound may also be preadapted, although they undoubtedly undergo further development. The process of adaptation may depend upon a considerable degree of plasticity in the nervous system (see PLASTICITY: PHYSIOLOGICAL CONCEPT). There is evidence that the nervous system adapts to repeatedly encountered characteristics of the environment during the early months of life. For example, cells in the visual cortex responsible for coding spatial orientation are subject to considerable modification in the first few weeks of life depending on the particular characteristics of the visual environment.   GEB

Bibliography
Walk, Richard and Pick, Herbert L. Jr. 1978: *Perception and experience*. New York and London: Plenum.

Adler, Alfred (1870–1937) After graduating in medicine in 1895, Adler soon took up psychoanalytical theory and became one of its most authoritative representatives. In 1910 he was president of the Psychoanalytical Society of Vienna but resigned the following year, thereby demonstrating his split with Freud. In 1926 he visited the United States where he became professor first at Columbia University (1927), and then at Long Island Medical College, New York (1932). Adler's theory of "individual psychology" is based on the concepts of "striving for superiority" and "inferiority feelings". Individuals from their childhood are led by a dominant drive to compensate and overcome their biological inferiority feelings (only symbiosis with the mother protects the child from the environment). Inferiority feelings sometimes continue into adult life because of psychological or social deprivations. The individual is therefore committed to a continuous process of self-realization in a social context.

"Style of life" is the term used for the forms of behavior through which individuals strive to affirm themselves. By moving the emphasis from the biological determinants of behavior to the psychosocial processes of self-affirmation, social interests and style of life, Adler's work has been very influential in post-Freudian psychoanalytical theory. (See also NEO-FREUDIAN THEORY.)   LM

Bibliography
Adler, A. 1927: *The practice and theory of individual psychology*. New York: Harcourt, Brace; London: Routledge and Kegan Paul.
—— 1939: *Social interest*. New York: Putnam; London: Faber and Faber.
Way, L. 1956: *Alfred Adler: an introduction to his psychology*. London: Penguin.

adolescence A transitional period of life between childhood and adulthood. There is more controversy than agreement among psychologists regarding the exact beginning and end of adolescence. Various physiological changes (e.g. growth spurts, maturation of reproductive organs, emergence of secondary sex characteristics – see PUBERTY) and psychological changes (e.g. emergence of logical thinking); increased interest in sexuality and the opposite sex; preoccupation with issues of identity, increased peer-conformity and increased responsibility have been identified as indicators of adolescence. However, no consensus exists on which changes define adolescence and which are frequent but non-essential characteristics of adolescents.

Adolescence is as much a social construction as an attribute of the individual. Some cultures and subcultures recognize a transitional period of a decade or more between childhood and adulthood while other cultures view the transition as occurring in the course of a brief initiation rite which may last only a few days or hours. The social construction of a lengthy adolescence has been traced to the creation of a juvenile justice system, child labor laws, and compulsory education laws during the nineteenth century emergence of an urban/industrial culture (Bakan 1971).

In practice, the study of adolescence encompasses all individuals who are psychosocially neither unambiguously children nor adults. An individual may be said to enter adolescence when he or she no longer views him/herself as a child (nor wants or expects to be treated as such), or when others begin to expect more mature behavior from him or her than they do from a child. Physical changes *or* psychological changes either in oneself *or* one's peers (or simply reaching a culturally specified chronological age) may precipitate this change in psychosocial status, which may then bring with it further psychological adjustments and modifications of social relations. An individual eventually achieves adult psychosocial status and leaves adolescence by successfully adopting some culturally specified adult role. This requires both the psychological capacity and willingness to perform the role on the part of the individual, and the culture's confirmation of the individual as a successful role-occupant. Historical factors often influence the difficulty of resolving the adolescent transition (e.g. high unemployment may decrease a culture's willingness to confer adult status).

MBa

Bibliography
Bakan, D. 1971: Adolescence in America: from idea to social fact. *Daedalus* Fall 1971, 979–96.
Canger, J.J. 1975: *Contemporary issues in adolescent development*. New York and London: Harper and Row.
Grotevant, H.D. and Cooper, C.R. 1985: Patterns of interaction in family relationships and the development of identity exploration in adolescence. *Child development* 56, 415–28. (See section on Family development and the child in this issue of *Child development*.)

adolescence: development in The period of human development beginning with puberty and culminating in the attainment of adult maturity. It cannot be given any precise limits, but in general it it covers the age-span from twelve to eighteen years.

It is a time of rapid physiological and psychological change, of intensive re-adjustment to family, school, work and social life and of preparation for adult roles. The processes of adolescent socialization and role-change are potentially stressful. Phase-specific maturational tasks can be identified, associated with these changes, particularly the physical, cognitive and emotional development. The sequence of physical changes at puberty involve an increased rate of growth in stature and weight (see ADOLESCENT GROWTH SPURT), development of the secondary sexual characteristics and the reproductive system (see MENARCHE) (Tanner 1962). The timing and effects of physical maturation have a number of psychological correlates and, in particular, rapid bodily change can have a powerful effect on self-concept. The variation in the age of onset and rate of the "growth spurt" and the impact of both early and late development have far-reaching effects. In boys, delayed maturation may lead to a feeling of low self-confidence and inferiority. Although the effects in girls are less marked, early menarche may be associated with negative feelings. Following puberty there is an upsurge of sexuality and an increase in heterosexual interests and behavior (Schofield 1965). There may be a passing phase of intense attachment to persons of the same sex but this does not appear to be related to adult homosexuality. The comfortable acceptance of appropriate sex-roles is an important part of identity development. Despite changing social attitudes toward sexual behavior in recent decades, in the direction of greater sexual freedom, and the pressures for early sexual experience, there is no evidence of increasing promiscuity and sexual behavior remains a major source of anxiety and uncertainty for young people. The value of sex education, and the effectiveness of different approaches, is difficult to assess. The majority of adolescents, however, favor sex education in a responsible way. Changes in intellectual function have far-reaching implications for behavior and attitudes. PIAGET described the transition from the stage of "concrete operations" to formal operational thinking following PUBERTY, enabling the adolescent to think in an abstract way, to construct hypotheses and to adopt a deductive approach in solving problems (see Inhelder and Piaget 1958; Elkind 1968). These changes in adolescent reasoning are reflected in scholastic learning, in personality development, in the growth of moral judgment (see Kohlberg 1969) and political thinking. (There are now some doubts about the psychological reality of alleged adolescent cognitive developments in moral reasoning (see Murphy and Gilligan 1980). They may be a reflection of socially defined norms of behavior.) The move toward maturity requires gradual emancipation from the home, the establishment of an independent life-style, a conscious sense of individual uniqueness, commitment to a sexual orientation and a vocational direction and the development of self-control. Self-concept development in adolescence is a complex process (see Coleman 1980). Erikson's contribution to the understanding of identity formation in adolescence has had a major influence (1968; see also Marcia 1980). He described the adolescent tasks of establishing a coherent identity and overcoming identity diffusion, but went further to indicate that some form of crisis was a necessary and expected phase in this process. This concept of a "normative crisis" has, nevertheless, been the most controversial part of Erikson's work and it has not been supported by research.

The course and successful completion of adolescence is influenced by a wide variety of factors. The function of parents is crucial in providing models of adult roles and in facilitating the individuation of adolescents (see Grotevant and Cooper 1985). Despite popular views to the contrary and frequent reference to the "generation gap", conflict between adolescents and parents is rarely substantial or long-standing (see Rutter et al. 1976; White et al. 1983) and parents remain a significant influence throughout adolescence. However, the adolescent's quest for independence and challenge of parental standards, values and attainments can pose a major threat and adolescent behavior can have a disequilibrating effect on marital and family homeostasis. Further, adolescence is often a time of idealism, when society's standards and morals are examined, challenged or rejected. Outside the home, adolescence is shaped by the school, the immediate peer group and contemporary youth culture. Wider social, cultural and political factors also have direct consequences, including increasing social complexity and moral confusion (Kitwood 1980), the ambiguity in the status and role prescription for adolescents, the prolonged dependence of adolescents engaged in further and higher education, the consequences of unemployment and the effects of mixed racial society. Friendships with other young people play an important part in adolescence particularly during the period of detachment from the family. The pattern of these relationships changes during early, middle and late adolescence (Coleman 1974). The peer group has a supportive function and a powerful influence on behavior, particularly in its pressure for conformity and social popularity and, in this way, it plays an important part in adolescent socialization. The relative attractiveness of the peer group is influenced by the quality of relationships within the home, parental attitudes toward it, and the nature of the adolescent problems, since adolescents perceive parents and peers as useful guides in different areas of experience.

Some degree of anxiety and the experience of tension is likely to be related to coping with maturational changes, and the acquisition of new roles, particularly since there are no clear-cut rules about how to progress to adulthood or when the process is complete. Disturbance is most likely to occur at times of transition and the extent of the anxiety is partly a reflection of the adolescent's perception of the balance of stress and support. The idea that adolescence is characterized by "storm and stress" has been a consistent feature of major theories of adolescence. The psychoanalytic view, expressed by Anna Freud (1958), was that 'adolescence is by its nature an interruption of peaceful growth' and this notion was in keeping with Erikson's concept of identity crisis. There is substantial evidence, however, that although rapid mood swings, feelings of misery, self-doubts and self-consciousness are common in adolescence and may lead to personal suffering, only a small number show emotional distress or do experience a disturbance of identity relating to their sense of self in the present. Psychiatric disorders occurring during adolescence include those present since childhood and those arising initially in this age-period (see Rutter and Hersov 1977). The full range of disorders occurring in later age-periods may be found. The key task in diagnosis is the differentiation of psychiatric disorders from age-appropriate reactions that may settle when stress is reduced or eliminated with further development and the passage of time.   WL.IP-J

Bibliography

Coleman, John C. 1974: *Relationships in adolescence*. London and Boston: Routledge and Kegan Paul.

—— 1980: *The nature of adolescence*. London and New York: Methuen.

Elkind, D. 1968: Cognitive development in adolescence. In *Understanding adolescent psychology*, ed. J.F. Adams. Boston: Allyn and Bacon.

Erikson, Erik H. 1968: *Identity, youth and crisis*. New York: Norton; London: Faber.

Freud, A. 1958: Adolescence. *Psychoanalytic study of the child* 13, 255–78.

Grotevant, H.D. and Cooper, C.R. 1985: Patterns of interaction in family relationships and the development of identity exploration in adolescence. *Child development* 56, 415–28.

Inhelder, B. and Piaget, J. 1958: *The growth of logical thinking*. London: Routledge and Kegan Paul; New York: Basic Books.

Kitwood, T. 1980: *Disclosures to a stranger*. London and Boston: Routledge and Kegan Paul.

Kohlberg, L. 1969: Stage and sequence: the cognitive developmental approach to socialization. In *Handbook of socialization theory and research*, ed. D.A. Goslin. Chicago: Rand McNally.

Marcia, J.E. 1980: Identity in adolescence. In

Handbook of adolescent psychology, ed. J. Adelson. New York: Wiley.

Murphy, J.M. and Gilligan, C. 1980: Moral development in late adolescence and adulthood: a critique and reconstruction of Kohlberg's theory. *Human development* 23, 77–104.

Rutter, M., et al. 1976: Adolescent turmoil: fact or fiction? *Journal of child psychology and psychiatry* 17, 35–56.

—— and Hersov, L. 1977: *Child psychiatry: modern approaches*. Oxford: Blackwell Scientific; Philadelphia: Lippincott.

Schofield, Michael G. 1965: *The sexual behaviour of young people*. London: Longman; Boston: Little, Brown.

White, K.M., Speisman, J.C. and Costos, D. 1983: Young adults and their parents: individuation to mutuality. In *Adolescent development in the family: new directions for child development*, eds. H.D. Grotevant and C.R. Cooper. San Francisco: Jossey-Bass.

adolescent growth spurt The period of acceleration in the rate of increase in height and weight associated with puberty. Changes in body composition take place in the adipose and lean body masses, bodily strength increases and the physique takes on an adult configuration. The growth spurt follows a phase of stable growth in late childhood and culminates in decelerating growth. It begins earlier in girls than in boys, who continue to grow at prepubertal rates for two years after the initiation of the growth spurt in girls. According to Frisch and Revelle (1971), the mean ages at the initiation of height and weight growth spurts in girls are 9.6 years, and 9.5 years, and in boys 11.7 years and 11.6 years respectively. Tanner et al. (1966) have indicated that peak height and weight velocities are reached at 12.1 and 12.9 years respectively in girls, and at 14.1 and 14.3 years in boys. Between growth spurt initiation and eighteen years approximately one-third of the growth precedes the peak height velocity and the rest occurs during the phase of growth deceleration. There is wide individual variation in the age of onset and this has psychological correlates. Early maturing boys have more favorable personalities than late maturers. WLIP-J

Bibliography

Frisch, R.E. and Revelle, R. 1971: The height and weight of girls and boys at the time of initiation of the adolescent growth spurt in height and weight and the relationship to menarche. *Human biology* 43, 140.

Tanner, James M. 1962: *Growth at adolescence*. 2nd edn. Oxford: Blackwell Scientific; Springfield, Ill.: C.C. Thomas.

——, Whitehouse, R.H. and Takaishi, M. 1966: Standards from birth to maturity for height, weight, height velocity, and weight velocity: British children, 1965. Parts I and II. *Archives of diseases of childhood* 41, 454 and 613.

aggression Aggression is one of those unfortunate terms in the behavioral sciences that have been taken over from everyday language and have a variety of meanings. Furthermore people tend to assume that the different uses of the term must have something in common since they are all covered by the same word. Most research-oriented psychologists define aggression as the intentional injury of another, and regard this form of behavior as quite different (i.e. governed by different processes) from the other actions often given the same label in ordinary speech (such as assertiveness, attempts to achieve mastery, or ritualized threat displays). What is most important about aggression is that the aggressor wants to hurt or perhaps even destroy the victim, either physically or psychologically, and is reinforced when this particular goal is achieved. Aggression in this sense has very little in common with the forcefulness shown by an "aggressive" salesman or the boastfulness demonstrated by a youthful male who is trying to impress someone by acting tough.

Distinctions have to be drawn among different types of aggression even within this somewhat limited definition. It is especially important to differentiate between instrumental aggression and what many psychologists refer to as hostile aggression. In both cases the aggressor seeks to injure someone, but when he is acting instrumentally the aggressive behavior is carried out for another, non-aggressive purpose (such as for money or social approval). The person who attacks his victim because he believes the rules of his group require him to do so is engaging in instrumental aggression, since compliance brings rewards and avoids punishment. Hostile aggression, on the other hand, is primarily directed toward the injury of the victim, and is typically a response to aversive stimulation, whether in the form of an insult, some illegitimate treatment, a frustration or a foul odor. Such behavior can be affected by learning. Inhibitions prompted by social norms often govern the intensity of open hostile aggression and frequently affect its exact nature. Moreover, this behavior can also be influenced by anticipated rewards and punishments independently of the group's rules. Nevertheless, the basic instigation to the hostile action stems from the aversive stimulation. A good many of the homicides or serious violent assaults in everyday life appear to be instances of hostile aggression; they are explosive outbursts resulting from an argument or perceived insult in which the violence is often more intense than the aggressor had initially intended. The threat of capital punishment is usually ineffective as a deterrent to this form of violence because the aggressors generally do not think of any possible consequences beyond their desire to hurt (or destroy) their antagonist.

It is clear that aggression does not always arise in the same manner. Learning influences all aggression to some extent, and it is especially important in human instrumental aggression. As is the case with other instrumental actions, people use aggression to obtain their objectives if they have found that this form of behavior gets them what they want. On the other hand, many animals, including humans, may have an inborn capacity for aversively stimulated aggression, so this form of aggression can occur without prior learning, although it can be modified, strengthened or weakened by experience. Aversively stimulated aggression (the term is substituted henceforth for hostile aggression) is also more apt to be affected in an involuntary fashion by environmental stimuli. In such instances a particular stimulus in the surrounding situation facilitates the occurrence of overt aggression. One example is the "weapons effect" in which the mere presence of a weapon elicits stronger aggression than would otherwise have occurred, particularly if inhibitions against aggression are weak at the time (see Turner et al. 1977). While it is not altogether certain what causes the "weapons effect", the stimulus's associations with either previously reinforced aggression or aversive events seem to be especially important.

The theoretical perspective taken here helps to explain the now frequently observed effects of violent movies and also the repeated failures to demonstrate a "hostility catharsis" as a result of engaging in either realistic or fantasy aggression. In regard to the former, scores of well-controlled studies in both laboratory and natural settings have shown that scenes of violence on the television or movie screen can increase the probability that children as well as adult viewers will behave aggressively themselves. This increased likelihood of aggression arises from several processes involving short-term influences or long-lasting learning. The temporary effects include a weakening of inhibitions due to screen-induced ideas that aggression can be rewarding or is morally justified under particular circumstances, and also the stimulation of aggression-facilitating ideas, feelings and motor reactions by the aggressive material on the screen (see Berkowitz 1973). As for hostility catharsis, a good many experiments have now contradicted the widely accepted notion that the display of either realistic or make-believe aggression "drains" a reservoir of supposedly pent-up aggressive "energy" somewhere within the person, thereby lessening the probability of further aggression. The aggressor may feel good when he finds that his intended victim has been appropriately injured and may even cease his attacks on this target for some time afterwards. However the accomplishment of this objective is reinforcing so that in the long run aggressive behavior is now more, not less, likely. We do not diminish the level of violence in society by encouraging people to act aggressively, even if this behavior takes place only in their imagination.   LB

Bibliography

*Baron, R.A. 1977: *Human aggression.* New York: Plenum.

Berkowitz, L. 1973: Words and symbols as stimuli to aggressive responses. In *Control of aggression: implications from basic research,* ed. J.F. Knutson. Chicago: Aldine-Atherton.

——, Cochran, S. and Embree, M. 1981: Physical pain and the goal of aversively stimulated aggression. *Journal of personality and social psychology* 40, 687–700.

Blanchard, R. and Blanchard, C. eds. 1984: *Advances in the study of aggression,* vol. 1. New York and London: Academic Press.

Brain, P.F. and Benton, D., eds. 1981: *Multidisciplinary approaches to aggression research.* Amsterdam, New York, Oxford: Elsevier/North Holland.

Geen, R. and Donnerstein, E. eds. 1983: *Aggression: theoretical and empirical reviews.* New York and London: Academic Press.

Turner, C.W. et al. 1977: The stimulating and inhibiting effects of weapons on aggressive behavior. *Aggressive behavior* 3, 355–78.

aggression: in developmental research A term which has several partially overlapping meanings, ranging from assertion of the self or forcefulness, to the motivation, feelings, or intent behind acts of violence, i.e., physical force used against another. These various facets have been studied developmentally by systematically observing the aggressive behavior of preschool and school children, by laboratory experiments involving aggressive play, by tests involving fantasy play, or by ratings of aggression by parents, children or peers.

Major areas of development research on aggression concern:
(a) The processes whereby children acquire specific aggressive actions, e.g. by reinforcement or imitation (Bandura 1973; see SOCIAL LEARNING THEORY; BANDURA).
(b) Socializing influences which may enhance aggression (e.g. the family, the school, television). Aggressive and punishing parents have aggressive children. Watching a great deal of violence on television is associated with increased aggression, particularly in boys (Huesmann et al. 1984a).
(c) The developmental continuity of aggression. There is evidence of great stability in individuals' (especially males') aggression from childhood to adulthood. Childhood aggression may also predict adult criminality (Huesmann et al. 1984b).
(d) The social rules and consequences of aggressive actions. Socialized aggression may be one of the role requirements in some adolescent SUBCULTURES (e.g. Marsh et al. 1978; Akamatsu and Farudi 1978).   JA

Bibliography

Akamatsu, T.J. and Farudi, P.A. 1978: Effects of model status and juvenile offender type on the imitation of self-reward criteria. *Journal of consulting and clinical psychology* 46, 187–8.

Bandura, A. 1973: *Aggression: a social learning analysis.* Englewood Cliffs, N.J. and London: Prentice-Hall.

Huesmann, L.R., Lagerspetz, K. and Eron, L.D. 1984a: Intervening variables in the TV violence-aggression relation: evidence from two countries. *Developmental psychology* 20, 746–75.

——, Eron L.D., Lefkowitz, M.M. and Walder, L.O. 1984b: Stability of aggression over time and generation. *Developmental psychology* 20, 1120–34.

Marsh, P., Rosser, E. and Harré, R. 1978: *The rules of disorder.* London: Routledge and Kegan Paul.

aging The general term for the study of old age. Gerontologists may be biochemists, physiologists, neurologists, psychologists or social scientists who attempt to discover how the body, brain and central nervous system change with age, how these changes affect mental abilities and behavior, and how the lives of people within society change as they grow old.

Social psychological and social studies have included, for example, how elderly people regard themselves and their changing role in society; how they feel that younger people regard them, and how they are in fact regarded; whether elderly people gradually withdraw from social contacts of all kinds ("disengagement theory") or whether they merely change the nature, and the pattern, of their social contacts.

A general question for gerontologists has always been whether old age can be indefinitely postponed, and human life indefinitely prolonged, or whether advances in medicine and social care cannot increase the maximum span of human life, though they can ensure that larger numbers of us manage to live out our full spans in good health and with our wits about us. There have been encouraging reports of spectacular longevity in isolated peasant societies such as those in Georgia in the USSR or Vilcanbanba in Ecuador, claiming that large proportions of the population are alive (and even achieve parenthood) at ages exceeding 160 or 170 years. Sadly these tales are myths. Reported ages greater than 123 years have never been satisfactorily documented. It is, of course, not impossible that science may yet find ways of prolonging life, but for the present most gerontologists believe that the overwhelming majority of us cannot expect to survive beyond our mid-eighties. The most reasonable social and scientific goals are to ensure that as many of us as possible happily live out our maximum spans.

The experience of western industrialized societies bears out these hopes, and also vividly brings home the enormous social adjustments which their realization will entail. In the west, most people now aged sixteen can expect to live, in good health, until they are about seventy-two years (if they are men) and about seventy-seven years (if they are women). While techniques for treating the illnesses of old age are increasingly effective, they are also increasingly costly and unlikely to be available to all. Realistic hopes rest on much cheaper, and more effective, techniques in preventative medicine and in personal health care and maintenance of fitness. Such techniques have already been almost embarrassingly successful. In the rich west one person in every five alive today is over sixty years old. This propor-

tion will grow, increasing the age gap, as well as the gap of prosperity, between rich societies and third world countries where average life expectancies range from forty to fifty-five years. Apart from the long-term consequences of such a painful disparity of human prospects, the rich west faces urgent problems in adjusting social and economic systems to this massive, quiet, geriatric revolution.

Experiments to study changes in human mental abilities with age date from mass observations carried out by Francis Galton on visitors to the International Exhibition of 1883. Galton's results on changes in efficiency of memory and speed of reaction time illustrate the fundamental, unsolved question in this science. Galton could only test each of the people who visited his booth at the exhibition once. He could thus only collect *average* data for age-groups, and found that these *average* scores steadily deteriorated with age. This finding occurs with depressing regularity in all similar comparisons, though some abilities (e.g. verbal ability and verbal IQ) change much less than others (e.g. memory test scores and performance IQ scores) as older groups are sampled. However, data obtained from separate successive "cross-sectional" samples of aged people do not allow us to conclude that every individual inevitably experiences a sad trajectory of progressive intellectual decline ending in senility. Recent work shows that when we look more closely at large cross-sectional samples we find that substantial numbers of people in groups aged from seventy-five to eighty-five perform as well as the average for young people aged from twenty to forty. This may mean that the clock runs faster for some of us than others, and that while some lucky people show little change in mental efficiency until they reach an advanced age, most show earlier declines. Unfortunately the only studies that can resolve this question are longitudinal surveys in which large numbers of individuals are each repeatedly tested over periods of twenty to thirty years as they pass beyond their comparatively youthful fourth and fifth decades. The evidence slowly accumulating now makes it increasingly probable that chronological age, *per se*, has little effect on human abilities. It is rather the accumulation of physiological damage over the life span, and the onset of diseases accompanying age, which bring a stable plateau of peak mental performance to an abrupt end in a "terminal drop" accompanying increasing pathology.

A happy and realistic goal for clinicians and psychologists is to discover what makes the fortunate "super aged" so lucky. Apart from choosing the right parents (survival runs in families), better health habits and effort to maintain intellectual as well as physical activity may allow most humans to keep their wits about them until they no longer need them.

These optimistic comments on the apparent normal course of human aging must be contrasted with information on pathological conditions of accelerated degeneration of the central nervous system which in some respects resemble changes seen in extreme, normal, old age (dementias, Alzheimer's syndrome, etc.).

PR

Bibliography

Birren, J.E., Cunningham, W.R. and Yamamoto 1983: Psychology of adult development and aging. *Annual review of psychology* 34, 543–75.

────── and Schaie, K. Warner 1985: *Handbook of the psychology of aging*. 2nd edn, ed. Susan Munger. New York: Van Nostrand.

assimilation In PIAGET's theory of cognitive development, assimilation is the process in which the child 'reduces the universe to its own terms' (Piaget 1936; 1952). Assimilation is 'common to physiology and psychology' since every organism assimilates objects in its environment by consuming them or making use of them. According to Piaget there is 'a fundamental tendency whose manifestations we shall rediscover at each new stage of intellectual development: the tendency towards repetition of behavior patterns and towards the utilization of external objects in the framework of such repeti-

tion. This assimilation ... [is] ... the fundamental fact of psychic development' (p. 55). Assimilation, however, is always associated with ACCOMMODATION, since attempts to assimilate objects or events to established SCHEMAS of action or thought lead to adjustments of the schemas. Development occurs through adaptation which consists of both assimilation and accommodation. The assimilation-accommodation model is basic to Piaget's theory and sets cognitive growth squarely in a biological context. (See Piaget 1983.)

RL

Bibliography

Piaget, J. 1936 (1952): *La naissance de l'intelligence chez l'enfant*. Trans. *The origins of intelligence in children*. New York: International Universities Press; London: Routledge and Kegan Paul (1953). Also published by Penguin, 1977.

────── 1983: Piaget's theory. In *Handbook of child psychology*, vol. 1. 4th edn, ed. W. Kessen. New York: Wiley.

attachment An affective tie between an infant and caregiver construed either as an indicator of dependence motivation or as an organizational construct within a systems theoretic view of development. Initially concerned with the psychiatric sequellae of disturbed early development Bowlby (1969) used an evolutionary perspective in recasting explanations of early infant-caregiver interaction. He proposed that smiling, clinging and vocal signaling be viewed as functionally-related proximity maintaining devices which ensured the safety of the infant and the reproductive success of the parents. Concern with safety from predation was broadened to include a view of the primary caregiver as a secure base which allowed exploration and which provided comfort in distress. The strength of an organizational approach lies in its ability to integrate a diverse set of behavior and provide a theoretical account of individual differences and developmental changes (Sroufe and Waters 1977). Bowlby's theory provoked much empirical research, particularly into the presumed privileged status of the mother. Evidence has since shown that the mother need not be the primary attachment figure and that an infant can form bonds with a number of responsive caregivers, including other children.

Ainsworth et al. (1978) suggested that there are three distinct patterns of infant attachment: Type A, *avoidant attachment* in which the infant ignores the mother and shows little distress at SEPARATION; Type B, *secure attachment* in which the infant turns to the mother for comfort, especially after separation (this is the healthy and most common pattern); Type C, *anxious, ambivalent attachment* in which the infant may appear anxious even in the mother's presence, and may resist contact at one moment and desire it the next. It is not wholly clear to what extent such different patterns result from temperamental differences among infants, and to what extent they result from the mother's behavior (see Connell and Goldsmith 1982). Belsky et al. (1984) found some evidence that the mother's role is more influential, since ratings of maternal behavior seem related to subsequent type of attachment. Weber et al. (1986) found that the responses of infants thirteen months old to an unfamiliar adult seem to be related to both the mothers' and the infants' own temperaments, and they felt that the mother's temperament does predict her child's attachment security, particularly in the case of Type A (avoidant) infants. (See also DEPRIVATION, PARENTAL; SEPARATION.)

BBL/RL

Bibliography

Ainsworth, M.D.S., Blehar, M.C., Waters, E. and Wall, S. 1978: *Patterns of attachment*. Hillsdale, N.J.: Erlbaum.

Belsky, J., Rovine, M. and Taylor, D.G. 1984: The Pennsylvania infant and family development project: III. The origins of individual differences in infant-mother attachment: maternal and infant contributions. *Child development* 55, 718–28.

Bowlby, J. 1969: *Attachment and loss*, vol. 1. *Attachment*. London: Hogarth Press; New York: Basic Books, 1969.

Connell, J.P. and Goldsmith, H.H. 1982: A structural modeling approach to the study of attachment and strange situation behaviors. In *The development of attachment and affiliative systems*, eds. R.N. Emde and R.J. Harmon. New York: Plenum.

Sroufe, L.A. and Waters, E. 1977: Attachment as an organizational construct. *Child development* 48, 1184–99.

Weber, R.A., Levitt, M.J. and Clark, M.C. 1986: Individual variation in attachment security and strange situation behavior: the role of maternal and infant temperament. *Child development* 57, 56–65.

attention: in infants Attention refers to the selective, goal directed properties of perception. An attentive state is characterized by alert orienting toward a source of stimulation and a readiness to receive information. Attention in infancy is sometimes described as though the baby is "captured" by the striking or immediately salient properties of the auditory or visual environment. This results in a characteristically flighty pattern of behavior, with attention caught by one object or event after another. However, although the young infant may be more distractable than the older child, even the neonate exercises selectivity in perception. Babies from birth show visual and auditory preferences for aspects of stimulation that are informative about objects and events. GEB

Bibliography

Banks, M.S. and Ginsburg, A.P. 1985: Infant visual preferences: a review and new theoretical treatment. In *Advances in child development and behavior*, vol. 19, ed. H.W. Reese. New York: Academic Press.

Gibson, E. and Rader, N. 1979: Attention: the perceiver as performer. In *Attention and cognitive development*, eds. G.A. Hale and M. Lewis. New York and London: Plenum.

autism Infantile autism is a rare condition, affecting about two children per 10,000, and was first described by Kanner in 1943. The main features are: a failure to develop social relationships; specific abnormalities of language; an insistence on "sameness"; and onset before thirty months of age. Three quarters of autistic children also have mental retardation. Stereotyped repetitive movements (e.g. finger flicking), overactivity and epilepsy are common. Although it is classified with the childhood psychoses, it bears little resemblance to adult psychoses such as schizophrenia. Autistic children come from predominantly middle-class families, and this observation was thought at one time to have causal significance. (For more recent research see Achenbach 1984.) The true nature of the condition remains obscure, and the current view is that autism is a non-specific syndrome of biological impairment. Treatment is aimed at helping social and linguistic development, often using behavior therapy. Involvement of the family in treatment is important and special schooling is usually necessary. Prognosis is closely linked to the degree of mental retardation present, and the severity of language impairment.   GCF

Bibliography

Achenbach, T. 1984: The status of research related to psychopathology. In *Research on school-age children*, ed. W.A. Collins. Washington, D.C.: National Academy of Sciences Press.

Rutter, M. and Schopler, E. 1978: *Autism – a reappraisal of concepts and treatment*. New York: Plenum.

———— and Garmezy, N. 1983: Developmental psychopathology. In *Handbook of child psychology*, vol. 4. 4th edn, ed. E.M. Hetherington. New York: Wiley.

Tinbergen, N. and E.A. 1983: *"Autistic" children: new hope for a cure*. London: Allen and Unwin.

Wing, L. and Ricks, D.M. 1976: The aetiology of childhood autism: a criticism of the Tinbergen's ethological theory. *Psychological medicine* 6, 533–43.

B

babbling *See* cooing and babbling.

baby talk Also termed motherese, or caretaker language, baby talk refers to that special, often stereotyped, reduced register of a language which is regarded as appropriate for talking to young children, lovers and sometimes the elderly. Conventionalized and conscious baby talk mainly comprises lexical items as *dindins* "food", *choochoo* "train", *geegee* "horse" or diminutive affixes, as in *girlie, housie, birdie*, etc. It has to be distinguished from unconscious grammatical operation found with caretakers such as the use of a higher pitched voice, changes in the statistical distribution of questions, commands and statements, reduction of grammatical complexity and increased use of repetition.

Under the impact of Chomsky's mentalist view of FIRST LANGUAGE ACQUISITION baby talk was widely disregarded by psycholinguists during the 1960s and early 1970s. More recently the importance of input in the study of language acquisition has been demonstrated by a number of researchers (e.g. Snow and Ferguson 1977).   PM

Bibliography

Fernald, A. and Simon, T. 1984: Expanded intonation contours in mothers' speech to newborns. *Developmental psychology* 20, 104–13.

Gleitman, L.R., Newport E.L. and Gleitman, H. 1984: The current status of the motherese hypothesis. *Journal of child language* 11, 43–79.

Snow, C.E., and Ferguson, C.A. 1977: *Talking to children: language and acquisition*. Cambridge and New York: Cambridge University Press.

Bandura, Albert Born in 1925 in Alberta, Canada, Bandura attended the University of British Columbia. After graduating (1949) he studied clinical psychology at the University of Iowa (PhD 1952) where he was influenced by Spence and the writings of Miller and Dollard. From Iowa Bandura went to Wichita for an internship, and then to Stanford. His importance as a theorist and experimenter on SOCIAL LEARNING THEORY lies in his development of ideas far beyond the reinforcement-contingency models with which it began. Bandura was particularly interested in the causes of AGGRESSION in children. He argued against the view that aggression is necessarily 'an impulsive, emotional, pathological manifestation' rather than 'a method for getting what [the aggressor] wants when other options have failed' (1973a). He also argued against earlier social learning theorists' ideas about the necessary connection between frustration and aggression.

Bandura's work with Richard Walters (1918–67) and others emphasized the central role of observational learning. They found that children could learn from watching an adult act aggressively (Bandura, Ross and Ross 1963). Children who had seen an adult punished for aggression were less likely than other children to imitate when given a chance; but if the children were then offered a reward for imitating the model, those who had watched the punished adult behaved no differently from the others. This showed that the children could learn to do things by watching someone who was not rewarded. Neither reward nor the observation of reward were therefore necessary for the acquisition of the learning, although reward or its observation would influence whether the child actually imitated what had been seen. Bandura therefore distinguished *acquisition* from *performance*. He also distinguished the process illustrated in this experiment from

IMITATION on the one hand, and IDENTIFICATION on the other. Imitation implies literal mimicry of another's behavior, while identification implies an attempt to be as completely like another person as one can. Bandura called the observational learning seen in his experiments 'modeling'. This process has proved effective in the treatment of various phobias (Bandura 1969a).

Bandura suggested that observational learning is indispensable in 'situations where errors are likely to produce costly or fatal consequences', and that reinforcement could hardly suffice to explain the acquisition of 'language, . . . customs, . . . and . . . educational, social and political practices' (1969b). Behavioral theories, in fact, cannot easily account for the appearance of entire organized patterns of behavior, for the acquisition of learning in the absence of reward, or for the fact that actions may be performed for the first time long after the observation of the model on which they are based. Cognitive social learning, on the other hand, recognizes processes which explain the demonstrable fact that observers 'abstract common features from seemingly diverse responses and formulate generative rules of behavior that enable them to go beyond what they have seen or heard' (1974).   RL

Bibliography

Bandura, A. 1969a: *Principles of behavior modification*. New York: Holt, Rinehart and Winston.

—— 1969b: Social-learning theory of identificatory processes. In *Handbook of socialization theory and research*, ed. D.A. Goslin. Chicago: Rand McNally.

—— 1973a: Social learning theory of aggression. In *The control of aggression*, ed. J.F. Knutson. Chicago: Aldine.

—— 1973b: *Aggression: a social learning analysis*. Englewood Cliffs, N.J.: Prentice-Hall.

—— 1974: Behavior theory and the models of man. *American psychologist* 29, 859–69.

—— 1977: *Social learning theory*. Englewood Cliffs, N.J.: Prentice-Hall.

—— 1985: *Social foundations of thought and action*. Englewood Cliffs, N.J.: Prentice-Hall.

——, Ross, D. and Ross, S. 1963: Vicarious reinforcement and imitative learning. *Journal of abnormal and social psychology* 67, 601–7.

behavior change in the classroom

An approach to problems of learning and behavior in the classroom which attempts to ameliorate problems through the systematic application of theory and techniques derived from research on animal and human learning. The approach, sometimes called BEHAVIOR MODIFICATION, or contingency management, was originally based in the radical behaviorist philosophy of B.F. Skinner (1974), and employed the principles and techniques of applied behavior analysis (Bijou and Baer 1978). This attempts to "explain" behavior change in terms of *respondent* and *operant conditioning* and the patterns of reinforcement (the rewards, natural consequences and punishments), which have been associated with the behavior over time. Its central concern is the identification of functional relationships between observable antecedent events, the context, a circumscribed pattern of behavior (behavior problem) and the observable consequences of that behavior. In essence, the concern is with the ways in which external or environmental events modify behavior.

In classroom applications of this approach, attention is focused on the unacceptable behavior of the pupil or class, and an attempt is made to identify how this is influenced by what the teacher and peer group do or do not do. This is known as a functional analysis and is the main tool of applied behavior analysis in classroom and other settings. It follows the model characteristic of laboratory studies of animal and human behavior and the theoretical and conceptual interpretative framework used by radical behaviorists. The problem behavior (target) is first described in behavioral terms ("pupil gets out of seat", "pupil hits other children", "only produces three or four lines of work during lesson") and an attempt is made to record its frequency, duration or other quantifiable characteristics before any intervention is made. During the pre-intervention phase, called "the baseline period", the behavior of the teacher and/ or peers is also monitored, the observer focusing on what they do immediately before and after the occurrence of the target behavior. When the observers have obtained a stable baseline (i.e. a reliable and representative picture of the target behavior over a period of time) the teacher is asked to follow the instructions of the behavior analyst for the "intervention phase" during which the behavior of both teacher and pupil continue to be recorded. In this way the observers are able to monitor the effects of their advice. If the target behavior changes in the desired direction an attempt may be made to re-instigate the problem behavior in order to ensure that it was the teacher's actions during the pre-intervention phase that were responsible for producing the unacceptable behavior. Finally, the teacher will be asked to re-introduce a program specified by the behavior analyst and will be further instructed in how to maintain, and if necessary generalize to other situations, the now acceptable behavior. If the initial prescription fails to produce the desired changes within a reasonable time, indicating that the original analysis of functional relationships was wrong, a further analysis is undertaken and the sequence repeated until the behavior changes to a more acceptable form.

The specific changes demanded of the teacher are determined by what emerged in the functional analysis. It is, for example, not unusual to find teachers giving attention, albeit by reprimands, to disruptive behavior and ignoring perhaps inadvertently, instances of acceptable behavior. The advice given by the behavior analyst under such circumstances might be to give clearcut attention, praise, smiles and the like when the pupil is behaving appropriately (i.e. reinforce the acceptable) and ignore, with due regard to the well-being of other pupils, the disruptions.

Although teacher attention (a common "social reinforcer") may work well for many pupils, there are occasions or circumstances where it has no impact. When this happens, material or other reinforcers will be introduced. A child who does not respond to teacher attention may be allowed to have an extended play time as a reinforcer for producing more work. Sometimes tokens, in the form of points or ticks on a card, are used in conjunction with the social reinforcer of teacher's praise. When a predetermined number of these is accumulated, they can be exchanged for a prize or some desired activity. Systematic token programs are called "token economies" and are used either with individuals or groups. In order to maximize the opportunities for reinforcement it may become necessary to introduce changes in the content or organization of the curriculum, structural changes in the classroom or even in the school. For instance if the learning tasks are too difficult, they will need to be structured into smaller components and the teacher will be asked to reinforce success on the smaller unit rather than the whole task.

Early applications of applied behavior analysis were implemented in selective settings, usually experimental classrooms attached to colleges or universities in the USA. Since then, there have been many studies reporting applications in a wide range of settings, including special education, focused on varied problems presented by pupils of all ages (see Sherman and Bushell 1975, O'Leary and O'Leary 1977, for illustrative studies and reviews). The central ideas and especially the techniques are being increasingly incorporated in the training of teachers and there are several textbooks for teachers on the subject (e.g. Clarizio 1971). The approach has several positive and important attributes.

One is the attention it has focused on the role of external (to the pupil) influences on classroom learning and behavior. It raises questions about the interplay between the teacher's management skills and the characteristics of pupils in trying to understand classroom problems. Having identified the set of critical factors, it provides clear procedures to attempt to bring about change.

A second feature of importance is that the approach provides a systematic way of investigating aspects of classroom interactions, particularly those concerned with management. Through an emphasis on careful description and recording, it has begun to clarify the problems many teachers encounter in their day to day work. The use of direct observation by an outside observer is an important aspect here. Another noteworthy feature, perhaps not given enough emphasis, is the underlying assumption that much behavior, including many forms of classroom behavior, is learned and retains some responsiveness to external changes. The problems are not seen as faults or disorders within the pupil.

Third, and perhaps most important, is the evidence that some classroom problems at least can be positively influenced by the use of techniques which can be taught to teachers and which do not lead to segregation of pupils into special units, classes or schools, from which they might not return to mainstream schooling.

Objections to the approach have been formulated at all levels. As a philosophy of science behaviorism is seen as narrow and out of keeping with contemporary views of science; as an orientation in psychology, its mechanistic conceptions of human behavior and experience are unacceptable to many; its views of learning, the emphasis on external determinants, and the implications it carries about the nature and solution of problems faced by teachers and pupils, are often thought simplistic. The presumed power of the classroom technology of behavior change has given rise to ethical objections, particularly when applied to the control of children in schools (see Clarke 1979, O'Leary and O'Leary 1977).

While published studies on classroom applications generally show successful outcomes it would be inappropriate to be optimistic. It is not possible to know the extent of failed applications and unsuccessful studies have a limited chance of publication. Also, even when successful, changes effected by one teacher in a particular classroom do not readily continue over time, or generalize to other teachers or other settings (Wahler 1980). It should also be emphasized that techniques and their rationale could readily be encompassed by a number of other theoretical accounts which do not necessarily give rise to the objections noted above (see Bandura 1974, Agras, Kazdin and Wilson 1979).

The increasing acceptance of behavioral techniques (if not the associated theory) among educationalists can be partly understood by considering the prevalence of learning and behavior problems in ordinary and special schools, and the limitations in the training of teachers to meet these problems.

It is difficult to obtain precise estimates of the nature and frequency of problems faced by teachers because there is no generally accepted taxonomy or classification of classroom problems. This in turn leads to a high degree of subjectivity on the part of teachers as to what they identify as problems: a "definite problem" for one teacher may be no more than a minor irritant for another. (See DISRUPTIVE PUPILS.)

Teacher-education is concerned primarily with curriculum matters and the foundation disciplines of philosophy, psychology and sociology. Although trainees will have some supervised teaching practice there is commonly little systematic guidance on the management of the classroom difficulties. Furthermore, while much has been written (usually by experienced teachers) on the subject (e.g. Francis 1975), this literature is pejoratively referred to as "tips for teachers".

It would of course be quite wrong to see classroom problems as arising solely out of deficiencies in TEACHER TRAINING. But it would be equally incorrect to ignore the possible contribution of teaching practices to the generation or maintenance of classroom problems. The approach offered by applied behavior analysis provides one way of trying to understand classroom processes and it has drawn attention to procedures which may well be integral to good teaching. (See also TEACHER-PUPIL INTERACTIONS.)   MBe

19

Bibliography

Agras, W.S., Kazdin, A.E. and Wilson, G.T. 1979: *Behavior therapy: toward an applied clinical science*. San Francisco: W.H. Freeman.

Bandura, A. 1974: Behavior theory and models of man. *American psychologist* 29, 859–69.

Bijou, S.W. and Baer, D.M. 1978: *Behavior analysis of child development*. Englewood Cliffs, N.J.: Prentice-Hall.

Clarizio, H.F. 1971: *Toward positive classroom discipline*. New York: John Wiley.

Clarke, C. 1979: Education and behaviour modification. *Journal of philosophy of education* 13, 73–81.

Doyle, W. 1986: Classroom organization and management. In *The handbook of research on teaching*. 3rd edn, ed. M. Wittrock. New York: Macmillan.

Francis, P. 1975: *Beyond control?* London: Allen and Unwin.

*O'Leary, D.K. and O'Leary, S.G. 1977: *Classroom management*. 2nd edn. New York: Pergamon.

*Sherman, J.A. and Bushell, D. 1975: Behavior modification as an educational technique. In *Review of child development research*, vol. 4, ed, F.D. Horowitz. Chicago: University of Chicago Press.

Skinner, B.F. 1974: *About behaviorism*. New York: Knopf.

Wahler, R.G. 1980: Behavior modification: applications to childhood problems. In *Emotional disorders in children and adolescents*, eds. P. Sholevar, R.M. Benson and B.J. Blinder. Lancaster: M.T.P. Press; New York: Spectrum Publications.

behavior modification A generic term referring to the applied use of behavioral psychology to bring about changes in human behavior by workers in the helping professions (e.g. clinical and educational psychologists, social workers, teachers). Based on Skinner's operant conditioning paradigm, its central tenet is that all behavior is primarily learned and maintained as a result of an individual's interaction with his or her environment, which includes other individuals, and is susceptible to change by control over features of that environment. The three-term analysis of behavior (or ABC model) indicates that behavior change may be achieved by manipulating either the antecedent conditions for behavior, or the consequences following behavior, in line with the law of effect. Simply stated, this means that rewarded behavior will tend to increase in frequency, while behavior followed by punishing consequences will tend to decline. (See also BEHAVIOR CHANGE IN THE CLASSROOM.)   KW

Bibliography

Bellack, A.S., Hersen, M. and Kazdin, A.E. 1983: *International handbook of behavior modification and therapy*. New York: Plenum.

Willis, J. and Giles, D. 1976: *Great experiments in behavior modification*. Indianapolis: Hackett.

Binet, Alfred (1857–1911) Worked with Charcot in the Salpêtrière hospital in Paris, founded with Beaunis the first French laboratory of psychology in 1884 at the Sorbonne and was its first director from 1895 to 1911. Binet founded the journal *L'année psychologique* in 1895. He wrote several works on the psychology of mental processes and of personality, but his main contribution was the development of mental tests. In 1905, together with Theodore Simon (1873–1961), Binet elaborated a scale to test the intelligence level of normal and mentally retarded children ("Binet-Simon scale"). Binet's theories on the relations between psychology and education are synthesized in his book *Les idées modernes sur les enfants* (1909).   LM

Bibliography

Bertrand, F.L. 1930: *Alfred Binet et son oeuvre*. Paris: Alcan.

Binet, A. and Simon, T. 1905: Méthodes nouvelles pour le diagnostique du niveau intellectuel des anormaux. *Année psychologique* 11, 191–244.

Pollack, R.H. and Brenner, M.W. eds. 1969: *The experimental psychology of Alfred Binet: selected papers*. New York: Springer.

Wolf, T.H. 1961: An individual who made a difference. *American psychologist* 16, 245–8.

bioprogram language This term was introduced and developed by Bickerton

(1981). In contrast to Chomsky's LANGUAGE ACQUISITION DEVICE which defines formal principles enabling children to select a possible grammar on the basis of restricted parental input, Bickerton's bioprogram refers to a well defined set of structures and structural developments, i.e. those which arise under conditions of creolization of an incipient pidgin. Ordinary FIRST LANGUAGE ACQUISITION is seen to involve the task of restructuring the innate bioprogram so as to approximate to adult grammar. Numerous creole constructions can therefore be expected in developing child language. A large number of the bioprogram categories (such as the punctual-non punctual distinction, that is the distinction between those processes consisting of determinate units and those made up of continuous transitions) are absent in most adult language systems. Bickerton explains this by pointing out that much of the grammar of so-called "natural" languages is in fact cultural. Consequently, the search for psychologically and biologically based linguistic universals in such languages is misguided. PM

Bibliography

Bickerton, Derek 1981: *Roots of language*. Ann Arbor: Karoma Publications.

Mühlhäusler, Peter 1984: Roots of language? A review article on a book by D. Bickerton. *Folia linguistica* 18, 263–77.

blind, the: psychology and education

There is no internationally-agreed definition of blindness, and in most countries the term is not restricted only to those who are totally lacking in sight. No reliable statistics are available, therefore, about global incidence, and even within any given nation the medico-legal criteria used for classification or registration purposes will encompass a very heterogeneous population. In some countries, for example the UK and the USA, the statutory regulations specify upper limits of acuity for distant vision and lower limits for width of visual field, and result in the majority of the "legally blind" having some potentially useful residual sight. A group

that is so heterogeneous in visual functioning will vary also in its educational and psychological needs, as is seen by the emergence of a term such as "educationally blind" which is used for those who have to use braille for reading and writing. The age of onset of the visual impairment and the presence of additional handicaps add to the heterogeneity of those labeled as blind.

Nevertheless, some order can be obtained by partitioning along the two independent dimensions of degree of residual vision and age of onset. The growing interest in the needs of the majority of the registered blind, those at the upper end of the blindness continuum, has its origins (1) in the confirmation of ophthalmologists that most ocular disabilities cannot be made worse by normal use of sight; (2) in the findings of experimental psychologists that various aspects of perception can be improved by training; and (3) in improvements in the quality and variety of magnifiers and low vision aids. Educators (e.g. Barraga 1964) seized upon the implications of these developments and proceeded to devise assessment and teaching procedures geared to encouraging greater reliance on and interpretation of quite meager visual information for orientation, mobility, object perception and even the reading of print (the latter now being facilitated by the use of closed circuit television magnifiers). The classification of a child or adult as blind is no longer regarded by teachers and rehabilitation staff as sufficient reason for assuming vision to be unusable, and when there are no contra-indications from the ophthalmologist, the common practice is for them to assess whether and how the learner uses, or could use, any remaining sight in recreation, classroom, and work and to devise training programs with that information in mind.

When the cut is made along the other axis – age of onset – a new set of problems arises. For those who become blind after extensive experience of operating visually, the concepts "re-adjustment" and "rehabilitation" are used but they seem less useful when applied to those who are born blind. This does not imply that congenital blindness has no impact on cognitive, perceptual and social development but rather that the growth of the total personality has its own unique shape and integrity. The handicapping consequences of blindness will be understood later, and then initially through the mediation of other people. There will be no sense of loss of body parts or functioning, nor the expectation by parents, family and advisers of overt or disguised feelings of hostility, depression and demoralization. These, however, are major problems for the newly-blinded, and are bound up with archetypal anxieties and attitudes about blindness that are themselves not just to do with the loss or absence of one of the major sensory modalities. Blindness has a symbolic content related to light and darkness, and to loss of power and control (see, for example, Monbeck 1973). It is perhaps for this reason that rehabilitation programs for the blind are a compound of skills training (to replace the lost power and control) and counseling, with the counseling sometimes extending to the members of the immediate family to enable them to accept the blindness and understand the feelings it evokes both in them and in the blind relative. But in relation to learning, great though the difficulties of the later-blinded may be in acquiring braille, independent mobility, and daily-living skills, there is ample objective and anecdotal evidence testifying to the value for the individual of having had the power of sight, even if only for a few years, as this provides a framework against which new experiences can be set and evaluated.

Extensive evidence from behavioral scales and checklists has shown that, as a group, congenitally blind infants and young children reach certain developmental milestones later than the normally sighted. Many of the items where delays are observed involve locomotor and self-care skills. In later childhood, there is evidence too of the slower growth of various perceptual and cognitive competencies, for which the expression "developmental lag" is often used. It has,

however, little explanatory value. More recent research is attempting to move on from merely recording these differences to an examination of the conditions that can mitigate the deleterious effects of visual loss. The wide variations among totally, congenitally blind children are being seen as informative about the constellation of necessary conditions for activating what Russian psychologists describe as the "safe analysers" (the remaining sensory channels). Western researchers may cast the procedure in terms of selecting alternative coding strategies, and then point to the role of the parents whose own feelings about the child's lack of sight may affect the initiation and development of their own parenting skills. As an example we may cite the importance for later language development of the ability of mother and baby to monitor one another's line of gaze and so share a frame of reference and know what the other is "thinking" about, before any mutual verbal communication is possible. In the absence of this visually-based component of pre-speech communication, the mother may herself be deprived of some important stimulus and feedback, and need to be taught how vocalization and then speech may have unusual functions for the blind child – for sensing objects, for maintaining contact, for obtaining attention, and for spatially locating himself in relation to others. The fact that language seems eventually to develop normally, that OBJECT PERMANENCE and constancy are achieved, that walking may be accomplished without a preceding crawling stage, and that some blind children achieve these and other attainments at ages not very different from those of their sighted peers, may be interpreted as proof that blindness is not inevitably a brake on development. This does not deny that it can very easily restrict opportunities for learning and interfere with the emergence of facilitative behavior on the part of the care-givers.

As with sighted children, reading (see READING: ORIGINS AND LEARNING) occupies a central place in the educational curriculum of the blind, and although modern technology is making access to information easier through cassette-recorders and devices that can convert print into a tactile format and into spelled-out or synthetic speech, braille remains the dominant system. This is because it is a reading-and-writing medium, and one that preserves the information-rich characteristics of whole-page lay-out (the ability to emphasize by indenting, paragraphing, italicizing, etc.) and the facility for rapid backward and forward checking and scanning. However, print can be read two to three times more quickly than braille, and makes smaller demands on storage capacity (short-term memory). The various explanations for the relative slowness of tactual reading can be seen to have physiological and psychological bases: the width of the finger-pad, the "tactual window", is smaller than the eye's visual field, thus reducing the amount of information that can be picked up in one fixation; the speed of movement and powers of acuity of the eye are inherently superior; the sensations in the finger leave fast-decaying traces, easily obliterated by succeeding stimuli and thus not accurately identified and transferred to longer-term storage centers; recognition of shapes by touch is akin to recognition through blurred vision; textural (dot density) features of braille are coded as well as the global and spatially-related characteristics, and especially in the early phases of learning, this can result in the adoption of inefficient strategies of coding; and the low levels of redundancy characteristic of the structure of the braille cell (as compared with printed letter shapes), combined with multiple meanings for the symbols and complex rules about the use of contracted forms, impose perceptual and cognitive loads of a higher order than those encountered in print reading. Some of these hypotheses are now being adequately operationalized (e.g. Millar 1981) and there is reason to expect significant advances in our understanding of the factors that influence braille letter and word recognition. Among the already well-attested findings are those of Nolan and Kederis (1969) to the effect that (i) growth

of some of the factors basic to reading readiness occurs very slowly in blind children, (ii) the correlation between INTELLIGENCE QUOTIENT and reading is significantly higher for braille than for print reading, and (iii) the recognition times for braille words are longer than the sum of the recognition times of the individual symbols in the words, a position which is the reverse of that found for print. Whatever the causation of the slower processing of tactually-presented information, the blind are at a disadvantage vis-à-vis their sighted peers, requiring considerably more time to cover the same curriculum content and finding graphical illustration in mathematics, geography, and other science subjects difficult to interpret.

(See also EDUCATION OF HANDICAPPED CHILDREN; INTEGRATION OF HANDICAPPED CHILDREN IN NORMAL SCHOOLS.)   MJT

Bibliography

Barraga, N. 1964: *Increased visual behavior in low vision children*. New York: American Foundation for the Blind.

Millar, S. 1981: Tactual shapes. In Portwood and Williams, op. cit.

Mills, A.E. ed. 1983: *Language acquisition in the blind child*. London: Croom Helm.

*Monbeck, M.E. 1973: *The meaning of blindness: attitudes toward blindness and blind people*. Bloomington and London: Indiana University Press.

Nolan, C.Y. and Kederis, C.J. 1969: *Perceptual factors in braille word recognition*. New York: American Foundation for the Blind.

*Portwood, P.F. and Williams, R.S. eds. 1981: *The visually handicapped child*. Division of Educational and Child Psychology, Occasional Papers, vol 5, no. 1. Leicester: The British Psychological Society.

*Warren, D.H. 1984: *Blindness and early childhood development*. 2nd edn. New York: American Foundation for the Blind.

blindness: in children A severe or complete loss of sight, sufficiently serious to impair the child's ability to process visual information. Only about 10 per cent of the legally blind are totally blind. Like deafness, it is not a unitary condition.

A central question in the development of blind children is whether experiential deficits, caused either by limited mobility or sensory deprivation, interfere with intellectual development. It was widely believed that the spatial concepts of the congenitally blind differ from those of the sighted, who retain the benefits of the "spatial sense". Recent research shows that blind children may have difficulty on tasks requiring "mental rotation" of spatial relations but that on other spatial tasks, such as estimation of length, their performance is equivalent to the sighted. Thus, there can be no general deficit in spatial representation, although some tasks may force the blind child to use inappropriate coding strategies that lead to error. Research with the blind is also important for understanding how children code *cross-modal* relations, since the blind may make use of information from an intact modality that is functionally equivalent to sight for the performance of complex tasks.

(See also BLIND, THE: PSYCHOLOGY AND EDUCATION.)   GEB

Bibliography

Millar, S. 1981: Cross modal and intersensory perception in the blind. In *Intersensory perception and sensory integration*. ed. Richard Walk and Herbert Pick, Jr. New York and London: Plenum.

bonding The affection and recognition between a mother and her child which is supposedly established by physical contact soon after birth. Klaus and Kennell (1978) reported that mothers who had such contact showed more physical affection to their newborn babies, and were more positive towards their children when they were a year old. Other researchers' attempts to replicate these results have not had great success (see Svejda et al. 1982). In general, mechanisms and possible critical periods for bonding have not been established (see Myers 1984). Nevertheless there is plenty of evidence that failure to form any secure emotional bonds in infancy does cause deviance and psycho-

pathology (see Rutter 1981; see also ATTACHMENT; SEPARATION).   RL

Bibliography

Klaus, M.H. and Kennell, J.H. 1978: Parent to infant attachment. In *Mother/child, father/child relationships*, eds. J.H. Stevens and M. Mathews. Washington, D.C.: National Association for the education of young children.

Myers, B.J. 1984: Mother-infant bonding: the status of the critical period hypothesis. *Developmental review* 4, 240–74.

Rutter, M. 1981: *Maternal deprivation reassessed*. 2nd edn. London: Penguin.

Svejda, M.J., Pannabecker, B.J. and Emde, R.N. 1982: Parent-to-infant attachment: a critique of the early "bonding" model. In *The development of attachment and affiliative systems*. New York: Plenum.

Bowlby, John An English psychoanalyst, born in London in 1907, who attempted to produce a synthesis of experimental, ethological and clinical approaches to explain the crucial role of early ATTACHMENT between mother and child. In a study of forty-four juvenile thieves (1946) Bowlby found that prolonged SEPARATION from the mother was a common feature of their histories. He pursued the idea that successful BONDING to one caregiver is absolutely necessary for healthy psychological development. His own and others' investigations of these ideas represent one of the major endeavors in developmental psychology of the last forty years (see Rutter 1981). There is no doubt that separation does occasion traumatic reactions in a young child, with agitation followed by depression, and frequently a disturbed initial reaction when reunited with the mother (see e.g. Field and Reite 1984). But the long-term effects are less clear. It is now thought that failure to form a secure attachment creates psychopathology, whereas disruption of established bonds need not have such a destructive impact (see Rutter 1981).

Bowlby's main works are his report for the World Health Organisation, *Maternal care and mental health* (1951), and his trilogy *Attachment and loss*: 1. *Attachment*

(1969); 2. *Separation, anxiety and anger* (1973); 3. *Loss, sadness and depression* (1980). London: Hogarth; New York: Basic Books. RL

Bibliography

Field, T. and Reite, M. 1984: Children's responses to separation from mother during the birth of another child. *Child development* 55, 1308–16.

Rutter, M. 1981: *Maternal deprivation reassessed.* 2nd edn. London: Penguin.

Bruner, Jerome S. An American psychologist born in New York in 1915, and educated at Duke and Harvard Universities. Bruner has spent much of his working life at Harvard although he was professor in Oxford from 1971–79. He did some early work on attitude and propaganda in the 1940s and on person perception during the 1950s. This was the area of research in which cognitive social psychology was developing. Bruner's most notable achievement in the 1950s was his collaborative *A study of thinking* (1956) with Goodnow and Austin. This was based on studies of people's problem-solving strategies in laboratory experiments. The focus of interest was the sequence of decisions made in reaching a solution. The book is generally cited as a first step in the growth of cognitive psychology. Later Bruner himself (1983b) described the problems as "non-natural" and believed that their non-naturalness determined the procedures which subjects adopted.

In the late 1950s Bruner became actively involved in problems of education and children's cognitive development. He published three books on education between 1960 and 1971, in which he put forward various pupil-centered ideas, such as the necessity for a pupil to *participate* in the educative process, and for his or her existing level of development to be taken as the starting point from which the process should begin. In 1960 Bruner and George Miller founded the Center for Cognitive Studies at Harvard. A product of this collaboration was *Studies in cognitive growth* (1966). In this book Bruner pre-sented a model of growth from "enactive representation" to "iconic representation", and from there to "symbolic representation". He argued that different cultures may produce different modes of thought because the "tools" they employ differ. Western cultures are highly symbolic and linguistic, whereas other cultures are perhaps iconic, and rely on images. This may explain why some rural African (Wolof) children are unable to do CONSERVATION tasks by the age of twelve, even though they deal successfully with liquids and objects in everyday life.

Latterly Bruner has been particularly interested in developmental studies, particularly of children's language. He follows the line of VYGOTSKY (opposed to PIAGET) that language skills help the child solve problems. His most important work, however, has been on the processes by which children pass from pre-speech communication to linguistic communication. He has stressed the way in which language is embedded in, and part of general communication. The interactions between the mother and her baby are routines in which the baby learns expectations about the mother's performance and also how to respond to it. Bruner has noted the shared direction of gaze between mother and baby, which is crucial for the child's grasp of reference, and comprehension of the mother's comments. He has also noted turn-taking games, and the general acquisition of social skills necessary for communication before any speech is acquired. The stress upon the *social* framework as an aid to language-learning is the most striking aspect of this approach. (See also COMPETENCE, LINGUISTIC; DEIXIS; DISPLACED SPEECH.) RL

Bibliography

Bruner, J.S. 1973: *Beyond the information given*, ed. J.M. Anglin. New York: Norton.

——— 1983a: *Child's talk. Learning to use language*. Oxford and New York: Oxford University Press.

——— 1983b: *In search of mind: essays in autobiography*. New York: Harper and Row.

—— , Goodnow, J.J. and Austin, G.A. 1956: *A study of thinking*. New York: Wiley.

—— , Olver, R.R., Greenfield, P.M. et al. 1966: *Studies in cognitive growth*. New York: Wiley.

Burt, Sir Cyril Lodowic (1883–1971) Professor of psychology in Liverpool (1909–1912), he held several public and teaching posts in London, including professor of psychology at London University from 1931 to 1951. Burt was considered one of the most important psychologists of this century for his research on aptitude tests in school, the inheritance of INTELLIGENCE, and on FAC-TOR ANALYSIS in psychology, as well as for his influence on British psychology and education. However, in recent years Burt has come to symbolize the use of psychological enquiry to justify a preconceived ideology and to give support for selective and elitist social and educational policies. The American psychologist Kamin (1974) was the first to accuse Burt of manipulating data on IQ to back the thesis of heredity. LM

Bibliography

Hearnshaw, L.S. 1979: *Cyril Burt, psychologist*. London: Hodder and Stoughton.

Kamin, L.J. 1974: *The science and politics of IQ*. Hillsdale, N.J.: Erlbaum; London: Penguin (1977).

C

child and adolescent psychiatry

Persistent disturbance of emotions or behavior which affects the child's social relationships or development, and is out of keeping with the child's sociocultural background and developmental level. Psychiatric disorder may be caused by factors within the child himself, his family, or his environment. In assessing disturbed children, therefore, it is necessary to examine not only the child but also the family, school and social circumstances. A multidisciplinary team approach is widely used to achieve this, with medically qualified child psychiatrists working closely with psychologists and social workers. This model forms the basis of Child Guidance Clinics.

The incidence of psychiatric disorder in school children has been estimated at between 5 and 15 per cent; and 10 to 20 per cent in adolescents (Rutter, Tizard and Whitmore 1981). These figures, however, do not reflect the number of children presenting for treatment, and factors such as parental anxiety may be as important as the severity of a child's disturbance when treatment is sought. Boys are twice as commonly affected as girls. Although the rate of disorder is highest in inner city areas there is no clear association with social class alone: other associated factors are parental mental illness and criminality, family discord and disruption, early SEPARATION experiences and SOCIAL DISADVANTAGE. Children with central nervous system abnormalities, mental handicap, or epilepsy, and children who have been abused, form a high risk group. There has recently been considerable interest in "protective factors" (Rutter 1981), which enable some children to survive gross deprivation and psychosocial stress. Examples are: an adaptable temperament; isolated rather than all-pervasive stress; a good relationship with one parent.

The two main groups of child psychiatric disorders, which together cover more than 90 per cent of psychiatric disorder seen in children, are disorders of conduct, where the child behaves in socially disapproved-of ways, e.g. lying, stealing, disobedience (see CONDUCT DISORDER) and emotional disorders, characterized mainly by anxiety symptoms, which may be accompanied by tearfulness, sadness, social withdrawal or relationship problems. They occur equally commonly in girls and boys, and are relatively short-lived compared with adult neuroses. They usually develop in response to stress in the child's environment, e.g. parental disharmony, illness in a family member. Certain children, those with especially anxious temperaments, are vulnerable to minor stresses, and it is thought that there are also critical periods in a child's life when specific stresses have a major impact, e.g. bereavement in the third or fourth years of life. Treatment usually consists of understanding the stress, and either modifying it or helping the child develop better resources to cope. The prognosis for recovery and adjustment in later life is very good.

Children diagnosed as "psychotic" are generally withdrawn and unable to form emotional relationships with adults or other children. They frequently have mannerisms such as finger flicking, twirling or spinning objects. Psychosis in childhood is very rare and is a confused area. This is partly owing to the difficulties inherent in applying adult diagnostic criteria to children who are usually unable to verbalize their inner feelings and experiences; and also partly because any process which affects relationship formation in infancy interferes with normal

27

development. It may thus be difficult to distinguish psychosis in young children from mental retardation. Three subgroups are recognized:

(a) Late-onset psychosis: these are adult-like psychoses (e.g. schizophrenia or bipolar depression) occurring in late childhood and adolescence. The treatment and prognosis is the same as for the adult condition.

(b) Disintegrative psychoses: these present around the age of four with social withdrawal and loss of skills, including speech. They are due to an underlying degenerative disorder of the central nervous system, and treatment is mainly palliative and symptomatic.

(c) Infantile autism.

The outlook for recovery from psychotic conditions in childhood is not good.

In *organic mental states* there is impairment of brain functioning with "delirium" – confusion and hallucinations, which are usually visual in children. The commonest causes in childhood are high fevers accompanying infections such as measles, meningitis or pneumonia. They may also be caused by accidental self-poisoning, by overdoses of drugs such as sedatives or anticonvulsants; and by drug abuse (e.g. glue sniffing, LSD or amphetamine intoxication). Treatment is directed at the underlying cause, and the episode of delirium is usually short-lived.

A number of conditions which occur on their own, not as part of a more widespread emotional or behavioral disturbance, can be grouped under the heading *monosymptomatic disorders*. They include tics, enuresis (bedwetting), encopresis (soiling), night terrors, head banging, thumb sucking. Many of these can be regarded as developmental, i.e. they arise as part of a developmental stage, and resolve spontaneously with increasing age and maturity. However, treatment may be sought because of parental anxiety, or because of the child's distress if symptoms are interfering with his functioning or relationships.

Educational problems form another group of conditions. There are many reasons for a child failing to learn.

(a) General intellectual impairment, which will affect all areas of learning.

(b) A specific learning disability, affecting only one area, such as reading or arithmetic. (See DYSLEXIC CHILDREN; REMEDIAL MATHEMATICS; REMEDIAL READING.)

(c) Temperamental factors: restless, fidgety chlldren with poor concentration and high distractibility often fail to learn in ordinary classroom settings.

(d) *Conduct disordered children* have a high incidence of reading retardation. The nature of this association is not well understood. Background family factors (e.g. dismissive attitudes to learning or authority) may be relevant; or the child's failure in the classroom may lead him to act out as an alternative strategy to impress his peer group and boost his own self esteem.

(e) *Stress* – such as divorce, bereavement, illness of a family member – may lead to loss of concentration and a temporary interruption of the child's progress.

(f) *Mental illness* – depressive disorder or schizophrenia arising in adolescence interferes with learning. The teacher may be the first to notice signs of the illness as school performance declines.

Wherever a child is failing educationally, there are likely to be secondary emotional problems – poor self esteem and loss of self confidence – which may need attention in their own right. (See also ABSENCE FROM SCHOOL AND TRUANCY; SCHOOL FAILURE; SCHOOL PHOBIA.)

Treatment of disturbed children, like assessment, requires a multidisciplinary approach, and inpatient, day patient or outpatient care may be necessary. The focus of treatment may be on the individual child, e.g. through individual psychotherapy, play therapy, behavior therapy, remedial tuition, or placement in a special school. On the other hand, the focus may be on helping the family to change, and for this family therapy, or parental counseling, may be required. Liaison with schools, nurseries, and play groups may be necessary, and close working relationships with social services departments are vital for children in care, or those who are suspected of suffering from emotional or physical neglect and abuse. The combined efforts of the child psychiatric team with pediatricians, physiotherapists, speech therapists, or teachers may be needed to help children who are physically or mentally handicapped in addition to any psychiatric disturbance. Drugs are little used in child psychiatry apart from the treatment of the hyperkinetic syndrome and the adult-like psychoses.

Child abuse; non accidental injury

Each year about six children per 1,000 are abused physically, emotionally or sexually. Such children may grow up to be permanently affected by their early experiences, with impairment of their capacity to form loving relationships. Abused children may present at accident departments with multiple fractures, burns and bruising; or with failure to thrive and developmental delay. They commonly show "frozen watchfulness" in the presence of adults. Research suggests that the failure of parent-child ATTACHMENT often predates the abuse, and a number of high risk factors have been identified which provide clues for possible early intervention (Lynch and Roberts 1982). These include young maternal age; a history of parental psychiatric illness; the parents themselves being abused as children; separation of mother and baby in the neonatal period; and multiple social problems. The management of child abuse may involve permanently removing the child from its parents; helping develop parenting skills in a mother and baby unit or special day center; or setting up early intervention programs for high risk mothers and their newborn babies to try to promote attachment. GCF

Bibliography

Adams, H.E. and Sutker, P.B. 1984: *Comprehensive handbook of psychopathology*. New York: Plenum, section 6.

*Barker, P. 1979: *Basic child psychiatry*. London: Granada.

Lynch, Margaret A. and Roberts, Jacqueline 1982: *Consequences of child abuse*. London: Academic Press.

Quay, H.C. 1987: Psychopathology of childhood. In *Annual review of psychology*, vol. 38, eds. M.R. Rosenzweig and L.W. Porter. Palo Alto: Annual Reviews Inc. (in prep.).

*Rutter, M. 1975: *Helping troubled children*. Harmondsworth: Penguin; New York: Plenum.

—— 1981: Stress, coping and development: some issues and some questions. *Journal of child psychology and psychiatry* 22, 4, 323–56.

——, Tizard, J. and Whitmore, K. eds. 1981: The Isle of Wight and its services for children. In *Education, health and behavior*. New York: Robert E. Krieber.

—— and Garmezy, N. 1983: Developmental psychopathology. In *Handbook of child psychology*, vol. 4. 4th edn, ed. E.M. Hetherington. New York: Wiley.

children's drawing Just over a century ago it was standard practice to stress the study of drawing as giving privileged access to the child's mind. The argument was that drawings are publicly-inspectable products; and since children's drawings are often peculiar, if one could but read the signs aright the peculiarity of the child's mental representation of the world would be revealed. Old texts contain a goldmine of insights ready to be rediscovered.

One strand of the tradition, arguably the most theoretically advanced one, was preserved and reworked in Piaget and Inhelder (1969); another strand, the collecting-and-classifying approach, by Kellogg (1970). But for half-a-century, the central dynamic of the research was lost. When interest in children's mental representation revived, most researchers concentrated on language, memory, reasoning and perception instead of on picture-production. It is only in the last two decades that researchers have broken with a product-oriented approach and turned to analysing production processes. This gives the topic its distinctive flavor: a mixture of old observations and brand new analytic techniques. Some useful modern books are by Beittel (1972), Freeman (1980), Gardner (1980), Golomb (1974), Goodnow (1977), MacGregor (1977) and Van Sommers (1984).

Most of the recent work is scattered in a variety of journals, though a number of the more important contributions can be found in a collection by Freeman and Cox (1985). The topics noted below may be found in the references cited so far.

The central thrust of most modern work is that finished drawings cannot be used to decode the child's mind. The psychologist cannot just act as a sort of collector-cum-critic, but must actively work with the child, either by giving different sorts of guidance or by setting different sorts of pictorial puzzle. Marks on the page are solutions to pictorial problems, and we shall only understand what the pictures mean if we define what problems are involved in their generation.

Young children almost universally go through a phase of drawing people looking like a face-plus-limbs. One old idea was that they were drawing what was important to them and for some reason the trunk wasn't important (giving a sort of "tadpole"); whilst another idea was that the trunk was indeed present but simply had not been divided off pictorially from the head (giving a sort of "humpty dumpty"). It should be possible to test between the two. If children be given a pre-drawn head and trunk, the former hypothesis would predict that arms would be drawn on the head, the latter, on the trunk. Neither occurs; instead arms go on whichever body-segment has been drawn larger. But legs always go on the trunk. The suggestion is that young children are skilled at decisions when planning the top and bottom of a figure but leave the middle to on-the-spot drawing decisions. A major topic in modern research is to disentangle the two levels of decision: getting the optimal balance is a problem for children.

Another topic can be exemplified by a modern approach to an equally old phenomenon. In one nineteenth-century study, given an apple transfixed by a hatpin, children up to the age of seven or so tended to draw a circle with a continuous line right across; a failure to implement hidden line elimination (HLE). If this reflects a concern to draw "what they know" then increasing the salience of what is hidden ought to strengthen the "error". Replacing the pin with two different-coloured sticks which are pushed into the sphere from opposite ends to meet with a click ought to suffice. It does not: in one study it actually reduced HLE-failure to zero. One suggestion is that the children mentally represented the scene as sphere-plus-two-sticks and this freed them to take the pictorial decision appropriately to draw the sphere with sticks at the side. "What they knew" was no longer in contradiction with "what they saw".

The tendency to draw sloping chimneys, perpendicular to an oblique roof, may result simply from a problem peculiar to the picture-plane. Children often cannot conquer "the perpendicular bias" even when the task is an abstract one: to copy two lines which form an acute angle. Gradually, every one of the old phenomena is being investigated. New research is devoted to distinguishing between what they typically try to do and how good they are at doing it. That forms a performance-analysis, in which one aim is to find experimental designs which help children take sensible pictorial decisions and another is to understanding their problem in coordinating "inward search" for a drawing-plan with "outward search" for shapes on the page which would realize the plan. All drawings are literally explanations (from the Latin ex-planere, to lay out on a flat surface) but they are not self-evident, and age-norms in explanatory expertise have been drastically revised downwards.   NHF

Bibliography

Beittel, K. 1972: *Mind and context in the art of drawing*. New York: Holt.

Freeman, N.H. 1980: *Strategies of representation in young children*. London: Academic Press.

—— and Cox, M.V. 1985: *Visual order*. Cambridge: Cambridge University Press.

Gardner, H. 1980: *Artful scribbles*. New York: Basic Books.

Golomb, C. 1974: *Young children's sculpture and drawing*. Cambridge, Mass.: Harvard University Press.

Goodnow, J. 1977: *Children's drawing*. London: Fontana.

Kellogg, R. 1970: *Analysing children's art*. Palo Alto: National Press.

MacGregor, R.N. 1977: *Art plus*. Toronto: McGraw-Hill.

Piaget, J. and Inhelder, B. 1969: *The psychology of the child*. London: Routledge.

Van Sommers, P. 1984: *Drawing and cognition*. Cambridge: Cambridge University Press.

Chomsky, Noam A. Born 1928, Professor of Linguistics at the Massachusetts Institute of Technology (MIT). Chomsky is the founder of one of the most influential schools in linguistics and psycholinguistics, that of transformational-generative grammar (TG). TG was presented to a wider audience in *Syntactic Structures* in 1957 and subsequently in *Aspects of the Theory of Syntax* in 1965. Chomsky's insistence that linguistics should be a branch of cognitive psychology and his mentalist views on language learning have provoked vivid interest among psychologists (see Greene 1972).

The most influential concepts introduced by Chomsky are those of deep and surface structure, *competence* and *performance*, *acceptability* and *grammaticalness*, and the notion of generative grammar. (See FIRST LANGUAGE ACQUISITION; LANGUAGE ACQUISITION DEVICE; COMPETENCE: LINGUISTIC; PSYCHOLINGUISTICS.) PM

Bibliography

Chomsky, Noam 1957: *Syntactic structures*. The Hague: Mouton.

—— 1967: *Aspects of theory of syntax*. Cambridge, Mass.: MIT.

—— 1986: *Knowledge of language*. New York: Praeger.

d'Agostino, F. 1986: *Chomsky's system of ideas*. Oxford and New York: Oxford University Press.

Greene, Judith 1972: *Psycholinguistics: Chomsky and psychology*. London: Penguin.

Lyons, John 1985: *Chomsky*. 2nd edn. London: Fontana/Collins.

chromosome abnormalities Chromosomes are those parts of the body cells which carry the genetic code. In humans, the normal cell contains 46 chromosomes, 44 of which are common to both sexes (autosomal chromosomes) and 2 of which differ between the sexes (sex chromosomes). In males these consist of one X and one Y (XY); in females, two matching X chromosomes (XX). A variety of abnormalities of both autosomal and sex chromosomes have now been identified, the commonest being too many or too few chromosomes. Autosomal chromosome abnormalities are generally associated with marked physical malformation and mental retardation (e.g. DOWN'S SYNDROME). Sex chromosome abnormalities are less closely associated with mental retardation; malformation of the sex organs are the most common physical abnormality and psychiatric disorder may occur. Prenatal diagnosis of chromosome abnormalities is possible by sampling the amniotic fluid surrounding the foetus (amniocentesis). Subsequent termination can thus prevent the birth of an abnormal child. GENETIC COUNSELING should be offered to parents and relatives of affected children to help them decide about future pregnancies. GCF

Bibliography

De Grouchy, J. and Thurleau, C. 1978: *Atlas of chromosome abnormalities*. New York: John Wiley.

Therman, E. 1980: *Human chromosomes*. Heidelberg and New York: Springer Verlag.

class size Refers to the size of teaching group in schools and in further education. The most extensive research has been carried out in school settings. Most professional teachers assume that children will learn more effectively and respond more easily to group leadership in smaller classes, but research results have repeatedly challenged these common sense assumptions, yielding either inconsistent or negative results.

Studies of children's attainments at various ages and in many countries have indicated that they are not improved when class sizes are reduced. This holds good when possible intervening variables such as school size and urban/rural balance are held constant (Davie et al. 1972; Little et al. 1972). There have been methodological problems in much of the research: the criterion of attainment has often been narrow, such as a single reading test (Maxwell 1977); there has been no agreement on the range of class sizes to be studied, and some investigators have focused on small differences in class size; for educational reasons classes with less able or difficult children are often made smaller, so that the pupil population variable confounds class size for research purposes. However, some recent studies (e.g. Shapson et al. 1980) have overcome these methodological problems, and their findings confirm the clear trend of the research evidence: the gains in basic academic achievement that are expected when school classes are reduced from 33–40 to 23–30 are not normally found – though there may be gains with groups of fewer than 16 (Glass et al. 1979).

Studies of children's behavior show similarly equivocal results (Little et al. 1972). These also suggest that teachers may not adapt their methods significantly to take advantage of decreases in class size, and Shapson et al. (1980) recently presented evidence supporting this view. However, an Australian observational study showed that in some larger first year secondary classes there was likely to be an emphasis on order and work habits with a high level of academic guidance and instruction (Keeves 1972).

A fruitful line of inquiry has been the examination of how *pupils* perceive the social climate of learning in classes of various sizes. For example in one North American study they appear to experience smaller classes as consistently more cohesive and more difficult, and frequently less formal and less diverse. One important feature of the work of this research group has been that it is based on a coherent and articulate theoretical model (Anderson and Wahlberg 1972). Too much of the literature on class size has reported survey findings with post hoc explanations of limited interest. This may explain why the results have been so inconsistent and the controversy thus far remains unresolved.

TIC

Bibliography

Anderson, G.J. and Wahlberg, H.J. 1972: Class size and the social environment of learning: a replication. *Alberta journal of educational research* 18, 227–86.

Davie, R., Butler, N. and Goldstein, H. 1972: *From birth to seven: second report of the national child development study*. London: Longman.

Glass, G. and Smith, M. 1979: Meta-analysis of research on class size and achievement. *Educational evaluation and policy analysis* 1, 2–16.

Keeves, J.P. 1972: *Educational environment and student achievement*. Melbourne: Australian Council for Education Research; Stockholm: Almquist and Wiksell.

Little, A., Mabey, C. and Russell, J. 1972: Class size, pupil characteristics and reading attainment. In *Literacy at all levels. Proceedings of the eighth annual study conference of the United Kingdom reading association*, ed. V. Southgate.

Maxwell, J. 1977: *Reading progress from eight to fifteen: a survey of attainment and teaching practices in Scotland*. Windsor, Berks: National Foundation for Educational Research.

Shapson, S.M. et al. 1980: An experimental study of the effects of class size. *American educational research journal* 17, 141–52.

clumsy children These children show a difficulty in performing skilled movements which is inappropriate for their age and cannot be explained in terms of general intellectual impairment or gross sensory defects. An alternative term sometimes used for this disorder is developmental apraxia (a disorder of movement) and agnosia (a disorder of perception).

The pattern of problems experienced by individual children may vary considerably but often includes difficulties in the mastery of ordinary physical skills such as eating, dressing and tying shoe laces. Associated educational difficulties include problems with handwriting and drawing and, of course, physical education. Although recognized some time ago (see Orton 1937) until recently the problems of this group of children have received very little attention.

It is likely that in many cases clumsiness results from minor brain damage occurring early in life, possibly because of birth difficulties or neurological disease. It is not surprising therefore that there may be a variety of other difficulties associated with clumsiness such as speech problems, reading problems, hyperactivity and epilepsy.

Recognition that clumsiness may often be of constitutional origin should not be taken to mean that remediation is doomed to fail. Physiotherapy and various training exercises may improve basic physical skills and remedial teaching may help with the child's educational difficulties. Simply diagnosing and explaining the problem to parents, teachers and the child may be particularly important in helping to reduce feelings of frustration which can in turn lead to further emotional problems.

(See also DYSLEXIC CHILDREN.)   ChasH

Bibliography

*Gordon, N. and McKinlay, I. eds 1980: *Helping clumsy children*. Edinburgh: Churchill Livingstone.

*Gubby, S. 1975: *The clumsy child*. London and Philadelphia: Saunders.

Orton, S.T. 1937: *Reading, writing and speech problems in children*. New York: Norton.

code The notion that language is a code implies that particular grammars for encoding conceptualizations may differ between languages or, put differently, that linguistic surface forms may have little to do with the underlying logic of an utterance.

Among the most widely debated issues in socio- and psycholinguistics is that of the influence of linguistic categories and cultural conceptualizations on the processes underlying human thought. According to Bernstein (1971) a distinction can be made between elaborated codes, giving access to a wide range of knowledge and important positions in a social hierarchy, and restricted codes, which limit the speaker's access to knowledge and power. Labov, on the other hand, argues that non-standard varieties of a language do not impose cognitive limitations. He provided anecdotal examples of logical thoughts expressed by a black speaker of non-standard English, and rather less logical thoughts expressed by a black speaker of standard English (Labov 1969; 1972).

Bernstein's suggestion about the limitations the restricted code places on cognitive processes depends heavily on the claim that speakers of the restricted code cannot switch to the elaborated code. Robinson (1965), however, found that they could do so at least when writing a letter. Collett et al. (1981) instructed lower working class and middle class English schoolchildren in a complex spatial task. Each child then had to instruct one other child from his or her own class, and the child so instructed had to complete the task. Although the middle class children did use elaborated code, and the working class children did use restricted code in giving their instructions, "learner" children from both classes completed the task with equal success. Taken together, these results suggest that the restricted code user is not limited cognitively or communicatively, nor necessarily bound to the restricted code.

Linguistic codes consist of subcomponents (e.g. the phonetic, phonological, lexical and syntactic components). The notion of "subcode" refers to regional, social or stylistic variants of the same linguistic system. Research which compares different *languages* rather than *codes* has not generally supported the view that language imposes the limitations Whorf and Bernstein claimed. (See Kay and Kempton 1984; see also WHORF.)   PM/RL

Bibliography

Bernstein, Basil 1971: *Class, codes and control*. London: Routledge and Kegan Paul.

Collett, P.C., Lamb, R., Fenlaugh, K. and McPhail, P.C. 1981: Social class and linguistic variation. In *Social situations*, eds. M. Argyle, A. Furnham and J.A. Graham. Cambridge: Cambridge University Press.

Kay, P. and Kempton, W. 1984: What is the Sapir-Whorf hypothesis? *American anthropologist* 86, 65–79.

Labov, W. 1969: The logic of nonstandard English. *Georgetown monographs on language and linguistics* 22, 1–31. Reprinted in *Language and social context*, ed. P.P. Giglioli. London: Penguin (1972).

Robinson, W.P. 1965: The elaborated code in working class language. *Language and speech* 8, 243–52.

cognitive development, non-Piagetian studies

Although current work on cognitive development is dominated by the ideas of PIAGET, there are nevertheless strands of thought about the subject whose origins owe nothing to his oeuvre, and these have an important place in the study of childhood.

One of these was the Gestalt school. Its members' main interest was in perception which they thought to be innately determined and which was in their view largely concerned with taking in patterns. This led them to argue that even very young children are aware of relative values, a belief that brought them into head-on conflict not only with Piaget and his supporters but also with the behaviorist school in America. In fact the pioneering experiments on judgments of relative size and brightness carried out in the early twentieth century by Köhler, a leading gestalt psychologist, have been largely vindicated, and there can be little doubt that young children are as adept as Köhler claimed in dealing with relative values.

At much the same time the work of VYGOTSKY in Russia launched a theory and a type of experiment which have played an important role in studies of child development and have produced conclusions quite different from Piaget's. Vygotsky's central idea was that language, and particularly what he called inner speech, transforms the child's cognitive abilities. To support his hypothesis Vygotsky observed children speaking in different situations and tried to relate what they said to what they actually did when they were solving problems. He was particularly interested in any direct connection between the two, as shown by his well known story of a boy drawing a picture of a car who broke his crayon, muttered "broken" and went on to draw a broken car.

The issue of the relationship between language and cognition was taken up by others, most notably at first by behaviorists in America and then in quite a different way by BRUNER. It is a question which still awaits an answer. But the study of language acquisition per se has produced some solid data. We know a great deal not only about how children's sentences develop, thanks to the observational work of Roger Brown and others, but also about the way in which adults talk to children.

A final major strand in studies of cognitive development takes as its inspiration the notion of information processing. The notion that humans can be regarded as limited information channels is a familiar one, and it has the advantage of leading to some precise predictions. By and large when these have been made about children the idea has been that there are no great qualitative differences between them and adults, but that the major cognitive changes in childhood are quantitative – the capacity of the information channel, the size of the memory store and so on. More recently a group of psychologists interested in what they call meta-memory and meta-cognition have argued that the changes are not so much in the machine's capacity as in the correct application of the right strategies at the right time. This takes the subject into the area of education because one of the most interesting parts of this recent concentration on the extent to which children are aware of the appropriate strategies has been its application to the study of learning to read and to write.   PEB

Bibliography

Fischer, K.W. and Silvern, L. 1985: Stages and individual differences in cognitive development. *Annual review of psychology* 36, 613–48.

Gardner, H. 1982: *Developmental psychology*. 2nd edn. Boston: Little, Brown and Co.

Vygotsky, Lev. S. 1962: *Thought and language*. Cambridge, Mass.: MIT; New York and London: Wiley.

cohort analysis

The search for systematic variability that is attributable to a group of individuals having experienced the same event during the same interval of time. Forms of cohort analysis are found in sociology, demography, economics, psychology and other social and behavioral sciences (see e.g. Ryder 1965). In psychology, especially developmental psychology, cohort analysis has focused almost exclusively on the *birth cohort*, individuals born during the same time interval, as a basis for categorizing sources of changes in, and differences among individuals. For example, differences in the average performance of twenty-year olds and seventy-year olds measured in the year 1980 on an intellectual task may be attributable to changes that are intrinsic to "aging processes" but such differences could also be due to other influences; those associated with the fact that the seventy-year-olds were born in 1910 and have spent their first twenty years in one set of educational, political, nutritional etc. circumstances whereas the twenty-year olds were born in 1960 and have spent their first twenty years in a different set of circumstances. Individuals who differ in chronological age simultaneously differ in experienced history-specific characteristics that may be related to differences in their behavioral attributes. Important birth cohort and age differences need not be fifty-year ones; differences as small as one year were found to be significant in adolescent personality development in the 1970s (Nesselroade and Baltes 1974). Additional support for the predictive validity of cohort and age classification is found in the areas of ability and personality, verbal learning and memory, sexual attitudes and behavior, and physical attributes.

In current developmental research, papers by Schaie (1965) and Baltes (1968) have been particularly influential in establishing the value of identifying cohort and other sources of variation within and between individuals. Schaie presented a General Developmental Model in which birth cohort, chronological age, and time of measurement were identified as representing fundamental sources of variability, the magnitude of which could be estimated by means of a carefully selected set of analysis strategies. In a critique of Schaie's model, Baltes emphasized the difference between description and explanation, argued that the Schaie model was more useful as a guide to data collection than data analysis, and developed a rationale for cross-sectional and longitudinal sequences as general data collection strategies for distinguishing cohort, age and time of measurement effects. Subsequently, Schaie and Baltes (1975) agreed on the value of sequential strategies for the purpose of data collection but not on the validity of causal inferences based on data derived from them.

The determination of the magnitude of cohort, age and time effects is hindered because of dependency among the three components as they are traditionally defined. That situation has led to several developments of, and critical exchanges concerning, analytical and statistical methods for estimating cohort, age and time of measurement effects (Horn and McArdle 1980).

The concepts of cohort and cohort effects, despite their limitations for formulating explanatory accounts, constitute an important step in the evolution of ideas about development. Their discovery and study have brought about alternative ways of conceptualizing developmental phenomena and more sophisticated appraisals of the traditional longitudinal and cross-sectional research designs and methods. The substantive and methodological research efforts associated with identifying and studying cohort, age and time of measurement effects have helped to foster a significant contemporary emphasis on the study of development as a phenomenon that occurs over the life span rather than being confined to the first eighteen or so years of life.

Cohort analysis, in explicitly recognizing the potential impact on the course of development of influences that are tied to social/environmental and biological changes has helped to focus attention on two important questions: which change phenomena are to be included in the province of developmental study and how general and permanent can one expect lawful relationships concerning development to be (Gergen, 1980). Definitive answers are yet to come but cohort analysis has underscored the importance of attending to context if developmental processes are to be more fully understood. Additional benefits of cohort analysis will be realized as cohort effects are analysed in process variable terms (Baltes, Cornelius and Nesselroade 1978).   JRN

Bibliography

Baltes, P.B. 1968: Longitudinal and cross-sectional sequences in the study of age and generation effects. *Human development* 11, 145–71.

———, Cornelius, S.W. and Nesselroade, J.R. 1978: Cohort effects in developmental psychology: theoretical and methodological perspectives. *Minnesota symposia on child psychology*, vol. 11. Hillsdale, N.J.: Erlbaum.

Gergen, K.J. 1980: The emerging crisis in life-span developmental theory. In *Life-span development and behavior*, vol. 3, eds. P.B. Baltes and O.G. Brim Jr. New York: Academic Press.

Horn, J.L. and McArdle, J.J. 1980: Perspectives on mathematical/statistical model building (MASMOB) in research on aging. In *Aging in the 1980s*, ed. L.W. Poon. Washington, D.C.: American Psychological Association.

Lerner, R.M. and Hultsch, D.F. 1983: *Human development: a life span perspective*. New York: McGraw-Hill.

Nesselroade, J.R. and Baltes, P.B. 1974: Adolescent personality development and historical change: 1970–1972. *Monographs of the society for research in child development*, 39 (serial no. 154).

Riley, M.W., Johnson, W. and Foner, A., eds. 1972: *Aging and society*, vol. 3. *A sociology of age stratification*. New York: Russell Sage.

Ryder, N.B. 1965: The cohort as a concept in the study of social change. *American sociological review* 30, 843–61.

Schaie, K.W. 1965: A general model for the study of developmental problems. *Psychological bulletin* 64, 92–107.

——— and Baltes, P.B. 1975: On sequential strategies in developmental research and the Schaie-Baltes controversy: description or explanation? *Human development* 18, 384–90.

compensatory education The effort to provide special education for children from poor backgrounds who have been found to be a high risk group for SCHOOL FAILURE. Although efforts in this area surged in the 1960s, the basic concept of intervening to optimize developments is not new. Education at the time of the French Revolution, for example, was marked by efforts to provide environments which would foster the development of skills in those who had until then been neglected and deemed hopeless (the mentally handicapped, the deaf, etc.; see Lane (1976) for a review of this work).

The sharp growth in compensatory efforts after the first world war can be traced to a variety of factors. First, in many industrialized western societies, there were major shifts in population with people moving from rural areas to the cities. Then after the war many middle-class families moved from the cities to the suburbs, leaving large concentrations of lower-class minorities within the inner cities. As a result increasing numbers of lower-class children were concentrated within the city schools. Since these children performed poorly in academic attainment the schools were confronted with increasingly high rates of school failure. At the same time there was increased enforcement of the laws which require all children to attend school throughout much of adolescence. As a result those children who might have dropped out of school because of failure or lack of motivation were retained.

A second major force behind the compensatory education movement derived from the changing occupational structure. As western nations became more technological there was a decline in the demand for unskilled labor and a rise in the demand for individuals who were literate and had other academic skills. The poor academic attainments of many from the lower classes therefore contributed to a high rate of unemployment among that group. The concept of compensatory education was advanced as a solution to this problem.

Third, the growing acceptance of democratic ideals led to increased demands for equality of opportunity for all. This trend was clearly shown in the Civil Rights Movement which was led by the black minority in the United States during the 1960s, and in which the demand for equal educational opportunity was central. It was felt that equality in other spheres, such as job opportunities, could not be met unless educational attainment was significantly enhanced.

These combined forces inevitably led to a focus on the school and more specifically, on the reasons for the high rate of school failure. Much use was made of a deprivation model put forward by Donald Hebb in the 1950s. The model, which stressed the concept of stimulus deprivation, was based on a series of studies documenting the environmental factors necessary for maintaining normal functioning in animals. It was found that when organisms were deprived of information to the various senses (vision, hearing and touch), their development in both the intellectual and affective realms was severely impaired. Further, studies of infants reared in the sensory-deprived environment of an institution showed comparable deficiencies in functioning. Because of its power in explaining deficiencies in behavior, the deprivation model was adopted as the explanation for the problems of lower-class children. They were said to have been reared in deprived environments (see SOCIAL DISADVANTAGE) and to be in need of more stimulating environments that would compensate for the deprivation. The term "compensatory education" logically followed from this reasoning.

Once the problem was considered within a deprivation framework, it was reasonable to focus the greatest effort on the preschool years. It was hoped that the earlier intervention was begun, the more likely it was that success would be achieved. Furthermore the dominant psychological theories, including those of FREUD, Skinner and PIAGET, stressed the importance of the early years in providing a foundation for all future development. Even though the failure was displayed by children of school age, it was thought that the difficulties could best be overcome by taking preventive measures during the preschool years.

A number of different efforts at early intervention were attempted. One type was based on techniques developed for the urban poor of Italy in the early 1900s by the physician Maria Montessori. The method emphasized the need for active involvement on the part of the child, in the three main areas of motor education (cutting paper, tying laces, etc.), sensory education (attention to texture, rhythms, etc.) and language, both oral and reading. Attractive and carefully structured materials were developed to foster learning while still allowing the child control over the pace and type of activity.

Other techniques used much more direct intervention. One of the most notable efforts was developed by Carl Bereiter and Siegfried Engelmann (1966). Using Skinnerian concepts of operant learning, they developed a language-focused method which emphasized drill, discipline and regimentation. Children worked in small groups where they were exposed to material presented in fifteen-to twenty-minute segments. The first unit might be on grammar, the second on phonics (recognizing the sounds of letters), the third on mathematics. This rigid structure stood in marked contrast to the ease and informality characteristic of most other pre-school approaches. There was an absence of free play which had long been viewed as the prime motivator of learning in young children. Instead, in line with operant principles, the rewards were externally-based motivators (e.g. food treats or praise) that had no intrinsic relationship to the tasks which the children were required to perform.

Still other methods aimed at the overall enrichment of the child. In some cases they were even called "bombardment approaches" in that they exposed the child to a vast array of stimuli in the hope of stimulating activity. (While the discussion of compensatory techniques has been limited to the educational components, it should be noted that many of them were designed for comprehensive intervention and included medical attention, nutritional enrichment and parent involvement (Zigler and Valentine 1979).)

Within a relatively short time considerable money and effort had been put into compensatory education, and efforts were also made to assess its effectiveness. Given the goal (the prevention of school failure), it would have been best to delay any assessment until the children had completed several years of formal schooling, but this was not considered feasible so it became typical for short-term evaluations to be conducted by means of tests such as INTELLIGENCE TESTS which have been shown to correlate with academic success. There were many reports of short-term gains in IQ scores and related cognitive tests. However, the gains often seemed to disappear over time; that is, as the children moved through school, there was a lessening of the differences between those who had, and those who had not, received compensatory instruction.

Long-term follow up studies have since been made to assess the effects of pre-school education on school performance and these results have been more promising (Zigler and Valentine 1979). The several hundred children who had participated in preschool programs were found to be 40 per cent less likely to be put into special education classes, and to be 20 per cent less likely to be kept back in a grade than were their peers in control groups. Further, when youths in the 16–21 year age range were studied, it was found that 37 per cent of those who had been in preschool went on to college or skilled jobs; only 8 per cent of the controls achieved this level of performance. The reason for the improvement is unclear; it could have been based upon such varied factors as changes in parents' attitudes and interactions with their children, and changes in the children's attitudes towards school and their abilities to meet the teachers' demands (see EDUCATIONAL ATTAINMENT AND EXPECTATIONS). Nevertheless the results stand in contrast to earlier reports and indicate the usefulness of continuing compensatory efforts.

While the later results are promising, their impact has not been great, for by the time they appeared considerable disillusionment had already set in and they soon became entangled in a major controversy.

On one side of the controversy was Arthur Jensen who, in a famous article (1969), argued that the difficulties of lower-class minority children who fail in school derive from genetic limitations. While this paper was, and continues to be, the subject of heated debate it has nevertheless served as an important rationale for the curtailment of preschool intervention programs. Another group of researchers also questioned the basis of the preschool intervention movement (see Cazden, John and Hymes 1972 for a review of this position). They rejected the assertions that the children were either genetically or environmentally deficient and, while acknowledging that the school performance was often poor, they attributed this failure to the structure of the school system, which they saw as a reflection of the culture of the dominant social group and as a force which devalued the culture in which minority children were reared. From this vantage point compensatory education was not what was needed. Instead it was claimed that schools had to be radically altered to meet the styles of the different populations they served. While many have found this approach appealing, it has for the most part remained academic in that workable alternatives remain to be developed.

The discussion until now, like much of the actual effort itself, has been directed at the pre-school years. However, some attention has also been devoted to older age groups. For example the Follow Through program in the United States was developed to offer a continuation of special services for disadvantaged children for the first three years of formal schooling. It was hoped that by establishing continuity between the preschool years and later schooling any initial gains would be maintained. In a major evaluation of this intervention it was indeed found that those children who were given continued compensatory services achieved a higher overall performance level in later schooling than did those who only had compensatory preschool (Weisberg and Haney 1977).

Much of the impetus for compensatory

education developed in the United States, which is not surprising since the States invests more time and money in education than any other country in the world. However, compensatory education for lower-class minority groups is provided in many other countries. (See for England, Tough (1977); for Holland, Groenendaal (1978); for Israel, Frankenstein (1970) and Minkovich et al. (1977).)   MB/JM

Bibliography

Bereiter, C. and Engelmann, S. 1966: *Teaching the disadvantaged child in the pre-school*. Englewood Cliffs, N.J.: Prentice-Hall.

Cazden, C.B., John, V.P. and Hymes, D. 1972: *Functions of language in the classroom*. New York: Teachers College Press.

Detterman, D.K. and Sternberg, R.J. eds. 1982: *How and how much can intelligence be increased?* Norwood, N.J.: Ablex.

Frankenstein, C. 1970: *Impaired intelligence: pathology and rehabilitation*. London: Gordon and Breach.

Groenendaal, H.J. 1978: *Vroegtijdige hulpverlening aan zwakfunktionerende kleuters*. Amsterdam: Vrije Universiteit te Amsterdam.

Heber, R. and Garber, H. 1975: The Milwaukee project: a study of the use of family intervention to prevent cultural-familial mental retardation. In *Exceptional infant*, vol. 3, eds. B.Z. Friedlander, G.M. Sterritt and G.E. Kirk. New York: Brunner/Mazel.

Jensen, A.R. 1969: How much can we boost IQ and scholastic achievement? *Harvard educational review* 39, 1–123.

Lane, H. 1976: *The wild boy of Aveyron*. Cambridge, Mass.: Harvard University Press.

Lazar, I. and Darlington, R. 1982: Lasting effects of early education: a report from the consortium for longitudinal studies. *Monographs of the society for research in child development* 47, 1–151.

Minkovich, A., Davis, D. and Bashi, J. 1977: *An evaluation study of Israeli elementary schools*. Jerusalem: The Hebrew University of Jerusalem.

Rutter, M. et al. 1979: *Fifteen thousand hours*. London: Open Books; Cambridge, Mass.: Harvard University Press.

Sommer, R. and Sommer, B.A. 1983: Mystery in Milwaukee: early intervention, IQ, and psychology textbooks. *American psychologist* 38, 982–5.

Tough, J. 1977: Children and programmes:
how shall we educate the young child? In *Language and learning in early childhood*, ed. A. Davies. London: Heinemann.

Weisberg, H.I. and Haney, W. 1977: *Longitudinal evaluation of Head Start planned variation and follow through*. Cambridge, Mass.: Huron Institute.

Zigler, E. and Valentine, J. eds. 1979: *Project Head Start: a legacy of the war on poverty*. New York: The Free Press.

competence: linguistic

According to CHOMSKY and other transformational-generative grammarians, competence refers to the ability of the idealized speaker-hearer to associate sounds and meanings in accordance with the rules of his or her language. A grammar of a language, in this view, is a description of this competence or knowledge. It is distinguished from the actual use of language in concrete situations, or performance (Chomsky 1965, 3–9). Transformationalist competence, like structuralist *langue*, refers to invariant self-contained systems. It differs from the latter notion in that it refers to a system of generative processes rather than a systematic inventory of items.

The principal objection to the concept of linguistic competence relates to its failure to refer to an identifiable psychological reality. Linguists of the variationist type (Bailey, LABOV) have shown that linguistic variation is highly constrained and regular and should therefore belong to competence rather than *performance*. Sociolinguistics investigating the ethnography of speaking (e.g. Hymes 1974) have pointed out that, in addition to grammatical competence, actual speakers also have communicative competence, i.e. they are able to distinguish between situationally appropriate and inappropriate language use.

There are a number of skills involved in this, such as grasping what the listener does and does not know. Children are not good at taking another person's perspective (see EGOCENTRISM), and only improve slowly (see Edelstein et al. 1984). Nevertheless, even young children seem to recognize the convention that different kinds of language should be used to different hearers. Children as young as three adjust their style to BABY TALK when addressing a younger sibling (Dunn and Kendrick 1982). Other aspects of communicative competence appear before speech. Infants respond to others' interest, since their attention is guided by their mothers' gaze (Butterworth and Cochran 1980). Furthermore, turn-taking, which is regarded as a necessary part of conversation, appears in interactions between mothers and their newborn infants (Kaye 1982). PM/RL

Bibliography

Butterworth, G.E. and Cochran, E. 1980: Towards a mechanism of joint visual attention in human infancy. *International journal of behavioral development* 3, 253–72.

Chomsky, Noam 1965: *Aspects of the theory of syntax*. Cambridge Mass.: MIT Press.

Dunn, J. and Kendrick, C. 1982: The speech of two- and three-year-olds to infant siblings: 'baby-talk' and the context of communication. *Journal of child language* 9, 579–95.

Edelstein, W., Keller, M. and Wahlen, K. 1984: Structure and content in social cognition: conceptual and empirical analyses. *Child development* 55, 1514–26.

Hymes, Dell 1974: *Foundations in sociolinguistics*. Philadelphia: University of Pennsylvania Press.

Kaye, K. 1982: *The social and mental life of babies*. Chicago: University of Chicago Press.

competence motivation

Refers to motives to master the environment. White (1959) believed children are born with such motivation, and that it explains their curiosity and persistence in difficult tasks. This amounts to a claim that children have an intrinsic motivation to learn, and will therefore do it for its own sake rather than for further reward. More recently Harter (1981) has offered a SOCIAL LEARNING explanation of why children differ in their curiosity and persistence on difficult tasks. her, encouragement and success will induce a child to seek challenges and give it high SELF-ESTEEM, whereas indifference or failure will have the opposite effect. On the basis of this assumption attempts have been made to relate perceived differences between children's curiosity and persistence to differences in parents' encouragement. For example, Yarrow et al. (1984) found that parents' sensory stimulation of their six-month-old infants correlated positively with the infants' persistence in dealing with a new toy. RL

Bibliography

Harter, S. 1981: A model of intrinsic mastery motivation in children: individual differences and developmental change. In *Minnesota symposium on child psychology*, vol. 14, ed. W.A. Collins. Hillsdale, N.J.: Erlbaum.

White, R.W. 1959: Motivation reconsidered: the concept of competence. *Psychological review* 66, 297–333.

Yarrow, L.J. et al. 1984: Developmental course of parental stimulation and its relationship to mastery motivation during infancy. *Developmental psychology* 20, 492–503.

computer-aided instruction (CAI)

A method for the systematic presentation of information which relies on a computer system for program storage and retrieval. In computer-aided instruction the prospective learner interacts directly with the computer in an attempt to master the program content. Cooley and Glaser (1969) describe a CAI system in the following six steps:

(1) The goals of learning are specified in terms of observable learner behavior and conditions under which the behavior is to be manifested.
(2) The learner's initial relevant capabilities are assessed at the beginning of a course of instruction.
(3) Suitable educational alternatives are then presented to the learner, who selects or is assigned one of them.
(4) The learner's performance is monitored, recorded and continuously assessed as the session progresses.
(5) Instruction proceeds as a function of the relationships between the student's performance, available instructional activities, and pre-established criteria of competence.
(6) As instruction proceeds, data relevant to the program are generated for monitor-

ing and improving the instructional system.

Advantages and disadvantages associated with CAI have been discussed by Goldstein (1974) and Seltzer (1971). Advantages include the tailoring of the instructional process to the unique characteristics of the learner, the immediate and accurate reinforcement, and the freeing of instructor time from the burdensome chore of bookkeeping. Among the major disadvantages associated with this form of instruction are the costs inherent in putting together a complete CAI system (including hardware and software), the degree to which learning under CAI has a carryover effect to other less structured environments requiring the same responses and the degree to which CAI is superior to other more traditional and less costly learning techniques. Another problem may be a tendency for students to make more effort when the instruction medium is "hard", and computers may appear not to be (Salomon 1983).

A number of analyses by the Kuliks and others (Kulik and Kulik 1985) have shown that computer-aided instruction seems to have positive effects in some contexts but not in others. Evidence and opinions are also divided about the general educational value of learning to program computers (see Salomon 1984). There has nevertheless been a great expansion of computer aid software both in general education, and in special education for pupils with handicaps and learning difficulties (see Mokros and Russell 1986). (See also MACHINE LEARNING; PROGRAMMED INSTRUCTION.)   RRJ

Bibliography

Cooley, W.W. and Glaser, R. 1969: The computer and individualized instruction. *Science* 166, 574–82.
Goldstein I.L. 1974: *Training: program development and evaluation*. Monterey, Calif.: Brooks/Cole.
Kulik, C.-L.C. and Kulik, J.A. 1985: *Effectiveness of computer-based education in college*. Ann Arbor: Center for Research in Learning and Teaching.
Mokros, J.R. and Russell, S.J. 1986: Learner-centered software: a survey of microcomputer use with special needs students. *Journal of learning disabilities* 19, 185–90.
Salomon, G. 1983: The differential investment of mental effort in learning from different sources. *Educational psychology* 18, 42–50.
—— 1984: On ability development and far transfer: reflections on Pea and Kurland's paper. *New ideas in psychology* 2, 169–76.
Seltzer, R.H. 1971: Computer assisted instruction – what it can and cannot do. *American psychologist* 26, 373–7.

concept learning Learning to categorize different experiences. This process has been much studied using the concept identification method. A person is presented with a series of stimuli, some of which have been designated by the experimenter as instances of a new category. Success in identifying the concept is demonstrated by the ability to classify new members of the category correctly. The stimuli used have often been composed of a small number of attributes (such as color and shape), as in the classic study by Bruner, Goodnow and Austin (1956). The category to be identified consists then of stimuli that possess a particular conjunction (e.g. both *black* and *circular*), a particular disjunction (e.g. either *black* or *circular*), or some other combination of attribute-values. Considerable evidence has accumulated that learning in this type of task occurs by the formation and testing of discrete hypotheses concerning the characteristics of the concept to be acquired. It is not possible, however, to characterize many common concepts, such as *furniture*, by a simple rule. In recent years it has been shown that the acquisition of such concepts appears to center around their best instances, or *prototypes*.   GVJ

Bibliography

Bruner, J.S., Goodnow, J.J. and Austin, G.A. 1956: *A study of thinking*. New York: Wiley.
*Reed, Stephen K. 1982: *Cognition: theory and applications*. Monterey, Calif.: Brooks/Cole.

concrete thinking Reasoning that is strongly tied to context or to immediate and tangible information. In Piaget's theory the concrete operational stage of cognitive development occurs between the ages of eight and eleven years. It is defined by the ability to think about problems in the "here and now" but not in the abstract and it marks a further step in the differentiation of the child from the world. The child can now reason logically in various domains such as conservation, classification and transitive inference, but only when all the information to be ordered remains immediately present. For example the child can work out the relative length of stick C by serial comparison of pairs of longer sticks A and B, to arrive at the solution by a transitive inference: A > B, B > C ∴ A > C. However, at the same age the child cannot solve a hypothetical version of the same problem: if John is taller than Mary and Mary is taller than Jane, who is the tallest? The ability to reason in the abstract awaits the acquisition of formal operations in early adolescence. (See PIAGET.)   GEB

Bibliography

Brainerd, C.J. 1978: *Piaget's theory of intelligence*. Englewood Cliffs, N.J.: Prentice-Hall.

conduct disorder The commonest type of child psychiatric disorder, characterized by behavior which is antisocial, e.g. lying, stealing, aggression, firesetting, truancy. Conduct disorder occurs more commonly in boys than girls, and children from large or disrupted families living in poor social conditions are especially at risk. There is a marked association with reading retardation, and there may be associated emotional symptoms such as anxiety and low self esteem. In up to 50 per cent of children, the disorder persists into adolescence and may develop into delinquency (cf. Spivack et al. 1986). Psychiatric treatment may take a variety of forms. Behavioral treatments consist of setting clear limits of acceptable behavior for the child, and encouraging parents and teachers to work together in a consistent approach. Individual therapy aims at developing the child's skills and self esteem and exploring any areas of conflict; family therapy may be aimed at trying to change rejecting family attitudes. If these approaches fail it may be necessary to remove the child from the home environment, by placing him or her in a residential school, children's home, or foster family.

(See also CHILD AND ADOLESCENT PSYCHIATRY; DELINQUENCY.)   GCF

Bibliography

Barker, P. 1979: *Basic child psychiatry*. London: Granada.

Epstein, M.H. and Cullinan, D. 1984: Behavior problems of mildly handicapped and normal adolescents. *Journal of clinical child psychology* 13, 33–7.

Robins, L. 1966: *Deviant children grown up*. Baltimore: Williams and Williams.

Spivack, G., Marcus, J. and Swift, M. 1986: Early classroom behaviors and later misconduct. *Developmental psychology* 22, 124–31.

conscience A set of personal rules and values that usually parallel the norms of society and guide individual social conduct. These rules are generally thought to be learned and are, therefore, initially implanted by external influences (e.g. through the rewards and punishment of authority figures). Once the rules are internalized, however, social conduct becomes privately regulated (e.g. guilt is experienced when these internalized rules are violated). (See also MORAL DEVELOPMENT.)   RHo

conservation A term in Piagetian theory that refers to the knowledge that physical properties of objects remain invariant under transformations that do not involve addition or subtraction. Such knowledge is acquired between the ages of eight and eleven years, during the concrete operational period.

In the classic conservation task, the child is shown two identical beakers of liquid A and B, and will affirm that they contain an equal amount of water. The water in B is then poured into a different container C, while the child is watching, so that the height and width of the liquid is changed. The child is asked whether A and C contain the same or different amounts of water. Children from about eight years, who conserve volume, will say that the amounts are equal despite the perceptual transformation. Younger children will generally say that the container in which the water level is highest contains most, they "center" upon or are dominated by the changing perceptual attributes of the display. Similar errors can be observed in tasks testing for conservation of length, number or weight. The question whether the child is truly dominated by appearances or simply fails adequately to understand the adult's questions, remains to be resolved. (See PIAGET.)

Bryant (1972) challenged Piaget's claims that young children are unable to understand invariances of quantity, but results continue to suggest that younger children do not perceive consistencies of number as older children do. Halford and Boyle (1985), for instance, asked children to say which of two rows of beads had more in it (following Bryant's experimental technique rather than Piaget's). The beads were then rearranged in their rows before the children's eyes, and the same question was asked again. Young children (3–4 years) showed no consistent tendency to pick the same row before and after the transformation, whereas older children (6–7 years) did. This kind of evidence does not support Bryant's challenge.   GEB/RL

Bibliography

Bryant, P.E. 1972: The understanding of invariance by very young children. *Canadian journal of psychology* 26, 78–96.

Halford, G.S. and Boyle, F.M. 1985: Do young children understand conservation of number? *Child development* 56, 165–76.

Piaget, J. 1952: *The child's conception of number*. New York: Humanities; London: Routledge and Kegan Paul.

contrastive analysis of linguistic systems It is claimed by a number of applied linguists and theoreticians of SECOND LANGUAGE ACQUISITION that the best second language teaching materials are based on a contrastive analysis of the learner's first language and the target language. This view derives from the assumption that positive transfer (facilitation) and negative transfer (interference) are the most important factors in the second language learning process.

Wardhaugh (1971) distinguishes between a strong and a weak version of the contrastive analysis hypothesis. The former claims that the errors and language difficulties of a learner can be predicted by a systematic comparison of the native and target languages. The weak hypothesis merely assumes that all errors can be accounted for by contrastive factors.

In spite of its superficial plausibility and wide acceptance by language teachers, neither version of the contrastive analysis hypothesis can be upheld. Empirical evidence from studies of INTERLANGUAGE suggests that contrastive errors account for only a small proportion of occurring errors. On the methodological side, contrastive linguists have failed to develop consistent criteria for the comparison of linguistic systems.   PM

Bibliography

Wardhaugh, R. 1971: The contrastive analysis hypothesis. *Tesol Quarterly* 5, 223–30.

cooing and babbling The first two stages in child vocal communication are those of cooing and babbling. Cooing refers to the squealing-gurgling sounds made by babies between the ages of six weeks and three to six months. Cooing sounds can be elicited first by a specific stimulus, i.e. a nodding object resembling a face in the visual field of the baby. After about the twelfth week it is necessary for the face to be a familiar one to elicit smiling or cooing (Lenneberg 1967, pp. 276 ff.).

Neither from the point of view of production nor from that of perception can cooing sounds be regarded as speech sounds, as the speech organs do not appear to move in a coordinated way at this stage.

Babbling, on the other hand, is clearly an example of speech sound production, though its precise relationship to later stages of FIRST LANGUAGE ACQUISITION and its communicational functions remain ill-understood. It is defined as the production of speech sounds characteristic of babies between the ages of about three months and two years. It usually peaks between nine and twelve months and with some children ceases when their first words appear. Other children continue to babble while their intelligible language develops.

During the babbling stage children produce a large variety of sounds many of which do not occur in the language of their caretakers and their peers. As babbling is also found with deaf children it is widely regarded as being related to physical maturation rather than exposure to speech. Gilbert (1982), however, questioned whether deaf infants start to babble at the same age as infants with normal hearing.

An important psycholinguistic issue is the relationship between babbling and the child's first words (de Villiers and de Villiers 1979, pp. 26 ff.). Some investigators believe that babbling is a prerequisite for normal FIRST LANGUAGE ACQUISITION in favor of a more indirect relationship between babbling and language. The study of babbling is also important in language universals research, in particular in the area of phonetic universals.   PM

Bibliography

de Villiers, P.A. and J.G. 1979: *Early language*. London: Fontana; Cambridge, Mass.: Harvard University Press.

Gilbert, J.H. 1982: Babbling and the deaf child: a commentary on Lenneberg et al. (1965) and Lenneberg (1967). *Journal of child language* 9, 511–15.

Lenneberg, Eric H. 1967: *Biological foundations of language*. New York and Chichester: John Wiley.

copula An overt verb such as English "to be" when used in normal neutral equational clauses (e.g. He is my brother).

It is regarded as semantically empty and many languages do not possess a lexical item corresponding to the English copula. Its principal grammatical function is to carry temporal, modal or aspectual information (see Lyons 1968, pp. 322 ff.).

The absence of an overt copula in certain varieties of English has been discussed by Ferguson (in connection with BABY TALK and foreigner talk) and for Black Vernacular English by LABOV (1969) in connection with claims made about the mental retardation of lower class black children. The development of the copula construction in FIRST LANGUAGE ACQUISITION has been studied by Brown (1970).

PM

Bibliography

Brown, Roger 1970: The child's grammar from 1 to 3. In *Psycholinguistics*, ed. R. Brown. New York and London: Macmillan.

Ferguson, Charles A. 1971: Absence of copula and the notion of simplicity. In *Pidginization and creolization of languages*, ed. D. Hymes. London and New York: Cambridge University Press.

Labov, William 1969: Contraction, deletion and inherent variability of the English copula. *Language* 45, 715–62.

Lyons, John 1968: *Introduction to theoretical linguistics*. Cambridge and New York: Cambridge University Press.

creativity Many diverse definitions have been proposed, but the following is probably representative: man's capacity to produce new ideas, insights, inventions or artistic objects, which are accepted as being of social, spiritual, aesthetic, scientific or technological value. This emphasizes novelty and originality in the production of new combinations of familiar patterns, as in poetry or music, or reorganization of concepts and theories in the sciences. But unconventionality is not sufficient: a lunatic's ravings are not creative. The product must be recognized by capable people, even if initially rejected and not appreciated until later.

Traditionally, creativity was considered a rare and mysterious phenomenon, occurring mainly in a few outstanding geniuses such as Da Vinci, Mozart or Einstein, although it was realized that many other generally more mediocre artists or scientists produced occasional or minor creative works. The present trend, however, particularly in the USA is to see creativity as spread through almost the entire population, though varying in degree. The dramatic play of the young child often appears as imaginative and creative. Indeed creativity can even be observed in young animals at play or among chimpanzees who, according to Köhler (1925), display inventive thinking or "insight".

The older view often linked creativity with insanity (e.g. Lombroso and Kretschmer), though Havelock Ellis's early survey of British geniuses in 1904 found only a very small proportion who could be called psychotic. Minor emotional difficulties, ill health and neuroses were more common. Even more extensive was Terman's study (Cox 1926) of 300 eminent historical figures including many artists and scientists. Terman expected them to have possessed outstanding intelligence, but on assessing their mental capacities from their recorded achievements he found only a few with very high IQs of 170 to 200. The average was 135, and some were as low as 100–110. The geniuses were distinguished more by the character traits of perseverance and drive and the encouraging environment in which most of them were reared. Neurotic tendencies were apparent only in a minority.

Anne Roe's intensive analysis (1952) of the personalities of sixty-four highly creative living scientists, and MacKinnon's (1962) and Barron's (1969) investigations of architects and other groups of professionals, have thrown much light on the psychology of creative individuals. Scientists, especially physical scientists, were characterized by intense absorption in their work and relative lack of interest in social or recreational activities. Though there were wide individual differences, they were the most emotionally stable group. Social scientists and Barron's writers showed more emotional disturbances, but Barron also found the writers high in ego strength, that is self-control and personal effectiveness. Many of these individuals were notably gifted as children, though not necessarily in the same special field; while others did not discover their talent and interest until early adulthood. On the other hand gifted children may be highly intelligent yet not specially talented or creative since they lack the mature technique and the strong inner drive characteristic of creative adults. Nevertheless those adolescents who do show artistic or scientific gifts, e.g. in science projects, are more likely to become involved in creative research and activities at university or in their subsequent jobs. The much lower frequency of creative accomplishments among women than among men is generally attributed to cultural expectations of sex roles, but women have also traditionally had to balance marriage and children against the ambition to follow a creative career.

A different approach is based on studying the creative process. Psychologists have reported many experiments on problem solving, a process which is certainly useful though not highly creative or original. Several writers, musicians, scientists and mathematicians have described their methods of work and the nature of their inspiration (see Ghiselin 1952).

Graham Wallas (1926) recognized four main stages: first that of preparation, including the acquisition of artistic skills or scientific information relevant to the particular problem. Although creative people may rebel against accepted conventions, they must be conversant with the methods and knowledge of their field in order to have something to be creative with. Secondly there is so-called unconscious cerebration, where a strong emotional drive to create interacts, largely subconsciously, with the skills or information. Next there is inspiration regarding the solution or the artistic product; this sometimes arises quite suddenly. Finally a long period of working out and elaboration occurs and, in science, of verification of the solution. This of course is an over-rigid formulation. There is often an interplay of all four stages spread over a considerable period, as in writing a symphony or novel, or developing a scientific discovery.

Much has been written on creativity by FREUD and his followers. In 1908 Freud pointed out the resemblance between children's play, fantasy or daydreaming and the work of the poet. In his view all these activities are expressive of people's inner needs and their imagined solutions. But the poet's feelings and conflicts are more repressed or inhibited, and they emerge in a disguised and socially acceptable form in his finished poems. Freud further distinguished "primary process" thinking, arising from the unconscious, from "secondary process", which is thinking under the control of the ego. He saw both as involved in creative production.

Other writers criticized Freud's implication that artistic and scientific creation derive from the sublimation of repressed and aggressive tendencies, and that creativity is essentially a neurotic defense mechanism, for there are innumerable neurotics who are not at all creative. Kris (1952) and Koestler (1964) have modified the original theory, paying more attention to the critical processes of the ego. They considered the creative artist to be a person who is more than usually in touch with his primary process fantasies and thus, like young children, more spontaneously imaginative. This underlies the original inspiration which is then taken over by the ego and fashioned through secondary process into the complete product. Moreover we gain aesthetic pleasure from a work of art because we are all prone to unconscious conflicts similar to the artist's. Kris refers to this as 'regression in the service of the ego'. It fits in with Barron's discussion of neuroticism and ego control among creative individuals and it helps to explain the greater part played by emotion in artistic as opposed to scientific production. Scientists do sometimes experience inspirations, but clearly most of their work is at the secondary level.

From about 1950 many industrial firms made use of schemes for stimulating creative thinking, such as Osborn's "Applied Imagination" and W.J. Gordon's "Synectics". These provide a fresh approach to such problems as designing and marketing a new product. Several staff members cooperate, and they are encouraged to put forward any suggestions that come to mind, however wild, not stopping to criticize or follow through. This is called "free wheeling", or the principle of deferred judgment. At a later session all ideas are considered critically by the group. This owes something to Freudian theory since the participants are told to relax all inhibitions and give free rein to creative imagination. Several other related techniques may be used. There is little or no scientific evidence that it works; but it has also spread from business into college courses where, it is claimed, training can be given in creative problem-solving with beneficial effects on academic work generally.

In 1950 Guilford drew attention to psychologists' neglect of creative abilities. Aptitude or achievement tests are "convergent" in the sense that the student's answers must converge to the one right solution. But some tests are available in which people are encouraged to put forward a variety of their own answers, i.e. to think "divergently". For example they may be asked to write down as many uses as they can think of for an empty tin can, and their responses are scored both for the quantity or fluency of ideas, and for quality as shown by the usefulness of the ideas. Many other similar divergent tests have been devised in the United States in the belief that American education has become too conventional and convergent, and that those children who will become the creative leaders of the next generation need to be discovered and encouraged. The tests, however, are rather trivial in content and they correlate very little with assessments or other criteria of creative behavior. As with most verbal tests girls tend to score more highly, whereas boys are more attracted to science, which chiefly involves convergent thinking. The tests are also very troublesome to score and they appear to have declined in popularity since the 1960s.　　PEV

Bibliography

Amabile, T.M. 1983: *The social psychology of creativity*. New York, Berlin, Tokyo: Springer-Verlag.

Barron, F. 1969: *Creative person and creative process*. New York: Holt, Rinehart and Winston.

Cox, C.M. 1926: *The early mental traits of three hundred geniuses*. Stanford, Calif.: California University Press.

Freud, S. 1908 (1959): Creative writers and day-dreaming. In *Complete psychological works of Sigmund Freud*, vol. 9. London: Hogarth Press; New York: Norton.

*Ghiselin, B., ed. 1952: *The creative process: a symposium*. Berkeley, Calif.: University of California Press.

Gordon, W.J. 1961: *Synectics: the development of creative capacity*. New York: Harper and Row.

Guilford, J.P. 1950: Creativity. *American psychologist* 5, 444–54.

Köhler, W. 1925: *The mentality of apes*. London: Kegan Paul; New York: Harcourt Brace; New York: Macmillan.

Koestler, A. 1964: *The act of creation*. London: Hutchinson.

Kris, E. 1952: *Psychoanalytic explorations in art*. New York: International Universities Press.

MacKinnon, D.W. 1962: The personality correlates of creativity: a study of American architects. *Proceedings of XIV Congress of Applied Psychology* 2, 11–39.

Osborn, A.F. 1953: *Applied imagination*. New York: Scribner.

Roe, A. 1952: *The making of a scientist*. New York: Dodd Mead.

Vernon, P.E. ed. 1970: *Creativity*. London: Penguin.

Wallas, G. 1926: *The art of thought*. London: Jonathan Cape; New York: Harcourt Brace.

critical periods: developmental Originally an ethological concept designating a fixed time in early development when the young organism is open to forms of learning that will be essential for social adaptation and adult life. A well known example is learning of conspecifics through imprinting in newly hatched goslings. In recent years the concept has been broadened to a sensitive period, to suggest simply a susceptibility for learning at a particular time rather than a crucial occasion for it.

It has been suggested by Bowlby (1969) that there may be a sensitive period for the development of ATTACHMENT in humans, whereby a particular caretaker comes to acquire emotional significance for the child. It is also possible that there may be a sensitive period for the acquisition of language in early childhood. However, a more useful concept in the study of human development may lie in the general PLASTICITY of the nervous system, rather than in a very specific readiness for learning implicit in the ethological approach. GEB

Bibliography

Bowlby, J. 1969: *Attachment and loss*, vol. 1 *Attachment*. London: Hogarth; New York: Basic Books.

Colombo, J. 1982: The critical period concept: research, methodology and theoretical issues. *Psychological bulletin* 91(2), 260–75.

cross-cultural studies: developmental The comparative investigation of experience and behavior across ethnic groups. Developmental studies examine the effects of the cultural milieu on patterns of physical and mental growth and are useful in distinguishing those aspects of human behavior that are universal from those which develop only in relation to specific cultural practices. An anthropological example is the work of Margaret Mead on sex role differentiation. She showed that even though behavior related to sexual role has definite biological roots, conditions of upbringing nevertheless accentuate or suppress components of sexuality in the adult. In the area of cognitive development, cross-cultural studies have also been useful in suggesting specific effects of literacy in the transition from concrete to abstract thinking. GEB

Bibliography

Lloyd, B. and Gay, J. 1981: *Universals of human thought*. Cambridge: Cambridge University Press.

Segall, M.H. 1986: Culture and behavior: psychology in global perspective. In *Annual review of psychology*, vol. 37, eds. M.R. Rosenzweig and L.W. Porter. Palo Alto: Annual Reviews Inc.

cross-lagged correlation A statistical procedure to shed light on causal relationships between variables in research settings where no experimental manipulation is possible. It has been widely used in occupational psychological research within organizations (Clegg, Jackson and Wall 1977). The correlation between two variables, x and y, is calculated on two occasions ($x_1 y_1$ and $x_2 y_2$), also permitting the calculation of correlations between x on both occasions ($x_1 x_2$), between y on both occasions ($y_1 y_2$), and the cross-correlations which are lagged in time ($x_1 y_2$ and $y_1 x_2$). In situations where $x_1 y_2$ is found to be substantially larger than $y_1 x_2$, it is often appropriate to infer causal priority from x to y rather than in the opposite direction.   PBW

Bibliography
Clegg, C.W., Jackson, P.R. and Wall, T.D. 1977: The potential of cross-lagged correlation analysis in field research. *Journal of occupational psychology* 50, 177–96.

cross-modal development Learning to use information derived from one of the senses as a standard, in order to make equivalence judgments about information from another (Jones 1981). Developmental studies throw light on assumptions about the relationships between sensory modalities and the nature of their coordination. For example, it was thought that "touch tutors vision" in development, i.e. tactual experience, is necessary for perceptual development, and that verbal mediation is necessary if information obtained in one sensory modality is to be related to another.

Recent studies of chimpanzees and pre-verbal human infants show that cross-modal coding is possible from an early age without benefit of verbal mediation. This has led to a greater appreciation of sensory processes as perceptual systems whose function is to obtain information that may be equivalent between modalities. On this view the developmental problem in cross-modal coding is one of attending to and remembering the appropriate information.

It is in attending to information that children may become more skilled with age, whether the equivalence judgment is to be made intra- or cross-modally, rather than in coordinating information. (See also PERCEPTUAL AND COGNITIVE ABILITIES IN INFANCY.)   GEB

Bibliography
Gibson, E.J. and Walker, A.S. 1984: Development of knowledge of visual-tactual affordances of substance. *Child development* 55, 453–60.
Jones, W. 1981: The developmental significance of cross-modal matching. In *Intersensory perception and sensory integration*, eds. R. Walk and H. Pick, Jr. New York: Plenum.

cross-sectional research A research design in which a range of variation in a given variable is examined by sampling several different cases at the same time: in contrast to longitudinal research in which a range of variation in a given variable is sampled by observing the same cases at different points in time. For example, a cross-sectional study of the relationship between a person's age and height would compare the heights of individuals who are at different ages, while a longitudinal study would compare the height attained by a given individual at different points in the lifespan. (See also LONGITUDINAL RESEARCH; DEVELOPMENTAL PSYCHOLOGY: METHODS OF STUDY; EDUCATIONAL RESEARCH: METHODOLOGY.)   SBe

crying: developmental Usually refers to a loud rhythmical vocalization associated with lowering or furrowing of the brows, which other than in neonates commonly involves tears; it is generally taken as denoting distress. Some researchers distinguish a milder behavior "fussing" or "fretting" on such bases as little or no rhythmicity, and the face being less contorted.

Three types of cry can be distinguished out of context, both by ear and when visually displayed as a spectrogram of the frequency distribution. These are the "birth cry", given as the newborn takes its first breaths, the "pain-cry", and the "hunger cry" given when the baby has not been fed for several hours. But apart from these gross differences, parents tend to rely heavily on the *context* of crying, such as how long ago the last feed was, to interpret many other possible meanings of a cry, like boredom, tiredness, stomach ache or wind.   AW

Bibliography

Dunn, J. 1977: *Distress and comfort.* London: Open Books; Cambridge, Mass.: Harvard University Press.

Kirkland, J. 1985: *Crying and babies: helping families cope.* London: Croom Helm.

Lester, B.M. 1984: A biosocial model of infant crying. In *Advances in infancy research*, eds. L.P. Lipsitt and C. Rovee-Collier. Norwood, N.J.: Ablex.

D

daydream Type of waking fantasy, independent of external stimulus, possibly gratifying wishes not being satisfied in real life. Daydreams differ from night dreams in that they are generally under voluntary control, with the daydreamer fully aware of being awake. As a result, daydreams tend to be experienced as less compellingly "real" than night dreams. Daydreaming is especially common among young people, but may continue throughout a lifetime. While often dismissed as a waste of time or mere escapism, daydreaming is not inherently pathological and may have a number of adaptive properties. For example, frequent daydreamers seem better able to cope with boredom and frustration. (See also FANTASY; EMOTION AND FANTASY.)　　　RPE

Bibliography
Singer, J.L. 1981: *Daydreaming and fantasy*. Oxford and New York: Oxford University Press (first published 1975).

deafness and hearing impairment in children A severe or complete loss of hearing that limits the child's ability to receive acoustic information. The incidence (in Britain) is approximately one per thousand births and it may be inherited or arise through environmental causes such as infectious diseases transmitted by the mother during pregnancy.

A primary effect is interference with communication through speech and this in turn has psychological consequences, especially for the comprehension and expression of spoken and written language. The disruptive effects on communication are most serious when deafness has its origins early in life. Remedial training may include physical aids to allow the use of residual hearing, training in lip reading, restricting the child to spoken language, training in a manual sign language or the use of "total" communication methods which comprise some combination of speech and sign. (See also HEARING IMPAIRED AND DEAF, THE: PSYCHOLOGY AND EDUCATION OF.)　　　GEB

Bibliography
Meadow, K.P. 1980: *Deafness and child development*. London: Edward Arnold; Berkeley: University of California Press.
Millar, S. 1982: Studies of the deaf and the blind. In *The pathology and psychology of cognition*, ed. A. Burton. London: Methuen.

deixis The notion of "deixis" refers to linguistic expressions which signal the contextual existence of persons, objects and similar orientational features. Deictic words include personal pronouns, adverbials of time and place and expressions signaling an honorific dimension. They are typically speaker-oriented and serve to create textual coherence.

The presence of deictic elements in all known human languages is taken as an indication that they developed out of face-to-face interaction. In studies of the development of communication there has been a great deal of interest in the related topic of children's ability to follow their mothers' gaze, and to understand pointing or to do it themselves (see Bruner 1983). In language development the question is how children learn that deictic words, such as the personal pronouns "I" and "you", change their reference when used by different speakers. Most children have learnt to use them properly by the age of two to two-and-a-half, but take longer to learn the correct use of positional pronouns like "here" and "there" (see Cox

1986). Continued misuse of personal pronouns is sometimes found in AUTISM.

PM/RL

Bibliography

Bruner, J. 1983: *Child's talk. Learning to use language*. Oxford and New York: Oxford University Press.

Clark, E. 1978: From gesture to word: on the natural history of deixis in language acquisition. In *Human growth and development*, eds. J. Bruner and A. Garton. Oxford: Oxford University Press.

Cox, M.V. 1986: *The child's point of view*. Brighton: Harvester.

Lyons, John 1977: *Semantics*. London and New York: Cambridge University Press.

delinquency Conduct disorder in young persons involving offenses against the law. In Britain, juvenile delinquents could be considered legally as persons under the age of seventeen with criminal convictions. However, no widely accepted definition exists, the term often including any antisocial, deviant or immoral behavior whether or not it forms part of a criminal offense. Delinquency is a serious cause for concern worldwide, but rates are difficult to estimate reliably. West and Farrington (1973) showed that 30.8 per cent of working-class boys in London had at least one conviction at twenty-one years. Boys have outnumbered girls in a ratio of up to ten to one. The most common offenses involve theft. A popular distinction is drawn between socialized and unsocialized delinquents (Hewitt and Jenkins 1946).

Causation is multifactorial, including genetic, psychological, social and cultural factors. Over-simplified causal explanations are misleading. Prevalence is high in depressed urban environments and one view relates delinquency particularly to disadvantaged subcultures. There is a well established connection between delinquency and disturbed home background and family conflict. Schools may have differing rates of delinquency and may play a part in fostering delinquent behavior (Reynolds 1976). Longitudinal studies suggest that future delinquents may be differentiated from others during late childhood on the basis of their attitudes and behavior (West and Farrington 1973). The "labeling" of children as failures and troublemakers, especially by teachers, contributes to the acquisition of deviant status (Hargreaves 1975). (See also CONDUCT DISORDER.)

WLIP-J

Bibliography

Hargreaves, David H., Hester, F. and Mellor, S. 1975: *Deviance in classrooms*. London and Boston: Routledge and Kegan Paul.

Hewitt, Lester E. and Jenkins, Richard L. 1946: *Fundamental patterns of maladjustment: the dynamics of their origin*. Springfield, Ill.: State of Illinois.

Loeber, R. and Dishian, T. 1983: Early predictors of male delinquency: a review. *Psychological bulletin* 94(1), 68–99.

Reynolds, D. 1976: The delinquent school. In *The process of schooling*, eds. Martyn Hammersley and Peter Woods. London and Boston: Routledge and Kegan Paul.

West, Donald J. and Farrington, D.P. 1973: *Who becomes delinquent?* London: Heinemann Educational.

*_____ 1977: *The delinquent way of life*. London: Heinemann Educational.

deprivation: parental This term covers the many ways, emotional and physical, in which parental care may be inadequate, and which may have immediate and long term consequences for the child. Bowlby (1951) suggested that separation of a young child from its mother not only causes immediate distress (protest followed by despair and detachment) but also predisposes to later psychopathic personality disorder and vulnerability to affective disorder. Since then it has become apparent that the effect of separation depends on many factors including the age of the child, its previous relationship with its mother and father, and the nature of the separation. It is also apparent that the various types of parental deprivation have quite difference long term consequences. For example, lack of environmental stimulation and encouragement to learn in infancy is associated with educational under-achievement, whereas

51

poor early emotional attachments may result in difficulties in adult social rela- tionships.

Awareness of the consequences of maternal separation and other forms of parental deprivation has been a major influence in the development of ideas of child care whether it is undertaken by the parents, by substitute parents or by any form of educational or residential institu- tion.   RAM

Bibliography

Bowlby, J. 1951: *Maternal care and mental health.* Geneva: WHO.

Rutter, M. 1981: *Maternal deprivation reassessed.* 2nd edn. Harmondsworth and New York: Penguin.

development: psychoanalytic theo- ries

A set of related, historical-causal accounts of the development of IN- STINCT and of OBJECT RELATIONS deriving from the internal psychological reality of the subject. Freud initially sought antecedents of his patients' nervous illnes- ses in their life histories but a theoretical turning point was his realization that the seductions which his patients described were not real events in childhood but phantasies that had been created when they were children (Rapaport 1960). It is the incorporation of this insight which makes psychoanalytic theories of develop- ment unique.

Psychoanalytic developmental or gene- tic theory must be placed within the abstract, conceptual "metapsychology" which Freud created as his psychological account of that which lay beyond con- sciousness. The topographical, the econo- mic and the dynamic perspectives, are, like the genetic, major parts of the meta- psychology. The topographical concerns the regions of the mind, in Freud's first system, the preconscious-conscious and the unconscious. The quantities and movements of psychic energy are concep- tualized within the economic perspective while the dynamic concerns the conflict of psychic forces, generally the instincts. These perspectives are interrelated and

interdependent in any explanation. For example, the term "dynamic unconscious" describes the struggle of unconscious forces, usually of an infantile sexual nature, to enter consciousness. Freud created this complex apparatus to account for his patients' past and present difficul- ties. He was concerned with many aspects of their lives; and his genetic theory differs from the more limited developmental theories constructed in academic settings.

Genetic theory and the topographic, economic and dynamic systems were cre- ated to explain the meaning of symptoms. In *Three essays on the theory of sexuality* (1905) Freud offered explanations of adult perversions and neuroses in terms of infantile sexuality. He described the ori- gins of adult genital sexuality in the component oral, anal and phallic sexuali- ties of infancy and early childhood. It is important to remember that the widely known oral, anal and phallic stages of libidinal (instinctual) development were constructed primarily from the accounts and analyses of adults.

A major step in the development of object relations as well as of instinct is the Oedipus complex, the term Freud chose to describe the child's conflicting wishes of love and hate toward its parents (see OEDIPUS AND ELEKTRA COMPLEXES). Clini- cally the Oedipus complex is crucial as 'the nucleus of the neuroses' (Laplanche and Pontalis 1973). Individuals who do not experience the three person conflicts typical of the Oedipus complex may develop more serious illnesses and are a therapeutic problem to psychoanalysis. But mental illness is not determined by experience alone. Freud believed that an individual's instinctual disposition contri- buted to the creation of neurotic symp- toms (*Outline of psychoanalysis*, Standard Edition, vol. 23). Both experiential and biological factors have a place in genetic theory; it is an interactionist account of development and has been compared with PIAGET's model in this respect (Greenspan 1979).

In *The ego and the id* Freud introduced a second model of the mental apparatus. The older topographic system of the preconscious-conscious and the unconscious was not abandoned but maintained alongside the model of mental agencies, the familiar id, ego and superego. The resolution of the Oedipus complex is significant in the development of the superego. It is through identification with the parents that Oedipal conflicts are successfully dealt with, that relations with the parental objects are internalized and the superego as the repository of parental ideals and prohibitions formed. A full understanding of the three agencies requires examination of them in terms of all the metapsychological perspectives but attention here is on the genetic. The ego is held to develop through the infant's adaptive encounters with reality. At birth the infant knows no reality and operates in terms of primary processes, condensation and displacement. These processes were first described by Freud in *The interpretation of dreams* and are characteristic of unconscious functioning. The ego differentiates out of the id which in the second model retained much of the identity of the unconscious. The ego functions in terms of the reality principle and its processes are described as secondary. It is this later model which is widely known in psychology, and development is often seen as an inexorable progression from id, to ego to superego as well as from oral to anal to phallic libidinal organization. Since much of metapsychological theory is ignored, these developments appear unintelligible as well as inexorable.

A further aspect of genetic theory which has wide currency is Freud's account of the development of gender identity. Freud held that human beings are bisexual and that the oral, anal and early phallic stages were essentially the same in boys and girls. Only after the child's sexual curiosity leads to the discovery that females are without a penis does further development take divergent paths (Freud 1925). Within the context of love/hate feelings for the parents in the Oedipus complex the young boy renounces his desires for his mother in fear that his father may deprive him of his penis and the young girl is alleged to turn away from her mother in disappointment that she too is without. Ever since Freud proposed the concept of penis envy it has been controversial (Sayers 1982).

Melanie Klein extended psychoanalysis as a therapeutic technique in the treatment of very young children. She provided them with carefully chosen play material, including small models of animals and people, with which they represented their inner world (Segal 1979). Klein worked intitially within Freud's later theory of instinct, that of Eros and Thanatos or sexual and destructive instincts, but emphasized the latter more than did classical Freudian theory. From her work with young children she evolved an elaborate account of pre-Oedipal development.

Moving beyond the stages of oral, anal and genital organization Klein proposed two constellations of processes, or positions as she called them. The earliest was described as the paranoid-schizoid position which characterized development in the first few months of life. The inner phantasy world of the infant was described as being unstable, made up of part objects, e.g. breasts, penises, but not the whole person of the parents. Denial, splitting into affectively good and bad, projection of the bad outward and introjection of the good were seen as dominant thought processes of the paranoid–schizoid position. These functions are metaphorically linked with the infant's bodily processes – ingestion, defecation, etc. Klein used concepts such as good and bad breasts to characterize the inner, phantasy world of the infant. That objects are not yet constituted as the symbolic wholes of the second year is an important aspect of early development and of paranoid-schizoid thought processes.

Klein suggested that by the middle of the first year the infant began to recognize that good and bad part objects emanated from a common source. The overwhelming greed for the good and the terrifying fear of the bad persecutory part object were thus moderated. The term "depressive position" marks the infant's dawning awareness of the permanence of its objects and its ambivalence about the consequences of its desires in relation to these objects.

Klein's work on pre-Oedipal development led to modifications in her views of gender identity. She described the origins of the Oedipus complex in the first year of life and held that the development of boys and girls differed. Not only were girls not phallic in the same sense as boys but she described them as more passively oral and with an early awareness of the vagina. Her views have stirred a great deal of controversy within the psychoanalytic community (Segal 1979) but through her therapeutic work with very disturbed young children and her willingness to speculate about early mental processes she has enriched genetic theory.

The treatment and study of children was also pioneered by Anna Freud, who worked within the theoretical system created by her father and developed the later topographical model, elaborating the function of the ego (1937). Careful descriptions of normal development were provided by her and her colleagues at the Hampstead Clinic (1966).

The function of infant and child observation in the construction and modification of psychoanalytic developmental theory has been a challenging one. Winnicott (1957) suggested that reconstructive work with patients provided insights about deep processes while observation offered information on early environmental events and functioned as a corrective indicating limits to infant capabilities. Nonetheless observation is not a substitute for reconstructive creation.

In recent years the extensive observation studies of Mahler and her co-workers (1975) have had an impact both on psychoanalytic and academic psychology. They describe stages of normal autism and normal symbiosis which occur prior to the psychological birth of the infant about five months after its physiological birth. The further development of self and other representations is detailed in four subphases of the separation-individuation process. These are: differentiation and body image development, practicing, rapprochement and consolidation of self plus

initial emotional object constancy. Reopening the issue of the relationship between reconstructive interpretation, the hallmark of genetic theory, and infant observation, Peterfreund (1978) has criticized Mahler's group for overextending clinical insights in creating concepts to explain infant behavior. Indeed, he characterizes the contemporary metapsychological edifice as lacking firm roots in biology and evolutionary thinking. If Peterfreund is correct, it is a curious reflection on its creator, Sigmund Freud, whom Sulloway (1979) has described as a 'crypto-biologist' and on his followers' difficulties in maintaining the complex, interactional theory he proposed.   BBL

Bibliography

Freud, Anna 1937: *The ego and the mechanisms of defence*. London: Hogarth Press; New York: International Universities Press.

—— 1966: *Normality and pathology in childhood: assessments of development*. London: Hogarth Press; New York: International Universities Press.

Freud, Sigmund: *Standard edition of the complete psychological works*. Interpretation of dreams, vols. 4 & 5 (1953); Theory of sexuality, vol. 7 (1953); The ego and the id, vol. 19 (1961); Anatomical distinction between the sexes, vol. 29 (1961); Outline of psychoanalysis, vol. 23 (1964). London: Hogarth Press; New York: Norton.

Greenspan, S.I. 1979: Intelligence and adaptation: an integration of psychoanalytic and Piagetian developmental psychology. *Psychological issues*, vol. 12, nos 3/4. Monograph 47/48. New York: International Universities Press.

Laplanche, J. and Pontalis, J-B. 1973: *The language of psychoanalysis*. London: Hogarth Press; New York: Norton (1974).

Mahler, M.S., Pine, F. and Bergman, A. 1975: *The psychological birth of the human infant*. New York: Basic Books; London: Hutchinson.

Peterfreund, E. 1978: Some critical comments on psychoanalytic conceptualizations of infancy. *International journal of psychoanalysis* 59, 427–41.

Rapaport, A.D. 1960: Psychoanalysis as a developmental psychology. In *Perspectives in psychological theory: essays in honor of Heinz Werner*, eds. B. Kaplan and S. Wapper. New York: International Universities Press.

Sayers, J. 1982: *Biological politics: feminist and*

anti-feminist perspectives. London and New York: Tavistock.

Segal, H. 1979: *Klein*. Glasgow: Fontana/Collins; New York: Viking Press, 1980.

Sulloway, F.J. 1979: *Freud, biologist of the mind*. London: Burnett Books and André Deutsch; New York: Basic Books.

Winnicott, D.W. 1957: On the contribution of direct child observation to psychoanalysis. In *The maturational processes and the facilitating environment*. New York: International Universities Press; London: Hogarth (1965).

development of motor skills Qualitative and quantitative changes in a child's motor skill repertoire as a function of age. As they grow older, children gradually acquire a broad repertoire of motor skills. Some skills emerge more-or-less spontaneously and are later perfected with practice. For example a normal child eventually begins to walk whether or not it is actively encouraged to do so. Once on its feet, it becomes more adroit in locomotion, moving around at various speeds in a changing environment. As another example, a child will spontaneously reach for and grasp an object. This fairly rudimentary act of prehension gradually becomes perfected so that the position of the fingers and the force exerted can be delicately varied depending on the shape and the nature of the object being grasped. Such skills, emerging perhaps through mimicry (see IMITATION), but without the need for specific tuition, may be termed endogenous skills. They are acquired quite early in life and there is a marked stereotypy among normal children in their basic motor repertoire and in the order of appearance of individual skills.

Other skills tend to emerge in response to a demand by an external agent such as a parent, teacher or another child, and are perfected only if there is deliberate practice. For example, a child can learn to modify its basic pattern of locomotion for skipping and dancing. Similarly, rudimentary finger and hand movements can be modified and greatly elaborated in the acquisition of hand-writing, and the playing of a musical instrument. These skills, which come to be superimposed on the basic repertoire, may be termed exogenous. They are acquired later in life, and normal children vary greatly in the number and the degree of perfection of such skills.

It is relatively easy to measure the motor development of children. There are two basic methods. The first involves the careful observation of a child moving freely in its natural environment, and noting how it manages the everyday tasks of locomotion, prehension, dressing and feeding. Developmental expectations can be established from observing many children. Parts of the assessment described by Gesell and Amatruda (1947) and Griffiths (1970) employ such a methodology. The advantage of an observational method is that one can be confident of examining "environmentally valid" behavior; that is, one is looking directly at the motor tasks that are of importance to the child. The disadvantage is that objective measurement of the quality of a child's performance is rarely achieved. The second method of measurement is to set up laboratory tasks that are relevant to everyday tasks demanded of a child, and ask it to perform under standard conditions (Bruininks 1978; McCarthy 1972). The advantages here are that the conditions of the task are relatively easy to control, performance can be objectively measured, and developmental norms can be established. The disadvantages are that it is difficult to choose test items that are relevant to everyday tasks, and even if they are relevant, a child's performance in the laboratory may not reflect its usual behavior (see DEVELOPMENTAL PSYCHOLOGY: METHODS OF STUDY).

While it is possible to observe and measure motor development in children it is not at all easy to account for that development, and for the marked individual differences typically seen at each age. At the base of the problem is our incomplete understanding of what determines skilled motor behavior. For example it is relatively easy to demonstrate a developmental progression in the skill of ball catching. Two-year-old children are generally very poor at catching. If you throw a ball to a child, it does not seem to track the movement visually and does not prepare its motor response in advance of the arrival of the ball. It begins its response too late and the ball is dropped. By three to four years of age, children begin to track the movement of the ball, some anticipatory arm movements are made, and there is partial success in catching. By six to seven years of age, eye-tracking of the ball and anticipatory movements of the arms and hands are accurate. Body and hand movements are appropriately timed and placed. While young children are not good at predicting the movement of fast moving objects and making quick anticipatory movements, they can catch slow moving objects (such as a balloon).

One has to look further than just the motor response to account for this kind of developmental progression. While a detailed task analysis of motor skills is not appropriate here, a brief account of ball catching will help to illustrate the point that motor behavior, and therefore development, depends on a complex of perceptual, attentional, cognitive and motor subskills (see PERCEPTUAL AND COGNITIVE ABILITIES IN INFANCY; PERCEPTUAL DEVELOPMENT; ATTENTION IN INFANTS; COGNITIVE DEVELOPMENT). Briefly, a child must visually track the movement of a ball, attend to and comprehend its speed and trajectory, and make predictions about its future locations. (See CROSS-MODAL DEVELOPMENT.) Finally there has to be a quick grasping action of the hands and fingers at the moment of impact with the ball. Young children seem able to predict movement and formulate anticipatory responses, albeit too slowly for ball catching (Laszlo and Bairstow 1985).

Detailed task analyses of different motor skills could highlight a number of different types of perceptual, cognitive and motor subskills contributing to performance. Each skill has its own set of subskills, but any one subskill is involved in a wide range of motor skills. The elucidation of the common and unique factors underlying skilled motor behavior could help in the understanding of motor skill development, though any suggestion that performance of the whole task is simply due to the additive contribution of a number of underlying factors would be an oversimplification. It is more likely that the different factors interact in their combined contribution to skilled motor performance.

From the above considerations it is clear that what we observe as a progressive change in a child's motor skill repertoire might be better termed perceptual-motor development. This point can be illustrated with a study that shows a link between the development of ability to perceive and memorize kinesthetic information and the ability to write and draw. It has been shown that training a child's kinesthetic perceptual ability results in improved drawing and writing (Laszlo and Bairstow 1983).

Given the complexity of behavioral factors determining skilled motor behavior, questions relating to possible underlying neurological factors are difficult to answer, or even formulate. A computer metaphor is useful though imperfect. As a child develops there are various genetically determined "hardware" changes in the neural-network of the central nervous system (see DEVELOPMENT OF THE NERVOUS SYSTEM) in addition to other physical changes in the structure of a child's body. These changes may critically determine the time and order of appearance of various endogenous skills. The physical structure of the body must ultimately determine the limits to skilled motor behavior at any given age, albeit in poorly understood ways. In addition it is likely that there are "software" changes in the central nervous system. A "functional structure" is superimposed on the basic physical structure of the central nervous system as a result of practicing motor skills, experiencing the sensory consequences, and receiving the concomitant rewards and punishments. These changes may underlie the appearance of exogenous skills. The metaphor breaks down when considering the longer term effects of practice and experience: the perceptual-motor experiences of a child may well (in turn) determine "hardware" changes taking place within the developing central nervous system.

Further studies of the development of motor skills need to proceed along two broad lines. The first should aim at an understanding of the behavioral factors underlying and determining skilled motor behavior, so enabling an examination of the relevant developmental changes in a child's behavior. The second would aim at elucidating the neurological bases for the development of perceptual-motor skills. If the behavioral and neurological processes behind the developmental progression were understood, developmental and other abnormalities in the skilled behavior of young children could be differentially diagnosed.   PJB

Bibliography

Bruininks, R.H. 1978: *Bruininks-Oseretsky test of motor proficiency*. Circle Pines, Minnesota: American Guidance Service.

*Connolly, Kevin, ed. 1970: *Mechanisms of motor skill development*. London and New York: Academic Press.

Gesell, Arnold L. and Amatruda, Catherine S. 1947: *Developmental diagnosis*, 2nd edn. New York: Hoeber.

Griffiths, B. 1970: *The abilities of young children: a comprehensive system of mental measurement for the first eight years of life*. London: Child Development Research Centre.

Laszlo, J.I. and Bairstow, P.J. 1983: Kinaesthesis: its measurement, training and relationship with motor control. *Quarterly journal of experimental psychology* 35A, 411–21.

——— 1985: *Perceptual-motor behavior: development assessment and theory*. London: Holt, Rinehart and Winston.

*Legge, David and Barber, Paul J. 1976: *Information and skill*. London and New York: Methuen.

McCarthy, D. 1972: *McCarthy scales of children's abilities*. New York: Psychological Corporation.

development of social cognition

The development of social cognition has typically been considered as a sub-category of cognitive development. Just as children come to conceptualize the physical world of objects and their rela-tions, so too children come to conceptual-ize the world of social objects and their relations. The content of social cognition thus includes everything there is to know about the social lives of people, including the psychological character of the indi-vidual (concepts of self, consciousness, intention, emotion), relationships between individuals (friendship, leadership), social conventions and norms (morality), and the characteristics of social institutions and systems (government, economics).

As cognitive phenomena, social con-cepts are governed by general principles of cognitive development. As Flavell (1985) explains, 'the head that thinks about the social world is the self-same head that thinks about the non-social world. All the basic mental tools ... (knowledge struc-tures, symbolic abilities, information-processing capacities etc.) can be used to categorize, remember, reason about, and otherwise manipulate social data as well as nonsocial data'. Thus, social cognition can be described in terms of age-related trends toward increasing conceptual sophistication. These trends, common to social and non-social concepts, include development from surface to depth (from a focus on overt perceptible attributes toward inferences about an underlying reality); from intuitive to reflective (from thinking about something to being aware of one's thinking), and from concrete to abstract.

There is, of course, another way of looking at social cognition. With emphasis on the social rather than the cognitive component, the field is equally a part of social psychology. From this standpoint, social understanding is viewed as an integral component of social experience and behavior. Instead of describing developmental trends toward increasing cognitive sophistication, emphasis in this case is on showing how social concepts both emerge from and contribute to the child's social life (see Higgens, Ruble and Hartup 1983).

Emphasis on the social side of social cognition raises two important issues: to what extent is social cognition socially and culturally relative, and how does social cognition function in social life? Productive approaches to these questions seek to examine how principles of cognitive development operate in conjunction with characteristics of the child's social life. Higgins and Parsons (1983), for example, have proposed that changes in social concepts represent a kind of collaboration between cognitive-developmental trends and major changes in the child's social experience. Another fruitful direction is the examination of relations between cognition and emotion in the child's dynamic efforts to establish and revise a valued sense of self in the world (see Harter 1983; Wozniak 1985). CNJ

Bibliography

Flavell, J.H. 1985: *Cognitive development.* 2nd edn. Englewood Cliffs, N.J.: Prentice-Hall.

Harter, S. 1983: Developmental perspectives on the self-system. In *Handbook of child psychology*, vol. 4. *Socialization, personality, and social development*, ed. E.M. Hetherington. New York: Wiley.

Higgins, E.T. and Parsons, J.E. 1983: Social cognition and the social life of the child: stages as subcultures. In Higgins, Ruble and Hartup, op cit.

———, Ruble, D.N. and Hartup, W.W. eds. 1983: *Social cognition and social development. A sociocultural perspective.* Cambridge: Cambridge University Press.

Wozniak, R.H. 1985: Notes toward a co-constructive theory of the emotion/cognition relationship. In *Thought and emotion*, eds. D. Bearison and H. Zimiles. Hillside, N.J.: Erlbaum.

development of the nervous system The growing ability of the nervous system to coordinate the organism's responses to simple and complex stimuli, together with the structural and physiological changes on which this ability depends. Development is most dramatic during intra-uterine and early postnatal life. This discussion will be confined to the central nervous system and excludes physiological topics which are too complex for the space available.

Gross structure
Two and a half weeks after conception the

disk-shaped human embryo is less than 1 mm in diameter. Some cells on the dorsal surface fold to form a gutter-like "neural groove". Adjacent cells multiply and form raised walls whose top edges bend toward each other and fuse to form the neural tube, the front end of which dilates to form the brain while the remainder gives rise to the spinal cord.

Six weeks after conception five separate regions can be identified in the enlarged front end of the neural tube (Patten 1968). The hindmost will become the medulla oblongata, the next will become the pons and in front of this lies the mesencephalon or mid-brain (fig. 1).

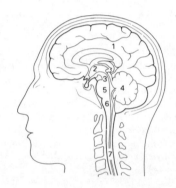

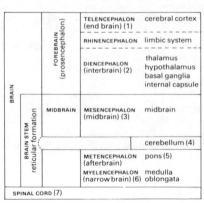

		TELENCEPHALON (end brain) (1)	cerebral cortex
	FOREBRAIN (prosencephalon)	RHINENCEPHALON	limbic system
		DIENCEPHALON (interbrain) (2)	thalamus hypothalamus basal ganglia internal capsule
MIDBRAIN	MESENCEPHALON (midbrain) (3)	midbrain
BRAIN STEM reticular formation		cerebellum (4)
	METENCEPHALON (afterbrain)	pons (5)
	MYELENCEPHALON (narrow brain) (6)	medulla oblongata
SPINAL CORD (7)		

Fig. 1 The regions of the brain

In front of the mid-brain lies the forebrain which is itself divided into the diencephalon, in which the thalamus and hypothalamus will eventually develop, and two enlargements which will become the cerebral hemispheres.

During infancy the brain grows rapidly but at a steadily decreasing rate. The brain stem, i.e. the mid-brain, pons and medulla oblongata, which contain centers essential for the maintenance of life, are quite well advanced in growth by the time of birth and show very little increase in size after the end of the first year. Nearly half the postnatal growth of the cerebral hemispheres has usually been completed by the end of the first year and they are close to their adult size by the tenth year. This growth is largely due to increase in volume of the white matter.

Cellular structure

Multiplication of "neuroblast" cells which will develop into neurons is most prominent from the tenth to eighteenth weeks of gestation (Dobbing 1981). The neurons grow rapidly through the remainder of pregnancy while cell multiplication declines. In late intra-uterine life, and during the first four years or so after birth, elaboration of dendritic processes (see fig. 2) is associated with development of increasing neuronal function. Simultaneously, proliferation of the glial cells continuing to the second postnatal year (Dobbing and Sands 1973), provides the main connective and supporting structure of the brain.

Myelinization begins at about the fourth fetal month, in the dorsal and ventral roots of the spinal cord. The fibers connecting higher centers in the cerebral hemispheres are generally later and some tracts are not completely myelinated for several years. After a fiber has become myelinated the thickness of the myelin sheath may continue to increase for a number of years.

The cerebral cortex develops rather slowly and it is not until the seventh fetal month that the six cell layers characteristic of the adult are apparent.

While the brain is developing its biochemical and electrical characteristics are also changing. These changes continue beyond childhood.

The development of function

Evidence of the degree of functional development in the central nervous system of the early embryo is provided by its movements in response to stimuli. For example, closing of the hand when the palm is touched has been demonstrated during the third fetal month. At about nine weeks, touching the mouth with a fine hair leads to bending of the whole body whereas by twelve and a half weeks, the mouth closes when it is touched and, if the touch is repeated several times, the fetus will exhibit swallowing movements. Thus a general response is replaced by a localized one appropriate to the stimulus and requiring a more highly developed nervous system.

Infants born prematurely have been studied at the gestational age of twenty-eight weeks. (Saint-Anne Dargassies 1966). They close their eyes if a light is shone on them. Nerve pathways in the midbrain and pons, which would be essential for this response, must therefore be functioning. A loud noise will awaken the infant and cause generalized movement. There is evidence of a sense of smell at this stage and there may be some taste sensation. The rooting reflex, i.e. opening the mouth and turning the head towards a part of the face which is touched, and the walking reflex are also present. The latter is demonstrated by

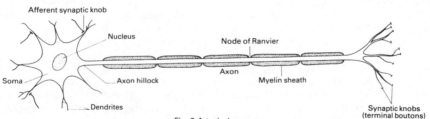

Fig. 2 A typical neuron

holding the baby upright with the feet on a flat surface and moving it forward. It will walk with high stepping movements. Thus the basic functional connections in the nervous system required for the movements of walking are well developed.

By thirty weeks the neuronal connections which allow the pupil to contract when a light is shone into the eye are established. The movements of sucking and swallowing are well coordinated in relation to breathing so that the infant can suck without choking. Also, the legs stiffen when the infant is held upright, an indication that the steady output of impulses from the lower end of the spinal cord, which will later be responsible for the maintenance of muscle tone, has begun.

Premature babies of thirty-two to thirty-five weeks' gestation usually appear much more alert than younger infants. This suggests that the "arousal" mechanism within the brain may be beginning to function. Improved coordination of movement shows further development within the nervous system.

When the prematurely born infant reaches a gestational age of forty-one weeks, it will follow a light with its eyes. This implies some form of vision but does not necessarily indicate that what the infant sees has great significance for it. It does suggest that further functional links have been established between the visual input to the brain and the outflow to the eye muscles. The infant tends to respond selectively to sounds such as that of the human voice. The differences in behavior between a child born at forty-one weeks and a premature infant who has reached this age are usually slight. Whether the infant has remained in utero or has been exposed to the external environment for the preceding month or two seems to have little effect on the development of the central nervous system. The movements of the newborn full term infant are largely reflexes but they become more controlled after about five or six months, as higher centers begin to process information and relate it to movement. Responses may be observed to many different stimuli, e.g. pain, touch or pressure, changes in temperature, taste, and certain odors.

By two months of age the visual system is sufficiently well developed to allow size and shape discrimination (Fantz and Miranda 1975). The vestibular apparatus, which provides the brain with information about the position and movement of the head in space, is functioning to some extent at birth but the child is usually ten or twelve weeks old before sensory input from the eyes, the vestibular apparatus and the receptor organs in the muscles and joints become fully integrated within the central nervous system. This integration is an essential basis for well controlled voluntary movement.

Infants over the age of twelve weeks show considerable variation in the rates at which their central nervous systems develop. Ages at which developmental "landmarks" are said to be reached are generalizations and many entirely normal children will reach them either earlier or later than the norm.

After the first three months the cerebral cortex begins to influence the postural reflexes which have recently become integrated. The action of the cortex is usually to inhibit these reflexes so that the child has more voluntary control of its posture.

Effective activity in the motor areas of the cerebral cortex is shown at about the fourth or fifth month by voluntary goal-directed movements, such as grasping at an object in the field of vision. These movements become increasingly skillful as the corpus striatum, motor cortex and pyramidal tracts develop further but even after two or three years the movements may still be clumsy.

The walking reflex, which is coordinated in the spinal cord, disappears completely some months before the infant begins to crawl or walk alone because it is inhibited by higher centers of the brain as these develop. The development of independent locomotion follows a sequence which reflects the order of maturation in the regions of the motor area of the cerebral cortex in which different parts of the body are represented. The infant can creep with the help of its arms before it can use its legs to crawl, stand or walk.

WAM

Bibliography

*Dobbing, J. 1981: The later development of the brain and its vulnerability. In *Scientific foundations of paediatrics*, eds. J. Dobbing and J.A. Davis. London: Heinemann.

—— and Sands, J. 1973: The quantitative growth and development of the human brain. *Archives of disease in childhood* 46, 757–67.

Fantz, R.L. and Miranda, S.B. 1975: Newborn infant attention to form and contour. *Child development* 46, 224.

Goldman-Rakic, P.S., Iseroff, A., Schwartz, M.L. and Bugbee, N.M. 1983: The neurobiology of cognitive development. In *Handbook of child psychology*. 4th edn, vol. 2, eds. M.M. Haith and J.J. Campos. New York: Wiley.

Patten, Bradley M. 1968: *Human embryology*. 3rd edn. New York and Maidenhead: McGraw-Hill.

*Saint-Anne Dargassies, S. 1966: Neurological maturation of the premature infant of 28 to 41 weeks' gestational age. In *Human development*, ed. F. Faulkner, Philadelphia and London: Saunders.

developmental psychobiology

Sometimes referred to as developmental biopsychology (e.g. Tobach et al. 1977), it is the study of biological processes that determine and constitute the development of behavior and its psychological components. As its name suggests, developmental psychobiology represents an amalgamation of *developmental psychology* and *psychobiology*. Developmental psychobiology encompasses all stages of life during which the foundations for behavior are established.

The roots of developmental psychobiology can be traced to the turn of the century when many ontogenetic issues were in the limelight of scientific debate. Experimental embryology had emerged as a discipline and from within it arose some model approaches to developmental studies that were to have broad and long-lasting influences. W. Preyer (1841–1897), in particular, attempted to unify developmental studies in physiology,

neuroanatomy and behavior. Preyer's celebrated works included comparative studies of behavioral embryology and developmental studies of the maturation of children.

Charles Darwin (1809–1882) can also be seen as an early advocate and practitioner of developmental psychobiology. In particular, his *The expression of emotion in man and animals* (1872) reflects some of his views of developmental study as a tool to an understanding of comparative-evolutionary aspects of behavior, as well as the nature of brain-behavior relations. Claparède (1911) was perhaps the first developmentalist to use the term "psychobiological" in his treatment of human attention, and asked 'is that which really interests us, which holds us enthralled, always that which *ought* to interest us from the point of view of our preservation, from the biological point of view?' Thereafter, as Konner (1977) points out, most of the major advances in twentieth century developmental psychology, notably those associated with Freud, Piaget, Hall, Baldwin, Gesell, Carmichael, Bower, Bowlby and Brown have been based on biological constructs.

Links with evolutionary theory and genetics

The Darwinian framework was incorporated into the thinking of many developmental psychologists (e.g. Baldwin 1895) during the later nineteenth century. Their acceptance of evolutionary views was influenced by those of contemporary embryologists who suggested that individual development (ontogeny) appears to replay (or recapitulate) the evolutionary development of the species (its phylogeny). To apply to mental development the doctrine that "ontogeny *recapitulates* phylogeny", it was assumed by many early developmental psychologists that studying the psychological development of children would provide an account of the otherwise inaccessible phylogenetic evolution of the human mind. Today, most developmentalists do not accept such views. Instead of asking what modern children can tell us about human evolution, contemporary interest tends to focus on how the nature of childhood and the developmental rules which guide it have themselves evolved (Bruner 1972; Konner 1977).

Some psychobiologically-oriented researchers conduct developmental studies because they are interested in problems derived from ethology, comparative psychology, or animal behavior. Indeed, ethological and comparative traditions, as articulated by Konrad Lorenz, Niko Tinbergen, T. C. Schneirla and Daniel Lehrman, placed great value on ontogenetic analyses. In particular, one goal of such behavioral approaches is to clarify *adaptive or functional* aspects of behavior, that is, to understand the means by which behavioral traits enable organisms to meet various environmental challenges and in the face of such forces of natural selection be maintained or reinforced in the species' repertoire. From this tradition comes interest in the behavior and behavioral development of young in relation to their social and physical environments. Parent-offspring relationships, affiliative behavior, the organization of motor patterns, play, imitation, recognition of parents, kin, food, prey, and basic vegetative activities have, for example, been involved in studies of the adaptive aspects of behavioral development.

The function of developmental processes is in general the achievement of adult competence. The adaptive significance of some aspects of the behavior of young, then, may lie in converting neonatal competence to adult competence: it is thought to be the case for infantile PLAY, for example, that adaptive benefits are realized *in later life*. By contrast, some of the behaviors of young may not perform this function at all, but instead have survival value *at that point* in development. Bowlby has proposed that one such function of the human infant's ATTACHMENT to its parents has been protection from predators and other threats of the environmental "niche" experienced by the infant at this vulnerable stage in its life.

The development of species-typical behavior and its evolutionary implications brings with it an appreciation of and interest in *heritable* factors that are expressed in behavior. Thus, the field of behavior genetics has a relevant alignment with developmental psychobiology. Heritability, however, is a parameter of populations, not individuals, so the role of some aspects of behavior genetics exists most precisely on the level of population characteristics. The historical persistence of the so-called "nature–nurture" controversy in developmental psychobiology can be understood, in part, as a problem that has been difficult to resolve because the adversaries in the controversy are often confronting one another with analyses that are appropriate either to individuals or to populations. Behavior genetics is, however, increasingly influenced by revelations of modern molecular biology and genetics.

The complexity of modern psychobiology: parent-offspring relations

Although developmental psychobiology has a tradition of comparative study that ranges across many species, mammalian development is emphasized. This can be understood in terms of its relevance to humans, and because mammalian offspring tend to present interesting ontogenetic pictures for study – their life histories usually include dramatic transformations from infancy to adulthood. It is possible to make such a generalization because mammals are defined, as a group, on the basis of common reproductive–developmental features: live birth and the provision of milk via specialized glands on the female's body. Mammary glands are an anatomical signpost for maternal behavior. The developmental psychobiology of mammals, therefore, necessarily includes the analysis of maternal behavior or, more accurately, *parental* behavior since in many species, including man, nurturance is provided by adults other than, and in addition to, the mother. Parental behavior is, in fact, a prominent feature of the reproductive efforts of many non-mammalian animals, such as some species of fish and many species of birds.

The inclusion of parental behavior in the mandate of developmental psychobiology brings with it special conceptual and methodological demands. Parental behavior is not a static or fixed form of input. The quantity and quality of parental attention tends to change over time, usually in a manner suited to the developmental status of the offspring. It is important to recognize the *developmental* nature of parental care.

The concept of developmental synchrony is very important because it stimulates awareness of the existence of the different means by which such interindividual synchrony is achieved. The effect of a parent (caregiver) on the offspring and the effect of the offspring on the parent often must be analyzed separately in order to understand the nature of their *reciprocal* controls. Developmental studies have been enhanced considerably by ability to understand the mechanisms of interactions within dyads, such as parent-offspring units.

Links with neuroscience

The problems and methods of contemporary psychobiology, physiological psychology, and the neurosciences in general, contribute to the scope and conduct of developmental psychobiology. Developmental analyses continue to be applied as *tools* to study other processes. Thus, many topics of psychobiological interest, such as learning and memory, feeding and drinking behavior, sensory processes, sleep, reproductive behavior and communication, are studied developmentally, with the aim of learning more about each problem as a result of better understanding the factors that contribute to its development.

In addition, the *methods* of contemporary neuroscience have influenced the conduct of the developmental work. In some instances a new technology has been applied to a developmental problem. This would include, for instance, basic studies of the development of neurochemical systems of the brain, behavioral pharmacology in immature animals, and neuroanatomical studies of the developing nervous system. Some of these efforts resemble or are identical to research in developmental neurobiology, a closely-

aligned discipline which is best discriminated from developmental psychobiology by greater emphasis on intrinsic properties of neural tissue and systems, rather than in their relations to behavior.

The application of modern anatomical and physiological techniques of neurobiology to behaviorally-oriented investigations is usually done through "descriptive–correlative" studies, which are typical of preliminary analyses. In developmental psychobiology there are several significant examples of this approach. Neural changes during development have been described with the aid of numerous neurobiological measures, ranging from molar levels of analysis such as brain size, cortical depth and myelination patterns, to more molecular analyses such as neuronal counts, cell size and shape, or arrangement of dendritic spines. Such morphological measures are then correlated with onset of function or level of performance. Alternatively, the same kinds of neural measures can be used correlatively to assess the consequences of different early environmental conditions for rate or level of neural development.

Relevance of early experience

Ontogenetic stages during which behavior and/or morphology undergo rapid or dramatic changes are, generally speaking, especially attractive to developmental psychobiologists. It is generally believed that periods of rapid changes are more susceptible to extrinsic influences than are ontogenetic stages of stability. The assumption is that living systems in the process of reorganization or change are more easily affected by environmental events, natural or artificial, than are systems that are operating in a relatively steady state. It is for this reason, at least in part, that developmental psychobiologists are attracted to analyses of "early experience", because the "early" period is usually part of the postnatal phase when development is rapid and dramatic.

The same assumptions that highlight early life as an important period during which development is shaped, also apply to the study of the early influence of toxins or teratogens (substances that can have detrimental effects on the organism). Hence, the methods and data of developmental psychobiology are often relevant to toxicologists and teratologists interested in some organismic effects of a toxin. Toxicologists who study, for instance, potentially harmful effects of drugs on developing animals are particularly aware of the special interpretive problems, particularly in organisms that engage in extensive parent-offspring interactions. The problem is that a drug can directly affect the young organism in at least two different ways. First, the drug can act directly on the organ systems of the young animal, and perhaps have more dramatic effects than on an adult, whose tissue is less susceptible to perturbation. The second potential source of effect is less direct but can be as significant. Alterations in physical or behavioral characteristics of offspring can produce changes in the quantity or quality of parental care. Moreover, many aspects of parental care are determined, in part, by responses to proximate cues from the offspring. Drug effects, even transient ones, can affect the parent's response which, in turn, can alter the condition of the young. These effects can produce chains of interaction that can extend beyond the immediate drug effect, in time and in kind of action.   JRAI/AW

Bibliography

Baldwin, J.M. 1895: *Mental development in the child and in the race*. London: Macmillan.

Bateson, P.P.G. 1981: 'Ontogeny'. In *The Oxford companion to animal behavior*, ed. D.J. MacFarland. Oxford and New York: Oxford University Press.

Bruner, J. 1972: The nature and uses of immaturity. *American psychologist*, 27, 687–708.

Claparède, E. 1910 (1911): Trans. Mary Louch and H Holman. *Experimental pedagogy and the psychology of the child*. London.

Darwin, C. 1877: A biographical sketch of an infant. *Mind* 2, 285–94.

Gottlieb, G. 1983: The psychobiological approach to developmental issues. In *Handbook of child psychology*. 4th edn, vol. 2, eds. M.M. Haith and J.J. Campos. New York: Wiley.

Gould, S.J. 1977: *Ontogeny and phylogeny*. London: Belknap.

Hall, W.G. and Oppenheimer, R. 1987: Developmental psychobiology.In *Annual review of psychology*, vol. 38, eds. M.R. Rosenzweig and L.W. Porter. Palo Alto: Annual Reviews Inc. (in prep.).

Hofer, M.A. 1981: *The roots of human behavior*. London: Freeman.

Konner, M. 1977: Evolution of human behavior development. In *Culture and infancy*, eds. P.H. Leiderman, S.R. Tulkin and A. Rosenfeld. London and New York: Academic Press.

Piaget, J. 1967 (1971): *Biology and knowledge*. Edinburgh: Edinburgh University Press; Chicago: University of Chicago Press.

Tobach, E., Aronson, L.R. and Shaw, E. 1971: *The biopsychology of development*. London and New York: Academic Press.

Trevarthen, C. 1980: Neurological development and the growth of psychological functions. In *Developmental psychology and society*, ed. J. Sarts. London and New York: Macmillan.

developmental psychology: methods of study

Developmental psychology is the study of the remarkable changes in behavior which happen as people grow older. These changes have been charted from the first moments in life, and though most of our current information about developmental changes concerns children, developmental psychology is also about the changes which take place during adulthood, since it is clear that in many ways older adults think and behave differently from younger ones.

Broadly speaking, developmental psychology has two independent aims. The first is to describe what developments there are: the psychologist sets out to establish what sort of things, for example, a six-month-old child does and is capable of doing, and how these differ from a one-year-old's behavior and capacities. The second aim is to discover the causes of developmental differences. What is it, the developmental psychologist must ask, that leads a one-year-old child to behave so differently from a six-month-old?

To discover a developmental change psychologists have to compare people at different ages. There are two quite different ways of doing this, longitudinal and cross-sectional. Longitudinal research studies follow the same people over time, and plot how their behavior changes as they grow older. For example, a study in which a group of children is seen just before they go to school and then several times again in their ensuing school years (there are several such studies) would be a longitudinal one. The great advantage of this type of research is that one can be reasonably sure that any behavioral change that is discovered is genuinely developmental. The only room for doubt is the possibility that testing the same child several times could artificially induce a change. But the major disadvantages of the longitudinal approach are practical ones. Such studies usually take many years, are expensive, and make great administrative demands in the area of keeping in touch with all the people involved. Furthermore losing participants is itself a major hazard. Even well organized projects sometimes end up with a small fraction of their original groups, and this of course raises the danger that there is some unknown underlying difference between the two groups (those remaining and those lost) which the study would not reveal and which might make its results at best biased and at worst wrong. A final reason why psychologists are often wary of longitudinal studies is their fear that after several years' hard work the results might not support the original hypothesis or even suggest a new one. Put together, these problems raise a considerable barrier for anyone considering doing longitudinal research, and this is probably why there are relatively few such studies. Most of the information about child development that is currently being produced relies on the other approach – cross-sectional research. This is a pity because cross-sectional studies also have their problems, and from the point of view of establishing developmental changes they are probably more serious.

CROSS-SECTIONAL RESEARCH studies deal with different people in different age groups (or *cohorts*). An example of a cross-sectional study is one in which different age groups of five-, six-, seven-

and eight-year-old children are given Piaget's well known conservation problem in two ways, and it is found that the two younger groups fail in one condition but succeed in another, while the older groups succeed in both conditions. This is a typical example of a cross-sectional study which, though it spans four years of childhood, can be completed within a matter of weeks. The advantages therefore are clear. Information is obtained very quickly, and if the study for one reason or another does not work very little time has been lost. But there are difficulties, and the major one is the awkward question whether the differences that emerge between different age groups are genuinely developmental ones. It is always possible that the five- and six-year-olds for example in any cross-sectional study are different from each other for quite other reasons than their age. If the project takes place in one school as such studies often do, it could be that the two age groups have had different teachers or different types of experience which have nothing to do with their ages (i.e. it is a *cohort effect* rather than an *age effect*). (See COHORT ANALYSIS.)

It can be seen that the strengths and weaknesses of the two approaches are to a great extent complementary. Longitudinal differences are genuinely developmental apart from the problem of the effects of repeated testing, while the one advantage of cross-sectional research, apart from its practical convenience, is that it does not have this particular problem. The ideal solution, which is tried very rarely indeed, is to combine the two.

We can now turn to the actual methods used. *Observation* is the oldest, most tried method in developmental psychology. The first major insights in the subject came from the so called "baby diaries" in which parents reported on their children's progress during the first few years. The best known of these is the meticulous account written by Darwin of one of his own children. As psychology developed in the early twentieth century people began to produce observational studies of older children and of children other than their own. The method was used to study both intellectual and emotional development, and it is probably the case that most studies in child psychology up to the beginning of the second world war were observational ones. But the method was less used after 1945 partly because of the growing popularity of the experimental method, but partly too because there seemed to be a general vagueness in observational reports. The trouble mainly centered around the lack of objective criteria. If a psychologist was reporting his observations on, say, aggressive behavior, there seemed to be no check at all that this use of the term was the same as everybody else's. The problem of objective criteria was taken up by "child ethologists" in the 1960s. Their answer, adopting methods used to study animals in their natural habitats, was to make no assumptions at all about broad categories such as aggression, but to record smaller, objectively defined pieces of behavior such as particular arm or face movements. Once these are recorded one can, using rather complex statistical procedures, see how particular acts hang together. From these consistent patterns one can infer and define the broader categories objectively. Using this method ethologists have shown that there are at least two types of apparently aggressive behavior in young children. One is genuinely aggressive, while the other, called "rough and tumble play" is playful and not meant to hurt (see ETHOLOGY).

Although the first systematic reports of developmental changes were observational, the method which finally established the subject as a separate entity was undoubtedly the psychometric test. This we owe to the distinguished child psychologist Alfred BINET, who was commissioned to produce an effective intelligence test, and did so by devising a set of ingenious problems for which the main criterion was that they should be developmentally sensitive. Binet only included items which were more likely to be answered by older than by younger children. His reason for this was that whatever intelligence may be it probably increases during childhood. His method worked; at any rate it was a pragmatic success because it predicted educational progress reasonably well, and still does so. But it obviously had important theoretical connotations as well, and one of these was that it highlighted in a very systematic way the extraordinary differences in the things which young and old children can manage to do. Here for the first time was an objective demonstration of development, and more such demonstrations came thick and fast during the ensuing years.

Although these tests dramatically established a question (as well as making useful predictions about individual children) they did little, however, to provide any answer. This was the challenge taken up by experimental psychology. Experimenters also give TESTS, but they can administer the same test under several different conditions, and this allows them to look at hypotheses about what underlies the often curious things that children do. The experimental method nowadays dominates child psychology, and it has made notable advances. It is to experiments that we owe,

It is to experiments that we attribute, since the pioneering work of Fantz in the 1950s, the demonstration that infants can perceive and can understand a great deal more than had been generally suspected till then. Most of PIAGET's best known work comes in the form of experiments, and it has been a mixture of experiments and observation which has been mainly responsible for the significant progress made in studies of the development of language over the last twenty years or so. Experiments have also helped to test theories about what causes developmental changes. If, for example, it is thought that the learning of a particular aspect of language changes the child's understanding of his environment, a very useful way of testing this would be to train children in the type of language in question and see whether this leads to any change in intellectual development. Provided the experiment is well controlled one then has a good test of the causal hypothesis. The only difficulty is that the experiment might not represent real life relationships, and so it is probably best to combine this method with others which do establish that the relationships are genuine ones.

The great advantage of experimental psychology is that it puts the psychologist in control: he can test his hypothesis by stipulating exactly what the different conditions will be in his experiments. But this is also its great disadvantage, because it means that the circumstances of the experiment often risk being artificial: to ask a child to bite on a board and then cover his head with extremely heavy equipment in order to study the movements of his eyes is splendidly scientific but it must be borne in mind that the procedure itself may influence what the child does with his eyes. Yet there seems to be little that can be done about this danger, apart from being aware of it, minimizing it where possible, and trusting in the end to the development of less intrusive techniques.

The artificiality of the experimental method has been noted by the child ethologists mentioned earlier and also by those who use more clinical methods. One that has a powerful and useful influence in child psychology is the questionnaire. Questionnaires held a very important place in child psychology during the 1950s when they were used in particular to study the ways in which children were treated by their parents. The well known study by Sears, Maccoby and Levin is a good example. These studies tended to relate the parents' behavior to the child's intellectual and emotional development. Too often, however, they assumed that any correlation must, so far as cause and effect are concerned, be one-way, and that the parents affect the child rather than the other way round. Recently, however, partly as the result of the impressive evidence from experiments that children are in many ways more aware of what is going on and more in control than had been believed earlier, it has been accepted that it could equally well be that the child is determining the parents' behavior. This makes the study of relationships between parent and child both more interesting and more difficult. Another use of questionnaires is more clinical; they have been

developed, most notably by Michael Rutter, to study disturbances in childhood. There is no doubt that the answers to these questionnaires, which are usually given to parents or to teachers, do produce extremely valuable information about the problems of development. One of the most promising possibilities in child psychology is that this kind of information will be related to direct observation of the children and also to data from experiments. Indeed combining different methods is almost certainly the best way to answer most of the problems of child psychology. Longitudinal and cross-sectional studies should be done together; training studies should be combined with correlations and experiments with data from naturalistic observation and from questionnaires. None of the main methods of child psychology is perfect, but their strengths and weaknesses are often complementary. They should be used together.   PEB

Bibliography

Baltes, Paul B., Reese, Hayne W. and Nesselroade, John R. 1977: *Life-span developmental psychology: introduction to research methods.* Belmont, Calif.: Brooks/Cole.

*Masters, J.C. 1981: Developmental psychology. *Annual review of psychology* 32, 117–51.

Mussen, Paul H. ed. 1983: *Carmichael's manual of child psychology.* 4th edn. New York and Chichester: John Wiley.

Vasta, Ross 1979: *Studying children: an introduction to research methods.* San Francisco: W.H. Freeman.

Dewey, John (1859–1952) Professor at the University of Michigan (1884–1886), Chicago (1886–1904) and at Columbia University in New York (1904–1929). As a philosopher and educationalist, Dewey contributed to the development of Functionalism with his article "The reflex arc concept in psychology" (1896). Dewey criticized the atomistic conception of psychic functions and the separate study of stimuli and organism's responses, stressing the adaptative meaning and unity of each act for the individual in his interaction with the environment. He is most famous in education as a proponent of child-centered teaching techniques stressing the cooperation between pupil and teacher in classroom learning.   LM

Bibliography

Boring, E.G. 1953: John Dewey: 1859–1952. *American journal of psychology* 66, 145–7.

Cremin, L.A. 1961: *The transformation of the school: progressivism in American education*. New York: Knopf.

Dewey, J.B. 1896: The reflex arc concept in psychology. *Psychological review* 3, 357–70.

discovery learning An approach to education which capitalizes on the child's natural curiosity and urge to explore the environment. The child learns by personal experience and experiment and this is thought to make memory more vivid and help in the transfer of knowledge to new situations. The method is especially widespread in primary school education and is associated with liberal educationalists such as Rousseau, Pestalozzi, Froebel, Dewey and Montessori. It has the support of Piaget's theory which stresses the importance of the effects of informal experience during childhood.

Limitations of the method are that there may not be sufficient time for the child to learn all it needs to know by personal discovery and that undesirable consequences, such as over-ready generalization, may ensue. Hence the teacher retains an important role in guiding the child and in supplementing teaching through more traditional methods.   GEB

Bibliography

Wittrock, M. ed. 1986: *The handbook of research on teaching*. 3rd edn. New York: Macmillan.

displaced speech The term was introduced by Bloomfield (1933) to refer to speech about events which do not relate to the immediate context of an utterance.

In their early stages of first language development children's speech is tied to the here and now. The majority of mothers' speech to their infants is not displaced. It describes or refers to objects to which the child is currently attending (Harris et al. 1983). It is probably only through being able to grasp the connection between what it perceives immediately before it and its mother's words that a child is able to "crack the code" of language (see Bruner 1983). Later at the one-word stage words become detached from their original stimulus. The capacity to produce displaced speech develops in well-ordered stages. Reference to the future, for instance, always appears later than reference to the past.

The capacity for displacement is universal in human languages, but much less developed or nonexistent in animal communication systems. (See also FIRST LANGUAGE ACQUISITION.)   PM/RL

Bibliography

Bloomfield, Leonard 1933: *Language*. New York: Holt, Rinehart and Winston; London: Allen and Unwin (1935).

Bruner, J.S. 1983: *Child's talk. Learning to use language*. Oxford and New York: Oxford University Press.

Harris, M., Jones D. and Grant, J. 1983: The non-verbal context of mothers' speech to children. *First language* 4, 21–30.

disruptive pupils Pupils whose behavior disturbs their teachers. Disruptive pupils are not a new source of concern, nor is there much evidence that their numbers have increased (see McFie 1934). There is division of opinion over the relative importance of psychosocial and sociological variables. Children whose disruptive behavior culminates in expulsion from school tend to come from highly stressful family backgrounds. Some severely disruptive pupils may also be constitutionally vulnerable by reason of atypical autonomic functioning (Davies and Maliphant 1974). Many have a history of serious illnesses or accidents and reception into the care of the local authority (Galloway et al. 1982).

There are wide differences between schools in the number of pupils expelled following disruptive behavior. Demographic variables do not predict these differences, which seem to reflect policies and expectations in the schools themselves rather than the nature of their pupil intake. (See EDUCATIONAL ATTAINMENT AND EXPECTATIONS.) Social psychologists have used the concept of secondary deviance to explain the development of disruptive behavior in some schools. Teachers' initial reactions to deviant behavior may increase the probability of further deviant behavior by uniting a subgroup of pupils in opposition to the school's value system (Hargreaves et al. 1975). Psychiatric assessment is likely to regard disruptive behavior as a CONDUCT DISORDER. Psychotherapy has a poor prognosis. Special groups or centers for disruptive pupils have become popular, but systematic evaluation studies are lacking. It is widely accepted that few pupils are disruptive in all settings. Assessment should aim to identify the variables which mediate disruptive behavior. The most promising approaches to treatment aim to change the situation, the pupils' responses to the situation, or both. (See also BEHAVIOR CHANGE IN THE CLASSROOM.)

DMG

Bibliography

Davies, J.G.V. and Maliphant, R. 1974: Refractory behavior in school and avoidance learning. *Journal of child psychology and psychiatry* 15, 23–31.

Galloway, D.M. et al. 1982: *Schools and disruptive pupils*. London: Longman.

Hargreaves, D., Hester, S. and Mellor, F.J. 1975: *Deviance in classrooms*. London: Routledge and Kegan Paul.

McFie, B.S. 1934: Behavior and personality difficulties in schoolchildren. *British journal of educational psychology* 4, 30–46.

Topping, K. 1983: *Educational systems for disruptive adolescents*. London: Croom Helm.

Down's syndrome This condition, known as mongolism until the early 1960s, accounts for 25 per cent of the severely mentally retarded and is caused by a chromosome abnormality. The main clinical features are a small round head, eyes which slant upwards and outwards (giving the "mongoloid" appearance); minor abnormalities of hands and feet, and moderate to severe mental retardation. There may also be abnormalities of the heart and digestive tract. It occurs in approximately 1 in 600 live births, and the incidence increases with maternal age. The chromosome abnormality consists in over 90 per cent of cases of an extra autosomal chromosome (Trisomy 21) with a recurrence rate of 1 in 100. More rarely, there is a translocation defect of chromosomes D/G, with a high risk of recurrence; or a mixture of some cells in the body with normal chromosomes and some with abnormal chromosomes (mosaicism). The diagnosis can be made in early pregnancy by examining the amniotic fluid surrounding the fetus (amniocentesis), and it is now common practice to offer this to all older women and those who already have an affected child. GENETIC COUNSELING is important. See also MENTAL HANDICAP.

GCF

Bibliography

Brandon, S. and Hauck, A. 1983: Down's syndrome: changing patterns. *Adoption and fostering* 7, 45–9.

Smith, G.F. and Berg, J.M. 1976: *Down's anomaly*. Edinburgh: Churchill Livingstone.

dyslexic children Controversies surrounding the concept of dyslexia have given rise to much heated argument, and there is no universally accepted definition for the group of children suffering from this handicap.

The term dyslexia generally refers to a developmental abnormality in which there exists a difficulty in reading which is out of all proportion to the individual's intellectual competence. The definition proposed in 1968 by the World Federation of Neurology's research group on the subject, chaired by Macdonald Critchley, implies a constitutionally based reading disability free from correlates of reading failure such as low intelligence, sociocultural deprivation and gross neurological deficits. While an exclusionary definition of this type is justifiable for practical reasons, it is unsatisfactory because of its failure to aid conceptual clarity and its limitations for diagnosis. An amended definition by Critchley includes erratic spelling and lack of facility in handling written language as identifiable symptoms and suggests that the defect is capable of improvement. Nonetheless, the negative correlates continue to be central to the definition. Although Critchley insists that the diagnosis is a medical responsibility, dyslexia is not viewed basically as a medical problem by the British Medical Association (1980), which states that most doctors are not competent or willing to diagnose dyslexia without the assessment of an educational psychologist.

The first reference to such a disorder was made in a report in the British Medical Journal in 1896 describing 'the paradoxical case of an intelligent boy of 14 who was incapable of learning to read'. The validity of supposing that dyslexia in children is a specific inherent disorder is based on the analogy of its symptoms to the acquired loss or impairment of the ability to read, caused by cerebral damage. In order to distinguish the two conditions, it is common practice to use the term alexia for all acquired forms of reading impairment and the term dyslexia for the inability to learn to read. In the vast majority of cases of dyslexia, there is hardly any evidence for anatomical or physiological brain deficits. The remarkable preponderance of boys who are dyslexic makes it more difficult to explain the condition on the basis of brain damage.

The primary basis for the sustained interest in dyslexic children is the promise that they hold as a distinct sub-group of reading disabled pupils. Although symptoms vary from child to child, case studies of dyslexic children refer to persistence in letter and word reversals (e.g. confusions between b – d; was – saw); difficulty in repeating polysyllabic words; poor recall of sequences of letters or digits; bizarre spelling; disordered writing; frequently a history of clumsiness and late speech development. The presence of similar characteristics in many children who experience difficulty in learning to read has caused scepticism about the existence of dyslexia in children as an identifiable sub-type of reading disability. Most psychologists and educators would agree that a small proportion of problem readers may in fact have a specific learning defect which is inherent and independent of intellectual shortcomings. The symptoms of the sub-type in its current use do not help to differentiate dyslexic from non-dyslexic failing readers.

Increasing recognition that reading disability is not homogeneous has sustained the search for homogeneous sub-groups of reading-retarded children. Eleanor Boden's attempt to break these children into those with psychological and those with visual problems is an example (Boden 1973). Theoretical notions about neuropsychological processes concerned with reading have been the basis for several studies using a variety of classification approaches (Vellutino 1979). No doubt these attempts provide insights on different sub-types. However, despite their appeal for clinical and educational practice, they require evidence to show that they really are distinctive sub-types. The more recent diversity models proposed for dyslexia, as part of a continuum of language learning difficulty, hold more promise because of the shift in emphasis from treating these children as victims of pathology to providing opportunities for optimal development.   SDS

Bibliography

Benton, A.L. and Pearl. D., eds. 1979: *Dyslexia: an appraisal of current knowledge.* Oxford and New York: Oxford University Press.

Boden, E. 1973: Developmental dyslexia: a diagnostic approach. *Developmental medicine and child neurology* 15, 663–87.

Malatesha, R.N. and Whitaker, H.A. eds. 1984: *Dyslexia: a global issue.* The Hague: Martinus Nijhoff.

Mathis, S. 1981: Dyslexia syndromes in children: towards the development of syndrome-specific treatment programs. In *Neuropsychological and cognitive processes in reading*, eds. E.J. Pirozzolo and M.C. Mittrock. New York and London: Academic Press.

Parlidis, G.T. and Miles, T.R. eds. 1981: *Dyslexia research and its applications to education.* John Liley and Sons Ltd. British Medical Association News Review.

Tansley, P. and Panckhurst J. 1981: *Children with specific learning difficulties: a critical review of research.* London: Nelson.

Vellutino, F. 1979: *Dyslexia: theory and research.* Cambridge, Mass.: MIT Press.

E

education: psychological assessment (US – evaluation) Refers to the investigation of educational, emotional, behavioral, developmental or other problems by applied (clinical, educational or school, and occupational) psychologists. It makes use of various procedures – interviews, observations, tests and even small-scale experiments – in order to collect and interpret information about clients and their circumstances in relation to the problem under investigation.

Assessment is a more comprehensive process than testing, and it may or may not use tests to gather the necessary information.

The assessment process is dependent to a great extent on the skills, experience and theoretical orientation of the assessor (Berger 1983). None of the differing theoretical and conceptual frameworks available has a clear position of superiority. In addition techniques such as psychological tests are prone to varying degrees and types of error, and the results they produce thus open to varied interpretations. Even the most well developed and commonly used techniques, such as tests of intelligence (see TESTS, INTELLIGENCE), are subject to these imperfections (Sattler 1982, Kaufman 1979). Finally there are no explicit rules for integrating the information obtained by these different means.

Historically, assessment was seen in narrow terms, aimed at the measurement of a limited range of attributes or characteristics by means of standardized tests. Testing and assessment were seen as synonymous. The measurement of intelligence or diagnosis of mental or physical pathology were the preponderant concerns of most applied psychologists. As some became involved in treatment and management the range of techniques required increased, with practitioners becoming aware of the need for procedures which would have immediate implications for directing treatment. Although there were several important analyses of testing much of the early work was concerned with narrowly conceived theory and practice of measurement (psychometrics). More recently, there has been a shift towards extending the range of procedures used in assessment (Nay 1979), the emphasis being on multi-method assessment. The reasons for this change stem mainly from the inadequacies of the one or two general purpose tests which psychologists commonly used. These general tests have been found to be inadequate as guides for practice and as ways of monitoring the effects of treatment. Additionally they have been found to be insensitive to the many consequences of psychological intervention.

Nevertheless, decisions made or influenced by such tests can exert a profound effect on the lives of individuals and their families. For instance, psychological assessments developed around one or two tests are influential in decisions about schooling, particularly the transfer of pupils between ordinary (mainstream) and special schools. Such transfers can circumscribe the future choices available to the individual, can lead to the stigmatization of pupil and family and absorb scarce resources. They can also be of immense benefit in helping to provide the individual and family with forms of support which would not otherwise be made available.

Some of the negative ramifications of psychological assessment have been highlighted by the use of tests on minority group children. (See Sattler 1982 for a discussion of the impact of tests in the USA, and Coard 1971 for some reactions in the UK.) It is argued that the tests, commonly of intelligence and attainments, are biased and prejudicial to the interests of the children, their families and others who may not share the norms of the dominant groups in the community. In some states in the USA the use of certain tests has been curbed by legislation. While there have been some recent attempts to refute the imputation of bias (Jensen 1980), the major problems arise because of the failure of test-givers to master the intricacies of test administration and interpretation (Berger 1983).

Although much of the critical debate has focused on intelligence tests, many of the issues raised are common to most if not all psychological procedures. For instance, assessment is very much dependent on informal or systematic observation. Mitchell (1979) among others has clearly documented the many limitations of observation, including the effect of observer bias and expectation, the reactivity of the people being observed and the limitations inherent in particular systematic observation techniques.

Another recent development has been an increasing awareness of the impact on people of the contexts in which they live. In the past the concern was with measuring characteristics (pathological or nonpathological) of or within the individual. It is now recognized that the intimate interplay between the individual and the physical and social environment has to be considered in order to obtain a realistic appraisal of problems and to formulate suitable treatment.

Assessment involves several other issues of outstanding importance. One is the conceptualization of the assessment process itself: little attention has been given to an analysis of what the process is about and why it takes the form it does. One view regards it as the application of scientific method in the investigation of the individual. This approach has been most clearly developed by Shapiro (1970). It sees investigation as being concerned with the generation and testing of hypotheses put forward to account for clinical phenomena – the presenting problems. The psychologist formulates hypotheses

and uses various means to test them experimentally. That is, assessment is essentially a form of research concentrating on an individual. In the framework of this approach the distinction between assessment and treatment is no longer clear-cut and may even be irrelevant. The treatment is seen as a test of the adequacy of the hypotheses and as such is an integral part of the investigations.

A somewhat related view has been developed from a different theoretical perspective in what is known as target assessment and entails the search for functional relationships between environmental events and the problem behavior. In this approach the problem is seen in terms of a specifiable set of behavior patterns which can be clearly defined. An attempt is then made through observation and manipulation to identify the environmental antecedents and/or consequences which exert some control over the problem behavior. In so doing, both the "causes" and the means of "treatment" are identified. (See BEHAVIOR CHANGE IN THE CLASSROOM for a more detailed description of this approach.) Target assessment is one aspect of a broader approach known as behavioral assessment which concentrates on the behavior-patterns that constitute the problem, a variety of procedures being used to identify the factors which influence its expression and form. The behavioral assessment process has several stages. The first consists of problem specification, the second of selecting, implementing and eventually terminating the intervention, and the third, follow-up evaluation. Other analyses of the process have additional stages and may emphasize different aspects of the investigation and intervention, particularly ecological influences. Behavioral assessment is generally concerned with the individual and psychologists have begun to examine and develop an experimental methodology for the investigation of individual clients (e.g. Hersen and Barlow 1976).

Another important issue concerns the role of theory in assessment: some forms of assessment are presented as pragmatic and empirical, essentially exercises in testing divorced from theory, while others are closely allied to a particular theoretical orientation but with little overt appreciation of the ways in which the theory influences practice.

It is not generally appreciated that theory selectively determines the form and nature of assessment. Behavioral assessment is one illustration of an approach which is closely dependent on a particular theoretical orientation. Theory provides the language, the content and the underlying models which will guide the investigations, what will be seen, and the interpretation of the outcome. It also influences the nature and evaluation of intervention. Even as common a practice as "testing intelligence" carries with it a network of assumptions and theoretical ideas about the "existence" and nature of intelligence, its measurement and its role in human functioning. A psychologist influenced by Piagetian theory and method would adopt an approach to intelligence differing substantially from that of someone whose view is based on one of several other views of intelligence (see Sattler 1982). Practitioners and the "consumers" need to be consistently aware of the implications for the individual of the adoption and adherence to a particular theoretical orientation.

Of particular relevance in the assessment of children, handicapped or not, is the need to adopt a developmental perspective and to consider the implications for assessment of the differential rates of development across the life span and the qualitative changes which occur at comparatively rapid rates in childhood. There have been some recent attempts to do so, for example in the assessment and treatment of problems in social relationships (Furman 1980).   MBe

Bibliography

*Berger, M. 1983: Psychological assessment and testing. In *Child psychiatry: modern perspectives*. 2nd edn, eds. M. Rutter and L. Hersov. Oxford: Blackwell Scientific; Philadelphia: Lippincott.

Coard, B. 1971: *How the West-Indian child is made educationally subnormal in the British school system*. London: New Beacon Books.

Furman, W. 1980: Promoting social development: developmental implications for treatment. In *Advances in clinical child psychology*, vol. 3, eds. B.B. Lahey and A.E. Kazdin. New York: Plenum Press.

Hersen, M. and Barlow, D.H. 1976: *Single case experimental design: strategies for studying behavior change*. New York and Oxford: Pergamon.

Jensen, A.R. 1980: *Bias in mental testing*. London and New York: Methuen.

Kaufman, A.S. 1979: *Intelligent testing with the W.I.S.C.-R*. New York: John Wiley.

Mitchell, S.K. 1979: Interobserver agreement, reliability and generalizability of data collected in observational studies. *Psychological bulletin 86*, 376–90.

Nay, W.R. 1979: *Multimethod clinical assessment*. New York: Gardner Press.

*Sattler, J.M. 1982: *Assessment of children's intelligence*. 2nd edn. Boston: Allyn and Bacon.

Shapiro, M.B. 1970: Intensive assessment of the single case: an inductive-deductive approach. In *The psychological assessment of mental and physical handicaps*, ed. P. Mittler. London: Tavistock; New York: Harper and Row.

education: psychology of The branch of academic psychological study concerned with schools and schooling. It is often referred to as the "psychology of education" rather than "educational psychology" to distinguish it from the applied research and professional practice associated with educational psychologists, who are employed (very largely) by the SCHOOL PSYCHOLOGICAL SERVICE.

There are many areas of psychological enquiry that have been pursued in the educational context. Studies of child development, especially those within a Piagetian framework, have been influential not only at the level of primary schooling, but also in secondary education, where it has been found for example that many concepts in school science presuppose a stage of cognitive development ("formal operations") that many pupils have failed to reach. (See PIAGET.) In the last few years post-Piagetian studies have begun to investigate more specific details of children's knowledge about the world, and about their own developing cognitive and social processes.

Perhaps the most central concern of the psychology of education has been with the development of intellectual processes, the acquisition of concepts and learning theory. The work of Bruner on DISCOVERY LEARNING and of Ausubel on "meaningful learning" proved particularly seminal, although more recently the study of school learning has been drawing on the theories and methods of information processing and cognitive psychology. Here again the focus has shifted to the details of children's representation of knowledge, and to the processes whereby that knowledge is expanded and amended. The fields of learning and problem-solving have drawn more closely together, and studies are being made of the ways in which school-children approach naturalistic or semi-naturalistic tasks.

Behavioral psychology, too, has contributed to our developing understanding of the child at school. The interest in the application of conditioning principles to the design of educational technology and teaching machines has given way to a more sensitive use of BEHAVIOR MODIFICATION techniques in helping children, teachers and parents with behavior problems, and this has been facilitated by the increasing rapprochement within mainstream psychology between the behavioral and cognitive traditions.

Finally, in this brief survey, the varied methods and approaches of social psychology have seen increasing application to understanding the interpersonal dynamics of schools. The interactions of children with children (in the formation and modification of friendship patterns, for example), children with teachers, and teachers with each other have all come in for investigation. The earlier attempts to assess the relative effects of different, very broadly conceived, "teaching styles" continue, but are now supplemented by more naturalistic, micro-observations of classroom (and staffroom) patterns and strategies of communication. (See SCHOOL AS A SOCIAL ORGANIZATION.)

The biggest change in the psychology of education over the last decade has been the development of models, theories and research methodologies that are purpose-built for the educational context. The earlier hope that high-level, content-free, general models of learning and other areas of performance could be taken from "pure" psychology and applied with accuracy and with profit to the study of schools has proved largely unfounded. Generations of students in TEACHER TRAINING have found the abstract principles so derived of little practical help, and researchers are tending to agree that models derived from laboratory-based studies frequently fail to capture the feel of what goes on in schools. It seems that the less ambitious attempt to understand particular tasks and situations that are familiar in schools will ultimately prove more fruitful.   GCI

Bibliography

Entwistle, N. ed. 1985: *New directions in educational psychology 1: teaching and learning.* Brighton: Falmer Press.

education of handicapped children Education may be provided in various ways for pupils with disabilities which affect their learning and development. Ideally it should be as normal as possible in terms of the aims, curricula and methods. Many handicapped children are satisfactorily educated in ordinary classes with varying degrees of support and specialist educational, psychological and medical surveillance (see INTEGRATION OF HANDICAPPED CHILDREN INTO NORMAL SCHOOLS). Others are taught in special classes or units with possibilities for participation in ordinary classes and provision for similar support and surveillance. Special schools are needed for others, at least for part of their school life and possibly with part-time attendance at a normal school. Education through the guidance and involvement of parents should be available from birth, should continue into preschool provision and, following the normal school period, further education and vocational training should be available as required.

The aims of education and curricula should, as far as possible, be the same as for non-handicapped children although severe sensory and intellectual impairments may dictate a different emphasis in aims or require special curriculum planning. In general, the more severe the sensory or intellectual handicap the greater the need for special teaching methods. These include, first, a thorough understanding of the consequences of visual, hearing or intellectual impairments for the child's cognitive, personality and educational development as well as his or her broader personal and social needs. Second, knowledge of the methods of structuring learning, of special methods of communication (e.g. braille language and speech signing systems) and a variety of technical aids (vision aids, sound amplification, electronic apparatus, microprocessors, etc.).   RG

Bibliography

Cope, C. and Anderson, E. 1977: *Special units in ordinary schools*. London: University of London Institute of Education.

Harvey, D.W., McGuire, J.M. and Plante, S.T. 1983: Meeting the needs of learning-disabled college students. *Journal of learning skills* 2, 29–34.

Mokros, J.R. and Russell, S.J. 1986: Learner-centered software: a survey of microcomputer use with special needs students. *Journal of learning disabilities* 19, 185–90.

Odom, S.L. and Fewell, R.R. 1983: Program evaluation in early childhood special education: a meta-evaluation. *Educational evaluation and policy analysis* 5, 445–60.

educational attainment and expectations

1. Parental expectations

Research in the sociology of education has shown that parental expectations, and children's perceptions of parental expectations, have a significant independent effect on children's educational attainment. Parental expectations have been shown to have a stronger effect on attainment than teacher's expectations.

A great deal of the research on parental expectations has been in the service of discovering causal factors to explain achievement differences among ethnic groups and among groups differing in socioeconomic status. While parental expectations correlate positively with social status, parental expectations alone cannot explain achievement differences among ethnic groups, even though ethnicity correlates with socioeconomic level.

Black parents of low socioeconomic status often have expectations for their children that are equal to or higher than those of middle-class parents, although the children of these groups significantly differ in achievement levels (see Tomlinson 1983; but also Maughan and Rutter 1986). One possible explanation for this is that high parental expectations are not enough; parents must also provide their children with time and attention, in addition to practical strategies which can be used to achieve educational goals. In some cases, high parental expectations may actually inhibit school performance. Relatively little research has been conducted to examine the strategies parents use to implement their expectations.

Researchers have also found that high parental expectations may differentially affect different abilities. Verbal and number abilities may be more susceptible to environmental influences, such as parental expectations, than spatial abilities. Also, parental expectations tend to influence the educational attainment of girls more than boys. (See also EDUCATIONAL ATTAINMENT AND PRESCHOOL EXPERIENCE; EDUCATIONAL ATTAINMENT AND SOCIAL CLASS; INTELLIGENCE AND ENVIRONMENTAL INFLUENCES).   JSC

2. Pupil expectations

The expectations that pupils have about their performance in an instructional setting have profound effects on their actual performance. The concept is closely related to Merton's notion (1948) of the self-fulfilling prophecy which holds that people who have expectations about what is to occur often act in ways likely to produce that occurrence. In an educational context, those who expect to perform well, do perform better than those who do not have that expectation (Zanna et al. 1975). What has made this line of research intriguing is that the successful performance occurs even though the expectation of success is based on factors that are not relevant to performance. The expectation of success or failure may come from random selection invoked by a researcher or by factors such as race, ethnicity or socioeconomic status. While most research has focused on the effect of successful expectations, two additional phenomena should be noted. First Aronson and Carlsmith (1962) found that pupils actively seek to confirm their expectations about themselves – even when that confirmation leads to failure. Second, the Zanna et al. study indicated that the expectations pupils have about themselves can interact with the expectations held by others. Pupils who had successful expectations, and about whom teachers also held positive expectations, actually performed worse than other students. The potentially helpful and potentially invidious effects of the expectations held by pupils has made this phenomenon an interesting one to researchers and educators (see also Eccles 1983; Weiner 1983). JCo

3. Teacher expectations

The study of the effect of teacher expectations on pupils' performance also derives from Merton's concept of the self-fulfilling prophecy. Rosenthal and Jacobson (1968) studied the prophecies or expectations that teachers had about children in their classes. They led teachers to believe that some of the children in their classes could be expected to do very well during the school year. Even though the children were randomly selected, those whom the teachers expected to do well actually performed much better on standardized tests at the end of the school year than did those children about whom the teachers had no expectations. This was particularly true of younger children and became less pronounced in the older

grades. Teacher expectations have been shown to affect pupils' performance in a variety of areas from mathematics to swimming. Current research has continued in at least two directions. One is to place the effect of teacher expectations in a larger theoretical framework (e.g. Darley and Fazio 1980; see also Minuchin and Shapiro 1983) and the other is the careful analysis of the ways in which teacher expectations are subtly communicated to students, and affected by the students' own perceptions or beliefs (Brattesani et al. 1984). JCo

Bibliography

Aronson, E. and Carlsmith, J.M. 1962: Performance expectancy as a determinant of actual performance. *Journal of abnormal and social psychology* 65, 178–82.

Brattesani, K., Weinstein, R. and Marshall, H. 1984: Student perceptions of differential teacher treatment as moderators of teacher expectation effects. *Journal of educational psychology* 76, 236–47.

Darley, J. and Fazio, R. 1980: Expectancy confirmation processes arising in the social interaction sequence. *American psychologist* 35, 867–81.

Eccles, J. 1983: Expectancies, values and academic behaviors. In *Achievement and achievement motives*, ed. J.T. Spence. San Francisco: Freeman.

Maughan, B. and Rutter, M. 1986: Black pupils' progress in secondary schools: II. Examination attainments. *British journal of developmental psychology* 4, 19–29.

Merton, R. 1948: The self-fulfilling prophecy. *Antioch Review* 8, 193–210.

Minuchin, P.P. and Shapiro, E.K. 1983: The school as a context for social development. In *Handbook of child psychology*. 4th edn, vol. 4, ed. E.M. Hetherington. New York: Wiley.

Rosenthal, R. and Jacobson, L. 1968: *Pygmalion in the classroom: Teacher expectation and pupils' intellectual development.* New York: Holt, Rinehart and Winston.

Tomlinson, S. 1983: *Ethnic minorities in British schools.* London: Heinemann.

Weiner, B. 1983: Some methodological pitfalls in attribution research. *Journal of educational psychology* 75, 530–43.

Zanna, Mark P. et al. 1975: Pygmalion and Galatea: The interactive effect of teacher and student expectancies. *Journal of experimental social psychology* 11, 279–87.

educational attainment and institutional care

Children reared in institutional care are usually the legal responsibility of a statutory or voluntary agency and live with other children in residences where they are looked after by a team of child care workers. John Bowlby has claimed that children under five who are reared in such institutions will suffer mental deficits because they lack the continuous relationship with the mother that is necessary to normal development. Some support for Bowlby's claim came from early studies showing low IQs among children reared in orphanages with poor staff ratios and few playthings (see BOWLBY).

Institutional upbringing is associated with intellectual deficit in handicapped children too. Children with DOWN'S SYNDROME reared in a residential setting score lower on measures of play maturity than Down's children at home (who had more social contacts and toys).

It is difficult to pinpoint the exact cause of intellectual deficits among institutionalized children because maternal absence, poor facilities and lack of social contact are often confounded. Tizard and Hodges (1978) followed the progress of children in high quality residential nurseries, those with excellent staffing ratios, home-like atmosphere, and educational playthings. At the age of four nursery children did not differ on IQ measures from home-reared children with similar social backgrounds. By eight, however, the IQs of the institutionalized children had decreased markedly; in fact they were lower than scores of children living in families who had been adopted from the institution before the age of four.

It appears that institutionalization before the age of four does not impair intellectual development but that after that age institutionalization may be associated with lower intellectual functioning and school attainment. This may be due to lack of personal involvement and continuity with adults rather than inadequate facilities. KS

Bibliography
*Tizard, B. 1977: *Adoption: a second chance.* London: Open Books.

—— and Hodges, J. 1978: The effect of early institutional rearing on the development of eight year old children. *Journal of child psychology and psychiatry* 19, 99–118.

educational attainment and locus of control

Locus of control of reinforcement refers to an individual's perception of reinforcement contingencies. The more a person sees a connection between his own behavior and what happens to him the more "internal" he is considered. Conversely, the more he does not perceive connections between his reinforcements and his actions but sees the consequences as due to luck, chance or the influence of others, the more "external" he is considered. Originating in Rotter's social learning theory (1966) locus of control orientation has been found to be related to an impressive array of significant behavior ranging from academic achievement to psychological adjustment. While there are multiple dimensional measures of locus of control available, the most popular measures for both children and adults provide a single global score.

Recent work has focused on antecedents of, and changing of, locus of control as well as on devising procedures that take advantage of the differences in information processing associated with internal and external orientations. For example, school curricula have been designed to be consistent with children's locus of control orientation, with resultant increases in academic achievement and liking for school. SN

Bibliography
Harter, S. and Connell, J.P. 1984: A model of the relationships among children's academic achievement and their self-perceptions of competence control and motivational orientation. In *The development of achievement motivation*, ed. J. Nicholls. Greenwich, Conn.: JAI.

Rotter, J.B. 1966: Generalized expectancies for internal versus external control of reinforcements. *Psychological monographs* 80.

educational attainment and preschool experiences

Preschool experience includes all that the child perceives or does, at home or in nursery, before compulsory schooling. A host of recent studies document the powerful influence of the home on children's preparation for school. The UK National Child Development Study found the strongest determinant of variations in reading and arithmetic attainment at seven years to be family background. Studies with even younger children show that social class influences linguistic skills and that children with more advanced language benefit the most when they go to school.

Many hypotheses have been put forward to explain the processes by which family factors affect school readiness. Observational studies indicate that high levels of maternal involvement, coupled with provision of age-appropriate and challenging playthings, foster sensori-motor competence (see PIAGET) in toddlers. Some mothers encourage intellectual development by using praise instead of criticism and allowing children to set their own pace and make decisions. Unfortunately the many factors associated with SOCIAL DISADVANTAGE such as poor jobs, housing and health make it difficult for poor families to provide a stimulating environment.

Nursery schools and playgroups have traditionally complemented middle-class homes by providing an informal curriculum of rich playthings and peer interaction. Because families living in circumstances of disadvantage rarely provide such learning opportunities, many programs of compensatory preschool education were developed to provide a "head start" for poor children before formal school (see COMPENSATORY EDUCATION). Follow-up studies (Darlington 1980) of pupils from American preschool programs show them to have higher rates of meeting school requirements (as measured by lower grade retention or assignment to special class) than children who had not attended preschool. Studies of children attending similar compensatory preschool programs in the UK showed significant cognitive and linguistic gains upon entry into school (Smith and James 1975).

Two factors are associated consistently with successful preschools: inclusion of sessions with structured play activities, high levels of adult-child conversation and parent involvement. Most educationalists now concentrate on the last in hopes that participating in nurseries will help parents develop confidence and skills for giving their own children a good start.   KS

Bibliography

Darlington, R.B. et al. 1980: Preschool programs and later school competence of children from low income families. *Science* 208 (April), 202–4.

*Mortimore, J. and Blackstone, T. 1982: *Disadvantage and education.* London and Exeter, N.H.: Heinemann Educational.

Ramey, C.T., Yeates, K.O. and Short, E.J. 1984: The plasticity of intellectual development: insights from preventive intervention. *Child development* 55, 1913–25.

Smith, G.A. and James, T. 1975: The effects of pre-school education: some American and British evidence. *Oxford review of education* 1, 221–38.

educational attainment and social class

Correlations have been found between parents' social class and their children's educational performance both in terms of years of schooling and level of academic achievement. The influence that a family's socioeconomic situation exerts over a child's educational attainment stems from a variety of sources, an important one being the value that a family places on education (see EDUCATIONAL ATTAINMENT AND PARENTAL EXPECTATIONS). Children of middle- to upper-class families tend to have high educational aspirations as a result of the pressure they perceive from home to continue their studies regardless of their own attitude towards school. Another factor is the effect of the values of the peer group on the children's developing standards and goals. (See further LEARNING AND MOTIVATION; see also SOCIAL DISADVANTAGE; COMPENSATORY EDUCATION.)   MB/JM

educational research: methodology Large scale surveys supported by extensive correlational analyses have traditionally been used. These have been extremely useful in defining the broad parameters of problem areas, an inevitable and necessary first-stage level of inquiry. Such an approach has a number of limitations, however. Among these are:
(1) The associations established and indexed by the correlations calculated between two variables permit no inference as to cause or the direction of effects. Furthermore they relate to group trends and not to individuals.
(2) The correlated variables almost inevitably (by definition) reflect the end-product rather than the nature of the processes themselves. However some surveys, through the use of supplementary data, can point up possible causal networks more precisely (see e.g. Rutter et al. 1970).
(3) Establishing the statistical significance of such correlations does not thereby establish their psychological value. Small correlations can be significant in statistical terms when large samples are used. Even large and highly significant correlations "explain" only a proportion of the variance between variables, for example a correlation of $+0.7$ explains only 49 per cent (0.7^2 x 100) of the variance, leaving 51 per cent as an index of ignorance or unexplained variance.
(4) Various forms of FACTOR ANALYSIS can help in the grouping and ordering of large numbers of correlations.
Factor analysis is a mathematical technique, and there is no necessity for the factors, however labeled, to be equivalent to any psychological entity or variable. Furthermore it is often not easy to fit individuals into factor patterns so derived. There are other techniques, of course, that analyse data in relation to persons rather than by discrete variables.

Some indications of change over time can be obtained through the use of LONGITUDINAL RESEARCH methods which follow the same group of children over a number of years. It is thus possible to indicate at what stage in development or in a child's school career specific difficulties were identified and what happened subsequently. These procedures can provide valuable data but the method has limitations, such as: (1) The studies are time consuming and rather expensive. (2) Samples contract in size over time for various reasons such as accident, change of address, or unwillingness to continue collaboration. This reduces the value of the data. The contraction may also occur disproportionately in vulnerable sections of the sample that are central to the objectives of the research (e.g. the effects of social factors on educational performance). (3) The size of the sample needs to be sufficiently large to permit analyses and generalizations from important subgroups contained within it (e.g. those who become delinquents or who are backward in reading). (4) Important changes may take place over time that have not been adequately monitored in the research (e.g. the rapid and recent widespread increase in unemployment across all occupational groups in the United Kingdom). (5) Introducing new variables or modifying others during the course of a longitudinal study has to be avoided if maximum use is to be made of the data without confounding the results.

CROSS-SECTIONAL RESEARCH methods using survey techniques at a given moment have an advantage in being more economical in both time and cost but cannot monitor changes over time. Some compromise arrangements merging cross-sectional and longitudinal methods in a limited way are possible.

Economic constraints, with the need to ensure more efficient and effective use of resources, will reinforce the need for more stringent evaluation of educational provision. An emphasis on more process-oriented psychological research on a smaller scale would be highly relevant to such purposes. This will require knowledge of advances within the mainstream of general psychology as well as in child development.   RM

Bibliography

Baltes, P.B., Reese, H.W. and Nesselrode, J. R. 1977: *Life-span developmental psychology: introduction to research methods*. Monterey, Calif.: Brooks/Cole.

Pintrich, P.R., Cross, D.R., Kozma, R.B. and McKeachie, W.S. 1986: Instructional psychology. In *Annual review of psychology*, vol. 37, eds. M.R. Rosenzweig and L.W. Porter. Palo Alto: Annual Reviews Inc.

Plowden 1967: *Report on children and the primary schools*. London: HMSO.

Rutter, M.L., Tizard, J. and Whitmore, K. 1970: *Education, health and behavior*. London: Longman; New York: Robert E. Krieber (1981).

Wittrock, M. ed. 1986: *The handbook of research on teaching*. 3rd edn. New York: Macmillan.

ego Although the word has a philosophical history in English as denoting the essential "self" or seat of identity, in psychology it has come to mean the system of rational and realistic functions of the personality. This usage is largely influenced by psychoanalytic personality theory in which the word ego is a translation of Freud's *Ich* (1923), where it is contrasted with the instinctually impulsive *id*, and with the evaluative *superego*; but it is not equated with consciousness, since FREUD argued that much of it would have to be unconscious or "preconscious". Its function in that theory leads to operationally definable concepts such as ego-strength and ego-control, whose development in childhood and efficacy in maturity can be assessed by means independent of psychoanalysis (Cattell 1965, ch. 3). Those theorists who give greater weight to ego-processes (such as reality-perception, conscious learning and voluntary control) in their accounts of personality development and in techniques of psychotherapy are known as ego-psychologists (Hartmann 1964).   RMC

Bibliography

Cattell, Raymond B. 1965: *The scientific analysis of personality*. Harmondsworth: Penguin.

Freud, Sigmund 1923: The ego and the id. *Standard edition of the complete psychological works of Sigmund Freud*, vol. 19. London: Hogarth Press; New York: Norton.

Hartmann, Heinz 1964: *Essays in ego-psychology*. London: Hogarth Press.

ego ideal Term in psychoanalytical personality theory for the ideal standard against which the ego evaluates its activity and qualities. Hence FREUD at one time gave it a role in dream-censorship, but for the most part he drops the term once he has attributed its function to the positive aspect of the superego (Freud 1923, esp. pp. 9–11). The young child sets up this psychic standard as part of that internalization of (or IDENTIFICATION with) parental values and controls which allows it to resolve the Oedipus and Elektra complexes. As such, it is 'the expression of the admiration for the perfection' which the child then attributes to its parents, as opposed to representing their forbidding and punitive aspect which the superego also embodies. Elsewhere the term is used, even by Freud, synonymously with SUPEREGO.   NMC

Bibliography

Freud, Sigmund 1923: The ego and the id. *Standard edition of the complete psychological works of Sigmund Freud*, vol. 19. London: Hogarth Press; New York: Norton.

egocentrism A term first proposed in 1926 by the French psychologist, PIAGET, to designate a cognitive state in which the individual comprehends the world only from his own point of view, without awareness of the existence of other possible points of view. Although typical of childish thought, egocentrism can be observed throughout the life span. It is a state of mind characterized by failure to differentiate between subjective and objective components of experience, with a consequent unwitting imposition of a personal point of view (see Cox 1980).

A classic example of spatial egocentrism in childhood is Piaget's "three mountains" task. The child of about five years is seated in front of a papier mâché model of three mountains and asked to imagine how the scene would appear to a doll at another position. The child consistently describes his own viewpoint as though it were characteristic of the doll's.

An example of social egocentrism from adulthood might be the case of the teacher with specialized knowledge who fails to take sufficient account of the lesser knowledge of his pupils, with the consequence that they fail to comprehend. This could be considered an example of egocentric speech, since the teacher intends but fails to communicate.   GEB

Bibliography

Cox, Maureen V. 1980: *Are young children egocentric?* London: Batsford; New York: St Martin's Press.

Ford, M.E. 1985: Two perspectives on the validation of developmental constructs: psychometric and theoretical limitations in research on egocentrism. *Psychological bulletin* 97(3), 497–501.

Piaget, Jean 1923 (1959): *The language and thought of the child*. 3rd edn. London: Routledge and Kegan Paul; New York: Humanities Press.

Waters, H.S. and Tinsley, V.S. 1985: Evaluating the discriminant and convergent validity of developmental constructs: another look at the concept of egocentrism. *Psychological bulletin* 97(3), 483–96.

emotion: environmental effects

Though some emotional reactions appear independent of former environmental stimulation, e.g. endogenous depressions, most theories postulate a high degree of interdependence between emotion and situations. Situations stimulate emotions, and emotions both color and generate situations. This interactive theme is reflected in evolutionary or ethological approaches which postulate that basic emotions reflect adaptive demands of key environmental situations; e.g. in-group and out-group identification links to acceptance-rejection; hierarchy to anger (high members) and fear (low members); territoriality to exploration and surprise; and the demands of temporal survival link

to affects of mourning and myths of survival. Sociologists generate similar situation-emotion models based on analysis of group structures. In addition to these structural or correlational models, both child psychologists and anthropologists describe the processes by which emotional states and expressions integrate social behaviors in mother-infant interactions, work and family interactions and situations involving role conflicts and interpersonal regulation. These analyses range across issues such as how emotional communication generates interpersonal ties to how social (situational) rules limit the expression and potential damage of uninhibited expressions of emotions such as anger and sexuality.   HL

Bibliography

Plutchik, R. 1980: A general psychoevolutionary theory of emotion. In *Emotion theory, research, and experience*, eds. R. Plutchik and H. Kellerman. New York: Academic Press.

Scherer, K. R. and Ekman, P. 1984: *Approaches to emotion*. Hillside, N. J.: Erlbaum.

emotion: Piagetian view

Piaget believed that cognition and affect are intricately entwined, but that neither process causes the other. Cognition is a matter of mental structures, while affect energizes behavior. Accordingly, affect can speed up or slow down intellectual development and influence what one attends to, but affect does not generate what one perceives, nor how one conceives of a problem. Similarly, cognition is linked to emotion via perception, learning and memory, but cognition cannot energize behavior.

Affect develops in six stages that roughly parallel the stages of intellectual growth. The first three stages are sensorimotor and involve (1) hereditary organizations such as alimentary instincts and curiosity; (2) the emergence of positive and negative affects linked to past experiences and circular reactions; (3) the beginnings of investment of interest in or valuation of objects. Three stages are post-representational and involve, respectively (1) the experience of the potential value that objects and persons may have; (2) the conservation of feeling states and emergence of will; and (3) the establishment of higher-order societal feelings. (See also PIAGET.)   JJCa

Bibliography
Piaget, Jean 1981: *Intelligence and affectivity: their relationship during child development*. Palo Alto, Calif.: Annual Reviews Inc.

emotion and fantasy Emotions are closely correlated with the emergence and the content of stimulus-independent thought, whether such thought is a fleeting image or an elaborate fantasy. The most common form of fantasy is daydreaming. Jerome L. Singer, his colleagues and students (e.g. Singer 1975) have repeatedly identified three separate patterns of daydreaming and have found that each pattern is characterized by both its own emotional tone and by content appropriate to that tone. Further, these patterns are relatively stable individual differences, or "trait" characteristics. The first style is that of unfocused mind-wandering, with fleeting stereotypical fantasies and an inability to sustain any prolonged or deep emotions. The second is marked by guilty and dysphoric affect and has appropriate content. The third pattern is positive, replete with both interest and joy, and it is marked by happy memories, explorations of possibilities, or sheer playfulness with stored images. See FANTASY.   RBT

Bibliography
Singer, Jerome L. 1975: *Daydreaming and fantasy*. Oxford: Oxford University Press.

emotional development This refers to several dissociable but related processes which occur over the life span. It cannot be understood independently of one's definition of emotions. These are central nervous system and feeling states which are intimately associated with involuntary expressive reactions in the face, voice and gesture. Emotions motivate the individual

and control numerous internal psychological processes, and are, in turn, controlled by them. Moreover, their external expressive patterns regulate interpersonal behavior in a variety of ways. They are continuous, active and adaptive processes, rather than intermittent, reactive and disruptive, as traditionally conceived. Perhaps because of their adaptive function, emotional expression patterns appear to be biologically based and pre-wired. For instance, blind infants and children with no opportunity to mimic expressions of others show remarkably similar patterns to those observable in sighted persons. At least six to eight patterns of facial expression such as anger, joy and disgust appear to be universally recognizable, and hence receptivity to these expressive patterns may also be pre-wired. In addition, emotional facial expression of adults, children and young infants are highly similar, permitting emotions to form a core of continuity throughout the life span.

Traditional conceptualizations have typically ignored many significant processes of emotional development, and been too simplistic about the ages of emergence of specific emotional states. Consider Bridges's widely-cited differentiation model, which posits an initial state of undifferentiated arousal in the neonate, from which first distress, then delight, differentiate at three to six weeks. At three months, anger differentiates out of distress; at four months, disgust from anger; and at six months, fear from disgust. At eight months, the positive emotion of elation differentiates from delight, and affection from elation at twelve months. Other more complex emotions such as jealousy, parental affection and envy are evident by five years.

Recent empirical work has called into question the differentiation model. There is evidence that neonates show both disgust to noxious, and delight to savory substances. They have remarkably well patterned expressions of surprise, fear, interest and possibly other fundamental emotions (see Feldman 1982). Moreover, the mechanism of differentiation proposed by Bridges is not persuasive. Fear, for instance, does not seem to have expressive components similar to but more specific than disgust, nor does affection seem to share many features in common with elation.

Perhaps the most significant inadequacy of traditional conceptions of emotional development is the failure to consider different domains of development that influence which emotions are observed at different ages. Emotional behavior can change in the course of life because of changes in (1) the situations that elicit emotions; (2) the instrumental (voluntary) behavior motivated by emotions; (3) the expressive reactions indicative of emotion; (4) the emotional states themselves becoming elaborated with development; and (5) changing social conventions as to what it is proper to experience, or express, or both, as an emotion. Let us consider each of these domains in turn.

1. *Emotions develop through changes in the efficacy of various eliciting circumstances, resulting from developments in perception, cognition, and learning.*

These changes may sharply increase the prevalence of a given emotion in an infant's response repertoire, but it is an error to assume, on the basis of these shifts in prevalence, that the response process is changing, or that the emotional expression is not observable earlier. For instance, the smiling response blossoms at four to eight weeks of age, the frequently cited "age of emergence". However it is observable under certain conditions much earlier. Blind infants smile at the mother's voice at three weeks; drowsy infants smile to many stimuli in the first month of life; and premature infants show extensive smiling in rapid eye movement sleep states. The blossoming of the smile at four to eight weeks seems to result from new ways of seeing the face (a prepotent elicitor of smiling at that age), and from the emergence of new memory capacities (effortful assimilation to new memory stores powerfully elicits smiling at all ages).

Similarly, fear is widely believed to emerge at seven to nine months because

fear of strangers, separation distress, and fear of heights and other stimuli are readily observable at those ages. However, fear is observable in response to other events much earlier: e.g. to looming stimuli by ten weeks of age, to prolonged scrutiny by a stranger at four months, and to separation from the mother in the home by five months. Accordingly, what emerges at seven months may not be a new emotion so much as a new cognitive capacity, like the ability to forecast future danger even in the absence of prior learning experiences with a specific stimulus.

Sadness is another emotional state not believed to be observable before six to eight months, when loss of a loved object is thought to be first understood by the infant. This expectation was at first supported by studies of maternal deprivation and anaclitic depression. Recent work, however, has demonstrated that sadness is observable as early as 3.5 months under conditions of severe parental abuse and neglect. Similar examples can be given for anger and other discrete emotional states. Changes in efficacy of eliciting circumstances thus constitute only one criterion of emotional development.

2. *Emotional development also takes place through changes in the coping reactions of the individual.*

As the infant becomes motorically and cognitively more competent, new response capabilities arise which permit new ways of reacting to old stressors. For instance, when the infant acquires the ability to crawl, it can control what happens when a stranger enters the room or the mother leaves it. Accordingly, an infant otherwise upset by a stranger can not only avoid distress, but even show friendliness. Similarly, new coping skills, such as the ability to move round objects, may prevent a child from crying or becoming frustrated with a problem. Instead of distress, the child may express joy over mastering the situation. As development continues, coping reactions become increasingly internalized, and defense mechanisms proper begin to play a role in regulating emotions.

In aging, some coping capacities may be lost, resulting in feelings of helplessness or depression.

Another major coping reaction that influences emotional development is paying attention to social cues. When infants and children are faced with ambiguous circumstances they typically look to important others for emotional information to help appraise the event (and thus to react emotionally to it). This permits emotions to be socially transmitted, by enabling individuals to mimic emotional responses without directly experiencing the positive or negative effects of the circumstances in which those responses occur.

Still another change in coping reaction to a stressor in the course of development involves the "targeting" of the object of the emotional expression. For instance, when newborns are restricted from movement, facial and vocal expressions of distress or anger are not directed at anybody, nor at the source of the distress, but by four months, infants clearly have a target – the immediate impediment – and by seven months, the target becomes both the impediment and the person who is permitting it. In adulthood, the defense mechanism of displacement illustrates a different type of coping response involving a shift in such targeting of emotions.

3. Emotional expressions can change with development.

One way is by becoming less "noisy" (e.g. facial expression patterns in the neonate frequently contain components not specific to the pattern, whereas at older ages this is less so). Facial expression patterns in response to restraint of movement are similar at one and four months. However, the one-month-old typically manifests components which are not typical of anger (eye closing, tongue protrusion). The four-month-old does not.

Emotional expression patterns also communicate more complex dimensions of affect with age, especially in the first two months of life. (After two months, hedonic tone and activation dimensions are identifiable in infant facial expression much as they are with adults). In the first two months, hedonic tone (i.e. whether the experience is pleasant or unpleasant) is identifiable quite readily, but level of activation is less clearly detected, perhaps because the range of intensities of infant wakefulness is so limited in the first two months.

Expressions also become instrumental with age. That is, an expressive reaction that was once involuntarily elicited now comes under the voluntary control of the child. Both crying and smiling clearly become instrumental very early in life, perhaps as early as two months. Anger, in the form of temper tantrums, become instrumental late in the second year. Other emotional expressions can likewise become instrumental, but little is known about when they do.

4. Emotional states undergo developmental transformations.

To the extent that changes in appraisal, in coping reactions, and in expressive patterning take place in the course of development, and to the extent that these processes influence the prevalence of the quality of emotional states, the feeling states of individuals must differ dramatically at different ages.

Moreover, feeling states themselves combine and synthesize in dramatic hierarchical fashion. The fundamental emotions intercoordinate into higher order, emergent emotions, and emergent emotions combine into even more complex states. Guilt is an instance of such a higher-order emotion. It is not fundamental, in so far as it shows no universally recognizable expressive pattern. It requires extensive representational abilities, may be observable by eighteen to twenty-four months of age, and seems to require the intercoordination of empathic distress with fear, sadness, and other emotions. Depression and anxiety also appear to be complex emotions which are intercoordinations of both fundamental and higher-order emotions. Anxiety seems to involve complex intercoordinations of fear, shame, anger, guilt, and interest. Depression, on the other hand, has elements of sadness, anger, disgust, contempt, guilt, and shyness. Shame, envy, and jealousy appear to be other instances of complex emotions.

5. *Emotional expressions become socialized.*

Every culture has display rules which govern the manifestation of the expression of emotions. In some societies, for instance, the response expected at a funeral is a smile. In others, weeping and exaggerated sadness are the rule. In others, emotions are inhibited. Ekman and his colleagues, for instance, (see Ekman 1982), found that Japanese and Americans who watched an unpleasant film had similar emotional expressions in private but not in company. Buck and his colleagues (see Buck 1984) found that women's facial expressions were more easily interpreted than men's, at least in so far as judges could better distinguish between women, who were viewing more and less pleasant scenes, than between men. There was no comparable difference between preschool girls and boys. This seems to show the socialization of different display rules for each sex within the same culture. Emotions are also socialized through the selection of appropriate channels for expression. For instance it is sometimes permissible to express anger through choice of words, but not through facial, vocal or overtly hostile behavior. Gnepp and Hess (1986) found that young children have a better understanding of verbal than of facial display rules, and they also understand prosocial rules better than self-protective ones. Older children understand better than younger ones.

JJCa/KSC/RNE

Bibliography

Bridges, K.M. 1932: Emotional development in early infancy. *Child development* 3, 324–41.

Buck, R. 1984: *The communication of emotion.* New York and London: Guildford.

Campos, J., et al. 1983: Socioemotional development. In *Carmichael's manual of child psychology: Infancy and development psychobiology*, vol. 2, eds. M. Haith and J. Campos. New York: John Wiley and Sons.

Ekman, P. ed. 1982: *Emotion in the human face.* 2nd edn. Cambridge and New York: Cambridge University Press; Paris: Editions de la Maison des Sciences de l'Homme.

Feldman, R.S. ed. 1982: *Development of nonverbal behavior in children.* Berlin and New York: Springer Verlag.

Gnepp, J. and Hess, D.L.R. 1986: Children's understanding of verbal and facial display rules. *Developmental psychology* 22, 103–8.

Sroufe, L.A. 1979: Socioemotional development. In *Handbook of infant development*, ed. J. Osofsky. New York: John Wiley and Sons.

emotional expression in infancy

The emotional life of young infants has often been characterized as undifferentiated arousal. That view is much oversimplified. Virtually all the specific facial muscles that enter into adult emotional expressions are functional in the neonate (Oster and Ekman 1978). Infants are also capable of many variations in voice and bodily posture. Expressive reactions serve to communicate the state of the infant, and they help to establish and maintain affectional bonds with caretakers. But that is not all. Infants of two to three months of age exert, by means of expressive reactions, considerable control over their interactions with other persons, and hence over the conditions of their own development (Trevarthen 1979). Before the end of the first year expressive or emotion-like states appear, including interest, happiness, distress, surprise, anger, disgust, and fear (Izard et al 1980). (See EMOTIONAL DEVELOPMENT.)

JRAv

Bibliography

Feldman, R.S. 1982: *Development of nonverbal behavior in children.* Berlin and New York: Springer Verlag.

Izard, C.E., Huebner, R.R., Risse, D., McGinnes, G.C. and Dougherty, L.M. 1980: The young infant's ability to produce discrete emotional expressions. *Developmental psychology* 16, 132–40.

Oster, H. and Ekman, P. 1978: Facial behavior in child development. In: *Minnesota symposia on child psychology*, vol. 11, ed. W.A. Collins. Hillsdale, N.J.: Laurence Erlbaum Associates.

Trevarthen, C. 1979: Communication and cooperation in early infancy: a description of primary intersubjectivity. In *Before speech: the beginning of interpersonal communication*, ed. M.

Bullowa. Cambridge and New York: Cambridge University Press.

empathy The understanding and sharing of another person's emotional experience in a particular situation. In the early nineteenth century Lipps described empathy (an English rendering of the German *Einfühlung*) as a process of "feeling into" the emotions expressed in the movements or dynamic postures of people, aesthetic objects or natural scenes. The spontaneous imitation of these cues produces kinesthetic sensations associated with corresponding emotions. The alternative theory of representation emphasized the need to understand the person's situation intellectually thereby evoking emotional memories previously associated with similar situations.

Empathy requires a receptive set ('taking the role of the other', Mead 1934), an appreciation of the meaning of the emotion-eliciting situation for the person and an accurate interpretation of the person's verbal and nonverbal behavior. Dymond (1949) created a measure of this kind of empathy; her test required people to make predictions about the feelings, thoughts or behavior of a person they had met briefly. Doubt has since been cast on Dymond's test, and tests which appear to be more valid have been developed by Hogan, and by Mehrabian and Epstein (see Chlopan et al. 1985). Empathy studies with young children have frequently used the *Feshbach Affective Situations Test* (Feshbach and Roe 1968). Empathetic reaction can range from involuntary nonverbal and/or physiological responses to the experience of an emotion similar to that experienced by the other person. Nonverbal reactions have been associated with motor mimicry, the spontaneous and unconscious IMITATION of facial movements and bodily postures. Physiological responses may include for example, muscle tension and heart rate or breathing changes. Very young children are claimed to be capable of facial imitation (Meltzoff and Moore 1983), and also to depress their behavior when their mothers'

behavior is depressed (Cohn and Tronick 1983). Empathetic emotional experience requires an imaginative reconstruction of the meaning of the situation for the person based on the experience of similar situations in the past and knowledge of the person, but such a reconstruction may not be sufficient to produce the emotion. Before a child can develop a more inferential understanding of others' emotional states, it must be able to take another person's perspective, but children are supposedly egocentric (see EGOCENTRISM) in early childhood. Nevertheless others' emotions seem to be one of the first topics of children's conversations (Bretherton and Beeghly 1982).

Hoffman (1976) has studied the development of forms of empathy through childhood. It is unclear whether, as Hoffman claims, empathy is an important part of MORAL DEVELOPMENT. The finding that Hogan's measure of empathy does not distinguish adolescent delinquents from other adolescents has been taken to show that empathy is unrelated to adolescents' moral character (Hudak et al. 1980). Attempts to find a relationship between Feshbach and Roe's measure and children's prosocial behavior have not been very successful.   SBe/GCC/RL

Bibliography

Bretherton, I. and Beeghly, M. 1982: Talking about internal states. *Developmental psychology* 18, 906–21.

Cohn, J.F. and Tronick, E.Z. 1983: Three-month-old infants' reactions to simulated maternal depression. *Child development* 54, 185–93.

Chlopan, B.E., McCain, M.L., Carbonell, J.L. and Hagen, R.L. 1985: Empathy: review of available measures. *Journal of personality and social psychology* 48, 635–53.

Dymond, Rosalind F. 1949: A scale for the measurement of empathetic ability. *Journal of consulting psychology* 13, 127–33.

Feshbach, N.D. and Roe, K. 1968: Empathy in six- and seven-year-olds. *Child development* 39, 133–45.

Hoffman, M.L. 1976: Empathy, role-taking, guilt and the development of altruistic motives. In *Moral development and behavior*, ed. T.

Lickona. New York: Holt, Rinehart and Winston.

Hudak, M.A., Andre, J. and Allen, R.O. 1980: Delinquency and social values: Differences between delinquent and nondelinquent adolescents. *Youth and society* 11, 353–68.

Lipps, T. 1965: Empathy and aesthetic pleasure. In *Aesthetic theories: studies in the philosophy of art*, eds. K. Aschenbrenner and A. Isenberg. Englewood Cliffs, N.J.: Prentice-Hall.

Mead, G.H. 1934: *Mind, self and society*. Chicago: University of Chicago Press.

Meltzoff, A.N. and Moore, M.K. 1983: New born infants imitate adult facial gestures. *Child development* 54, 702–9.

enuresis A medical term applied to the involuntary passage of urine by persons more than three years old. Distinctions are made between enuresis which occurs only during the night, nocturnal, and that which happens during the day, diurnal. Two thirds of the reported cases among children involve nocturnal enuresis. The reported frequency of enuresis in childhood is a function of the social characteristics of the sample studied. Rates vary for normals as well as for children with behavior problems, institutionalized and retarded children. Rates also vary with cultural background and training. Among children whose parents have sought psychiatric advice enuresis is almost twice as common in boys as in girls and peaks between the ages of eight and eleven years. In adulthood and old age a lack of voluntary control over the discharge of urine and feces is labeled incontinence.

BBL

Bibliography

Adams, H.E. and Sutker, P.B. 1984: *Comprehensive handbook of psychopathology*. New York: Plenum.

environmental influence *See* intelligence and environmental influences.

epigenetic sequence The biological or psychological development of the individual within his lifespan, conceived as a series of stages, each of which results from the interactions between the person and the environment and among the parts of the organism or psyche, and each of which contains new phenomena or properties not present in earlier stages. Distinguished from *phylogenetic sequence*, the development of properties in the species through biological evolution, and from *preformism*, the doctrine that all properties which arise in development are present in miniature form in the original organism. Major examples of views of psychological epigenesis are FREUD's description of PERSONALITY DEVELOPMENT and PIAGET's description of cognitive development. SBe

epilepsy (childhood) Recurrent, transient, brain dysfunction with altered consciousness, associated with paroxysmal electrical discharges in the brain which may be detectable by an electroencephalograph and diverse objective and subjective phenomena depending upon developmental age and the location of the discharge within the brain. It is best understood as one form of brain dysfunction which may betoken the existence of other forms of dysfunction or damage especially where the epilepsy starts early in life (particularly in the first year where there is a mortality of about 10 per cent) and is persistent. Most children survive and recover. Those who do not recover are more likely to show evidence of other cerebral impairments in cognition and in behavior. Otherwise behavior disorder and psychiatric disorder are increased as a function of: the socially aversive nature of seizures leading to dread and to prejudice; the general problems of living with a chronic illness; impaired parenting of a vulnerable child; the unwanted effects of drug treatment and restrictive regimes; and poorly managed treatment programs.

Such factors in combination readily account for the 60 per cent rate of psychiatric abnormality found in children with epilepsy and brain lesions. The child's development may be biased by the brain abnormality before the onset of seizures or as a function of the disturbances in parenting engendered by the seizures. These will vary with the child's developmental age at their onset. Increased irritability and dependency, reduced learning capacity and some increased tendency towards psychosis are noted. Apart from brain dysfunction, the abnormality of parenting includes extreme over-solicitude or severe rejection, or, what is worse, intense ambivalent wavering between these two responses to the remembered, imagined, or ever present threat of death which seizures inspire and which their mortality intermittently reinforces.   DCT

Bibliography

Adams, H.E. and Sutker, P.B. 1984: *Comprehensive handbook of psychopathology*. New York: Plenum.

Quay, H.C and Werry, J.S. eds. 1979: *Psychopathological disorders of childhood*. New York: Wiley.

Erikson, Erik H. American psychoanalytic theorist who produced a LIFESPAN PSYCHOLOGY of human development. He was born in Germany in 1902. He was an art teacher before becoming psychoanalyst (trained by ANNA FREUD). While resident in the USA after 1933, Erikson worked at the universities of California, Yale and Harvard, and at the Western Psychiatric Institute in Pittsburgh. He died in 1979.

Unlike SIGMUND FREUD, Erikson brings the individual's entire lifetime into his theory of development. He also differs from Freud in his belief in the positive aspects of the EGO, and its central role as more than an unhappy intermediary between the warring ID and SUPEREGO. In Erikson's view a healthy ego is in touch with basic desires and also with the cultural values embodied in the superego. Conflict between the id and the superego is played down. But Erikson follows Freud in claiming that the ego has the task of reconciling the biological needs of the organism with the demands of the culture in which the person lives. He visited American Indians (Sioux and Yurok) with social anthropologists. He was therefore able to compare different cultures' child-rearing practices, to see the different demands they make, and to appreciate the importance of the integration they offer. Parents' ways of guiding their children are socially given, and the parents must themselves be socially integrated 'to represent to the child a deep ... conviction that there is meaning to what they are doing' (1963). According to Erikson, 'children become neurotic not from frustrations, but from the lack or loss of societal meaning in these frustrations' (ibid).

Within the EPIGENETIC SEQUENCE of personality development Erikson suggests there are eight stages (or "ages"; 1963), from the *oral sensory* stage of the first year to *maturity*, i.e. declining years. (The eight ages are summarized in LIFESPAN PSYCHOLOGY.) Each age has its particular task which must be negotiated successfully if the child's emotional and mental health are to be maintained. In the first year, for instance, there is a *crisis* between basic trust and basic mistrust. 'The infant's first social achievement ... is his willingness to let the mother out of his sight without undue anxiety or rage' (1963). Each stage is a crisis because it involves a 'change of perspective' (1959), and the possibility of failure, which at this stage would be the development of basic mistrust. Each stage and its crisis are related to one of the basic elements of society (1963). The trust which the child develops, if successful at this stage, has its societal counterpart in organized religion.

The succeeding stages have their crises in which the positive pole is one of self-acceptance and activity (e.g. autonomy and industry), and the negative pole is one of bad feeling and inability to cope (e.g. shame and inferiority). Erikson (like SULLIVAN) places far more emphasis than Freud on development after the first few years of life, and believes in the particular importance of adolescence as the period at which adult *identity* is formed. Adolescence is said to be a *moratorium*, or period of delay granted by society for the definition of oneself relative to society before one takes on adult obligations. In childhood one identifies with others (see IDENTIFICATION). In adolescence ego identity 'develops out of a gradual integration of all identifications' (1959), but it 'alters them in order to make a unique and reasonably coherent whole of them' (1968). This alteration is forced on the adolescent by rapid bodily changes and genital maturity which cause him or her to question 'continuities relied on earlier'. Success in identity formation gives one confidence in one's inner sameness and confidence that others recognize one as having function and status. Failure leads to what Erikson variously calls role confusion (1963), identity diffusion (1959) and identity confusion (1968).

Erikson's eight-stage sequence is described in textbooks, but the adolescent identity crisis is the part of his theory which has received most serious attention. It has led to the successful framing and testing of empirical hypotheses about individual differences (e.g. Marcia 1980; Slugoski et al. 1984).   RL

Bibliography

Erikson, E.H. 1959: Growth and crises of the healthy personality. *Psychological issues* 1, 50–100.

———— 1963: *Childhood and society*. 2nd edn. New York: Norton; London: Hogarth (1965).

———— 1968: *Identity: youth and crisis*. New York: Norton; London: Faber and Faber.

Marcia, J.E. 1980: Identity in adolescence. In *Handbook of adolescent psychology*, ed. J. Adelson. New York: Wiley.

Slugoski, B.R., Marcia, J.E. and Koopman, R.F. 1984: Cognitive and social interactional characteristics of ego identity statuses in college males. *Journal of personality and social psychology* 47, 646–61.

error analysis As a method in applied linguistics and SECOND LANGUAGE ACQUISITION research, error analysis gained impetus in the late 1960s (see Corder 1973, pp. 256–94), partly as a reaction against contrastive linguistics, partly as a means of supplementing it. It is assumed that, by systematically studying the errors of a second language learner, one can make inferences about his or her competence in that language.

Charting a second language learner's linguistic development through error analysis has psycholinguistic importance in that it submits the transfer hypothesis (see CONTRASTIVE ANALYSIS) to critical testing. The close links of error analysis with transformational grammar is reflected in its acceptance of the competence-performance distinction. Accordingly, a distinction is made between competence "errors" and performance "mistakes".

Error analysis has been seriously hampered by the lack of adequate devices for the description of linguistic development and has therefore been replaced by studies of INTERLANGUAGE. It does, however, continue to be used for some purposes, such as the comparison of first and second language learner's spelling difficulties (Bebout 1985).   PM

Bibliography

Bebout, L. 1985: An error-analysis of misspellings made by learners of English as a first and as a second language. *Journal of psycholinguistic research* 14, 569–93.

Corder, S. P. 1973: *Introducing applied linguistics*. Harmondsworth and Baltimore: Penguin Books.

ethnic minority children: education Concern for the education of ethnic minority children has arisen as a result of research over the past twenty years in the United States and Great Britain indicating that these children often perform more poorly in school than the majority population. Performance differences have been documented on both intelligence tests and academic achievement measures, although differences vary depending on the ethnic group under study. The group most heavily studied has been black children.

The research prompted a number of investigators, committed to the environmentalist view of intellectual development, to devise and implement compensatory education programs. These programs, the most notable of which was Headstart in the United States, took a variety of forms but all attempted to enrich the academically-related environment of the ethnic minority child to stimulate intellectual development. As a result of contemporary trends in developmental psychology, these programs tended to concentrate on preschool-age children. Program content varied greatly; some concentrated on the child alone while others attempted to intervene and change the whole family environment.

Relatively little work has been done on educational programs for older ethnic minority children. Work in Britain suggests that in secondary school children of both West Indian and Asian descent do not get the highest grades in exams. But they do *better* in terms of numbers of exams passed than their IQ scores would lead one to predict (Mackintosh and Mascie-Taylor 1985; Maughan and Rutter 1986). Children from racial minority groups are also more likely to go on to further education or vocational courses than are whites, but they are less likely than white children to attend university (Craft and Craft 1983).

While a great deal of controversy surrounds the usefulness of compensatory education for ethnic minorities, evaluations to date have indicated that these programs have achieved qualified success. (See also COMPENSATORY EDUCATION; INTELLIGENCE AND ENVIRONMENTAL INFLUENCES.)   JSC

Bibliography

Craft, M. and Craft, A. 1983: The participation of ethnic minority pupils in further and higher education. *Educational research* 25, 10–19.

Lazar, I. and Darlington, R. 1982: Lasting effects of early education: A report from the consortium for longitudinal studies. *Monographs of the society for research in child development* 47, 1–151.

Mackintosh, N.J. and Mascie-Taylor, C.G.N. 1985: The IQ question. In *Education for all.* Department of Education and Science Report. London: HMSO.

Maughan, B. and Rutter, M. 1986: Black pupils' progress in secondary schools: II. Examination attainments. *British journal of developmental psychology* 4, 19–29.

ethology: human The application of ideas from ethology and sociobiology to the study of human behavior. The models and concepts of both classical and modern ethology began to be applied systematically in the 1960s; after a series of meetings, the International Society for Human Ethology was formally founded in 1978. Through the 1970s, human ethology was increasingly influenced by sociobiology, and a specialist journal devoted to human applications, *Ethology and sociobiology*, commenced publication in 1979.

Despite their simplicity, some ideas of classical ethology have found human application. Theorists such as Lorenz, Tinbergen and Eibl-Eibesfeldt have looked for the presence of "sign stimuli" in humans; for example, elevated shoulders or posture-releasing submissive behavior, or babylike expressions releasing parental care. The concepts of displacement activity and vacuum activity have been used, for example in Lorenz's controversial book *Human aggression* (1966). Eibl-Eibesfeldt has filmed and documented many "fixed action patterns" (for example facial expressions and gestures) found cross-culturally; an extensive article of his with open peer commentary (Eibl-Eibesfeldt 1979) exemplifies this fairly traditional approach to the ethological study of human behavior.

In the UK and USA, human ethologists concentrated on the observation of behavior in natural settings, without such a tight theoretical framework. Blurton Jones (1967) described the differences between rough-and-tumble play, and real aggression, in a study of nursery school children. This proved the precursor to a large number of observational studies on children, and renewed interest in sampling techniques and the problems of category definitions and the effects of the observer on behavior. These were approaches and issues which had been undeveloped since the observational studies of child development in the USA in the 1930s. Blurton Jones's edited volume, *Ethological studies of child behaviour*, proved a landmark in these respects. Because of the ease of observation, preschool children have been a goldmine for human ethological studies; other examples are aggression and dominance, attention structure, and altruism. For similar reasons, several ethological studies were carried out in medical or mental institutions. Several ethological studies have been made on autistic children.

Besides utilizing ethological concepts such as dominance hierarchy or attention structure, such studies were characterized by attempts at child or human ethograms. An ambitious example of an attempt at an ethogram for preschool children is that of McGrew (1972). Ekman and Friesen (1976) attempted to analyze human facial expression. Both these approaches, and the cross-cultural work of Eibl-Eibesfeldt, have been important influences in the study of non-verbal communication.

Following the interests of animal ethologists in the influence of the environment on social structure and behavior, some human ethologists have investigated areas such as the effects of crowding on behavior (McGrew 1972). Smith and Connolly (1980) combined observational methods and a child ethogram based on those of McGrew and others, together with experimental methodology, to assess the impact of different environments on the behavior of children in different preschool settings.

Some investigations were more explicitly concerned with the functional significance of certain human behaviors. The work of Bowlby (1969) on the parent-infant attachment system is a most notable example. These and other studies have considered the adaptiveness of behavior in the natural environment, often assuming that the "natural environment" of the human species – what Bowlby calls 'the environment of evolutionary adaptedness' – is similar to the environment of present-day peoples living in a hunter-gatherer subsistence economy.   PKS

Bibliography

Alexander, R.D. 1980: *Darwinism and human affairs*. London: Pitman.

Blurton Jones, N.G. 1967: An ethological study of some aspects of social behaviour of children in nursery school. In *Primate ethology*, ed. D.

Morris, London: Weidenfeld and Nicholson, pp. 347–68.

*——— ed. 1972: *Ethological studies of child behaviour*. Cambridge and New York: Cambridge University Press.

Bowlby, John 1969: *Attachment and loss*, vol. 1. *Attachment*. London: Hogarth Press; New York: Basic Books.

Chagnon, N.A. and Irons, W. 1979: *Evolutionary biology and human social behavior: an anthropological perspective*. Massachusetts: Duxbury Press.

*Eibl-Eibesfeldt, I. 1979: Human ethology: concepts and implications for the sciences of man. *Behavioral and brain sciences* 2, 1–57.

Ekman, P. and Friesen, W.V. 1976: Measuring facial movement. *Environmental psychology and nonverbal behavior* 1, 56–75.

Hinde, R.A. 1983: Ethology and child development. In *Handbook of child psychology*. 4th edn, vol. 2, eds. M.M. Haith and J.J. Campos. New York: Wiley.

Lorenz, K. 1966: *On aggression*. London: Methuen; New York: Harcourt, Brace and World.

Lumsden, Charles and Wilson, Edward 1981: *Genes, minds and culture*. Cambridge, Mass.: Harvard University Press.

McGrew, W.C. 1972: *An ethological study of children's behaviour*. London and New York: Academic Press.

Ruse, M. 1979: *Sociobiology: sense or nonsense?* Dordrecht, Holland: D. Reidel Pub. Co.

Smith, P.K. and Connolly, K.K. 1980: *The ethology of preschool behaviour*. Cambridge and New York: Cambridge University Press.

Wilson, Edmund O. 1978: *On human nature*. Cambridge, Mass.: Harvard University Press.

exploration: In a specific sense, exploration consists in actively seeking out and investigating novelty by means of the sensory apparatus or through motor responses or both. Its adaptive value may be that specific exploration allows the organism to test situations of potential significance and hence to reduce uncertainty concerning the properties of a complex environment. It has also been argued that exploration may, in a general sense, serve the purpose of increasing physiological arousal through active seeking of stimulation. Hence, exploration may dispel uncertainty and maintain the activation level of the nervous system at an optimum.

In developmental psychology exploration has been closely linked with PLAY and curiosity. Individual differences in exploratory behavior during infancy have also been related to security of ATTACHMENT. The child who is securely attached is more willing to venture on exploratory forays in strange environments, perhaps because it knows that it can always return to a safe base.   GEB

Bibliography

Bruner, J.S., Jolly, A. and Sylva, K. 1976: *Play: its role in development and evolution.* Harmondsworth: Penguin; New York: Basic Books.
Vandenberg, B. 1984: Developmental features of exploration. *Developmental psychology* 20, 3–8.

F

factor analysis A method of simplifying data by reducing the number of variables. The technique provides a summary of the intercorrelations among variables in a data set. It may be exploratory to discover underlying patterns, or confirmatory to test whether expected patterns emerge from the data. The starting point is the matrix of correlations among the variables which may, for instance, be subjects' scores on tests or on different items in a personality questionnaire.

The procedure is based on two principles. The first, which was pointed out by GALTON, is that the correlation between two variables equals the products of their correlations with a third hypothetical variable: $r_{ij} = r_{ig}r_{jg}$. In the ideal case in which there was only one factor which accounted for all the variance in the two variables, the partial correlation between the two, after that factor had been controlled for, would be zero. If there are several factors underlying the correlations in the matrix, the correlation between any two variables is the sum of the cross-products of their common factor loadings: $r_{ij} = r_i F_1 r_j F_1 + r_i F_2 r_j F_2 + \ldots + r_i F_n r_j F_n$ (where i and j are the variables and $F_1 \ldots F_n$ are the common factors). The second factor analytic principle is that the total variance in a set of data is the sum of the variance contributed by the common factors, the specific factors (unique to individual items) plus error. (The error may be calculated from the reliability (see TESTS, RELIABILITY OF).) If the reliability (e.g. correlation between the scores of the same subject on the same item on different occasions or "test-retest reliability") is 0.67, the error of the item is $1 - 0.67 = 0.33$.)

There are two methods for extracting the first factor from the correlation matrix: principal components analysis and clas-

sical factor analysis. In principal components analysis the first component is defined as the best linear combination of the variables (i.e. the combination which accounts for more of the variance than any other). The second component is the second best linear combination, under the condition that it is orthogonal to (i.e. uncorrelated with) the first component. This means that it accounts for the maximum amount of the residual variance after the removal of the effect of the first component. Subsequent components are extracted in the same way, until all the variance in the matrix is accounted for. Each accounts for the maximum amount of residual variance and is orthogonal to the already extracted components. Unless at least one variable is entirely predictable from some or all of the other variables, there will be as many factors as there are variables. Each observed variable can therefore be described as a linear combination of the n components: $z_j = a_{j1}F_1 + a_{j2}F_2 + \ldots + a_{jn}F_n$. In this equation z_j is the observed variable, $F_1 \ldots F_n$ are the n components (factors), and $a_{j1} \ldots a_{jn}$ are the factor loadings of the variable j on factors $F_1 \ldots F_n$.

Classical factor analysis is based on the assumption that the correlations are the result of an underlying regularity in the data. Each variable is therefore influenced by common factors which influence other variables, but each variable also contains unique and error variance. Each observed variable can therefore be described as follows: $z_j = a_{j1}F_1 + a_{j2}F_2 + \ldots a_{jm}F_m + d_jU_j$. In this equation everything is the same as in the previous equation except for the addition of the expression d_jU_j. In this expression U_j is the unique factor for variable j, which is orthogonal to all common factors and to all other unique factors; d_j is the factor loading (standardized multiple regression coefficient) of variable j on the unique factor U. Whether defined principal components or inferred classical factors are employed depends on whether there is assumed to be unique variance. At each step in principal components analysis the procedure extracts the maximum of the total variance, regardless of whether it is true or error variance, whereas classical factor analysis makes specific allowance for unique variance and error.

The factors are reference axes and may be rotated for the purpose of interpreting the data. Rotation is to *simple structure* (Thurstone), that is to a position in which each item loads on as few factors as possible. This allows interpretation of the factors. For example, if verbal tests load heavily on one factor and arithmetical tests load heavily on another, they may be defined as a verbal and an arithmetical factor. If, on the other hand, an item loads on more than one factor, it does not help in labeling the factors. Orthogonal rotation retains the lack of correlation between the factors. Oblique rotation allows factors to be moved to positions in which they fall among clusters of items. This may clearly ease the task of interpretation, although it means that factors are no longer accounting for discrete portions of the variance in the data. As Thurstone pointed out, however, there is no reason to believe that useful classificatory dimensions in the real world are unrelated to each other. He used the example of height and weight, which are useful as separate dimensions on which to classify people even though they are correlated. When factors have been rotated obliquely they are correlated with each other. This allows the researcher to extract second-order factors from the matrix of correlations among the factors. It is possible, for instance, to extract second-order factors from Cattell's 16 first-order personality factors, and the second-order factors include two which are similar to Eysenck's introversion-extraversion and neuroticism dimensions.

There are many criticisms of interpretations which treat factor analytic results as if they revealed underlying structure (see Lykken 1971). It is true that "you get out what you put in" since the analysis provides a summary of the inter-correlations in a set of data. But a summary may be enlightening when a correlation matrix is not. It is also true that if tests or items are added or taken away from the battery or the questionnaire, the factor structure may change. But again this is only to be expected since the analysis reveals the relationships among the variables which are there. A researcher would infer that factor analysis might be revealing "real" causes of the observed correlations only if the same factors could be reliably extracted from the same tests, and similar factors could be extracted from different tests of a similar kind. Even then a good theory would require that the factors be related to other phenomena.

A different sort of criticism has been offered by Buss and Craik (1985), who point out that traits which do not correlate with others will tend to be overlooked by researchers who use factor analysis since they will not load on any of the main factors. This, however, is a danger with any technique which reduces or summarizes data. RL

Bibliography

Buss, D.M. and Craik, K.H. 1985: Why *not* measure that trait? Alternative criteria for identifying important dispositions. *Journal of personality and social psychology* 48, 934–46.

Lawley, D.N. and Maxwell, A.E. 1971: *Factor analysis as a statistical method*. London: Butterworth.

Lykken, D.T. 1971: Multiple factor analysis and personality research. *Journal of experimental research in personality* 5, 161–70.

family, the The human group centrally concerned with biological and social reproduction and generally considered a universal unit of social organization in its nuclear or primary form as constituted by a man, a woman and their socially recognized children. Its broader composition varies with social structural and cultural factors, and its meanings reflect its use in psychological as well as in sociological and biological theories. Within psychoanalytic theory the term "family romance" refers to the fantasies of a child, e.g., that he or she is adopted, which distort the child's relationship with its parents, but which have their origins in the OEDIPUS COMPLEX. The family, and particularly the mother-child relationship, is held to be extremely important in early development. Psychological and social development occurring as the result of living in the family are described as primary socialization. (See also ATTACHMENT.)

There is a great deal of anthropological historical and sociological work on the family in the context of the wider society (see e.g. Anderson 1971), but there has been comparatively little contact between this and the work of developmental psychologists (see Maccoby 1984). Psychologists, however, have not ignored the effects of different family structures on the development of children. There is now also a fairly substantial body of observational or quasi-experimental studies of family interaction (e.g. Blechman and McEnroe 1985).

Potentially one of the most fruitful approaches to studying the family is that of family therapists, who use ideas drawn from systems theory and Bateson, and 'focus on the patterns that are developed and maintained in the family through time and that regulate the behavior of system numbers' (Minuchin 1985). The family, in other words, is treated as a system of which the members are (primarily) interdependent parts, whose behavior is to be understood by reference to the regulatory processes of the system rather than as a product of their individual psyches. BBL/RL

Bibliography

Anderson, M. ed. 1971: *Sociology of the family*. Harmondsworth: Penguin.

Blechman, E.A. and McEnroe, M.J. 1985: Effective family problem solving. *Child development* 56, 429–37.

L'Abate, L. ed. 1984: *Handbook of family psychology and psychotherapy*. Homewood, Ill.: Dow Jones-Irwin.

Maccoby, E.E. 1984: Middle childhood in the context of the family. In *Development during middle childhood*, ed. W.A. Collins. Washington, D.C.: National Academy Press.

Minuchin, P. 1985: Families and individual development: provocations from the field of family therapy. *Child development* 56, 289–302.

fantasy Fantasies are sequences of mental images occurring when attention is transferred from the external environment or some primary goal and channeled towards an unfolding series of private responses. They usually concern possible events which have varying likelihoods of actually happening.

The study of fantasy has had a checkered history in psychology. Behaviorist psychology, with its emphasis on observable behavior, neglected the study of fantasy because of its private nature. Cognitive approaches, especially information processing models of man, have returned psychology to the study of mental processes.

On this view emphasis is placed on the cognitive-affective functions of fantasy. Mental imagery is seen as playing a key role in learning and adaptive behavior enabling the individual to alter emotional arousal (increasing or decreasing) in anticipation of future situations, providing feedback for the self-regulation of behavior, and exploring future possibilities without commitment to action. In children three to five years old a positive relationship has been found between fantasy in play and social competence (Connolly and Doyle 1984).

Normative studies reveal that while there are individual differences in the development of this skill, almost all subjects report engaging in some form of daydreaming daily. Visual imagery is the most common modality and fantasy occurs when individuals are alone and in restful motor states. The most frequently reported daydreams concern future interpersonal situations. There is some evidence suggesting that as individuals pass from adolescence through young adulthood into middle age the content of fantasy changes to become more realistic, with at least a possibility of fulfillment.

Unpleasant and bizarre fantasies also decrease with age. (See DAYDREAM.)

The use of mental imagery has been incorporated into diverse psychotherapeutic techniques with different theoretical orientations ranging from insight psychotherapy, e.g. psychoanalysis to behavior modification treatments. It has been used successfully in the relief of irrational fears (phobias) in systematic desensitization therapy as well as in the elimination of unwanted behavior by aversive conditioning. The effectiveness of these treatments suggests the power of fantasy to modify behavior (see Bellack et al. 1983).   RBP-S

Bibliography

Bellack, A.S., Hersen, M. and Kazdin, A.E. 1983: *International handbook of behavior modification and therapy*. New York: Plenum.

Connolly, J.A. and Doyle, A.B. 1984: Relations of social fantasy play to social competence in preschoolers. *Developmental psychology* 20, 797–806.

Singer, Jerome L. 1981: *Daydreaming and fantasy*. Oxford and New York: Oxford University Press (1975).

fantasy: Freudian theory An imaginary and organized scene or episode dramatically fulfilling a conscious or unconscious wish, in which the subject appears as one of the actors. English psychoanalysts proposed the systematic use of two spellings and employed fantasy to refer to conscious constructions and phantasy to describe the content of unconscious processes. This distinction has been ignored in American and French writings.

For Freud fantasies can operate at either a conscious or unconscious level. Unconscious fantasies are intimately tied to repressed infantile desires; they are the structures that underpin such unconscious products as dreams and symptoms. Conscious fantasies include daydreaming and fictions which fulfill wishes that are more accessible to the conscious mind mainly because they are given coherence by the process of secondary revision. Nevertheless in analysis even conscious fantasies

can be seen to be connected to unconscious ones and the wishes they articulate. (See DAYDREAM.)

Fantasy is given a central place in OBJECT RELATIONS theories, particularly in the writings of Melanie Klein. The term comes to mean the person's inner world of unconscious feeling and impulse – the effective source of *all* human behavior. It is believed that these phantasies are the unconscious content and that the content begins in the first minutes of the infant's life when his instinctual demands have to be met by the objects in his environment. The infant's phantasies are also connected with his need to satisfy unmet needs; early phantasies articulate instinctual urges both libidinal and destructive. As the child grows phantasies are elaborated; they are found in both normal and abnormal people and are seen to be *real* to the extent that they shape the person's interpersonal relationships. It is this dynamic reality of phantasies that prompted Isaacs to distinguish conscious fantasies from primary unconscious phantasies.

A connection between conscious mental activity and unconscious wishes is exploited in projective tests which employ a variety of ambiguous stimuli, e.g. inkblots, pictures or clouds, to assess unconscious motivation.   BBL/JWA

Bibliography

Laplanche, J. and Pontalis, J-B. 1973: *The language of psychoanalysis*. London: Hogarth; New York: Norton.

Rivière, J. ed. 1952: *Developments in psychoanalysis*. London: Hogarth.

field dependence/independence A dimension of individual differences in the perception of self as separate from the environment. The field dependent individual relies heavily on the visual context to establish his or her own spatial orientation, whereas the field independent person relies more on postural and gravitational cues. The dimension was first described by Witkin (1949) who used the rod and frame test (among others), to dissociate visual from gravitational cues.

This test requires a rod to be adjusted to the upright position when perceived in a frame, itself at some degrees of tilt from the upright. Witkin found stable differences in adherence to the orientation of the surround (i.e. field dependence) between individuals, between the sexes (with females being more field dependent than males) and with development (with field dependence decreasing with age). There is some evidence that these differences in perception also correlate positively with other personality factors, such as authoritarianism. The other major test used has been the embedded figures test in which the subject must find a simple form in a complex background. Those who find the form more quickly are regarded as field-independent. More recent evidence suggests that the embedded figures test and the rod and frame test do not measure the same thing. McKenna (1984) reviews a number of studies which lead him to conclude that the embedded figures test is a measure of cognitive ability rather than cognitive style.   GEB/RL

Bibliography

McKenna, F.P. 1984: Measures of field dependence: cognitive style or cognitive ability. *Journal of personality and social psychology* 47, 593–603.

Witkin, H.A. 1949: The nature and importance of individual differences in perception. *Journal of personality* 18, 145–60.

first language acquisition A term broadly used to denote the description of the acquisition by individuals of their native language. It is therefore usually confined to the study of children and their developmental progress in the acquisition of their first language as opposed to the learning of a second language or the re-learning of a language by an adult after traumatic injury.

Psychologists became especially interested in language acquisition in the late 1950s when B.F. Skinner and Noam Chomsky clashed over the theoretical assumptions necessary to explain the language acquisition process.

Skinner had attempted to formulate a theory of language acquisition in strictly behaviorist, stimulus-response terms. CHOMSKY, from a background in structural linguistics, argued forcibly against such a view. One of the earliest empirical studies growing out of this debate was the longitudinal study by Roger Brown who recorded in detail the language of three children throughout the early 1960s (see Brown 1973 for an overview of the early stages of language acquisition). The work of Brown and others showed that the child was actively engaged in acquiring a system of rules that allow the generation of novel word combinations. As such they lent greater support to modern linguistic views than to behaviorist accounts of the language acquisition process. Other early studies included work on the notion of pivot grammar to account for the regularities observed in early child utterances. (See PIVOT-OPEN GRAMMAR.)

The fact that modern language acquisition studies arose from the general debate over theories of acquisition resulted in an almost total preoccupation with the structure of language.

It has become increasingly recognized by child language researchers that language acquisition encompasses a range of phenomena far beyond the bounds of syntax. While the earlier studies concentrated on the patterns of word combinations, later research began to focus on the meanings expressed by these combinations. An increasing number of studies investigated the semantic component of the grammar during language acquisition. Semantics is concerned with the meaning of words and sentences.

The renewed interest in the semantic component of language had two major consequences for the study of language acquisition. The first was the development of cognitive theories of language acquisition (Bloom 1970; Cromer 1974) in which it was proposed that the child's language development was dependent on prior development of particular cognitive abilities. In a Piagetian version (see PIAGET), the very ability to form word combinations was viewed as dependent on the achievement of the completion of the SENSORI-

MOTOR STAGE of cognitive development between one-and-a-half and two years of age. But though the studies engendered by such views were of interest in the continuing investigations of the relation between language and thought, they proved inadequate to explain the acquisition of the syntactic component of the grammar. It was later argued that particular developments in cognitive processes may be necessary but not sufficient to explain language acquisition. It has even been argued that the acquisition of the syntactic component of language and cognitive development are more independent than had been formerly believed, and that the development of complex linguistic forms can occur in severely retarded children with very limited conceptual knowledge.

The second consequence of the interest in semantics has been the extension of the period studied back into early infancy. Whereas some studies had concentrated on ages at which the child first begins to combine words into structured multiword utterances, others became more interested in the processes involved in the acquisition of first words. Some work indicated that children differ in the types of the first words they begin to use, with some children tending first to acquire referential terms while others first use primarily socially expressive terms.

Much research on early word use has been directed at discovering the procedures children use when they extend their early words to refer to new instances, sometimes erroneously (overextensions). Clark (1973) found evidence that generalization of words occurs on the basis of perceptual similarities, while Nelson (1974) argued that generalizations were more often based on functional similarities. There has also been some controversy over whether children acquire criterial features that can be considered definitional of their concepts as encoded in language or whether a theory of prototypical features is more accurate.

The interest in earlier stages of language acquisition has given renewed impetus to the study of another component of language – phonology. Some studies have been concerned with processes involved in the first sounds a child makes (see COOING AND BABBLING). Others have been concerned with the acquisition and development of the phonological component of language. Of these latter studies, some have been concerned with the analysis of infant perception of auditory stimuli. Evidence has been found that speech is analyzed differently from non-speech sounds even in infants as young as four weeks of age.

In studies of speech production, large individual differences have been found both in the age at which children can produce various sounds and in the order of acquisition of these sounds. Children show individual preferences for specific articulatory patterns, for particular classes of sounds, and for particular kinds of syllable structures, and use varying processing strategies. Such differences, however, do not extend beyond certain limits. While the evidence is that children actively construct their own phonologies during early development giving rise to these individual differences, there appear to be constraints and limits on their phonological output. These constraints are thought to be due both to the child's mental hypotheses and to his production and perceptual abilities at a given point in development (Leonard et al. 1980).

Various language disordered groups may differ in some aspects of the phonological component of their language perhaps due to differences in perceptual processing strategies. Phonological coding problems may be important at later stages of language acquisition. For example recent research on cognitive processes underlying SPELLING ability implicates phonological coding problems in various language disordered groups including developmental dyslexics.

A great deal of recent research on infants has been concerned with the effects of early interaction between mother and child on language acquisition (e.g. Camaioni and Laicardi 1985). While research on mother-child interaction has failed to demonstrate convincing effects on the acquisition of syntax, such research appears to be particularly valuable for understanding the acquisition and development of pragmatics. The pragmatic component of language concerns the way in which language is used. It includes the study of the way sentences function in communication and the way the context of an utterance interacts with grammatical structure in determining meaning. Research on pragmatic acquisition has been carried out by Bates (1976). It has been recently argued that some language-disordered children (for example some high level autistic children) can be characterized as having primarily pragmatic dysfunctions and may be more deficient in language use than their vocabulary and syntactic structure would suggest.

Researchers in language acquisition have become aware that language acquisition studies must be concerned with all the major domains of language – syntax, semantics, phonology and pragmatics – and the interrelations of these components with other aspects of cognitive development. At present the field is becoming increasingly complex as researchers explore problems in all these areas, as well as taking account of differences between comprehension and production in language acquisition, and the large individual differences children show in acquiring their first language. There are at present few firm conclusions regarding the processes by which language acquisition occurs. Language acquisition currently remains a mysterious process engendering a good deal of exciting research.   RFC

Bibliography

Bates, E. 1976: *Language and context: The acquisition of pragmatics*. New York: Academic Press.

Bloom, L. 1970: *Language development: form and function in emerging grammars*. Cambridge, Mass.: MIT Press.

*Brown, R. 1973: *A first language*. Cambridge, Mass.: Harvard University Press.

Camaioni, L. and Laicardi, C. 1985: Early social games and the acquisition of language. *British journal of developmental psychology* 3, 31–9.

Clark, E.V. 1973: What's in a word? On the child's acquisition of semantics in his first language. In *Cognitive development and the acquisition of language*. New York: Academic Press.

Cromer, R.F. 1974: The development of language and cognition: the cognition hypothesis. In *New perspectives in child development*, ed. B. Foss. Harmondsworth: Penguin (reprinted in Cromer, R.F. 1986: *Language and cognition in normal and handicapped children*. Oxford: Blackwell (in press)).

*de Villiers, J.G. and P.A. 1978: *Language acquisition*. Cambridge, Mass. and London: Harvard University Press.

Leonard, L.B., Newhoff, M. and Mesalam, L. 1980: Individual differences in early child phonology. *Applied psycholinguistics* 1, 7–30.

*Maratsos, M. 1983: Some current issues in the study of the acquisition of grammar. In *Handbook manual of child psychology*, ed. P.H. Mussen. 4th edn. New York and Chichester: John Wiley.

Nelson, K. 1974: Concept, word and sentence: interrelations in acquisition and development. *Psychological review* 81, 267–85.

Skinner, B.F. 1957: *Verbal behavior*. New York: Appleton-Century-Crofts; London: Methuen (1959).

Freud, Anna (1899–1982) The last child of Sigmund Freud from whom she received her interest in psychoanalysis to which she dedicated herself as organizer and researcher. From 1925 to 1938 Anna Freud was director of the Vienna Institute of psychoanalytical training. In 1938 she moved with her father to London where she founded the 'Hampstead child therapy course and clinic' for the treatment of children and adolescents with mental disorders. An important aspect of Anna Freud's activity was her attempt to apply the concepts of psychoanalysis to the fields of education, social work and pediatrics. The description of *defense mechanisms* in her 1936 book was fundamental for the development of psychoanalysis.   LM

Bibliography

Freud, A. 1937: *The ego and the mechanisms of defence*. London: Hogarth; New York: International Universities Press (1946).

Freud, Sigmund (1856–1939) Founder of the branch of psychological theory and psychotherapeutic practice known as psychoanalysis. Born on 6 May 1856 in Freiberg, Moravia, which was then within the Austro-Hungarian Empire (now Pribor in Czechoslovakia), Sigmund was the first child of the second marriage of a Jewish wool-merchant Jakob Freud, whose two sons by a previous marriage were already grown up; one of them was married and the father of a small boy, so that Freud was an uncle at birth. He had seven brothers and sisters.

The family moved to Vienna when Sigmund was only three, and the half-brothers emigrated to England (Manchester) at this time. Thereafter Freud lived in Vienna for the rest of his life, except for the last fifteen months when he too settled in England (London) after being forced to flee from Nazi persecution at home. Although family finances were very limited, the eldest son's education was fostered, and his intelligence and academic industry won him a place at the local *Gymnasium*. Here, in addition to German literature and some English, he studied mainly the language and literature of the Greek and Latin classics. In his latter years at school he was consistently top of his class, putting to good use an exceptionally retentive visual and auditory memory, and his flair for writing was singled out as unusual by one of his teachers. Formal recognition of his literary achievement as an adult came with the award of the Goethe Prize at Frankfurt in 1930, three years before Hitler ordered his books to be burned in Berlin.

By the time he left school, his career plans had changed from becoming a lawyer to 'desire to eavesdrop on the eternal processes' of nature, as he wrote to his boyhood friend Emil Fluss (Schrier 1969, p. 424). In practice this meant registering in the medical faculty of Vienna University to study biology, physiology and anatomy. But Freud did not abandon his earlier interest in cultural and philosophical matters, for during his first few years he also sat at the feet of Franz Brentano whose theories about the object-

orientation of mental processes may have influenced his own later psychological formulations. As a third-year student he did laborious work on the reproductive system of the eel, but was later able to concentrate under Ernst Brucke upon neuroanatomy, the field in which he published his first scientific observations (1877). It was Brucke who eventually had to persuade Freud that he could not make a living as a research-worker and had therefore better take his medical degree. This he did in 1881.

The need for a financially gainful career became more urgent the following year when he became engaged to Martha Bernays of Hamburg. The next four years, which it took him to establish a career as a basis for marriage, produced an assiduous two-way correspondence which is a rich source for biography as well as for glimpses of Freud's view of women. The couple were married in 1886 and eventually had six children; the marriage lasted until Freud's death. During his engagement he was working in the Vienna General Hospital, mainly on neurological problems, and trying to make a mark in the medical world. He did so in 1884 with his pioneering paper on the medical and psychotropic properties of cocaine, and he consolidated this success by acquiring in the following year a teaching post at the university (*Privatdozent*) and a traveling scholarship to visit the eminent psychiatrist Jean-Martin Charcot in Paris. Charcot was well known for his particular interest in the pseudo-neurological symptoms (such as anesthesia, amnesia, paralysis, dysphasia) produced by some patients suffering from hysteria, and in using hypnosis for their treatment. He also intuited the sexual component in many of these disturbances. It may almost be said that Freud went to Paris as a neurologist and came away as a psychotherapist. For although, when back in Vienna, he worked for another two years or so in brain-pathology (especially with children) and gathered material for an important later monograph (1891) on speech disorders arising from brain-damage (aphasia), he soon began to collaborate with Joseph

Breuer in the psychological treatment of a number of hysterics. From these case-studies, published in 1895, emerged several hypotheses which have remained central in psychoanalytic theory. The question of the relation between Freud's early neurological preoccupations and his later psychological theories also remains, but at the outset he was certainly concerned to sketch an elaborate and detailed neurological model for his psychological postulates. This seminal *Project for a scientific psychology*, as it is now known in English, was written only four years after the study of aphasia, but not published until 1950 (*Standard edition*, vol. 1).

Crucial ideas to emerge from these first psychotherapeutic researches were:
1. that the neurotic symptom, and the pattern of such psychological disturbance as a whole, are a symbolic reaction to an emotional shock;
2. that the memory of this shock, and its associated feelings, are so distressing that they have been banished from conscious recall by the mind's processes of defending itself against anxiety;
3. that these repressed elements, now located in "the unconscious", are not dormant but are part of a system of non-rational associations and transformations (the "primary process") which can indirectly influence and disrupt conscious feelings, trains of thought, recollections and perceptions, and which are most clearly evident in dreams;
4. that the business of therapy is to identify the repressed material and the reasons for its repression, and to enable the patient to accept them consciously and rationally.

The greater part of Freud's subsequent work consisted of the investigation, modification and elaboration of these central ideas, and of addressing the questions that they raise not only about the origin and treatment of emotional disturbance but also about normal personality development, motivation, thinking and the organization of mental life in general. For he was after a *general* psychology, whose principles would apply equally to the sick and the healthy, to the individual and to society. The early clinical observations

had already suggested to him some more fundamental hypotheses about the structure and processes of the mind.

The idea of an emotional "trauma" in (1) and (2) above, which Freud initially identified with sexual interference by a parent-figure (the "seduction hypothesis" which he soon gave up), raised questions about the origins of anxiety, why some anxieties are intolerable, what agency initiates the defense of repression, and whether there are other defenses. Again, the assumptions in (3) compel one to ask how the contents of the unconscious are organized, how this evidently active system is energized, and what principle governs its indirect incursions into conscious mental life. Already by the turn of the century Freud was thinking of a motivating force (*libido*) whose aim is the satisfaction of instinctual drives towards survival, pleasure and the avoidance of pain, and whose psychological manifestation is in wish-fulfillment (see INSTINCT). This libido is in constant tension with an adaptive agency, the EGO, whose function is to regulate our actions according to reason and reality. Since the "reality principle" of the ego often requires us to delay impulse-gratification, it may conflict with the "pleasure-principle" of the libido. The frustration of libidinal gratification ultimately underlies anxiety, he argued, only to revise the idea later; and the philosophically uneasy anthropomorphic and hydraulic metaphors in which Freud depicts the psychobiological interaction between bodily instinct and mental energy are characteristic.

By the turn of the century also, the form taken by infantile sexuality in the OEDIPUS AND ELEKTRA COMPLEXES had been sketched, and he was ready to illustrate in *The interpretation of dreams* (1900; *Standard edition*, vols. 4 and 5), how "latent" unconscious feelings, images and desires are symbolically transformed and organized into the "manifest", wish-fulfilling content of normal dream-life in accordance with the "pleasure-principle".

Freud generalized his concept of libido-motivation in the theory that, in the normal course of development, the growing child gets instinctual gratification from different zones of the body at different age-levels (see DEVELOPMENT: PSYCHOAN-ALYTIC THEORIES). At about the time that these views were published in *Three essays* (1905; *Standard edition*, vol. 7), the incipient psychoanalytic movement was joined by Carl Jung of Zurich, who accompanied Freud on a lecturing invitation to Clark University in 1909, but broke away for theoretical and personal reasons some five years later. That was three years after Alfred ADLER had done the same (see McGuire 1974 and *Standard edition*, vol. 14, pp. 48–66).

The post-war influenza epidemic killed his beautiful, happy and healthy daughter Sophie, mother of two young children, at the age of twenty-six. Three years later he learned of the cancer of the jaw which kept him in constant pain and frequent surgery for his last sixteen years. The first theoretical revision of his work was to some extent also a consequence of the war. The "pleasure-principle" did not allow him to explain *inter alia* why soldiers who had been traumatized in battle and removed from combat retained their recurrent nightmares. He concluded that there must be a fundamental compulsion to repeat which is just as basic as the pleasure-principle, and which is in the service of a more general destructive motive called the "death instinct" or *Thanatos*. A group of constructive motives contend against this. It makes up the "life instinct" or *Eros*. Many of Freud's sympathizers have misgivings about these reformulations in *Beyond the pleasure principle* (1920; *Standard edition*, vol. 18), but are much happier with the structural revision of psychoanalytic personality theory in *The ego and the id* (1923; *Standard edition*, vol. 19), which introduce the ID as the reservoir of instinctual impulses, and the SUPEREGO or EGO IDEAL as the source of the evaluative regulation of actions and mental activity in addition to the Ego's controls. Consequently Freud can now express the goal of psychoanalysis as 'where Id was Ego shall be'. The theory that anxiety is transformed libido was revised in *Inhibitions, symptoms and anxiety*

(1926; *Standard edition*, vol. 20) in favor of a more discriminating view in which it can be an expedient signal which calls up one or more of a range of defense mechanisms.

Freud plainly thought that both his theorizing and his therapeutic investigations were "scientific". Doubting critics, however, stress the lack of objectivity in observation, the difficulty of deriving specific testable hypotheses from the theory, the likelihood that the analyst selectively elicits certain sorts of actions or ideas from the patient, and the at least equal effectiveness of therapy based on other psychological theories (Farrell 1981; Cheshire 1975, chs. 4–7; Eysenck 1985). Others argue that Freud was mistaken to think that he was giving a *causal* account of the origins of our mental life. What he provided, they say, was a way to explore and construct the idiographic meanings of that experience for each individual, as one might come to understand a linguistic text. This is the "hermeneutic" or "semiotic" approach, developed obscurely by Lacan (1973); but see also Ricoeur (1970), Blight (1981) and Rycroft (1985). On the other hand, there is now a considerable literature, by no means all unfavorable, about the empirical testing of Freudian theory (Kline 1981). And Einstein, having come across some events that could be explained only, as he believed, by Freud's theory of repression, concluded: 'it is always delightful when a great and beautiful conception proves to be consonant wih reality' (Jones 1961, p. 628). Freud died in London on 23 September 1939.   NMC

Bibliography

Blight, J.G. 1981: Must psychoanalysis retreat to hermeneutics? *Psychoanalysis and contemporary thought* 4, 147–205.

Cheshire, N.M. 1975: *The nature of psychodynamic interpretation*. London and New York: Wiley.

Eysenck, H.J. 1985 *Decline and fall of the Freudian empire*. London and New York: Viking.

Farrell, Brian A. 1981: *The standing of psychoanalysis*. Oxford and New York: Oxford University Press.

Freud, Ernst L. ed. 1961: *Letters of Sigmund Freud, 1873–1939*. London: Hogarth.

Freud, J.M. 1957: *Glory reflected: Sigmund Freud – man and father*. London: Angus and Robertson.

Freud, Sigmund 1895–1938: *Gesammelte Werke*. Frankfurt am Main: S. Fischer. *Standard edition of the complete psychological works of Sigmund Freud*. 24 vols. London: Hogarth; New York: Norton.

*Jones, Ernest 1961: *The life and work of Sigmund Freud*. New York: Basic Books; London: Penguin (1964).

Kline, Paul 1981: *Fact and fantasy in Freudian theory*. 2nd edn. London and New York: Methuen.

Lacan, Jacques 1973 (1979): *The four fundamental concepts of psychoanalysis*. London: Penguin.

McGuire, William ed. 1974: *The Freud-Jung letters*. London: Hogarth; Princeton, N.J.: Princeton University Press.

Ricoeur, Paul 1970: *Freud and philosophy*. New Haven and London: Yale University Press.

Rycroft, C. 1985: *Psychoanalysis and beyond*. London: Chatto and Windus.

Schrier, I. 1969: Some unpublished letters of Freud. *International journal of psychoanalysis* 50, 419–27.

Sulloway, F.J. 1979: *Freud, biologist of the mind*. New York: Basic Books; London: Fontana (1980).

G

generation A term originating from biology with distinct uses in social and political theory. In its strictly biological sense it refers to the coming into existence of a new organism from the time of fertilization to its full reproductive maturity.

In socio-political terms a generation consists of persons in a common age group sharing the same cultural and historical experiences. The term "generational conflict" refers to the problems and conflicts observed between the younger generation trying to effect change, and the older generation trying to maintain the status quo. Many theorists have discussed the interconnection of this concept and the concept of social change. The Spanish philosopher José Ortega y Gasset, for example, considers the coexistence of various generations and the relations established between them as representing the dynamic system that makes up historic life. For Ortega, the key generational struggle takes place between those moving into middle age and those moving out of it (Sheleff 1981; Esler 1974). The German sociologist, Karl Mannheim, on the other hand, emphasized that a generation becomes an actuality when a common consciousness is aroused, i.e. when individuals participate in the social and intellectual currents of their society and period. There has been a recent resurgence of interest in the concept of generation in social and political theory. For the most part it seems that conflicts between parents and adolescents concern the latter's claims to various adult rights rather than values or aims in life (see Hartup 1983). (See also ADOLESCENCE: DEVELOPMENT IN.)   MG

Bibliography

Esler, A. ed. 1974: *The youth revolution: the conflict of generations in modern history*. Lexington, Mass.: D.C. Heath.

Farley, J. 1977: *The spontaneous generation controversy from Descartes to Oparin*. Baltimore and London: Johns Hopkins University Press.

Hartup, W. 1983: Peer relations. In *Handbook of child psychology*, vol. 4, ed. E.M. Hetherington. New York: Wiley.

Mannheim, Karl 1974: What is a social generation? In Esler.

Ortega y Gasset, José 1974: The importance of generationhood. In Esler.

Sheleff, L.S. 1981: *Generations apart: adult hostility to youth*. New York: McGraw-Hill.

genetic counseling Advice about the risk of recurrence of congenital abnormalities. It may be offered to parents after the birth of an abnormal child, or to anyone who may be a carrier of an inheritable condition such as haemophilia. Assessment of the risk of recurrence involves an accurate diagnosis of the condition, including a search for CHROMOSOME ABNORMALITIES; a knowledge of the genetic transmission of the disorder, and a search among other family members for affected individuals or carriers. It is as important to be able to reassure parents that their child's abnormalities are not likely to recur in subsequent pregnancies as it is to warn them of a high risk of recurrence.   GCF

Bibliography

Harper, P.S. 1981: *Practical genetic counselling*. Bristol: John Wright and Sons.

genetic epistemology The aim of genetic epistemology was to establish a new branch of philosophy and it has as its subject matter both the origin and the structure of knowledge. James Ward (see Ward 1883) outlined the genetic methods required by this philosophical subdiscipline, and James M. Baldwin (see e.g. Baldwin 1915) formulated its task as the reconstruction of logic from a developmental point of view, the establishment of experimental logic and the theory of the origins of cultural values.

In contemporary thought, the term genetic epistemology refers to the work of Jean PIAGET as well as to the empirical and experimental research, carried out in a Piagetian framework, on the development of concepts, logical operations and symbolic thinking in children.

Piaget's synthesis of philosophy of science and psychology draws a parallel between the evolution of the sciences and the ontogeny of thinking; in both realms there is a development from practical operations toward mathematical logic and axiomatization. Piaget thus transforms the allegedly speculative or metaphysical philosophy of science of the French constructivists into a set of testable problems in cognitive development (see Piaget 1967, 1970, 1983).

Most developmental psychologists influenced by Piaget have lost sight of this link between psychology and the philosophy of science. They limit themselves largely to elaborating on the stage-features of sensori-motor, concrete operational, pre-operational and formal operational thinking, while the processes of transition from one level to the next remain to be determined.   AM

Bibliography

Baldwin, J.M. 1915: *Genetic theory of reality*. New York and London: Putnam.

Piaget, J. 1967: Nature et méthode de l'épistémologie. In *Logique et connaissance scientifique*. Paris: Gallimard.

——— 1970: *L'Épistémologie génétique*. Paris: Presses universitaires de France.

——— 1983: Piaget's theory. In *Handbook of child psychology*, vol. 1. 4th edn, ed. W. Kessen. New York: Wiley.

Ward, James 1883: Psychological principles I. *Mind*.

genetics, evolution and behavior

Genetic and evolutionary influences on human behavior remain controversial areas of study more than a century after Mendel's discovery of particulate inheritance and Darwin's original exposition of evolutionary theory. In the 1970s and early 1980s acrimonious debate reached new depths following, for example, Jensen's publication (1969) of a review paper combining the topics of genetics, intelligence, and race, and Wilson's treatise (1975) on behavioral evolution. The current debates often involve heavy doses of polemical politics and *ad hominem* attacks. However, at the same time they often represent attempts by practitioners of academic disciplines such as anthropology, biology, genetics, psychology, and sociology to come to grips with a plethora of new information which crosses their traditional disciplinary boundaries.

Two fundamental approaches have been applied in the study of genetics. One is mechanism oriented and involves Mendelian segregation combined with physiological and cellular studies of genetic influences on the development of the phenotype of individuals. The second is a statistical approach, variously labeled biometrical or quantitative genetics, which attempts to understand the influence of genetic variation on phenotypic variation by analyzing the patterns of distribution of characteristics among the members of populations. Both approaches have been applied to the investigation of psychological phenotypes.

That genetic variation can have profound influences on behavioral phenotypes of humans was unequivocally demonstrated by the discovery and subsequent investigations of phenylketonuria (PKU) beginning in the 1930s. This now-treatable form of profound mental retardation is related to a metabolic block of a particular enzymatic pathway which is itself due to homozygosity for a particular genetic allele at a single autosomal locus. The discovery of a specific genetic etiology for a particular set of retardates constituted a true breakthrough in investigations of the causes of retardation. PKU is now a classic model for a large set of genetically distinct "aminoacidurias" and further single-gene causes of retardation. Another "breakthrough" in understanding the genetic underpinnings of human variation was the discovery in 1959 that an extra chromosome was the cause of DOWN'S SYNDROME. It was only in 1956 that the normal diploid human chromosome number was established to be 46 (44 autosomes plus two sex chromosomes, X and Y). Having 47 chromosomes with the supernumerary being an extra copy of the chromosome labeled number 21, hence "trisomy-21", is the cause of Down's syndrome. Females having one X chromosome rather than the normal two (45X0) were, also in 1959, discovered to display Turner's syndrome, the symptoms of which include a specific cognitive deficit and failure to mature sexually. Klinefelter's syndrome males (47XXY) have an extra X chromosome, and display sexual and personality disturbances. These and many other chromosomal anomalies associated with behavioral symptoms have been discovered in recent decades. At the present time human chromosome studies (cytogenetics) is one of the fastest expanding areas of genetic investigation with implications for psychology. Literally many hundreds of genetic alleles are now known to influence various aspects of psychological function, ranging from sensory abilities to cognition.

The biometrical approach to understanding hereditary contributions to individual differences in human behavior antedates the discovery of Mendelian genetics, having begun with investigations by Sir Francis Galton. Recent advances in methodological sophistication, especially techniques involving path coefficients and utilizing twin and adoptive family data, continue to contribute to an unraveling of the complexities of genetic and environmental influences on psychological individuality. Bouchard and McGue (1981) reviewed 111 studies, many of them recent, containing an aggregate of 526 familial correlations including 113,942 pairings dealing with genetic involvement in intellectual functioning as assessed by IQ tests. The general interpretation of the outcomes of carefully conducted studies

has not changed since the inception of IQ tests early in the century; a substantial proportion of the variation in IQ appears to be mediated genetically. However, numerical estimates of the technical heritability statistic, which indexes the proportion of trait variance which is attributable to genetic variance of the population, has changed. Recent large studies point to a heritability of IQ in the vicinity of 0.5, rather than the 0.75–0.8 values which were widely cited in previous decades. Large scale adoption and TWIN STUDIES, some utilizing the extensive national records available in some countries (such as Denmark), are being conducted for many psychological variables. An inherited susceptibility or predisposition has been documented for many behavioral dimensions, ranging from smoking and alcoholism to homosexuality and likelihood of criminal activity, as well as diverse psychopathologies and variation in normal-range personality traits. Although specific mechanisms remain undiscovered, the evidence is unequivocal for a strong genetic dimension in the etiology of both schizophrenia and affective psychoses. Somewhat surprisingly to many, Plomin et al. (1980) point out that when genetic background is taken into account there remains no evidence for an important role of any known environmental variables in the development of schizophrenia. Although the details vary, and in most cases are poorly understood at present, it is perhaps not surprising that genetic individual differences appear to play a role in the development of individual differences on every psychological variable that has been investigated (Whitney 1976). At the present time the rapidly accumulating knowledge of genetic influences on behavior has exceeded its incorporation into general psychological theory.

Although data now outstrip general theory in the realm of psychological genetics, in the realm of human behavioral evolution theoretical speculations greatly exceed empirical data. Phenotypic variation influenced to some degree by heritable genetic variation, combined with differential reproductive success (individual Darwinian fitness or inclusive fitness) is the essence of evolution. While it is clear that heritable variation does influence most (perhaps all) dimensions of human behavior it is usually difficult to relate behavioral variation and concomitant genetical variation, at least within the normal range of variation, to differential reproductive success. Bajema (1971) has drawn together a number of papers which attempt to measure ongoing genetic evolution in contemporary societies. Unfortunately virtually every serious study is met with a wide range of criticism, much of it not scientifically grounded. Nevertheless, theoretical speculation and accounts of plausible possibilities abound in both the technical and popular literature.

Most recent accounts of human behavioral evolution remain at the level of comparisons between species and largely restrict their treatments of human behavior to species-general typological concepts. This is the case even though natural selection depends on heritable variation among individuals within the species. It has become impolite and exceedingly controversial even to discuss heritable individual differences which could involve human behavioral evolution, and academics tread lightly. Nevertheless possibilities abound, many based on quite extensive data. As an example, phenotypic INTELLIGENCE as measured by the controversial IQ tests displays many of the characteristics to be expected of an evolutionarily-relevant phenotype. Phenotypic individual differences are large, measurable, and have substantial genetic influence; extreme individuals, at least at the low end of the trait continuum, are severely depressed in reproductive performance; the trait displays inbreeding depression as do many other fitness relevant traits; and a reproductive difference favoring individuals of above average intelligence is demonstrable even within some modern industrialized populations. The latter finding, replicated in various independent studies (e.g. Waller 1971), is surprising to many laymen who share the common observation that "less bright" people tend to have larger families. The

actual data are consistent with that observation. However, a larger proportion of the "less bright" people also have no children at all. When account is taken of the reproductive performance of all the members of a group, including those that do not reproduce, the general outcome has been that higher intelligence is positively related to reproductive performance.

Racial variation is another taboo topic that could shed considerable light on human behavioral evolution. Of course existing biological races of humans display considerable overlap of distribution for many behavioral traits and share many of the same genes. Some geneticists and anthropologists have stated that the vast preponderance of genetic variation is among individuals within race and not among races, leading to suggestions that investigations of racial subgroups within the species would not be fruitful with regard to evolutionary interests. However, Neel (1981) points out that from simultaneous consideration of only 8 genetic loci one can be correct about 87 per cent of the time in assignment of an individual to race, and greater accuracy can be obtained when dealing with small groups. Races differ in the frequency of many genes, including many of relevance to behavior. Well known examples include the genes responsible for PKU, which are predominantly found among Caucasians; Tay-Sachs disease which is almost exclusively limited to Jewish populations; and sickle cell anemia which is most common in Blacks. The incidence of many behavioral phenotypes also differs substantially among races. Examples are many: the distribution of IQ scores has been found in studies from the 1920s through the 1980s to differ among races in an ordering of Americans of Asian ancestry, Americans of European Caucasian ancestry, Americans of Black African ancestry; rates of psychologically relevant phenomena such as homicide, schizophrenia, affective psychoses, and suicide differ substantially among races. Although studies of racial variation within other species have shed much light on the processes of evolution in general, the recent social climate has tended to stifle investigations of human behavioral genetics and behavioral evolution from this potentially informative perspective.   GW

Bibliography

Bajema, Carl J. (comp.) 1971: *Natural selection in human populations.* New York and Chichester: Wiley.

Bouchard, T.J. and McGue, M. 1981: Familial studies of intelligence: a review. *Science* 212, 1055–9.

Fuller, J.L. and Simmel, E.C. eds. 1984: *Behavior genetics: principles and applications.* Hillside, N.J.: Erlbaum.

Jensen, A.R. 1969: How much can we boost IQ and scholastic achievement? *Harvard educational review* 39(1), 1–123.

*Lumsden, Charles J. and Wilson, Edward O. 1981. *Genes, mind, and culture.* Cambridge, Mass. and London: Harvard University Press.

Neel, J.V. 1981: The major ethnic groups: diversity in the midst of similarity. *The American naturalist* 117, 83–7.

*Plomin, Robert, DeFries, John C. and McClearn, Gerald E. 1980: *Behavioral genetics, a primer.* San Francisco: W.H. Freeman.

*Vogel, F. and Motulsky, A.G. 1979: *Human genetics.* Berlin and New York: Springer-Verlag.

Waller, J.H. 1971: Differential reproduction: its relation to IQ test scores, education, and occupation. *Social biology* 18, 122–36.

Whitney, G. 1976: Genetic considerations in studies of the evolution of the nervous system and behavior. In *Evolution, brain and behavior: persistent problems*, eds. R. Bruce Masterton, William Hodos and Harry Jerison. Hillsdale, N.J.: Erlbaum, 79–106; London: Wiley.

Wilson, Edward O. 1975: *Sociobiology: the new synthesis.* Cambridge, Mass.: Harvard University Press.

Genie The name of a girl discovered by Los Angeles social workers at the age of thirteen and a half in conditions of almost total social isolation. At the time of her discovery, in 1970, she had not acquired language. Genie's linguistic development, although it began so late, showed normal progress through the initial use of single word utterances and overgeneralization of features. But she never asked spontaneous questions, or mastered past tense markers, word order or intonation. At nineteen she could not speak as well as a normal five-year-old. Her development implied the adaptability of language learning, but also the limits to that adaptability beyond CRITICAL PERIODS.   PM/RL

Bibliography

Curtis, S. 1977: *Genie: a psycholinguistic study of a modern-day "wild child".* New York and London: Academic Press.

gerontolinguistics Concerns the nature of the linguistic systems used by old people and their communication problems in general. At the moment it can hardly be called a separate field within PSYCHOLINGUISTICS, but for both social and linguistic reasons it is likely to become one in the near future. Areas of particular interest include the decrease in stylistic flexibility and reading skills in the elderly and the loss of second languages in bilinguals (Clyne 1977). There has been a great deal of work on language disorders, including those which are more prevalent in older people (see Oxbury et al. 1985). There have also been many studies of the processes which may be involved in older people's apparent deficits in memory for linguistic material (e.g. Duchek 1984). Discussions of recent work on the language used by (and to) the elderly take up the whole of number 1/2 of *Language and communication* 6,1986.   PM/RL

Bibliography

Clyne, Michael G. 1977: Bilingualism of the elderly. *Talanya* 4, 45–56.

Duchek, J.M. 1984: Encoding and retrieval differences between young and old: the impact of attentional capacity usage. *Developmental psychology* 20, 1173–80.

Helfrich, Hede 1979: Age markers in speech. In *Social markers in speech*, eds. K.R. Scherer and H. Giles. Cambridge and New York: Cambridge University Press.

Oxbury, J., Wyke, M., Whorr, R. and Coltheart, M. 1985: *Aphasia.* London: Butterworth.

gerontology *See* aging.

gifted children Children who display superiority in one or more fields of human activity, in comparison with their peers, in such a way that their abilities seem to be endowed by nature. There is no doubt that children differ in their natural abilities from birth, but the degree to which these abilities are exploited and enhanced by the child's experience and teaching has been the focal point of much debate. The early research on identical twins by Galton and Pearson led the way to other such studies, from which a ratio of about 9:1 of genetic to environmental influence on INTELLI-GENCE has been suggested.

The existence of a general intellective factor called g, which is independent of other particular abilities that individuals possess was suggested independently by BINET and Simon in France and SPEARMAN in England in the early 1900s. Tests of intelligence designed to measure this factor have since been used to classify children within their age group. Predictive validity of these tests, particularly of the Stanford developments of Binet's original scales, by Terman between 1916 and 1937 has been established in many kinds of intellectual activity. This has meant that a gifted child has been taken to mean one who scored in the top percentiles of a test of intelligence within his age group. Studies such as the longitudinal research of Terman focused attention on this category of gifted child and provided much in the way of general insights into the characteristics that they possessed. More recently, however, attention has been focused on a broader definition of giftedness. Guilford (1982) has suggested a model of the intellect which has 150 distinct abilities. Strengths in a particular combination of these endows an individual with his abilities in a certain field of human endeavor. The concept of CREATIVITY has evolved and is associated with giftedness in the arts and the ability to invent novel solutions to problems, both scientific and artistic.

The present meaning of giftedness is, therefore, by no means completely clear. The characteristics that a gifted child may display are those appropriate to his particular abilities. Gifted children have, in general, many characteristics and behavioral traits in common with those of lesser abilities, so that they may well, for example, wear spectacles, be thin, be pale, be impatient, but they may equally well not. The multidimensional model of the human intellect prevents the psychologist or educator from looking for general characteristics that can identify gifted children, but encourages looking at each individual and the particular combination of abilities that he or she has in large measure so that he or she can be assessed as "gifted" or not in a particular field of endeavor. The nurturing of these gifts then has to be tailored to that individual's particular needs, particular stage of development and particular environment (see Gardner 1983).   CJD

Bibliography

Barbe, Walter B. and Renzulli, Joseph S. 1975: *Psychology and education of the gifted.* New York: Irvington.

Borkowski, J. and Day, J. 1985: *Intelligence and cognition in special children.* New York: Ablex.

Freeman, J. 1979: *Gifted children.* Baltimore: University Park Press.

Gardner, H. 1983: *Frames of mind: the theory of multiple intelligences.* New York: Basic Books; London: Heinemann (1984).

George, W.C., Sanford, J.C. and Stanley, J.C. 1977: *Educating the gifted: acceleration and enrichment.* Baltimore and London: Johns Hopkins University Press.

Guilford, J.P. 1982: Cognitive psychology's ambiguities: some suggested remedies. *Psychological review* 89, 48–59.

Povey, R. 1980: *Educating the gifted child.* New York and London: Harper and Row.

Sternberg, R.J. and Detterman, D.K. eds, 1986: *What is intelligence?* Norwood, N.J.: Ablex.

guilt and shame Guilt is the condition attributed to a person (including oneself) upon some moral or legal transgression. Shame is occasioned by an object which threatens to expose a discrepancy between what a person is and what he or she ideally would like to be. Thus, a person may be guilty of a crime but ashamed of the self. The degree of guilt is usually proportional to the offense committed: by contrast, the act that precipitates shame is often inconsequential in itself; its importance lies in what it reveals about the self. Both guilt and shame presume internalized standards of conduct, but guilt has a more abstract, judgmental quality than shame (e.g. one can admit to being guilty without feeling guilty, but one cannot be ashamed without feeling ashamed); and guilt is less tied to the threat of exposure. In terms of its experiential immediacy and its close relationship to self-identity, shame may be considered the more fundamental of the two emotions. In western cultures, however, guilt has been the more highly valued because of its implications for autonomous action. This prejudice is reflected in psychological theories, which tend to ignore shame as a phenomenon distinct from guilt. Psychoanalytic theories trace the origins of guilt to INTERNALIZATION of prohibitions imposed by early authority figures; behaviorist theories view guilt as a conditioned emotional response to actions that in the past have led to punishment; and existentialist theories conceive of guilt as a reaction to behavior that impedes the realization of one's full potential, however that potential is defined (biologically, socially, or spiritually).

Higgins et al. (1985) have tried to compare feelings associated with discrepancies between what one believes oneself to be and the ideal person, or person one ought to be in one's own or others' opinions. They found that failure to live up to significant others' ideals is associated with shame, whereas failure to live up to one's own ideals is associated with dissatisfaction and a sense of powerlessness. Failure to do what one believes one ought is associated with guilt, whereas failure to do what significant others think one ought is associated with spells of terror and concern about one's health.

Evidence suggests that men may be more prone than women to experience guilt, and conversely with respect to shame (Lewis 1971). No single explanation can account for this and other (e.g. socioeconomic) group differences in the tendency toward guilt and/or shame. Social expectations, family dynamics, and child-rearing practices all undoubtedly play a role. It has been suggested that a sense of worthlessness is created by an upbringing which sets high standards, and by parents who imply that affection and acceptance depend on reaching these standards (see Higgins et al. 1985; see also MORAL DEVELOPMENT). Entire societies have been contrasted on the extent to which they foster guilt-like or shame-like reactions as a means of social control. However, cross-cultural comparisons are made difficult by varying conceptions of guilt and shame. For example, even such cognate terms as *Scham* in German and shame in English have somewhat different meanings, the former connoting modesty as well as shame.   JRAv

Bibliography

Graham, S., Doubleday, C. and Guarino, P.A. 1984: The development of relations between perceived controllability and the emotions of pity, anger and guilt. *Child development* 55, 561–5.

Higgins, E.T., Klein, R. and Strauman, T. 1985: Self-concept discrepancy theory: a psychological model for distinguishing among different aspects of depression and anxiety. *Social cognition* 3, 51–76.

Lewis, H. 1971: *Shame and guilt in neurosis*. New York: International Universities Press.

*Smith, R.W. ed. 1971: *Guilt: man and society*. Garden City, N.Y.: Doubleday.

Thrane, G. 1979: Shame. *Journal for the theory of social behavior* 9, 139–66.

H

Hall, Granville Stanley (1844–1924)
After obtaining his doctorate with a thesis
on the "muscular perception of space"
under the supervision of William James in
1878 Hall studied in Leipzig with Wundt
and Ludwig. Hall was the organizer of
psychology in the United States. In 1883
he founded the first American psychology
laboratory at Johns Hopkins University in
Baltimore; in 1887 he founded the *American
journal of psychology*, and in 1892 he
founded the American Psychological
Association of which he was the first
president. Hall's work deals with the
development of psychic processes from
adolescence to old age (*Adolescence* 1904;
Youth 1907; *Senescence* 1922) using a
theoretical framework of an evolutionary
kind and questionnaires as a technique of
enquiry. In 1909, Hall invited Freud and
Jung to the United States for a series of
conferences, thus contributing to the
diffusion of psychoanalysis there.   LM

Bibliography

Hall, G.S. 1904: *Adolescence*. New York: Appleton.
——— 1907: *Youth*. New York: Appleton.
——— 1922: *Senescence*. New York: Appleton.
Starbuck, E.D.G. 1925: G. Stanley Hall as a
psychologist. *Psychological review* 32, 103–20.

Halliday, Michael A.K. Born in
1925, studied Chinese language and literature at London, and general linguistics at
Cambridge and Peking. Halliday is currently Professor of Linguistics at the
University of Sydney. He is regarded as
the leading figure in neo-Firthian linguistics and has recently made significant
contributions to sociolinguistics and child
language acquisition studies.

In *Categories of the theory of grammar*
(1961) Halliday develops a number of
notions already found in Firthian linguistics. The application of his scale-and-
category grammar to language teaching is
discussed in Halliday, McIntosh and
Strevens (1964).

Of great importance to psycholinguistics are Halliday's studies on the development of linguistic functions in FIRST LAN-
GUAGE ACQUISITION and his research into
the relationship between function and
structure.   PM

Bibliography

Halliday, M.A.K. 1961: Categories of the
theory of grammar. *Word* 17, 241–92.
——— 1973: *Explorations in the functions of
language*. London: Edward Arnold.
——— 1985: *An introduction to functional grammar*. London and Baltimore: Edward Arnold.
———, McIntosh, A. and Strevens, P. 1964:
The linguistic sciences and language teaching.
London: Longman; Bloomington: Indiana University Press.

handicapped children *See* education
of handicapped children.

Harlow, Harry F. (1905–81) Born in
Fairfield, Iowa, Harlow studied at Stanford University, where he took a doctorate
in psychology in 1930. He was professor
of psychology at the University of Wisconsin where he founded the famous primate
laboratory. Harlow's first studies concerned processes of learning and the
effects of cortical lesions in monkeys.
These investigations led to the concept of
learning to learn, a process of rapid
acquisition of a problem-solving strategy.
This idea is not compatible with the
behavioristic models of learning as a chain
of associations. Harlow also studied the
roles of curiosity and motivation in the
learning process.

In the 1950s Harlow and his wife, Margaret, carried on a program of research on ATTACHMENT and mother-infant socialization. In the laboratory they investigated how very young macaque monkeys behaved towards surrogate-mothers made of wire or covered in terry-cloth. The young preferred contact with the terry-cloth mother even if it was not the source of food like the wire-mother. The Harlows extended their research on the nature of "love" in an attempt to understand the effects that early SEPARATION between mother and child has on psychodynamic development and sexual behavior. They also tried to discover how to promote recovery from the behavior disorders, such as depression, which the separation caused. Their study of primate behavior helped to highlight the characteristics of human psychological development and the causes of the onset of psychopathology (Harlow and Mears 1979).   LM

Bibliography

Harlow, H.F. 1950: Learning and satiation of response in intrinsically motivated complex puzzle performance by monkeys. *Journal of comparative and physiological psychology* 43, 289–94.

—— 1958: The nature of love. *American psychologist* 13, 673–85.

—— 1962: The development of affectional patterns in infant monkeys. In *Determinants of infant behavior*, vol. 2, ed. B.M. Foss. London: Methuen; New York: Wiley.

—— and Harlow, M.K. 1965: The affectional systems. In *Behavior of nonhuman primates*, vol 2, eds. A.M. Shrier, H.F. Harlow and F. Stollnitz. New York: Academic Press.

—— and Harlow, M.K. 1969: Effects of various mother-infant relationships on rhesus monkey behaviors. In *Determinants of infant behavior*, vol. 4, ed. B.M. Foss. London: Methuen; New York: Wiley.

—— and Mears, C.E. 1979: *The human model: primate perspectives*. Washington, D.C.: Winston and Sons.

hearing impaired and deaf, the: psychology and education Hearing impairment is a term used to encompass and describe all types and conditions of hearing loss, hearing problems or deafness.

Severe to total congenital (at birth) or prelingual (before language develops) hearing impairment or deafness occurs in approximately 1 to 2 per 1,000 children, excluding those who have fluctuating, intermittent or temporary conductive hearing loss caused by problems of the middle ear. The occurrence of severe to total hearing impairment in adults is approximately 3–5 per cent. As suggested by these figures, the incidence of hearing loss increases with age.

Hearing impairment or deafness usually takes one, or both, of two forms: conductive or sensory neural/perceptive hearing impairment.

Conductive hearing loss is due to a disorder in the conduction of sound from the external ear to the inner ear. It is most commonly caused by middle ear problems (Ballantyne 1977, Knight 1981).

Sensory-neural hearing loss is usually due to damage or lesions in the inner ear, i.e. cochlea, auditory nerve, and/or auditory centres of the brain. Sensory-neural hearing loss may be caused by a variety of conditions, e.g postnatal causes including infection, viruses, ototoxic drugs, trauma etc. Prenatal and birth causes include: genetic factors; viral infections via the mother (e.g. maternal rubella, cytomegalovirus); ototoxic drugs taken during pregnancy; jaundice; low birth weight; anoxia, etc. (Ballantyne 1977, Knight 1981).

The degree and nature of hearing loss in childhood is usually assessed and diagnosed by an otologist and/or an audiologist. The degree of hearing loss is commonly shown on an audiogram in decibels (d.b.), a logarithmic scale on the vertical axis over the range of frequencies (horizontal axis) in which speech normally occurs i.e. 1.25–8.0 kilohertz (Ballantyne 1977). Other information about a subject's hearing may be obtained through freefield audiometric techniques or objective measures of hearing e.g. impedance or evoked response audiometry or electrocochleography (Knight 1981).

Categories of hearing loss based on the degree of hearing loss indicated on the audiogram tend to fall into five general categories: mild (up to 40 decibels (d.b.)), moderate (41–65 d.b.), severe (66–80 d.b.), very severe (81–100 d.b.), and profound (101 d.b. or greater).

Because of the heterogeneity of the population of the hearing impaired, factors which are crucial to the understanding of the psychological, educational, auditory, linguistic, learning and behavioral needs and function of the hearing impaired, include: cause, degree and nature of hearing loss; age at onset; age at diagnosis and fitting of appropriate hearing aids; age at, and appropriateness of, audiological, educational and communicational intervention; non-verbal (practical) and verbal skills, function and abilities; motivation and aptitude; presence of additional handicapping conditions; and either enabling or handicapping nature and conditions imposed by those within the hearing impaired person's environment, or by the environment itself (Levine 1981, Moores 1978).

The psychological, educational, communicational, linguistic and social problems and needs of the prelingually hearing impaired (i.e. those whose hearing loss occurs before language is developed or established) tend to be more complex than the needs and difficulties of those who lose their hearing after language is established (Jackson 1981, Levine 1981).

Additional handicaps tend to occur more frequently in cases of congenital sensory-neural hearing impairment which may include: visual acuity, visual field, peripheral visual and visual perceptual difficulties; mental/intellectual handicap; specific learning disorders; physical and physiological difficulties (Bond 1979, Vernon 1969). Hearing impaired persons tend to have an above-average incidence of significant visual problems. (See BLIND, THE: PSYCHOLOGY AND EDUCATION.)

The first few years of life are critical in communication, speech and aural language development (see Moores 1978). The normally hearing person's verbal and non-verbal or practical abilities tend to show a close positive relationship. Hearing loss occurring before language develops generally results in retardation of language and aural communicational skills, and consequently significant retardation in verbal-educational skills, in comparison with hearing peers of similar non-verbal or practical ability (Moores 1978, Levine 1981, Myklebust 1964). Even temporary, fluctuating, and intermittent hearing losses may cause retardation of verbal educational attainments and skills.

Some educators of the hearing impaired argue (with supportive evidence) that careful early diagnosis, appropriate amplification of sound through individual hearing aids, intensive enriching exposure to developmentally normative patterns of aural (auditory-oral) language and careful, consistent, parent and family guidance and training, should assist hearing impaired children to develop intelligible speech, adequate aural communicational and linguistic skills and more normative verbal-educational attainments (Nolan and Tucker 1981, Jackson 1981, section 4). Educators who are aurally (auditorily and orally) biased may suggest that there is no place for signing or natural gesture in the education of the hearing impaired.

Hearing aids (Jackson 1981) do not correct or compensate for hearing problems. The hearing aid amplifies sound to enhance whatever useful residual audition the hearing impaired person has. Even with hearing aids, the pattern of sound may be distorted, uncomfortable and intermittent. It may not be a pleasure for the hearing impaired child to listen or to use his residual hearing.

Failure in, or inability to cope in, an aural environment usually leads to problems of attainment, adjustment and behavior (see INTELLIGENCE AND ENVIRONMENTAL INFLUENCES, and DISRUPTIVE PUPILS). Inadequacy or inappropriateness of some environments in which the hearing impaired exist would appear to be a major factor in the higher incidence of maladaptive or disturbed behavioral and emotional patterns among the hearing impaired (Levine 1981; Mindel and Vernon 1971; Moores 1978; Myklebust 1964).

Evidence of higher, but still significantly

retarded, verbal-educational attainments of hearing impaired children of hearing impaired parents (Moores 1978); severe retardation of hearing impaired children's verbal-educational attainments; above-average levels of emotionally and behaviorally maladaptive, disturbed and disturbing behaviors among the hearing impaired (Levine 1981, Mindel and Vernon 1971, Moores 1978, Myklebust 1964); and concern about possible disintegration or deterioration in the "deaf cultural group" are among factors which have motivated some educators and psychologists to advocate and support the use of sign "languages" in the education of the hearing impaired (Mindel and Vernon 1971, Moores 1978).

Sign language of the hearing impaired is a language in its own right, and consequently has different linguistic structure from other languages. Some educators of the hearing impaired have extracted the sign vocabulary for "deaf sign language" to incorporate the vocabulary into normative "hearing" aural language patterns which are acoustically amplified (individual hearing aids) and simultaneously supported with signs in normative "hearing" grammatical structure. Systems of signing which follow the above procedure include "Signed English" and "Total Communication" (Jackson 1981, section 4).

There is a diversity of educational placement and preschool services available to the hearing impaired (see INTEGRATION OF HANDICAPPED CHILDREN IN NORMAL SCHOOLS) in Britain and North America. Approximately 10 per cent or less of hearing impaired children in Britain are educated in special schools for the hearing impaired. The remainder are educated through facilities such as special classes, or small tutorial groups in ordinary schools; and many hearing impaired children, some with very severe hearing losses, cope adequately in mainstream classes. North American facilities for the hearing impaired have a similar range of preschool and school services. A few colleges in North America cater specifically for the hearing impaired. There have recently been efforts to exploit the visual aids offered by computers in several areas of their education (see Stoker 1983; Prinz and Nelson 1985).

Psychological studies of the hearing impaired appear to have moved from a pathological normative model which appeared to concentrate on features of similarity to or difference from the hearing population (Myklebust 1964) to a model based on organizing the environment and communication system to meet the needs of the hearing impaired (Levine 1981; Moores 1978).

Psychological assessment of hearing impaired children requires a clear understanding of the elements, construction, validity, reliability and purpose etc. of any test which is used, as well as understanding what the test actually measures. (See TESTS.) Tests which have verbal instructions, questions or content, including language which must be read, place the hearing impaired child at a disadvantage owing to linguistic retardation in comparison with non-verbal abilities. In contrast to significant retardation of verbal skills and attainments the hearing impaired tend to show a normative distribution of non-verbal or practical abilities (Bond 1979, Levine 1981, Moores 1978).

This does not mean that verbal tests should not be used with the hearing impaired as verbal tests may provide useful base-line information for comparison with peers – both hearing and hearing impaired – and for remedial programming in comparison with previous performance etc. (See TESTS: NORMATIVE AND CRITERION REFERENCED.)

Careful and appropriate early assessment, diagnosis, intervention, communication and placement, based on the hearing impaired individual's needs, abilities and aptitudes, remain crucial to enabling both the hearing impaired individual and his environment to succeed. DEB

Bibliography

Ballantyne, J. 1977: *Deafness*. 3rd edn. Edinburgh, London and New York: Churchill Livingstone.

Bond, D.E. 1979: Aspects of psychoeducational assessment of hearing impaired children with additional handicaps. *Journal of the British association of teachers of the deaf* 3,3.

English, J., ed. 1978: Usher's syndrome: the personal, social and emotional implications. *American annals of the deaf* 123, 3.

*Jackson, Anne ed. 1981: *Ways and means 3 – hearing impairment*. Somerset Education Authority: Globe Education Publications.

Knight, N. 1981: *A medical view of hearing loss*. In Jackson, op. cit.

*Levine, E.S. 1981: *The ecology of early deafness: guides to fashioning environment and psychological assessments*. New York: Columbia University Press.

Mindel, E.D. and Vernon, McCay 1971: *They grow in silence: the deaf child and his family*. Maryland: National Association of the Deaf.

*Moores, D.F. 1978: *Educating the deaf: psychology, principles and practices*. Boston: Houghton Mifflin.

Myklebust, H.R. 1964: *The psychology of deafness: sensory deprivation, learning and adjustment*. 2nd edn. New York and London: Grune and Stratton.

Nolan, M. and Tucker, I.G. 1981: *The hearing-impaired child and the family*. London: Souvenir Press.

Prinz, P.M. and Nelson, K.E. 1985: "Alligator eats cookie": acquisition of writing and reading skills by deaf children using the micro-computer. *Applied linguistics* 6, 283–306.

Stoker, R.G. 1983: On computers and the hearing impaired. *Volta review* 85, 364–5.

Vernon, McCay, 1969: *Multiply handicapped deaf children: medical, educational, and psychological considerations*. CEC Monograph, Washington D.C.: Council for Exceptional Children.

holophrases Single-word utterances having one primary stress and one terminal intonation contour. In early child language such one-word utterances contain the meaning of what adults would normally express in a longer string of words, not necessarily a sentence as is widely claimed. Thus, the word apple uttered by a fourteen-month-old baby may mean "I want an apple" or "give me your apple".

Related to the emergence of holophrases in FIRST LANGUAGE ACQUISITION is the emergence of prefabricated pattern in SECOND LANGUAGE ACQUISITION

and pidginization, where utterances such as "that is all" and "I don't know" are memorized as unanalyzed wholes.   PM

Bibliography
Hakuta, K. 1974: Prefabricated patterns and the emergence of structure in second-language acquisition. *Language learning* 24, 287–97.

Rodgon, M.M. 1976: *Single word usage: cognitive development and the beginnings of combinatorial speech*. Cambridge and New York: Cambridge University Press.

Wanner, E. and Gleitman, L.R. eds. 1983: *Language acquisition: the state of the art*. Cambridge and New York: Cambridge University Press.

humanistic education An approach to education of the whole person, originating from humanistic psychology, and due in large measure to the pioneering work of Carl Rogers. Rogers's work as a psychotherapist led him in the 1950s to the view that human beings have an innate potential for growth and learning and that this potential could be released by the companionship of a "teacher" if the latter possessed the essential qualities of genuineness, warmth and EMPATHY. Genuineness referred to the ability to reveal oneself and one's true feelings. Warmth referred to the ability to accept and value another person unconditionally. Empathy referred to the ability to see someone else's situation through their own eyes, and to communicate that understanding with a gentle, non-authoritarian clarity. Rogers preferred the word "facilitator" to that of "teacher", and came to extend his ideas about the facilitation of learning from the psychotherapeutic to the school context, arguing that these same personal qualities were invaluable in an educator of whatever sort.

One of the problems with humanistic education is that it often encompassed both descriptive and prescriptive attitudes to human development. Its values are "child-centered", assuming that a child in a climate of benign freedom can and will choose to learn in ways that are appropriate and healthy; and as a movement it argues that it is the proper business of education to provide such a climate of maximal support and minimal direction. Its concerns are centrally with the development of personality and a realistic and congenial self-image and a humanistic educator would tend to criticize most current educational provision for its relative failure to attend to and foster these crucial areas.

Humanistic education inherits from its psychological parent an explicit emphasis on the quality of personal relationships and on the open and responsible expression of feelings, both positive and negative. Although these emphases have failed to shift the overall content of the school curriculum very much, they have filtered through strongly into the current concern with "personal and social education", tutoring, pastoral care, and counseling. These areas of school life rely heavily on techniques of inter-personal communication, group work, role play, guided introspection and so on that were originally developed by humanistically oriented psychologists and psychotherapists in their work with adults. And there is an increasing awareness of the role of feelings and emotions in the normal learning process.

GCl

Bibliography

Roberts, T.B. ed. 1975: *Four psychologies applied to education*. New York: Wiley.

Rogers, C.R. 1983: *Freedom to learn for the eighties*. Columbus, Ohio: Charles Merrill.

hyperkinetic states These childhood states are characterized by motor restlessness, fidgetiness, poor attention, distractability, impulsiveness and excitability. They occur more often in boys than in girls, and may be accompanied by clumsiness, learning difficulties, emotional disturbance and antisocial behavior. They are diagnosed much more frequently in North America than in Britain, possibly owing to some overlap in the diagnostic criteria used for hyperkinetic states and CONDUCT DISORDER. Research into etiology has indicated a number of relevant factors, including genetic, structural or physiological brain abnormalities, toxic or allergic reactions, and family factors (maternal depression, early deprivation and poor family organization). Treatment with stimulant drugs and behavior therapy produces improvements in many children. Diets low in allergens or food additives (e.g. the Feingold diet) are also used, but are still at an experimental stage. The outlook for hyperkinetic children with associated behavior problems and learning difficulties is not good; although overactivity itself decreases in adolescence. GCF

Bibliography

Black, D. 1982: The hyperkinetic child: two views. *British medical journal* 284, 533–4.

Thorley, G. 1984: Review of follow-up and follow-back studies of childhood hyperactivity. *Psychological bulletin* 96(1), 116–32.

I

id Latin word used in English translation of FREUD for *das Es* (literally, the "It"). Freud (1923) contrasted it with the EGO and the SUPEREGO. It is the major portion of the unconscious mind, and the seat of INSTINCT. As such it is the source of energy and desire which the ego must constantly try to control and direct towards realistic possibilities of gratification. (See DEVELOPMENT: PSYCHOANALYTIC THEORIES.)   RL

Bibliography

Freud, S. 1923 (1961): The ego and the id. In *The standard edition of the complete psychological works of Sigmund Freud*, vol. 19. London: Hogarth; New York: Norton.

idealism The belief that there is a clearly perceptible ideal or perfect state in which the world should and could be. Idealism is often cited as an important aspect of moral development in ADOLESCENCE. Many writers on adolescence (e.g. Havighurst 1979) argue that setting the values to live by is a major task as one enters adulthood. Espousal of ideals may be part of this process. It has been argued that the desire that the world should fit one's ideals is an adolescent form of EGOCENTRISM (Kitchener 1983). Kohlberg, perhaps in contrast, sees judgment of actions which is based on clear, abstract ethical principles as the peak of mature moral reasoning. There have, however, been many critics of his views (see Kurtines and Gewirtz 1984; see also MORAL DEVELOPMENT). Adelson (1975) found that idealistic views decline as adolescence progresses and pragmatism and realism increase.   RL

Bibliography

Adelson, J. 1975: The development of ideology in adolescence. In *Adolescence in the life cycle*, eds. S.E. Dragastin and G.H. Elder. Washington, D.C.: Hemisphere.

Havighurst, R.J. 1979: *Developmental tasks and education*. 4th edn. New York: McKay.

Kitchener, K.S. 1983: Human development and the college campus: sequences and tasks. In *Assessing student development*. San Francisco: Jossey-Bass.

Kurtines, W.M. and Gewirtz, J.L. eds. 1984: *Morality, moral behavior and moral development*. New York: Wiley.

idealization In the widest sense, this is the process of regarding a person as perfect. It involves overlooking or denying attributes of the person that do not fit the idealized picture and, in this respect, it differs from admiration.

In Freudian psychoanalytic terminology it refers to the mental process whereby objects may be construed as ideally good. The love-object 'is aggrandised and exalted in the subject's mind' (Freud). This over-evaluation involves the transfer or displacement of an excessive quantity of libido from the ego to the object. IDENTIFICATION with idealized objects, especially parents, plays a part in the construction of ideal models that contribute to the formation of character. Some authors emphasize the defensive functions of idealization, e.g. Klein's conception of splitting of objects into "good" and "bad" as a defense against anxiety.   WLIP-J

Bibliography

Freud, S. 1953–74: On narcissism: an introduction. In *The standard edition of the complete psychological works of Sigmund Freud*, vol. 14. London: Hogarth Press; New York: Norton.

Klein, M., 1952: In *Developments in psychoanalysis*, ed. Joan Rivière. London: Hogarth Press.

identification A core concept in psychoanalytic theory denoting the process through which the subject assimilates aspects of others (objects) and constitutes its personality from the resulting products. A legacy of FREUD's use of the term in successive theoretical formulations is a set of related meanings. Noting that the assimilative process may involve extension of the subject's identity into another, a fusing with another or the borrowing of identity from another, Rycroft (1968) lists four types of identification. *Primary identification* in infancy is problematic in that the subject is scarcely differentiated from the other. The sense of the term most widely employed in psychology is *secondary identification*. It functions as a defense best known in the Oedipus complex where assimilation of the parents replaces the ambivalent feelings of love and hostility towards them and leads to the formation of the superego. (See OEDIPUS AND ELEKTRA COMPLEXES.) *Projective* and *introjective identification* are also defenses and involve fantasies in which the subject either is inside and in control of another or has taken the object, or part object inside the self. Identification is distinguished from incorporation which is linked with the oral stage of development and fantasies of ingesting the object, and from internalization which denotes the assimilation of relations such as that of the subject to the authority of the father. (See also INTERNALIZATION.) ERIKSON (1968) believes that the child must identify with many people, and that the successful development of its personality depends on that. SOCIAL LEARNING THEORY emphasizes *modeling* in socialization. This is similar to identification, but is a less thorough attempt to be like the model.   BBL

Bibliography

Bandura, A. 1985: *Social foundations of thought and action*. Englewood Cliffs, N.J.: Prentice-Hall.

Erikson, E.H. 1968: *Identity in youth and crisis*. New York: Norton; London: Faber and Faber.

Rycroft, C. 1968: *A critical dictionary of psychoanalysis*. London: Nelson; New York: Basic Books.

imagination The word "imagine" and its cognates are commonly used to express a variety of differing but closely interrelated concepts. Philosophers have often found it convenient to discuss the general topic of imagination under three principal headings, the imaginative, the imaginary, and mental imagery. The term "imagination" has also been given by some philosophers, notably Hume (1738) and Kant (1781, 1787), to a faculty claimed to be necessarily involved in sense-perception.

The notion of imaginativeness is closely akin to those of inventiveness and creativeness. A person is said to be imaginative in so far as he or she is able to think of things which other people cannot think of. This capacity may be exercised in any sphere where thought of a more than purely routine nature is required, whether in composing a piece of music, performing it, thinking of a scientific hypothesis or devising a way of testing it, writing a poem or novel, acting in a play, and so on. It is, however, a wider notion than inventiveness or CREATIVITY. It is also required for the understanding and appreciation of the imaginative creations of others, the feelings of other people, and so forth (see EMPATHY). In this aspect imagination shows itself as perceptiveness and sensitivity rather than as inventiveness or creativity. Not that these two aspects can be very clearly separated one from another. Sensitivity to another is akin to a readiness to make hypotheses about him (see Chlopan et al. 1985), and it has been claimed (Croce 1902) that to appreciate a work of art one must be able to recreate something of the experience of the original artist. However, such freedom must operate within some appropriate discipline if imaginativeness is not to degenerate into mere fancifulness. The nature of these disciplines will vary with the activity involved and what exactly they are is at its clearest where that activity has a clear and definite purpose. I may think of a highly novel way of routing the traffic through a town center, but it hardly counts, except ironically, as "imaginative" if it is clear that it would not work. On the contrary, my inability to see that it will not work is a good indicator of my lack of imagination.

If it is not possible to compare the effectiveness and economy of offered solutions, it is difficult to say which are imaginative. This is one possible problem with the validity of tests "divergent" thinking (see Wallach and Kogan 1965).

Kant held that more was required for the perceptual experience of a self-conscious being than the passive reception of sensations, and he ascribed some of this extra – just how much of it is rather obscure – to the work of imagination. Our perceptions are fragmentary and fleeting. But such a fleeting and fragmentary perception has typically the character of being a perception of a more enduring object of some sort. This is true even if I can characterize my experience only as, for example, seeing a dark patch against the foliage. Where this is not so my experience will be one of complete bewilderment. "Imagination" is the name given by Kant to the power, or perhaps to part of the power, so to connect one perception with other possible perceptions, or with other perceptions not currently occurring, that it can have this typical character of being the perception of an enduring object, and of an enduring object of a certain type.

The imagination is therefore given the job of explaining several perceptual and cognitive processes which have become contentious in empirical psychology. Kant's ideas form the background to constructive and *gestalt* theories of perception, and also to cognitive psychologists' "information processing" concept of mind. The problems Kant was discussing are still an issue in developmental psychologists' disputes about CROSS-MODAL DEVELOPMENT and OBJECT PERMANENCE (e.g. Gibson 1979; Piaget 1983; see Caron and Caron 1982). (See also FANTASY). JMS

Bibliography

Abrams, M.H. 1953: *The mirror and the lamp: romantic theory and the critical tradition*. New York and Oxford: Oxford University Press.

Caron, A.J. and Caron, R.F. 1982: Cognitive development in early infancy. In *Review of human development*, eds. T.M. Field et al. New York and Chichester: Wiley.

Chlopan, B.E., McCain, M.L., Carbonell, J.L. and Hagen, R.L. 1985: Empathy: review of available measures. *Journal of personality and social psychology* 48, 635–53.

Croce, B. 1902 (1922): *Aesthetics*. Trans. D. Ainslie. London: Macmillan.

Engell, J. 1981: *The creative imagination: enlightenment to romanticism*. Cambridge, Mass. and London: Harvard University Press.

Galton, F. 1883: *Inquiries into human faculty and its development*. London: Macmillan.

Gibson, F.F. 1979: *An ecological approach to visual perception*. Boston: Houghton Mifflin.

Hume, D. 1738: *A treatise of human nature*. Bk I, pt IV, sect. II.

Kant, I. 1781 (1950): *Critique of pure reason*. Trans. Norman Kemp Smith. London: Macmillan.

Piaget, J. 1983: Piaget's theory. In *Handbook of child psychology*. 4th edn, vol. 1, ed. W. Kessen. New York: Wiley.

Wallach, M.A. and Kogan, N. 1965: Modes of thinking in young children: a study of the creativity-intelligence distinction. New York: Holt, Rinehart and Winston.

*Warnock, Mary 1976: *Imagination*. London: Faber and Faber; Berkeley: University of California Press.

imitation Can be defined as placing one's own actions into correspondence with the behavior of others, implying an active process of matching or rendering equivalent behavior. Such a definition stresses the social functions of imitation in maintaining interpersonal relations and group identity.

Imitation may also serve the useful purpose of disseminating knowledge acquired by individuals to other groups or across generations. In the latter case, what is inherited is not the particular, adaptive behavior itself, but a generalized capacity to imitate and thus rapidly benefit from the accumulated learning of others.

BANDURA (1985) and other exponents of SOCIAL LEARNING THEORY have stressed the crucial importance of imitation in learning social behavior such as AGGRESSION. Bandura prefers to call the process "modeling" or "observational learning" to distinguish it from imitation of the surface features of others' actions.

Recent evidence from developmental

studies suggests that the ability to imitate may be innate. It has been shown that babies in the first month of life can imitate movements of the mouth and tongue (Meltzoff 1981) but this result has not always been replicable (Koepke et al. 1983). Such an ability may be very useful in helping the infant rapidly to produce the particular sounds of the language into which it is born. Later, however, the errors children make in learning syntax show that they are *over-regularizing*, i.e. using regular forms too much, as in "goed" or "thinked" for the past tense. This again demonstrates extraction of a rule rather than imitation of what a child has heard (see Platt and MacWhinney 1983).   GEB/RL

Bibliography

Bandura, A. 1985: *Social foundations of thought and action*. Englewood Cliffs, N.J.: Prentice-Hall.

Koepke, J.E., Hamm, M., Legerstee, M. and Russell, M. 1983: Neonatal imitation: two failures to replicate. *Infant behavior and development* 6, 97–102.

Meltzoff, A.N. 1981: Imitation, intermodal co-ordination and representation in early infancy. In *Infancy and epistemology*, ed. G.E. Butterworth. Brighton: Harvester; New York: St. Martin's.

Platt, C.B. and MacWhinney, B. 1983: Error assimilation as a mechanism in language learning. *Journal of child language* 10, 401–14.

innate behavior Behavior that is present at birth; an inborn control system for action. The term innate is sometimes used interchangeably with the concept of instinct to designate pre-programmed behavioral systems, the implication being that such activities are not learned. In recent years, however, the distinction between innate and acquired behavior has been superseded by an interactionist approach. Even innate behavior may have some learned components (e.g. thumb sucking may have been learned in the womb). Other inborn behavior that does not appear until later in the life cycle, such as nest building in birds, has also been shown to depend upon an interaction between endogenous and environmental factors.

In the case of the human infant the repertoire of innate behavior was until recently thought to be limited to a few reflexive responses, but it is now clear that infants are capable of fairly complex behavior soon after birth. For example, newborn babies can imitate facial movements such as tongue protrusion (but see McKenzie and Over 1983); they show complex coordinations between seeing and hearing and will search with their eyes for a sound.   GEB

Bibliography

Castillo, M. and Butterworth, G. 1981: Neonatal localisation of a sound in visual space. *Perception* 10, 331–8.

McKenzie, B. and Over, R. 1983: Young infants fail to imitate facial and manual gestures. *Infant behavior and development* 6, 85–95.

Meltzoff, A. and Moore, M.K. 1977: Imitation of facial and manual gestures by human neonates. *Science* 198, 75–8.

inner speech The study of inner speech is concerned with:

1. The measurement of latent articulatory movements accompanying silent reading, listening or thinking;
2. The determination of its grammatical and semantic properties;
3. Its relationship with overt speech in FIRST LANGUAGE ACQUISITION;
4. Its role in speech production.

Experimental evidence such as electromyographic measurements, carried out mainly within Soviet psycho- and neurolinguistics, suggests that different forms of thinking are accompanied by differential physiological activity of the articulatory organs. Less reliable evidence is available, mainly from speech disorder research, on the grammatical and semantic properties of inner speech. It is widely held that it is a condensed and reduced form of language.

As to its role in child language acquisition, it is seen as a development out of interpersonal communication rather than out of the egocentric monologues of young children. Its principal function is that of programming a special class of non-speech acts, such as problem solving. Consequently, it cannot be regarded as a stage in external speech production which is controlled by different grammatical processes.

One of the most fruitful areas of inner speech research is its comparison with other reduced forms of language such as sign language and pidgins.   PM

Bibliography
Furrow, D. 1984: Social and private speech at two years. *Child development* 55, 355–62.
Průcha, Jan 1972: *Soviet psycholinguistics*. The Hague: Mouton.
Rubin, K. and Dyck, L. 1980: Preschoolers' private speech in a play setting. *Merrill-Palmer quarterly* 26, 219–20.
Vygotsky, L.S. 1962: *Thought and language*. Trans. E. Haufmann and G. Vakar. Cambridge, Mass.: MIT.

insight A term used by the gestalt psychologist Wolfgang Köhler (1925) to denote a form of intelligent problem solving. Köhler set adult chimpanzees tasks that required solution by indirect means, for example, retrieval of bananas out of reach by means of a stick or by stacking boxes to form a step ladder. The chimpanzees succeeded only when all the constituent elements of the problem had first been seen within the same field of view. They behaved as though their perception of the problem had undergone a sudden radical restructuring and they would then rapidly arrive at an appropriate solution. When the elements were widely separated in space, "insightful" learning did not occur and the chimpanzees continued to attempt ineffective "trial and error" strategies.

Insightful problem solving similar to that observed by Köhler can be seen in human infants at about eighteen months. Thereafter, with the acquisition of language, this capacity may be greatly extended since language as a medium of representation may allow the child to "bring together" elements of a task which would otherwise remain spatially distinct in immediate perception.   GEB

Bibliography
Köhler, Wolfgang 1925: *The mentality of apes*. New York: Kegan Paul.
Yursen, S.R. ed. 1985: *The development of insight in children*. New York and London: Academic Press.

instinct Those patterns of experience and behavior which – as universally distinctive among the members of a species as their anatomical features – emerge within the process of maturation, are adapted to normal environmental conditions, and are inherited (not learned, though learning is significantly related to them). They comprise: (a) specific neuro-physiological conditions, and elements of (b) perception (sign stimuli), (c) conation (drive), motivation, exploratory and appetitive behavior, (d) consummatory acts (fixed pattern reactions and associated reflexes) and (e) emotion attendant upon fulfilment or thwarting. Their maturational order marks CRITICAL PERIODS of development and learning (e.g. imprinting), the effects of which seem enduring and irreversible. The presence of instinct does not signify the absence of intelligence or learning (a common misunderstanding); its degree of flexibility being related to the degree of complexity of the species-organism. Before, in, and after the work of Darwin, instinctual experience and behavior has been held to exist in man, though here the element of drive in particular, and flexibility in relation to learning, are emphasized. Also, man's biological inheritance being always overlaid by a cultural heritage, the accommodation of the one to the other leads to the establishment of *sentiments*, entailing non-rational as well as rational elements. The significance of instinct for sentiment-formation, learning, personality and character development, and the operation of cultural influences has entered psychological and sociological theories in many ways. Examples are: McDougall (Social Psychology); Shand (Foundations of

Character); FREUD (see INSTINCT: PSYCHODYNAMICS and DEVELOPMENT: PSYCHOANALYTIC THEORIES); Cooley and Mead (the importance of primary group communications during the early years of family and play-group experience in the growth of the self" in society); Pareto (regarding the instinctual dispositions of the human mind as "residues" exerting continual and powerful influences of a "non-logical" kind in the many theories ("derivations") which men construct about the world and society, and in the struggles between elites); and Westermarck (*Origin and development of the moral ideas*). Always criticized in its application to man, the concept of instinct remains important in the human sciences.   RF

Bibliography

Cooley, Charles Horton 1902 (1964): *Human nature and the social order*. New York: Schocken.
—— 1909 (1962): *Social organization*. New York: Schocken.
Davey, G.C.L. 1983: *Animal models of human behavior*. New York and Chichester: Wiley.
Fletcher, Ronald 1968: *Instinct in man*. London: Allen and Unwin.
McDougall, William 1908: *An introduction to social psychology*. London: Methuen.
Shand, Alexander, F. 1914: *The foundations of character*. London: Macmillan.
Westermarck, Edward 1903: *The origin and development of the moral ideas*. 2 vols. London: Macmillan.

instinct: psychodynamics A term which refers both to innate and fixed behavior patterns common to most members of a species and to a motivational force usually distinguished by its goal. In his writing Freud used the German word *Instinkt* for the former and *Trieb*, sometimes translated as drive, for the latter. He developed his theory of instinct (*Trieb*) in the context of his psychoanalytic investigations of sexuality. Freud described an instinct as having a source within the body and a pressure or quantity of energy which was seeking release, related both to its somatic source and to its object. A subject's choice of object and method of

gaining satisfaction or aim are constructed in the course of development and represented psychologically. Freud viewed instinct as 'a borderline concept between the mental and the physical' (Freud 1915). In a wider sense Freud was a dualist, initially placing Ego or self-preserving, and sexual or species perpetuating instincts in competition, but in his final formulations opposing *eros* (love, both self and sexual instincts) and *thanatos* (instinct of death and disorder). (See DEVELOPMENT: PSYCHOANALYTIC THEORIES; OBJECT RELATIONS.)   BBL

Bibliography

Freud, S. 1915 (1957): Instincts and their vicissitudes. *The standard edition of the complete psychological works of Sigmund Freud*, vol. 14. London: Hogarth Press; New York: Norton.
Grünbaum, A. 1984: *The foundations of psychoanalysis: a philosophical critique*. Berkeley: University of California Press.

instructional technology Mechanical, optical, electronic and computer aids to information presentation in education. Instructional technology ranges from simple aids such as the blackboard, through film projectors to complex computer systems. Most of this technology has originated for business and entertainment purposes and been applied to education as part of the continuous search for stimulating learning environments.

The most widely used examples of electronic instructional technology are *audio-visual aids* such as the slide projector, overhead projector, movie projector, tape recorder, television, video tape and video disk. The uses of such audio-visual media are generally to give pupils classroom experience of situations which cannot be experienced at first hand on account of cost, time or distance.

Variants of the tape recorder in the form of *language laboratories* have made a major impact on language training. Digital computers, and in particular low-cost microcomputers, are the latest additions to the range of instructional technology and are already in widespread use at all levels

of the educational system (see PROGRAM-
MED INSTRUCTION). MLGS

Bibliography
Dale, E. 1969: *Audiovisual methods in teaching.*
New York: Holt, Rinehart and Winston.

integration of handicapped children in normal schools

A method of providing education for handicapped children while maintaining direct and regular contact with non-handicapped peers, referred to in the USA as "mainstreaming". While both physically and mentally handicapped children have special educational needs, their social needs can probably best be met by mixing with normal peers. Successful integration consists of achieving the optimal balance between the provision of specialized teaching and equipment, and work and leisure contact with peers. Schemes have varied from special units on a school campus to complete membership by handicapped children in normal classes. Modifications often have to be made to curriculum, timetabling and staffing arrangements (Hodgson, Clunies-Ross and Hegarty 1984). As more handicapped children are educated in normal schools, the special schools will increasingly have to take on the role of resource centers (Fish 1985). The arguments in favor of segregating handicapped children have been: first, that their educational and physical needs can be met more efficiently; and second, that they can be protected from possible social rejection. The arguments in favor of integration are based essentially on the moral argument that an integrated society must not have segregated schools, whatever the basis for segregation, and that there are benefits for both handicapped and non-handicapped children. There is no evidence that segregation produces better educational results than integration. Evidence on the attitudes of normal children towards handicapped peers with whom they have had contact indicates that acceptance or rejection depends on many variables, including the level of integration achieved, and the attitudes of teachers.

Integration should not be seen as a cheap option, or it will be achieved at the expense of education. Schemes of integration need to be carefully designed and properly funded. Given this, special educational needs can be met while achieving levels of social contact which can be beneficial to both handicapped and non-handicapped participants. SJK

Bibliography
Fish, J. 1985: *Special education: the way ahead.*
Milton Keynes: Open University Press.
Hodgson, A., Clunies-Ross, L. and Hegarty, S. 1984: *Learning together. Teaching pupils with special educational needs in the ordinary school.*
Windsor: NFER-Nelson Pub. Co.

intelligence

The all-round mental ability (or thinking skills), either of human or of lower animal species. The term derives initially from the Greek philosopher's distinction between cognitive or intellectual, and affective or emotional, faculties of mind. In more recent times intelligence was often regarded as the quality which distinguishes man's adaptability, his capacity to learn and to reason, from the instinctive and reflex processes of animals. Though intelligence is already present in the ability of lower species to sense and react to objects and to learn at a primitive level, it evolved with the enormous growth in size and complexity of the higher brain centers and the cortex. Mammals can generally adapt more readily and cope with more complex tasks than fish and insects; while monkeys and apes are more intelligent than other mammals, apart from man.

To try to define intelligence in terms of mental powers or faculties such as memory, imagination, reasoning, etc. is of little help since these too are vaguely defined and non-observable. Modern psychology is concerned more with the analysis of behavior and mental processing than with some hypothetical causal entity in the brain. It is not a "thing" like red hair; but a quality of diverse forms of human activity. By measuring the success or failure of children of different ages, or adults, in a wide range of cognitive tasks, it is found that some persons are consistently more successful than others. The common element in all such performances was designated by SPEARMAN as the General or *g* factor; and he showed how to determine what mental functions are most characteristic of intelligence, e.g. grasping relationships, abstracting, problem solving; or which are relatively independent, e.g. rote memory, sensory processes, etc. Thus it is possible to measure intelligence by appropriate tests, although one cannot see it or define it precisely. American psychologists tend to lay less stress on this general intelligence than on more specific types or factors of ability, verbal, memorizing, spatial, etc., which may be called group factors or primary factors.

Many writers consider that the term intelligence has outlived its usefulness since it gives rise to much misunderstanding and controversy (see Gardner 1983). An alternative approach is the experimental study of mental processes involved in taking in information, coding and storing it, and using this knowledge in coping with problems and in thinking.

Attempts have been made to produce reaction-time tests which correlate with other, more traditional measures of intelligence. Jensen (1986) has used a very simple apparatus which consists of an array of buttons with lights next to them. "Reaction-time" is the time between a light coming on and the subject's finger *leaving* the home button to move to the button next to the light. It is therefore not a matter of speed of movement, nor, according to Jensen, does it presuppose any knowledge or make demands on the subject's memory. Yet reaction times are said to correlate negatively with general intelligence measured by standard TESTS. The theory which supports this research is that *speed* of processing might reasonably be expected to be a major factor in superior intelligence. Other researchers have used more "cognitive" reaction-time tests (e.g. Vernon et al. 1985). Doubt has been cast on the validity of the assumption that Jensen's apparatus measures *speed* (Longstreth 1984). It also appears that

different measures of processing speed do not always correlate with each other or with test scores (Irwin 1984).

Intelligence was regarded as an innate capacity, dependent on the genes inherited from the parents. But, in the light of such work as PIAGET's on child development, and D.O. Hebb's neurological theories, it was realized that inborn brain power does not develop into effective intelligence without stimulation from the environment; also that an unstimulating or deprived environment can inhibit its growth (see INTELLIGENCE AND ENVIRONMENTAL INFLUENCES). Like all other genetic attributes it is the product of interaction between the organism and its environment.   PEV/RL

Bibliography

Gardner, H. 1983: *Frames of mind: the theory of multiple intelligences*. New York: Basic Books; London: Heinemann (1984).

Hebb, D.O. 1949: *The organization of behavior*. New York: Wiley.

Irwin, R.J. 1984: Inspection time and its relation to intelligence. *Intelligence* 8, 47–65.

Jensen, A.R. 1986: Intelligence: definition, measurement, and future research. In *What is intelligence?* Eds. R.J. Sternberg and D.K. Detterman. Norwood, N.J.: Ablex.

Longstreth, L.E. 1984: Jensen's reaction-time investigations of intelligence: a critique. *Intelligence* 8, 139–60.

Piaget, J. 1950: *The psychology of intelligence*. London: Routledge and Kegan Paul.

Spearman, C. 1927: *The abilities of man*. London and New York: Macmillan.

Vernon, P.A., Nador, S. and Kantor, L. 1985: Reaction times and speed-of-processing: their relationship to timed and untimed measures of intelligence. *Intelligence* 9, 357–74.

intelligence and environmental influences The growth of an individual's intelligence from the fetal stage to adult maturity is affected by many aspects of the environment in which he or she is reared. Even before birth the infant's development is hindered if the mother's health or nutrition are inadequate; and environmentally produced injury to the brain may occur at birth. However, it is difficult to assess the effects of such perinatal conditions since they tend to be more frequent among lower class or minority group families than in white middle class families. Hence they may be confounded with genetic or social class differences. Malnutrition, leading to poor growth of body and brain, is particularly characteristic of children in under-developed countries.

Recent investigations of infancy show the importance of mother-child inter-actions in the first year for perceptual, linguistic and conceptual development. The mother's (or other main caretaker's) conversations and play with the child stimulate his vocalization and other responses; while poorly educated or harassed mothers are much less effective. The value of a rich and varied environ-ment in early life was demonstrated by Hebb's work with dogs and rats. There is evidence that a complex environment may be stimulating and beneficial later in life too (see Schooler 1984). Those reared in a restricted environment show poorer learning capacities later on than those with a more stimulating environment. Severe deprivation occasionally occurs if a child's environment provides no social contacts or access to the world of people and things. The resulting mental and even physical retardation may be almost irremediable. However there are recorded cases of severely deprived children who were transferred to a more normal environment at six or seven years old, and did catch up with other children in speech and intelli-gence within a few years. A striking study in this area is that by Skeels (1966), who tested twenty-four orphaned children at an average age of eighteen months, when they were living in a very unstimulating institution. Later thirteen of them were transferred to another home where there was better care and attention, and then adopted into foster homes. When traced twenty-five years later, the transferred group were normal, self-supporting adults, some in highly skilled jobs; whereas the non-transferred were still institutionalized, or in very low grade jobs.

Another study which has received con-siderable publicity was carried out in Milwaukee by Garber and Heber (1977). Here twenty black infants living in very poor homes were brought daily to a center for an intensive program designed to stimulate sensori-motor, perceptual, lan-guage and thinking skills. They were compared on numerous tests with another twenty matched infants who had no such treatment, and who were expected to reach an IQ of 80 or below in later childhood. Initially the two groups scored the same on developmental scales, but from two to four years their IQs averaged 122 and 96 respectively. The program ceased when the children entered school at six; and when tested at eight to nine years the experimental group averaged IQ 104, the controls 80. This is a very large improvement; but we cannot tell how permanent it is going to be until the results of further follow-up and fuller details are reported. We are not entitled to claim that an IQ deficit of over 20 points can be completely eliminated by psychologically planned child-rearing. A more sceptical view of the program appears in Sommer and Sommer (1983). In any case the program was far too elaborate and costly to be applied to large numbers.

Other, more haphazard types of "intervention" have proved generally ineffective, notably the American Head Start programs which were provided for thousands of preschool children from poor environments in the 1960s, in the hope that this COMPENSATORY EDUCATION would improve their learning capacities and adjustment to schooling. The schemes varied quite widely, but though some have been claimed to be beneficial, careful follow-up investigations showed that any gain in mean IQ or achievement in the first year at school usually faded out in another year, till there was no differ-ence between Head Start children and others with comparable background who had received no special treatment. (See COMPENSATORY EDUCATION on longer term effects).

Several less ambitious experiments have been reported where children aged one to three years gained on average some 10–15 IQ points (Bronfenbrenner 1974). These programs were likewise planned to stimulate mental growth, but they generally involved training the mothers, either at home or in a clinic, to interact more effectively with their children (see Slaughter 1983). These projects have mostly lacked adequate control groups, and there is little evidence as to the permanence of the gains. Kagan and others (1976) showed that children reared largely in daycare centers obtain the same IQ levels as others reared entirely at home (cf. Clarke-Stewart 1984). Much has been written about the dangers of maternal DEPRIVATION, e.g. separation of child from mother because of prolonged hospitalization of either. Later investigations have not confirmed them; children may show considerable anxiety and even become apathetic; but they seem to overcome these effects quite rapidly. Much depends on the age at separation, its length and particularly on the provision of a substitute mother figure.

Parental socioeconomic class always shows some relationship to children's mental growth. Those from wealthy homes where there is more care, more materials such as educative toys and books, and more stimulating activities, obtain higher IQs and school attainments on average. But the effect is probably due in part to parental genes, not wholly to superior environment. The parents' education, in fact, is more influential than their material wealth and home comfort. A possible major factor is the kind of language used in the home. Bernstein (1971) has claimed that middle class, as contrasted with lower class, speech tends to develop more logical thinking and abstract concepts, rather than just expression of feelings; also to convey such values as planning for the future, self-responsibility and motivation for education. Doubt was cast on this thesis by the work of LABOV (1973; see also CODE). In the USA some work has been done in recent years on the effects of different kinds of home upbringing on children's development, though there are immense difficulties in this follow-up research. Probably the most influential factors are the warmth, accept-

ance and emotional security provided by the parents; varied experiences and contacts with other children, avoidance of overprotectiveness and encouragement of independence; and a "democratic" discipline (which expects high standards of conduct), rather than permissiveness or authoritarianism. (See SELF-ESTEEM.)

While it has been proved that lack of any schooling hinders the development of intelligent thinking, there seems to be little difference attributable to different kinds of schooling (see SCHOOL DIFFERENCE). Many measures believed to foster educational development, such as small classes, open plan classrooms, individualized instruction, use of visual and other aids, streaming or not streaming by ability, additional incentives, provision of nursery schools and kindergartens, drilling in arithmetic or spelling, etc., have not been shown to have any consistent effects. Intensive remedial work with retarded children may produce some gains in reading and arithmetic – usually rather temporary; but it does not affect the overall ability level that we call intelligence. This is not because some children are genetically superior to others so that schooling makes no difference, but because, by the age of five or six, the genes interacting with the home environment have laid down a certain level of mental functioning, which the school cannot do much to alter. This level, however, as measured by intelligence tests, is by no means constant. It can fluctuate quite widely between, say, six and eighteen years; and though tests given at six can forecast eighteen-year IQ fairly accurately in the majority of cases, earlier tests from one to five have very little predictive value. Some of the variations occur because tests for different ages vary in content, or because of chance irregularities in administration and other conditions of testing. The main factor is likely to be the changes in development following on changes in environment; but we know little about which features of environment bring about speedier, or slower, growth.

There are indeed difficulties in isolating the major components of good or bad environments and measuring their effects. Far too often if one factor is shown to be ineffective, psychologists think up some other explanation without adequate proof (see Jensen 1973). Also there is so much overlapping between factors of health, family climate, education, etc. that it is hardly possible to prove which are the major causes. Admittedly, changes of thirty points or over in IQ can result from much improved environment, but this does not mean that genetic factors are not also important. Indeed the modification of intelligence level by environment does seem to be limited. We have no recipe for improving, or lowering, children's intelligence at will. Many investigations based on resemblances and differences among twins, siblings, foster children etc. have tried to specify the relative influence of heredity and environment, but without reaching a consensus. There are too many complications, such as environmental differences *between* different families, and differences between siblings *within* the same family. Often heredity and environment cooperate, or "co-vary"; that is, children born of parents with superior intelligence are more likely to be supplied with a stimulating environment than those of duller parents. Moreover, to quite an extent, children make their own environments, as well as being made by the environment. The intelligent child provokes more interaction from his mother, seeks out stimulating experiences as in reading advanced books, is more curious and more inventive; whereas the duller child is relatively apathetic and does little to develop his own thinking.

No mention has been made of differences attributable to the cultural environments of different racial or ethnic groups. The topic is highly controversial (see JENSEN CONTROVERSY) and is hardly soluble in so far as intelligence always develops through the interaction between genes and environment (see Pellegrino 1986). The concepts and the thinking styles of, say, children in China reflect a different environment from that of American whites. They would require different tests to measure adequately their own

levels of intelligence. On the other hand, Chinese-Americans and Caucasians can be compared on the same test, because their environments are largely identical.

PEV

Bibliography

Bernstein, B.B. 1971: *Class, codes, and control.* London and Boston: Routledge and Kegan Paul.

*Bronfenbrenner, U. 1974: Is early intervention effective? *Teachers college record* 76, 279–303.

Clarke-Stewart, A. 1984: Day care: a new context for research and development. *Minnesota symposium on child psychology* 17, 61–100.

Garber, H. and Heber, R. 1977: The Milwaukee project. In *Research to practice in mental retardation*, ed. P. Mittler. Baltimore: University Park Press, 119–27.

Hebb, D.O. 1949: *The organization of behavior.* New York: Wiley.

*Jensen, A.R. 1973: *Educability and group differences.* New York: Harper and Row.

Kagan, J., Kearsley, B. and Zelazo, P.R. 1976: Day care is as good as home care. *Psychology today* May, 36–7.

Labov, W. 1973: The logic of non-standard English. In *Language and social context*, ed. Pier Paolo Giglioli. London: Penguin.

Pellegrino, J.W. 1986: Intelligence: the interaction of culture and cognitive processes. In *What is intelligence?*, eds. R.J. Sternberg and D.K. Detterman. Norwood, N.J.: Ablex.

Schooler, C. 1984: Psychological effects of complex environments throughout the life span: a review and theory. *Intelligence* 8, 259–81.

Skeels, H.M. 1966: Adult status of children with contrasting early life experiences: a follow-up study. *Monographs of the society for research in child development* 31, no. 105.

Slaughter, D.T. 1983: Early intervention and its effects on material and child development. *Monographs of the society for research on child development* 48, no. 202.

Sommer, R. and Sommer, B.A. 1983: Mystery in Milwaukee: early intervention, IQ, and psychology textbooks. *American psychologist* 38, 982–5.

*Vernon, P.E. 1979: *Intelligence: heredity and environment.* San Francisco: W.H. Freeman.

intelligence quotient (IQ) A number or "score" derived from performance on an intelligence test which expresses an individual's success on that test relative to the performance, on the same test, of a comparable group. There are several methods for computing an IQ, each of which can give a slightly different number. Most current tests adopt a standard procedure. This expresses an individual's score in terms of its deviation or distance (i.e. above or below) the average of the scores of the reference or normative group. By convention, the group average is commonly set to 100.

(See also TESTS: INTELLIGENCE; TESTS: NORMATIVE AND CRITERION-REFERENCED.)

MBe

interlanguage The term was introduced by Selinker (1972). It refers to a separate dynamic linguistic system and can be regarded as a reflection of the psycholinguistic process of interaction between the learner's mother tongue and the target language in SECOND LANGUAGE ACQUISITION. Interlanguage systems are described in terms of time-incorporating grammatical rules, i.e. rules which describe developments and rule-changing creativity, such as those developed by Bailey.

Interlanguage research concentrates on natural sequences of second language acquisition. One of the most startling results so far is that this acquisition appears to follow a natural language-independent "syllabus" where contrastive factors (see CONTRASTIVE ANALYSIS OF LINGUISTIC SYSTEMS) play only a minor role. This syllabus parallels the development of pidgin languages from less complex to more complex systems and nativized creoles.

PM

Bibliography
Corder, S. P. and Roulet, E. eds 1977: *The notions of simplification, interlanguage and pidgins and their relation to second language pedagogy*. Geneva: Librairie Droz.

Ellis, R. 1985: *Understanding second language acquisition*. Oxford and New York: Oxford University Press.

Selinker, L. 1972: Interlanguage. *International review of applied linguistics* 10, 219–31.

Tarone, E. 1983: On the variability of interlanguage systems. *Applied linguistics* 4/2, 143–63.

internalization In social psychological terms the adoption of attitudes or behavior patterns by an individual. Indeed much of socialization and education is involved with encouraging the individual to internalize the behavioral norms, morals and values of his or her group. A child's behavior is shaped or guided by example, encouragement, rewards and punishments, and hence directed into particular channels by external instruction and intervention. However, as the child develops he or she becomes able to give him or herself these instructions. Full internalization is reached when the behavior takes place not just because it is rewarded or punished, but because it is seen to be correct or appropriate. In psychoanalytic theorizing the term is often used synonymously with introjection or IDENTIFICATION and describes the process by which objects or norms in the external world are molded into permanent mental representations. The ego defense mechanism of identification is the way in which an individual attempts to take on the characteristics of someone who is more important than himself. Identifications may be made on the basis of guilt feelings, the need for punishment, or strong emotional attachments.

AF

Bibliography
Aronfreed, J. 1969: The concept of internalization. In *Handbook of socialization theory and research*, ed. D.A. Groslin. Chicago: Rand McNally.

Bandura, A. 1985: *Social foundations of thought and action*. Englewood Cliffs, N.J.: Prentice-Hall.

Fisher, S. and Greenberg, R.P. 1977: *The scientific credibility of Freud's theories and therapy*. New York: Basic Books; Brighton: Harvester.

J

Jensen controversy The contributions of hereditary and environmental factors to general INTELLIGENCE, as measured by standard tests, has been disputed since the 1920s. By the 1960s the majority of American psychologists and sociologists believed that differences in intelligence were mainly due to children's home upbringing and learning. They particularly rejected any genetic differences between racial or ethnic groups. Hence the uproar in 1969 when Arthur Jensen published an article in the *Harvard educational review*, which marshaled the extensive evidence of innate individual differences, and hypothesized that the large IQ difference between American blacks and whites was partly due to genetic factors. Leftwing student groups and black activists threatened him with physical violence, and many reputable social scientists condemned him more on ideological than scientific grounds. His subsequent writings have shown that much of the evidence they cited was unsound. Some researches have supported and others rejected his hypothesis, and Jensen now admits that we lack an adequate methodology for proving it. More recently, however, he has claimed that his use of reaction-time experiments as measures of intelligence overcomes many of the objections to traditional tests. This has again brought up the issue of racial differences, as Jensen claims that these tests underline the fact that racial differences are a difference in *g* (or general intelligence) rather than 'narrower group factors associated with . . . particular item content' (Jensen 1985). This claim has not gone unchallenged (e.g. Humphreys 1985).

(See INTELLIGENCE AND ENVIRONMENTAL INFLUENCES.)   PEV

Bibliography

Humphreys, L.G. 1985: Race differences and the Spearman hypothesis. *Intelligence* 9, 275–83.

Jensen, A.R. 1972: *Genetics and education*. London: Methuen; New York: Harper and Row.

—— 1985: The nature of the black-white differences on various psychometric tests: Spearman's hypothesis. *Behavioral and brain sciences* 8, 193–219.

K

Klein, Melanie (1882–1960) In extending psychoanalytic techniques to study the inner worlds of two- and three-year-olds Klein provided one of the earliest detailed accounts of pre-oedipal development and a clinically fruitful description of primitive thought processes. She created a method to treat severely disturbed young children and to gain access to their fantasies through the use of carefully chosen play material.

Klein worked within Freud's final theory of sexual and aggressive instincts. Although she employed concepts derived from the theory of psychosexual development and the stages of oral, anal and phallic-genital organizations these erotogenic zones achieved psychic importance earlier and often, according to her developmental timetable, simultaneously. Klein's identification of the Oedipus complex in primitive form within the first year was a major departure from classic psychoanalytic theory.

Her introduction of the concept of *position*, an organized constellation of mental processes, provided a new way of describing mental structures and objects. The *paranoid-schizoid position* characterized development in the first few months of life. The fantasy world of the infant was described as being unstable and made up of *part-objects*, fragmentary perceptions, e.g. breasts, penises, but not the whole persons of either parent. Denial, splitting into affectively good (satisfying) and bad, projection of the bad outward and introjection of the good, were seen as dominant thought processes of the paranoid-schizoid position. These mental functions are metaphorically linked with the infant's bodily processes – defecation, ingestion etc. Klein used terms such as good and bad breasts to characterize the unconscious fantasies of the very young infant. That objects are not yet constituted as the symbolic wholes of the second year is an important aspect of early development and of paranoid-schizoid thinking. The identification and description of the thought processes of this psychic constellation proved fruitful in later extensions of psychoanalytic techniques to treatment of severely disturbed adults (Rosenfeld 1965).

Klein claimed that by the middle of the first year the infant became aware that the good breast which it loved, and the bad persecutory breast which was the repository of its hate and which it feared, were one. Sadness thus accompanied thoughts of the destruction wrought by aggressive impulses and from its love of the object a need to make reparations developed. This achievement, which she described as the beginning of the *depressive position*, marked the infant's creation of whole objects and its ambivalence about the consequences of its desires in relation to these objects. The precarious nature of this achievement and a return to the more primitive mental processes of splitting, projection and introjection is evidenced in the everyday life of individuals and groups (Bion 1961).

Klein's later theories concerning the importance of *primitive envy* in mental life were as controversial as her description of infantile mental life in terms of unconscious fantasies. She postulated that primitive envy arose with early deprivation; the part object was viewed as possessing and enjoying something desirable but unobtainable. This primitive envy resulted in a wish to destroy the part object. Thus jealousy was seen as a developmental achievement for it allowed a desired object continued existence even though it was unobtainable.   BBL

131

Bibliography

Bion, W.R. 1961: *Experiences in groups and other papers*. London: Tavistock Publications.

Rosenfeld, Harold 1965: *Psychotic states: a psychoanalytic approach*. London: Hogarth Press.

Segal, Hanna 1979: *Klein*. London: Fontana/Collins.

L

Labov, William Born in 1927, Labov is Professor of Linguistics at the University of Pennsylvania. He is best known for his work on linguistic variation theory. In *The social stratification of English in New York City* (1966) he develops a descriptive apparatus capable of handling variable data. Linguistic variation is no longer relegated to performance but seen as a normal aspect of linguistic competence.

In demonstrating the logic and regularity of allegedly confused language of Black American children, Labov proposes a "difference hypothesis" to replace Bernstein's "deficit hypothesis" (see CODE).

Labov's studies on semantic boundaries and fuzzy semantics are now being used in aphasia research (Zurif and Blumstein 1978). The application of variation theory to FIRST LANGUAGE ACQUISITION is discussed by Labov and Labov (1976).   PM

Bibliography

Labov, William 1966: *The social stratification of English in New York City*. Washington D.C.: Center for Applied Linguistics.

—— 1972: *Language in the inner city*. Philadelphia: University of Pennsylvania Press; Oxford: Basil Blackwell.

—— and Labov, Teresa 1976: Learning the syntax of questions. Paper presented at the Conference of Psychology and Language, Stirling, Scotland.

Zurif, Edgar B. and Blumstein, Sheila E. 1978: Language and the brain. In *Linguistic theory and psychological reality*, eds. M. Halle et al. Cambridge, Mass. and London: MIT Press.

language acquisition *See* first language acquisition.

Language Acquisition Device The notion of LAD (Language Acquisition Device) was introduced by CHOMSKY (1964). This device is said to enable the native speaker to acquire his/her internalized grammar for a language on the basis of primary linguistic input data. The function of the LAD can be represented as follows:

Input   Device   Output
Primary Data → LAD → Internalized
                            Grammer

The LAD is independent of individual languages as children can acquire any natural language.

An important aspect of Chomsky's views on FIRST LANGUAGE ACQUISITION is that the primary data to which a child is exposed are full of performance errors.

The question to what extent children are equipped with a biologically-based innate capacity for language acquisition is not settled (see also BIOPROGRAM LANGUAGE). The limitations of Chomsky's views on this question include: the neglect of the important role of structured input (BABY TALK); the unsuitability of a static transformational-generative model of description to capture dynamic development; and the inability to account for the discrepancy between production and perception in language acquisition.   PM

Bibliography

Chomsky, Noam 1964: *Current issues in linguistic theory*. The Hague: Mouton.

Lieberman, P. 1984: *The biology and evolution of language*. Cambridge, Mass.: Harvard University Press.

language and cognition Traditionally conceived of as a field of research which attempts to answer such questions as "How far is language necessary for thought?" and "What intellectual capacities are required for an individual to develop and sustain language?". In practice, further questions have been raised concerning both "language" and "cognition". "Is language confined to humans?", "At what point can young children be said to have acquired language?", and "Are sign languages (or other communicative systems based on non-verbal symbols) really types of language?" are all questions which test our understanding of the concept of language. They force us to decide whether, and where, to draw lines across the terminological continuum from "linguistic" through "paralinguistic" to "non-linguistic" communication. It may prove impossible to point to formal properties which serve as critical attributes of language (Lyons 1972).

Questions have also been raised about "cognition". The modern field is wider in scope than the study of thinking: a reasonable definition would refer more generally to "the mental processing of information", and contributing disciplines include psychology, linguistics, artificial intelligence and neurology. There are many different, and some widely divergent, subfields within it, including speech perception, visual perception, word recognition and reading, memory, learning and attention, and so on. Consequently one person's view of cognition may be very different, both in content and methodology, from another's; controversial issues from one point of view are pseudo-controversies from another (Ades 1981): and precious few attempts are made these days to present an overall picture (though Campbell 1979, for language acquisition, attempts a stimulating dualistic statement, with "inner", truly cognitive, processes interacting with "outer", sensori-motor processes, and with a flexible boundary between these two domains).

Much work has centered on the theory of language developed by CHOMSKY and his associates during the last quarter-century, and Chomsky (1981) represents, for many, the flowering of a truly cognitivist linguistics at last. But many linguists have dissented from this approach, warning that grammar-writing, like map-making, crucially involves selection, abstraction and distortion (Matthews 1979). For many psycholinguists, the Chomskyan notion of a "mental organ" of language is misguided, inasmuch as presently-known language abilities can be accounted for by appeal to nonlinguistic properties of human cognition; thus, just as there are no "organs of speech" as such (rather, organs for eating, breathing, drinking, etc.) so we have no specifically linguistic cognitive capacities (rather, other capacities are recruited to linguistic ends – Bever 1970).

Developmentally, the Behaviorist view of language acquisition as a triumph of human learning has been effectively challenged by Chomsky. His position stresses the difficulties faced by the child in constructing an appropriate grammar, given (a) the complexity of the linguistic system and (b) the apparently inadequate nature of the primary linguistic data (the forms of language the child is exposed to). Accordingly, the Chomskyan view looks to some innate potential for language acquisition, which is part of the cognitive endowment of the "prelinguistic" child (see also LANGUAGE ACQUISITION DEVICE). Further, this capacity is specifically linguistic, hence differs radically from Piaget's concept of language (1959) as an outgrowth of general cognitive development.

Extreme difficulties lie in the way of resolving such issues. The existence of child language forms such as *sitted* (for *sat*), *foots* (for *feet*), etc., which cannot have been modeled by adult speech, suggests that very simple learning processes are not adequate; but it is still an open question how far aspects of learning are involved in, and interact with, other, possibly innate, cognitive skills in the language acquisition process. While certain language/cognition parallels (such as the coincidence of early vocabulary growth with the ability to search for displaced objects) are compatible with the Piagetian view, it is not easy (a) to establish a sufficient number of such correlations, nor (b) to determine the direction of the causality, cognition → language. Research by Donaldson (1978) into such areas as conservation and class inclusion has uncovered the importance of the interaction between linguistic forms and the perceived context for these forms; not only can children be shown to "have" these concepts much earlier than conventional Piagetian estimates allow, but (more importantly) the possession of these concepts cannot be realistically disentangled from their linguistic means of expression.

This might seem to favor the Chomskyan view of language as part of a richly structured cognitive system at the outset; but there are procedural difficulties (at the very least) here also, inasmuch as the nature of the child's specific linguistic resources is gauged on the assumption of the inadequate properties of the linguistic input to the child. Recent studies on the language addressed to young children ("motherese" and related phenomena such as BABY TALK – Ferguson and Snow 1977) have considerable potential in this connection, in uncovering aspects of clarification and simplification in speech to children which are not present in speech to adults. However, it is not yet clear whether the role of input language is crucial in language acquisition; it *might* represent such an effective (albeit unconscious) teaching strategy that learning theory once more becomes viable, or it might turn out to be a massive epiphenomenon, bound by culture and geography. The answer probably lies somewhere between these extremes, in which case we may have to consider a selective role for input – perhaps in providing enhanced contexts for the acquisition of certain types of linguistic features over others (e.g. abstract formal features which play only an indirect role in message structure, such as subject-verb inversion in English question forms).

Thus far we have considered the ontogenesis of language; we now turn to what we may call its microgenesis (the moment-by-moment, or "on-line", processing of language, both in comprehension and production), where language/cognition interactions also take place. If language abilities in adults are sustained through the operation of some stable and discrete mental organ, we should expect them to be in immune from variation in relation to modality and task differences (just as they are predicted to be independent of other aspects of cognition in development). Against this view, there is the "cognitive resources" position already referred to, according to which context (along with other pragmatic factors) continues to play a role in language processing beyond the point of maturity, and modality differences (e.g. reading vs. writing, speech vs. auditory processing) may at least partially determine the nature of the processing that takes place. For instance, it may seem reasonable to assume a "search for message" strategy in comprehension, but a "search for expression units" strategy in production, and such strategies seem to involve radically different types of ability (and can indeed be differentially impaired in language pathology). Conversely, parallels in strategies may be found between language processing and other aspects of cognition (e.g. the perception of ambiguity in utterances and in visual stimuli). Again, these issues are not easy to resolve, since it appears to be impossible to develop techniques of investigation that are at once rich and non-intrusive, and to devise models of linguistic behavior that are simultaneously adequate to account for observational facts and precise enough to bear on specific hypotheses.

For example, consider the fundamental opposition between "top down" (analysis-by-synthesis) vs. "bottom up" (analysis-by-analysis) models of language perception (Fodor, Bever and Garrett 1974). Evidence exists, in both reading and auditory processing studies, to support and deny each type of model, and a good guess would therefore be that we actually employ a mixture of processing strategies; that largely automatic feature detectors call out stimulus properties for the operation of higher level synthesizing abilities, within a hierarchy towards the head of which stand "attention" and even "consciousness". Such a "model" currently beckons, but no formulation of it has rigor, and hence it has none of the properties we require of a model; most importantly, it cannot be falsified.

Finally, we should emphasize the richly differentiated nature of language. Even restricting our discussion to conventional verbal communication, we find a hierarchy of skills, rooted in more than one sensory modality and extending across a wide range of motor control functions, yet reaching up to the highest levels of intellectual operations. In view of this, the importance of language as an object of study in the field of cognition is not surprising; but by the same token we should not expect it to yield up its secrets easily. MAGG

Bibliography

Ades, T. 1981: Time for a purge. *Cognition* 10, 7–15.

Bever, T.G. 1970: The cognitive basis for linguistic structures. In *Cognition and the development of language*, ed. J.R. Hayes. New York: Wiley.

Campbell, R.N. 1979: Cognitive development and child language. In *Language acquisition: studies in first language development*, eds. P. Fletcher and M. Garman. London and New York: Cambridge University Press.

Chomsky, N. 1981. *Lectures on government and binding*. Dordrecht: Foris.

Clark, H.H. and E.V. 1977. *Psychology and language: an introduction to psycholinguistics*. New York: Harcourt Brace Jovanovich.

Cox, M.V. 1986: *The child's point of view. The development of cognition and language*. Brighton: Harvester.

*Donaldson, M. 1978. *Children's minds*. London: Croom Helm; New York: Norton.

Ferguson, C. and Snow, C. 1977: *Talking to children: language input and acquisition*. London and New York: Cambridge University Press.

Fodor, J.A., Bever, T.G. and Garrett, M.F. 1974. *The psychology of language: an introduction to psycholinguistics and generative grammar*. New York: McGraw-Hill.

Harris, M. and Coltheart, M. 1986: *Language processing in children and adults*. London and Boston: Routledge and Kegan Paul.

Lyons, J. 1972: Human language. In *Non-verbal communication*, ed. R.A. Hinde. London and New York: Cambridge University Press.

Matthews, P.H. 1979. *Generative grammar and linguistic competence*. London: George Allen and Unwin.

Mehler, J. ed. 1981. *Cognition* 10. (Tenth anniversary volume.) Lausanne: Elsevier Sequoia S.A.

Piaget, J. 1926, 1959. *The language and thought of the child*. London: Routledge and Kegan Paul; New York: Humanities.

learning and memory: methods of studying
Any attempt to list all the empirical methods which have ever been used to study human learning would produce an endless catalogue of little help or interest to anyone. A more plausible goal is a sketchy history of assumptions which have been made about the nature of human memory and forgetting, and the kinds of experiments which have been carried out to test and extend these assumptions.

Applied research into human memory dates at least from the third century BC when associational mnemonic techniques were taught in schools of philosophy and rhetoric to help speakers remember catalogues of details or complex events, or to deliver long speeches without notes. These techniques depended heavily on the use of imagery. For example students learnt to image at will arbitrary structures (e.g. "The Palace of Memory", the "Theater of Memory", etc. etc.) with detailed imaged "locations" into which they mentally placed images of concrete objects as cues for particular topics which they wished to recall (e.g. an anchor for naval matters; a bag of grain for farm prices etc. etc.). Such techniques have proved remarkably successful and many hundreds of years later have been investigated by Bower (1970), and others in modern laboratories.

In the intervening centuries many vivid adventurers such as "Colonel" Benkowski, of Prague, and academics such as Dr Richard Pick of Magdalen College, Oxford, incremented their incomes by developing and teaching mnemonic systems. Perhaps the most famous was Gregor von Feinagle, immortalized in Byron's *Don Juan*. This rich background of general information about very successful, practical memory aids may have contributed, indirectly, to the Lockean idea that the efficiency of retention in human memory is determined by the number and diversity of "associations" which can be made between stored "facts". Alas, as in other areas of science the existence of this highly developed and successful *technology* of memory had remarkably little impact on hypotheses formulated about the nature of memory or on experiments made to test these hypotheses. It is no exaggeration to say that Feinagle's (1812) (pirated) published lectures could have launched an extremely effective experimental program anticipating work carried out by Bartlett by a hundred and twenty years. Bartlett's work, in turn, has taken a further fifty years to find proper appreciation.

As so often in psychology a rich harvest of "unofficial" knowledge about human abilities was lost because of the influential pertinacity of a brilliantly misguided scientist. Herman Ebbinghaus (1850 to 1909) conceived the idea that memories are stamped in by "mental work". He was aware that words or concepts frequently associated with each other might be very rapidly learned under experimental conditions. Thus he tried to use items with no existing associations, inventing "nonsense syllables" (usually a consonant, a vowel and a consonant selected at random from the alphabet) for this purpose. Ebbinghaus was his own subject, laboriously discovering how many repetitions it took him to learn lists of nonsense syllables of different lengths, how the learning of one list interfered with the learning of a subsequent list (proactive interference), or how subsequent learning interfered with retention of previous material (retroactive interference). He also showed that attempting to learn many lists immediately after each other ("massed practice") is much less efficient than learning lists at spaced intervals ("distributed practice"). It would be wrong to assume that Ebbinghaus neglected the possible effects of the associative structure of material to be learned upon the efficiency of its learning and retention. He was careful to check his results with nonsense syllables by teaching himself very long passages from *Don Juan*.

He confirmed that much the same general principles applied.

The experimental techniques developed by Ebbinghaus set the pattern of laboratory work until 1930, because they were so easily assimilated to the investigation of hypotheses of mutual inhibition and facilitation between learned responses developed from work by animal learning theorists such as Pavlov, Watson, Hull and later Skinner. Indeed this tradition persisted, especially in Mid-Western Universities in the United States, until the late 1950s and mid 1960s in spite of more naturalistic experiments carried out by Sir Frederick Bartlett in Cambridge, England, and published in his book *Remembering* (1932). Bartlett gave his subjects prose passages and naturalistic pictures to inspect and recall. His interest in social psychology made him sensitive to the fact that people from different cultures recall entirely different details of the same passage or picture and, as time passes, details become "conventionalised" to fit increasingly closely into their idiosyncratic expectations. Bartlett was the first to suggest that our knowledge of the world becomes incorporated into dynamic structures which he termed "schemata". These are not passive, knowledge storage devices, but rather active encoding structures which selectively assimilate and transform new information from the perceptual world.

In 1932 the ideas of computing systems and of information processing technology, let alone the concepts of "Artificial Intelligence Theory" were far in the future. Bartlett's vivid originality inspired his students at Cambridge but was not immediately appreciated elsewhere. During the 1950s it had been noted that syllables were not completely "nonsensical". Some were more "word-like", and so had more associations than others, and were correspondingly easier to learn. There followed Bousfield's discovery that lists of nouns made up of instances of easily recognized superordinate categories such as animal names, precious stones, etc. etc., were more easily recalled than random lists. From this modest beginning came a revolution in the 1960s and early 1970s with an increasing interest in subjects' use and description of relationships and of organizational structures within verbal material. If the structures which people detected, and which made their recall easier, could be discovered, it was supposed that the rules used by the brain to order and store experience might become accessible. CHOMSKY had pointed out that sentences in any language can be described in terms of higher order structures. Much effort was expended following up Chomsky's idea that the rules of thought could best be deduced from the rules of syntactic structure. This approach is now seen to be too limited. Allowance must also be made for semantic and propositional content, and for the use of "knowledge of the world".

The 1970s also saw an interest in memory for other types of material than words. Verbal learning had become the stock in trade of psychologists studying memory because materials were so easily collected, standardized and presented. The discovery by Haber and Standing that quite ordinary people can recognize up to 90 per cent of 5,000 or more pictures each of which they have inspected, briefly, only once before, forced psychologists to appreciate that human brains are not primarily adapted to recognize and recall words. Rather we are visual creatures who have an extraordinary facility in recognizing and imaging complex scenes. It became implicitly clear that to study the organization of memory we must be able to describe organization schemata for complex pictures as well as for lists of words and connected sentences.

At present the main difficulty facing psychologists is to find descriptions for knowledge structures which are applicable not only to techniques of data storage and retrieval in computers, but to the ways in which the human brain assimilates and retrieves information. At this juncture experimentation is, perhaps, less useful than originality in the development of abstract models for the ways in which knowledge about the world, and propositions about relationships between things in the world, can be represented in data-storage systems. Until such models become more sophisticated experiments on memory will be very trite and limited essays, hardly increasing the fragmentary understanding of complex processes which we have so far gained.   PR

Bibliography

Bartlett, Frederick 1932: *Remembering: a study in experimental and social psychology*. Cambridge: Cambridge University Press; New York: Macmillan.

Bower, G.H. 1970: Analysis of a mnemonic device. *American scientist* 58, 496–510.

Johnson, M.K. and Hasher, L. 1987: Human learning and memory. *Annual review of psychology*, vol. 38, eds. M.R. Rosenzweig and L.W. Porter. Palo Alto: Annual Reviews Inc. (in press).

Kintsch, W. 1977: *Memory and cognition*. New York and London: Wiley.

learning and motivation: in children

Motivation in the sense in which one person may be highly motivated and another lack motivation, is a concept used to explain different amounts of effort or persistence shown by different people on the same task. At one time psychologists conceptualized motivation in terms of drives or needs, i.e. something upsetting the homeostasis of the organism. Later there was more concentration on the ways in which the environment could arouse, or motivate a person or an animal. Some things would operate as incentives which would produce effort. Much of the experimentation on animal learning has involved the interaction between rewards such as food and the animal's needs such as hunger. The animal is induced to learn something by being rewarded for its trouble. The response it makes is the instrument by which it obtains what it wants. On the other hand animals explore their environment out of curiosity. Although such exploration may be phylogenetically related to survival through the discovery of dangers or potential rewards, the individual animal's efforts may be continued with no reward (Harlow et al. 1950). Children are also explorers (see EXPLORA-

TION; COMPETENCE MOTIVATION). But formal education may present disincentives in the form of hard work and self-denial. One major problem in education is to encourage curiosity beyond the point at which its returns are intrinsically rewarding. The attempt to do this by offering extrinsic reward in the form of approval or prizes may diminish a child's interest in what it is doing (Lepper, Greene and Nisbett 1973).

Difficulties are also created by the fact that school success may be instrumental in producing undesired as well as desired ends. Lacey, for instance, quotes a grammar school boy: 'When . . . I had passed [the 11+] . . . I was treated as a "puff" and was a "brainy soft-arsed mardy".' This difficulty does not only involve PEER GROUP pressure, although, as Beloff and Temperley (1972) report, 'the relatively adult-oriented and socialized children are . . . the unpopular ones'. There are also assumed to be pressures or encouragements from the home. In 1948 Davis suggested that different goals are regarded as desirable in different social classes. Middle class children generally do better than working class children in school. The middle class children also score better on IQ tests, but Douglas reported (1964) that 26 per cent of upper middle-class children worked "very hard" as against 7 per cent of working class children. Since hard work does affect exam success (hard workers doing better and poor workers worse than IQ scores would predict) the motivation which affects the effort is an important variable in improving such success. If it is assumed that exam performance measures learning, this motivation is clearly influencing learning.

It has been suggested that middle-class children have more stimulating home environments and are encouraged to do well at school. From the time of Froebel attempts have been made to make schools stimulating, to feed the child's natural curiosity. The success of such attempts to increase intrinsic motivation has been dubious. Programs of DISCOVERY LEARNING in British schools have been reported in government publications to produce minimal improvements and to be detrimental in some subjects, although there is evidence that more able or knowledgeable learners do very well when they are given latitude and are not too strictly guided (Snow and Lohman 1984). If the school cannot offer successful rewards the child with high ACHIEVEMENT MOTIVATION has an advantage in coping with learning.

McClelland is the most famous student of achievement motivation, despite some doubts about his use of projective tests. His well known cross-cultural studies were influenced by Winterbottom (1958) who found that boys with high need for achievement had mothers who claimed that they had demanded independence from their sons. For twenty-two countries McClelland (1961) discovered a high correlation (r = 0.53) between the average number of achievement themes in children's readers published in 1925 and the increase in electric power consumption per head (used as an index of economic growth) between then and 1950. The themes in the children's readers were taken to show the emphasis the society placed on achievement. Further studies within societies, using different measures, tended to support this assumption. This naturally implies that one's culture (or sub-culture) may instill or repress the need for achievement. This was the implication of Winterbottom's work, and Rosen and D'Andrade (1959) provided support in a study in which parents could help their sons in experimental tasks. Parents of boys with high achievement needs had higher expectations and involvement, as well as rewarding and punishing more than parents of those with low needs. But later research has had very mixed results, and has certainly not confirmed these theories about the learning of achievement motivation. Moreover the idea that parents' behavior may be a response to children's behavior as much as a cause of it has been a commonplace in recent years (Bell 1968). Meanwhile doubt has been cast on the usefulness of need for achievement scores by their failure to predict school success (Entwisle 1972).

Yet it remains a natural assumption that parental attitudes, values and involvement will influence children's motivation. If the parents simply assume that their child must be interested in and do well at school, the child is unlikely to be unaffected by this. Many researchers have said that parental interest influences school progress. Fishbein has built into his model of the connexion between attitude and behavior the assumption that the attitudes of "significant others" should be included in the predictive equation. Interestingly Kolb (1965) found that only boys of high socioeconomic status showed long term benefits from a program designed to increase underachievers' motivation. The implication was that the low status boys lost their initial improvements because of their background values.

On the other hand, according to Swift (1966), there is no class bias (in Britain) in the assumption that school is "a good thing". There is also evidence that immigrant families put great stress on academic achievement (D.E.S. 1985). Although assumptions about the role of the school might differ according to class, other factors will presumably influence the individual's effort to succeed academically. Anxiety for instance has been implicated in achievement. Holt (1964) has detailed anecdotes about children's fears in the classroom, while experimental evidence has shown that highly anxious people have more difficulty in learning (but see McKeachie 1984). The problem of anxiety was taken into account by Atkinson (1964) who hypothesized that "achievement-oriented activity" would be affected by approach and avoidance forces, viz. the motive to succeed and the fear of failure. This fear is said to be learnt through previous failure and its attendant shame.

More recent work has concentrated on the perceptions of success and failure, and the expectations of future performance. Clearly if one expects to fail one's anxiety and fear of failure may well be greater than if one expects to succeed. Rosenbaum (1972) found that attributions of failure to stable causes (inability, or diffi-cult task) led to lower expectation of future success than did attributions to unstable causes (lack of effort, or bad luck), while attributions of success to stable causes led to higher expectations. Dweck and Reppucci (1973) showed that subjects who persevered and produced good performance after repeated failures tended to ascribe failure to low effort (a controllable, unstable cause).

Katz in Australia and Bernstein in England both suggested that working class children are not encouraged to have a sense of control over their environment, and that they perceive success as 'limited in possibility of attainment by factors over which the individual has no control'. It seems possible, therefore, that social class may affect pupils' motivation by affecting their beliefs about what they can and cannot achieve. But the neat attributional account of motivation has not been without critics, especially in its applications to educational problems (see Weiner 1983; Brophy 1983). Nicholls (1984) proposed that effort should not be conceptualized as something distinct from ability. Heider (1958) and Weiner (1980) treated them as separate factors, ability being fixed and immutable, while effort is under the agent's control. Nicholls suggested that pupils who think of ability as fixed, approach study differently from those who think of it as something which the process of learning may improve. In this model effort and ability are entwined together. It is still an attributional model, however, in which the motivation depends on expectations about the possibility of success on the immediate task. It should therefore be contrasted with expectancy-value models like Eccles's (1983), which also take into account the pupil's beliefs about the usefulness of success. It is possible that disbelief in their ability to gain success by their own efforts may be prevalent in lower class children more than in middle class children, but they may also be more prone to scepticism about the worth of education or tend to perceive school as a repressive institution rather than an instrument for success. (See also EDUCATIONAL ATTAINMENT AND EXPECTATIONS.)   RL

Bibliography

Bell, R.Q. 1968: A reinterpretation of the direction of effects of socialization. *Psychological review* 75, 81–95.

Beloff, H. and Temperley, K. 1972: The power of the peers. *Scottish educational studies* 4, 3–10.

Bernstein, B. 1962: Social class, linguistic codes and grammatical elements. *Language and speech* 5, 221–40.

Brophy, J. 1983: Conceptualizing student motivation. *Educational psychology* 18, 200–15.

Davis, A. 1948: *Social class influences upon learning.* Cambridge, Mass.: Harvard University Press.

Department of Education and Science 1985: *Education for all.* London: HMSO.

Douglas, J.W.B. 1964: *The home and the school.* London: MacGibbon and Kee.

Eccles, J. 1983: Expectancies, values and academic behaviors. In *Achievement and achievement motives,* ed J.T. Spence. San Francisco: Freeman.

Harlow, H.F., Harlow, M.K. and Meyer, P.R. 1950: Learning motivated by a manipulation drive. *Journal of experimental psychology* 40, 228–34.

*Holt, J. 1964: *How children fail.* London: Pitman.

Katz, F.M. 1964: The meaning of success. *Journal of social psychology* 52, 141–8.

Lacey, C. 1970: *Hightown grammar school.* Manchester: Manchester University Press.

McClelland, D.C. 1961: *The achieving society.* Princeton, N.J.: Van Nostrand.

McKeachie, W.J. 1984: Does anxiety disrupt information processing or does poor information processing lead to anxiety? *International review of applied psychology* 33, 187–203.

Nicholls, J.G. 1984: Achievement motivation. *Psychological review* 91, 328–46.

Snow, R.E. and Lohman, D.F. 1984: Toward a theory of cognitive aptitude for learning from instruction. *Journal of educational psychology* 76, 347–76.

Swift, D.F. 1966: Social class and achievement motivation. *Educational research* 82, 83–95.

*Weiner, B. 1980: *Human motivation.* New York: Holt, Rinehart and Winston.

—— 1983: Some methodological pitfalls in attributional research. *Journal of educational psychology* 75, 530–43.

Winterbottom, M.R. 1958: In *Motives in fantasy, action and society,* ed. J.W. Atkinson, Princeton, N.J.: Van Nostrand.

For other references see Weiner 1980.

learning difficulties (Note: For the sake of brevity the word "child" includes "young person".)

The term "learning difficulties" may be used either to refer to particular aspects of learning, in which a child may have difficulty, or in a more general way, to the fact that a child has difficulty in learning. This latter use of the term was introduced in the British Report of the Committee of Enquiry into the Education of Handicapped Children and Young People (Warnock Report, DES 1978). In this Report it was recommended that the previously used categories of handicap should be discarded and that children should be considered in terms of their special educational needs. Consequently it was suggested that the term "educationally subnormal" should be replaced by "children with learning difficulties", and qualified by the terms "severe", "moderate" and "specific". "Severe" and "moderate" learning difficulties were intended to refer respectively to severe and moderate levels of subnormality. The term "learning difficulty" was subsequently incorporated into the wording of the British 1981 Act on Special Education, where a child with special educational needs was described as one who had a 'learning difficulty which calls for special educational provision to be made for him'. Furthermore, a child with learning difficulty was defined as one who 'has a significantly greater difficulty in learning than the majority of children of his age' or who 'has a disability which either prevents or hinders him from making use of educational facilities of a kind generally provided in schools'.

The concept of learning difficulty adopted in the Act's definitions is not elaborated further, but would appear to include the level and nature of curricular content which would be regarded as appropriate for the children concerned, in line with the administrative connotation of the definition of "special educational need".

In the USA the term "learning disability" has been incorporated into the Education for all Handicapped Children Act of 1975 (PL 94–142). The Act includes a definition of the term indicating that it refers to deficiencies in processes underlying educational performance but excluding other forms of primary causation (e.g. environmental deprivation). This "definition by exclusion" has been criticized by Hallahan and Bryan (1981) among others.

"Learning difficulties" in the sense of a term referring to difficulties in particular aspects of learning has been used in a number of ways. One of the most common themes in its definition has been concerned with discrepancies in the levels of a child's performance. It has been noted that a child's level of performance in certain aspects of educational attainment, of communication, or of behavioral adequacy, may be lower than in other aspects of his performance or functioning, and that in certain instances these are assumed to be the result of *specific* difficulties in learning which are primary, and not the consequence of emotional disturbances, of deprivation of experience, or of sensory or motor impairment. In so far as the difficulties represent *discrepancies* in levels of performance, it is also assumed that they are not a concomitant of a generally low level of intelligence (Wedell 1975). These considerations involve two sets of assumptions – those concerned with the nature of the difficulties, and those concerned with their causes.

The account of the nature of learning difficulties outlined above has to be seen in the context of a growing doubt about INTELLIGENCE as a unitary concept. Historically, learning difficulties had been defined in terms of "backwardness" and of "retardation" (Tansley and Pankhurst 1981). These terms tended to be defined in terms of the discrepancy between a child's educational attainment and either his chronological age (backwardness) or his level of "intelligence" (specific retardation: retardation in this sense should be clearly distinguished from "mental retardation"). Specific retardation, therefore, contrasted a child's attainment with his "potential" (intelligence) and these children were therefore called "under-achievers". Experts in psychometrics have questioned the validity of the

concept of under-achievement and of the discrepancy model in general (Thorndike 1963). Learning difficulty as defined in terms of a discrepancy between actual and expected performance is an uncertain concept.

Children's difficulties in learning have been manifested and described in a variety of ways. A common description has been in terms of syndromes of difficulties, such as dyslexia (see DYSLEXIC CHILDREN). These syndrome names are derived from clinical neurological studies of adults who have lost the capacity to perform in particular ways as the result of various forms of neurological impairment. The extension of the use of these terms to children is questionable since in these cases they refer not to a loss of a capacity, but to a failure to develop or acquire it (Wedell 1975). Furthermore, in clinical neurology, syndromes are established on the basis of the demonstrated co-occurrence of symptoms, and the evidence for this, for example, in children described as dyslexic, is contradictory (eg. DES 1972). Doubt also applies to syndrome terms such as "hyperactivity", used to describe restlessness and short attention-span in children. Schacher, Rutter and Smith (1981) have pointed out that hyperactivity in many children is situation- or task-specific and cannot be used to describe a child in a general way.

The above accounts of learning difficulties also have associations with assumptions about their cause, and much of the literature refers to learning "disabilities". This is already often implicit in the discrepancy model of learning difficulty. Accounts of the syndrome models almost invariably also refer to disabilities underlying the symptomology. These disabilities are described in terms of the dysfunction of psychological processes which is thought to cause the impaired performance, such as defects in perceptuo-motor functions, in language and in memory. Difficulties in reading and spelling are ascribed, for example, to defects in intermodal association, and attention difficulties to defects in perception. Much research has been devoted to investigating these associations, but the evidence, while supporting many of these hypotheses, has not proved conclusive. Wedell (1973) pointed out that the causal relationship between the hypothesized underlying processes and performance on the target tasks was likely to be more complex than had been acknowledged. For example, any particular performance might be subserved by different combinations of processes and the ways in which a child had been taught the task was also likely to exert an important influence.

Much research has been devoted to attempts to discover the organic bases of learning difficulties, and some of the early studies were particularly concerned with this. In the face of insufficient evidence for associations with demonstrable neurological impairment, some have put forward the notion of "minimal cerebral dysfunction"; a hypothesis that some forms of learning difficulty might be caused by subclinical forms of neurological impairment.

Approaches to the assessment and treatment of learning difficulties have been derived from the various conceptualizations mentioned above. Delacato (1966), for example, devised means of assessing delayed and impaired neurological function, and also training procedures aimed at rectifying these. However, doubt has been expressed about these approaches by the American Academy of Cerebral Palsy. Many batteries of tests to assess the psychological processes thought to underlie learning difficulties have been produced, for example the Illinois Test of Psycholinguistic Abilities and the Frostig Developmental Test of Visual Perception. These batteries have been linked with remedial programs for the particular functions assessed. However, studies designed to investigate the effectiveness of these programs have only partly substantiated their effectiveness in improving children's performances on the test batteries, and only rarely shown the children to improve significantly more in the target educational performances (eg Hammill and Larsen 1974). Similarly, attempts by means of early identification procedures to assess

these functions in children at the early stages of schooling, in order to predict which children would later have difficulties in learning, have had little success (Lindsay and Wedell 1982).

The above findings have contributed to the conclusion already mentioned above, that the causation of learning difficulties is very complex and this, in turn, has led to attempts to help children with learning difficulties through "direct instruction". These approaches involve the specification of the target task which the child is required to learn in terms of "behavioral" objectives. The sequence of instruction is based on task-analysis aimed at identifying the successive steps necessary for the child to master the target task. The methods employed in teaching are derived from operant learning theory, but many of the approaches to task analysis are based on notions similar to those underlying the "process" approach to learning difficulties (Wedell 1973). An important feature of this teaching approach is the detailed recording of the child's progress towards each objective, by means of "precision teaching" (Haring et al. 1978). This teaching approach is still at the early stages of development, but has the advantages that the evaluation of its effectiveness is integral to it.

This brief account of learning difficulties has indicated that the phenomenon to which the term refers is well demonstrated, but that the understanding about how the difficulties are caused and how they should best be remedied is still a matter of controversy. The issues involved represent an interesting aspect of the meeting of psychology and education. DMG

Bibliography

Delacato, C.H. et al. 1966: *Neurological organisation and reading*. Springfield. Ill.: Thomas.

Department of Education and Science 1972: *Children with specific reading difficulties*. London: HM Stationery Office.

——— 1978: *Special educational needs (The Warnock Report)*. London: HM Stationery Office.

Hallahan, D.P. and Bryan, I.H. 1981: Learning difficulties. In *Handbook of special education*, eds. J.M. Kaufman and D.P. Hall. Englewood

143

Cliffs, N.J.: Prentice-Hall.

Hammill, D.D. and Larsen, S.C. 1974: The effectiveness of psycho-linguistic training. *Exceptional children* 41, 5–14.

Haring, N.G. et al. 1978: *The fourth R: research in the classroom*. C.E. Merrill.

Lindsay, G.A. and Wedell, K. 1982: The early identification of educationally "At Risk" children revisited. *Journal of learning disabilities* 15, 212–17.

Schacher, R., Rutter, M. and Smith, A. 1981: The characteristics of situationally and pervasively hyperactive children: implications for syndrome definition. *Journal of child psychology and psychiatry* 22, 375–420.

Tansley, P. and Pankhurst, J. 1981: *Children with specific learning difficulties*. National Foundation for Educational Research.

Thorndike, R.L. 1963: *The concepts of over and under achievement*. New York: Columbia University Teachers' College.

Wedell, K. 1973: *Learning and perceptuo-motor disabilities in children*. New York and London: Wiley.

—— 1975: Specific learning difficulties. In *Orientations in special education*. New York and London: Wiley.

learning strategies Activities that are engaged in with the goal of increasing learning. Since they are goal directed they are executed intentionally. Such strategies may be those of a learner in which case they are either internal cognitive strategies (e.g. imagery) or external strategies (e.g. note-taking). Alternatively, they may be the strategies of authors who modify materials to make them easier to learn (e.g. by providing pictures, by adding italics to important points in a text or by organizing the material in a helpful way).

There is a long history of research on the types of strategies that people spontaneously use when they are attempting to learn. During the last two decades researchers have traced out the development of this spontaneous use of strategies. An excellent example is the work on the development of rehearsal in recall (e.g. when learners are presented with a list of words and must recall them in a test). A second example of the development of the spontaneous use of a strategy involves semantic-elaborative strategies in associa-

tive learning. These strategies include elaborative imagery (e.g. imagining a turkey sitting on a rock for the paired associate turkey-rock) and verbal elaboration (e.g. thinking "the turkey sat on the rock" for the pair turkey-rock). When late adolescents are asked to learn such paired associates, they are much more likely than younger children to employ these elaborations. Recently, the spontaneous use of strategies in everyday tasks (such as learning from text) have been examined. For a review, see Pressley et al. (1982).

Some theorists have argued that sophisticated strategy deployment on occasions when it is appropriate is at the very heart of intelligence (e.g. Borkowski 1985). A great deal of effort has also been expended in order to determine when children who do not spontaneously produce an efficient strategy can be taught to use learning strategies (see Weinstein and Mayer 1986). For instance young schoolchildren often do not spontaneously produce rehearsal strategies when they are given a list of words to learn so that it can be reproduced later, but it is usually possible to increase these children's recall by instructing them to use rehearsal strategies. This can be the case even with late adolescents. It is also possible to instruct young schoolchildren and even preschool children to use elaborative strategies in associative learning. On the other hand children's imagery-elaborative skills lag behind (e.g. Pressley 1982), a point which emphasizes that not all failures at spontaneous strategy usage can be remedied by instruction. Sometimes the learner is unable to generate a strategy because of cognitive-developmental constraints (probably the case with imagery), and sometimes for other reasons.

Just as those interested in spontaneous strategy usage have turned their attention in recent years to more practical everyday tasks, so have those interested in strategy instruction. Researchers have been instructing learners to paraphrase text, to make internal mental images of concrete stories, and to use a variety of rehearsal and imagery strategies to prepare for multiple-choice tests. In addition learning strategies are being developed for a variety of tasks such as vocabulary learning, spelling, learning social studies and the learning of face-name associations. (See Pressley et al. 1982 for examples of research in all these areas).

One particularly heartening aspect of research on strategy usage is the usefulness of strategy instruction in improving the learning of deficit populations. Disabled children do not develop some strategies until later than normal children. Retarded children are even more profoundly deficient with respect to spontaneous strategy usage. However, simple instructions to use strategies produce increased learning for these populations at least with respect to some strategies some of the time (Pressley et al. 1982 reviews work on these topics; also Pressley and Levin 1983 and Levin and Pressley 1983). However it must be emphasized that simple strategy instruction does not always work. See Bender and Levin (1978) for an example of ineffective strategy instructions with retarded children.

A variety of material aids have been designed to increase learning. In virtually every case the benefits associated with a particular type of aid have been found to be situationally specific. To illustrate this point, consider the learning gains associated with two types of adjunct aids for prose learning – questions and pictures.

When an author adds questions to a text they can be put either before the relevant material or after it, and their positioning will have a great effect on which aspects of the text are especially well learned. The presence of questions, either before or after the text, enhances the retention of material specifically covered in the questions. However, the effects of pre- versus post-questions are very different for material not specifically covered in the questions. In the case of post-questions, recall of material other than the question-relevant material is enhanced. However, pre-questions tend to reduce recall of material not specifically included in the questions, presumably because the pre-questions focus the learners' attention on the question-relevant material at the

expense of the material incidental to the questions. Anderson and Biddle (1975) provide a comprehensive discussion of questioning effects.

Do pictures aid prose learning? Levin and Lesgold (1978) carefully reviewed this issue and concluded that improvement in learning happens only when young children are the learners and when the pictures accurately represent the text. Also, the prose should consist of concrete stories, orally presented, and the test should consist of short-answer questions. Thus, as in the case of questions, there are specific limitations on the extent to which learning gains are associated with pictures.

In addition to questions and pictures, a number of other aids can be added to text, and in every case positive effects are observed only some of the time. For instance, Ausubel (1963) proposed that texts be accompanied by advanced organizers which are designed to relate to-be-learned materials to already available knowledge, but research has only occasionally confirmed the effectiveness of organizers. There is great debate about whether the strategy is ineffective or whether researchers have failed to construct organizers consistent with Ausubel's theory. Recent evidence indicates that advanced organizers affect memory of higher-level conceptual knowledge, but have no impact on lower-level knowledge (see Mayer and Bromage 1980 for an overview of advanced organizer effects). Similarly, the available research indicates that overviews and behavioral objectives are effective only some of the time (Melton 1979).

There are many issues left to be resolved. The testing of learning strategies is increasingly being conducted in the classroom rather than the laboratory with many new methodological difficulties (e.g. Pressley et al. 1982; Pressley and Levin 1983; Levin and Pressley 1983; McKeachie et al. 1985). Nonetheless, there is enough positive evidence in support of the learning strategies approach to warrant the effort necessary to do real-world studies of learning strategies' effects. MP

145

Bibliography

Anderson, R.C. and Biddle, W.B. 1975: On asking people questions about what they are reading. In *The psychology of learning and motivation*, vol. 9, ed. G. Bower. New York, San Francisco and London: Academic Press.

Ausubel, D.P. 1963: *The psychology of meaningful verbal learning*. New York and London: Grune and Stratton.

Barclay, C.R. 1979: The executive control of mnemonic activity. *Journal of experimental child psychology* 27, 262–76.

Bender, B.G. and Levin, J.R. 1978: Pictures, imagery, and retarded children's prose learning. *Journal of educational psychology* 70, 583–8.

Borkowski, J.G. 1985: Signs of intelligence: Strategy generalization and metacognition. In *The development of insight in children*, ed. S.R. Yussen. New York: Academic Press.

Levin, J.R. and Lesgold, A.M. 1978: On pictures in prose. *Educational communication and technology journal* 26, 233–43.

—— and Pressley, M. eds. 1983: *Cognitive strategy research: educational applications*. New York: Springer-Verlag.

Mayer, R.E. and Bromage, B.K. 1980: Different recall protocols for technical text due to advance organizers. *Journal of educational psychology* 72, 209–25.

McKeachie, W.J., Pintrich, P.R. and Lin, Y-G. 1985: Learning to learn. In *Cognition, information processing and motivation*, ed. G. d'Ydwelle. Amsterdam: Elsevier.

Melton, R.F. 1979: Resolution of conflicting claims concerning the effect of behavioral objectives on student learning. *Review of educational research* 48, 291–302.

Pressley, M. 1982: Elaboration and memory development. *Child development* 53, 296–309.

—— et al. 1982: Memory strategy instruction. In *Progress in cognitive development research*, vol. 2, eds. C.J. Brainerd and M. Pressley. New York: Springer-Verlag.

—— and Levin, J.R. eds. 1983: *Cognitive strategy research: psychological foundations*. New York: Springer-Verlag.

Weinstein, C.E. and Mayer, R.E. 1986: The teaching of learning strategies. In *The handbook of research on teaching*. 3rd edn, ed. M. Wittrock. New York: Macmillan.

Lenneberg, Eric H. (1921–1975)

Professor of psychology at the University of Michigan, Lenneberg trained in the psychology of language and in general neurological and medical sciences. He made a number of important contributions to the understanding of the relationship between language and the brain. The findings presented in his *Biological foundations of language* (1967) became a major source of information for both transformational-generative grammar (see CHOMSKY) and PSYCHOLINGUISTICS.

While Lenneberg's most important function was to serve as a synthesizer of knowledge found in the disciplines of psychology, linguistics, anthropology, neurology, physiology and genetics, he also made important contributions in the areas of localization of speech in the brain, child language development and speech disorder research.   PM

Bibliography

Lenneberg, Eric H. 1967: *Biological foundations of language*. London and Sydney: J. Wiley and Sons.

Miller, George A. and Lenneberg, Elisabeth eds. 1978: *Psychology and biology of language and thought: essays in honour of Eric Lenneberg*. New York and London: Academic Press.

lifespan psychology

The lifespan perspective in developmental psychology is relatively recent. The study of development began in the nineteenth century as the study of growth-related change in infancy, childhood and adolescence. Maturational changes were thought to occur in a universal ONTOGENETIC SEQUENCE, paralleled by universal stages in psychological development. For example it is reasoned that while there is some variation in the age at which walking or talking begins, or the age of first menstruation, both sequence and timing are relatively predictable within broad bounds. Furthermore, in a given culture, it can be expected that children or adolescents will, at any given age, be working on the same set of developmental tasks, tasks representing the intersection of biological readiness and social institutions. For example, six-year-olds in one culture may be starting school, in another learning to hunt.

The lifespan perspective recognizes the need to search for a general sequence of change over the entire life course, notwithstanding the absence of maturational markers (the menopause in women is considered the only universal maturational change in adulthood), and the diversity of social roles in a pluralistic age-graded system. One cannot become a parent, for example, before puberty, nor contract a marriage independent of parental consent before reaching the age of political majority. Child labor laws restrict the participation of the young in the labor force, and mandatory retirement in certain occupations excludes the elderly.

Within these very broad bounds, however, there is much possible variation and no single sequence of roles. First marriage and parenthood may occur at twenty or earlier, at thirty, at forty, or later; the peak of a career will occur early for those in certain fields (for example professional athletes, musicians and mathematicians) and later in others (art, literature, the social sciences). The sequence of roles is not invariant: a first marriage may be followed by a second; career peaks may be followed by career changes. Consideration of the entire life cycle is complicated by the fact that the maturational timetable of the first portion

of the life span is absent in adulthood, and the range of variation so great.

The scientific study of the life span began in the 1940s, building on such bases as G. Stanley HALL's book *Senescence: the last half of life*, published in 1922; Charlotte Buhler's distinction between the biological and the biographical life curves, published in 1933; and Else Frenkel-Brunswik's studies of the life span, begun in Berkeley during the 1930s. The concept of developmental tasks was developed by Robert Havighurst at the University of Chicago during the 1940s, combining the drive toward growth, or maturational timetable, of the individual with the constraints and opportunities in the social environment. In 1950 Erik ERIKSON published *Childhood and society*, widely considered to be the most influential book of the period and an introduction for many readers to the concept of development over the life cycle.

Although Erikson's work built on that of others, his model of eight stages of the life cycle was the first widely received model of development extending the notion of developmental stages into adulthood. Paralleling Freud's ontogenetic sequence for the first part of the life cycle, Erikson poses the following "nuclear crises" or stages in psychosocial development:

Stage	Approximate age	Freudian equivalent
basic trust vs. mistrust	infancy	oral
autonomy vs. shame and doubt	toddler	anal
initiative vs. guilt	preschool	phallic/ oedipal
industry vs. inferiority	school age adolescence/ young adulthood	latency none
intimacy vs. isolation	young adulthood	genital
generativity vs. stagnation	middle adulthood	none
ego integrity vs. despair	later adulthood	none

Erikson's theory is an extension of Freud's in the following ways: first, he expands the concept of stages of development to embrace the entire life cycle; second, he recognizes more explicitly the interaction of the individual with the social context; third, the content of those stages for which there is no Freudian equivalent adds new substance to our understanding of development over the life span. The stage of identity vs. role confusion is the stage at which the young adult finds a place in society; generativity vs. stagnation marks the stage of responsibility for the next generation, not only through parenthood but through any form of care and concern for the young; the stage of ego integrity vs. despair marks the point when one's one and only life cycle is accepted, when one can look back over the life course without despair.

Recognition of personality development in adulthood was greatly enhanced by the work of Bernice Neugarten and her colleagues at the University of Chicago in the Kansas City Study of Adult Life, carried out over the decade 1954–64. Although she found a regular progression toward increased interiority of personality, there was no comparable regularity of change in social behavior. On the basis of these findings, she challenged the disengagement theory of Cumming and Henry, suggesting that life satisfaction was associated with sustained activity throughout the life cycle. A major contribution of Neugarten's work is expanded understanding of the developmental changes in middle age, hitherto thought to be a period of stability. Her work marks the beginning of a lifespan perspective, uniting child developmental studies at one end of the life cycle with gerontology at the other.

Since its beginnings in the study of personality development over the life course, lifespan psychology has seen major advances in the study of family and intergenerational relations; cognitive development; age grading and the social system; and social policy. Not only does lifespan psychology encompass the life course of the developing individual, but the broader social and political context in which the individual's development occurs. ND

Bibliography

*Baltes, Paul B. and Schaie, K. Warner, eds. 1973: *Life-span developmental psychology: personality and socialization.* New York and London: Academic Press.

Datan, Nancy and Ginsberg, Leon H. eds. 1975: *Life span developmental psychology: normative life crises.* New York and London: Academic Press.

*——— and Lohmann, Nancy eds. 1980: *Transitions of aging.* New York and London: Academic Press.

———, Rodeheaver, Dean and Hughes, Fergus 1987: Lifespan psychology. In *Annual review of psychology,* vol. 38, eds. M.R. Rosenzweig and L.W. Porter. Palo Alto: Annual Reviews Inc. (in press).

*Erikson, Erik H. 1963: *Childhood and society.* 2nd edn. New York: W.W. Norton: Harmondsworth: Penguin.

Goulet, L.R. and Baltes, Paul B. eds. 1970: *Life-span developmental psychology: research and theory.* New York and London: Academic Press.

Honzik, M.P. 1984: Lifespan development *Annual review of psychology* 35, 309–31.

*Neugarten, Bernice L. ed. 1968: *Middle age and aging.* Chicago and London: University of Chicago Press.

linguistic backsliding According to Selinker (1972, p. 216) backsliding is 'the regular reappearance of fossilized errors' that were thought to be eradicated in SECOND LANGUAGE ACQUISITION. It usually results from the learner's difficulty in expressing particular semantic notions and from stress-provoking social settings. Otherwise a learner will produce more advanced and correct forms of the second language.

Hyltenstam (1977) has shown that backsliders strictly adhere to the overall implicational pattern ("inbuilt syllabus") underlying the sequential appearance of grammatical constructions in second language acquisition.

Research into backsliding behavior can shed light on both the relationship between pragmatic and structural considerations in language development and the concept of structural difficulty in linguistics.

While the term backsliding is usually reserved for second language acquisition, the use of simplified registers such as BABY TALK can be associated with a reversal to earlier learning stages of a speaker's first language. PM

Bibliography

Hyltenstam, Kenneth 1977: Implicational patterns in interlanguage syntax variation. *Language learning* 272, 283–411.

Selinker, L. 1972: Interlanguage. *International review of applied linguistics* 10, 209–31.

linguistic naturalness A property often claimed for linguistic rules, categories or analyses proposed since the mid-1960s. Those interested in naturalness have been concerned to define and apply the notion "natural" in the treatment of some linguistic level or subdiscipline, e.g. one speaks of "natural" phonology, "natural" morphology, "natural" syntax, "natural" rules, etc.

In order to justify employing an attribute such as natural as a measure of evaluation, one must first establish how to recognize it. Generally, the evidence proffered by linguists can be divided into two subtypes: *system-internal* and *system-external* evidence. Language system-internal properties that count as natural include: (a) *change* A natural category or rule is more resistant to change than unnatural category or rule; (b) *creolization* In the loss of function-words during pidginization natural rules or categories survive longest and reappear first during creolization; (c) *typology* Natural rules or categories are more frequent in the world's languages; (d) *frequency* Tokens of natural categories or applications of natural rules are more frequent within one language; (e) *neutralization* Natural categories are the surviving members of a merger between two categories; (f) *analogy* Natural categories are the templates of change; unnatural categories undergo the change; (g) *phonology* Natural categories or rules are ones easier to produce or perceive; (h) *morphology* Natural categories

are not zero encoded, i.e. they have some exponent; (i) *syntax*: Natural rules or categories are ones with a perceptual or production function; and (j) *mappings* Natural rules do not produce intermediate forms that are not also acceptable surface forms. Language system-external properties include: (a) *language acquisition*: Natural rules and categories are acquired earlier or less subject to suppression; (b) *speech errors*: Natural rules or categories are less subject to error; (c) *language disturbance*: Natural rules or categories resist breakdown longer; (d) *language death*: Natural rules or categories are longer survivors in the dissolution of a language.

The area of linguistic naturalness with the largest literature is undoubtedly phonological naturalness. Much of this interest arose from reactions to the influential *The sound pattern of English* (SPE) by Chomsky and Halle (1968). According to Darden (1974) these reactions can be divided into controversies about five issues.

One specific and voluminous area of controversy in generative phonology in the post SPE era bears on the degree of *abstractness* of phonological representation. The SPE model assumes that an underlying or abstract form is mapped by rules onto a concrete, surface phonetic form. If no restrictions are placed on potential rules or representation then nothing prevents one from assuming underlying forms quite "distant" from the surface. Some of the major research supporting a more abstract phonology includes especially Gussmann (1980). Those works favoring a more restricted and concrete "natural generative phonology" include Hooper (1976) and Vennemann (1974).

The central ideas in neutral generative phonology (NGP), according to Hooper and Vennemann, are threefold: (a) The *True generalization condition* requires that speakers formulate generalizations about the sound structure of their language to relate surface forms one to another, not rules relating underlying to surface forms; (b) the *No ordering condition* bars any (extrinsic) rule ordering; and (c) *Lexical representation* contains the words of a language, not just the stems plus rules on how to change them, e.g. *sing, sang* and *sung* would all be listed separately. These three conditions severely (the first named group of linguists above would say too severely) limit the type of grammars available to describe natural language phonology. In particular there could be no cases in NGP of *absolute neutralization*, sound segments that never survive to the surface of a language but which influence derivations, e.g. there would be no "silent *e*" in English phonology in *mute* that could be appealed to in accounting for the lack of *yu* in *mut* and *moot*.

A second area of controversy about naturalness in phonology concerns the manner of *evaluating competing analyses*. In SPE counting phonological features was considered the primary criterion. Therefore, the rounding of front vowels e → ö and the rounding of back vowels γ → o would require the same number of feature changes, i.e. the features (− round) would change to (+ round) or vice versa. However, in terms of natural properties such as frequency, change, acquisition etc., back vowels round far more easily than front vowels. What is needed, say those favoring a more natural approach, is some universal theory of phonological markedness, a set of principles assigning segments "markedness values" and characterizing the "markedness status" of rules.

The third area addressed by those advocating naturalness in phonology concerns *distinctions in types of rules*, and Vennemann (1974) argues that one must treat differently phonetically conditioned and morphologically or lexically conditioned changes. For instance, the first can be illustrated with the backing of a nasal when followed by a back consonant, e.g. *ban* vs. *bang*; the second by the insertion of vowels before an *s*-plural whenever the noun stem ends in an *s*-like-sound, e.g. rat*es*, mod*es*, wav*es* vs. fa*ces*, ca*ges*, chur*ches*. In the first example reference need be made only to the phonological composition of the string; in the second reference has to be made to a morphological category *plural*. Vennemann (1974) advocates a lexicon of "words" (instead of morphemes, affixes, etc.) listing all forms of a paradigm separately with rules within the lexicon relating the various forms. For regular paradigms the rules are highly redundant; for suppletive paradigms, such as *go:went:gone*, the rule would be correspondingly idiosyncratic. These two rule types would be in different components of the grammar and would fulfill different functions.

The fourth area of interest of natural phonology is *sound change*. Bailey (1982) divides change into two subtypes: *connatural* and *abnatural* change. The first corresponds to system-internal unmarking, the reduction of markedness ("unnaturalness") because of internal pressure. Some sounds are less frequent, more subject to change, acquired by children later, etc. These tend to alter to forms with less cognitive cost (because less marked) by means of well-known phonological processes. For example, in old English a qualitative suffix -*th*[þ] was added to adjectives and some verbs, e.g. *long:length broad:breadth, wide:width*. If, however, the stem ended in a spirant such as -f or -x, which was spelled -*gh* and later disappeared from English, then this -*th* qualitative suffix changed via a phonological process called *dissimilation* into a -*t*, e.g. *high:height, drive:drift, dry:drought*. The system-internal motivation for this change rests in the phonetically implausible and difficult sequence of two spirants. Abnatural change, on the other hand, is change brought about by borrowing, for example. English has taken initial v-, z-, j-, as in *very, zest*, and *just*, from French, enlarging the inventory of distinctive sounds in the language, cf. Bloomfield (1933, p. 447). Bailey pleads that both natural changes, connatural and abnatural, are needed to maintain the natural balance of synthesis and analysis.

Finally, natural phonology has emphasized the role of *language acquisition* in theory construction. Especially prominent in this area have been the works in natural phonology, e.g. Stampe (1979). Stampe's major claim is that a child acquires the phonological rules and representations of his language by restricting and suppressing an innate, "language-innocent" inventory of unrestricted sounds and rules to just those of his environment. Three strategies children employ are: (a) *suppression* of one of two contradictory processes; (b) *limiting* the set of segments to which a rule applies; and (c) *ordering* a previously unordered pair of rules. Consonants become voiceless because oral constriction impedes the airflow required to cause phonation. Therefore, children must learn to suppress this pole of a pair in order to be able to produce a voice-voiceless contrast. As an example of limiting, children tend to devoice all final consonants as soon as they learn to produce postvocalic segments. Children acquiring English must then limit this rule's application just to those cases of voiceless consonants. German children do not need to learn to limit this rule, as German always devoices such final consonants. Examples of ordering in children's speech are too involved to present here, see Stampe (1979, pp. xiv-xv) for illustrations.

Naturalness in morphology is a more recent development than phonological naturalness. It has primarily been the product of European linguists. As Dressler (1982) characterizes it, morphological naturalness incorporates notions from: (a) language universals; (b) perception; (c) acquisition; (d) functionalism; (e) aphasia; and (f) language change. The most important investigator in this area is Mayerthaler (1980, 1981). In assessing morphological naturalness, he first assigns a cognitive value to a linguistic category, e.g. cognitively plurality is more marked (less natural) than singularity. Mayerthaler assigns a markedness value to the encoding of this cognitive category. The assessment of "natural" encoding of words is based upon laws. The Law of Iconicity demands, for instance, that something cognitively more marked be encoded iconically, by an additive exponent marking that asymmetry. Thus *boy:boys* is an unmarked encoding of plurality, whereas *foot:feet* is a marked encoding, since the contrast relies only on a modulatory and not an additive

strategy. The plural formation *fish:fish* is least desirable, i.e. is overmarked and quite subject to change, late acquisitions and errors.

A corollary to the Law of Iconicity is often called Humboldt's Universal and can be stated as: one form, one meaning. Encodings in the unmarked case should preserve perceptual constancy. A single exponent should not be used for more than one morphological function and each morphological category should, in the ideal case, have at most a single exponent. The English inflectional -*s* provides a striking counterexample to this universal, since it encodes three morphological categories: plurality, possession and third person singular present tense. A more typical instance of the pressure of Humboldt's Universal can be seen in the dislike native speakers have for those adverbs in -*ly* from adjectives that already end in -*ly*, cf. *Drive friendly!* (an actual US road sign) not *?Drive friendlily*.

Encoding is also subject to the effects of *Markedness Reversal*. A marked encoding may become unmarked in a marked environment, just as a person wearing clothing is marked in a nudist camp. Some objects naturally come in groups and rarely as individuals. These are examples, of marked environments and markedness reversal may occur. In English *police* is a natural plural and has an additively encoded singulative form *policeman*.

Naturalness in syntax has certainly played a less prominent role than naturalness in the previously discussed subdisciplines. Bartsch and Vennemann in unpublished work have proposed that the True Generalization Condition should be valid for syntax as well as for the phonology of natural language, claiming, for example, that *passive* is a rule relating two surface structures, not one connecting underlying forms. While use has been made of the properties of a natural rule, change, acquisition, breakdown etc., no comprehensive proposal has been made.   JAE

Bibliography

Bailey, Charles-James 1982: *On the yin and yang nature of linguistics*. Ann Arbor: Karoma Press.

Bloomfield, Leonard 1913: *Language*. New York: Holt, Rinehart and Winston.

*Brock, A., Fox, R. and LaGaly, M. eds. 1974: *Papers from the parasession on natural phonology*. Chicago Linguistics Society.

Chomsky, Noam and Halle, Morris 1968: *The sound pattern of English*. New York, Evanston and London: Harper and Row.

Darden, Bill J. 1974: Introduction. In *Papers from the parasession on natural phonology*, eds. A. Brock, R. Fox and M. LaGaly. Chicago Linguistics Society.

Dressler, Wolfgang 1982: *Plenary session papers*. The XIIIth International Congress of Linguists. Tokyo. Japan.

Gussmann, Edmund 1980: *Studies in abstract phonology*. Cambridge, Mass. and London: MIT Press.

*Hooper, Joan 1976: *Introduction to natural generative phonology*. New York and London: Academic Press.

*Mayerthaler, Willi 1980: Morphologischer Ikonismus. *Zeitschrift für Semiotik* 2, 19–37.

—— 1981 : *Morphologische Natürlichkeit*. Wiesbaden: Athenaion.

Stampe, David 1979: *A dissertation on natural phonology*. New York and London: Garland.

Vennemann. Theo 1974: Words and syllables in generative grammar. In *Papers from the parasession on natural phonology*, eds. A. Brock, R. Fox and M. LaGaly. Chicago Linguistic Society.

logical thinking: developmental

Reasoning according to the formal rules of inference so that conclusions follow validly from premises. The most influential account of the development of logical thought is that of PIAGET. He argued that children between the ages of eight and eleven years, in the concrete operational period, are in possession of reversible mental operations which allow logical reasoning with respect to things and events in the immediate present. The concrete operational child is aware for example, that a superordinate class must include a subordinate class or that properties of substances are conserved despite changes in their appearance. However, the systems of mental operations remain relatively isolated from each other until adolescence and the advent of formal operations. Now the child can consider the possible as well as the actual and makes systematic deductions concerning the truth or falsity of relations between propositions. The developmental transition is from an intra- to an interpositional logic with an accompanying shift from concrete to abstract content. (See also REASONING.) GEB

Bibliography

Brainerd C.J. 1978: *Piaget's theory of intelligence*. New Jersey: Prentice-Hall.

Fischer, K.W., Hand, H.H. and Russell, S. 1983: The development of abstractions in adolescence and adulthood. In *Beyond formal operations*, eds. M.L. Commons, F.A. Richards and C. Armon. New York: Praeger.

Flavell, J.H. 1963: *The developmental psychology of Jean Piaget*. Princeton, N.J. and London: Van Nostrand.

longitudinal research *See* developmental psychology: methods of study; educational research: methodology.

M

machine learning The emulation of human knowledge acquisition processes through algorithms programmed for a digital computer system. The possibility of machines learning about the world and how to control it has been significant in engineering studies for many years with recent developments in control, communication and computer systems stemming from Norbert Wiener's concept of a science of *cybernetics* encompassing both man and machine.

In the past decade computers have been used increasingly for such studies and the scope has been broadened to cover all aspects of artificial intelligence including pattern recognition, perceptual-motor skills and linguistic activity (Winston 1984). The switch in emphasis has made it apparent that learning is only one aspect of human intelligence and that we have little hope of emulating the learning of a task if we are not able to emulate the final performance of that task.

The significance for education of work on machine learning and artificial intelligence is the insight into the processes of human learning and instruction. This has led to the use of the term cognitive science to cover all aspects of the study of intellectual processes whether in people or machines. For example much of the material published by Andreae (1977) on his *Purr Puss* learning system is concerned with the training techniques necessary to help the system to acquire knowledge. Work on expert systems (Michie 1979; Clancey 1985) which encode and emulate human skilled activity for practical purposes has led to new understanding of these skills which in turn makes it easier to teach them to people. More advanced COMPUTER-AIDED INSTRUCTION systems also incorporate artificial intelligence techniques in their operation (Sleeman and Brown 1981) but given the limited information available from the student–computer interaction there is still the problem of measuring even part of the student's knowledge structure. (See also PROGRAMMED INSTRUCTION.)   MLGS

Bibliography

Andreae, J.H. 1977: *Thinking with the teachable machine*. New York and London: Academic Press.

Clancey, W.J. 1985: Heuristic classification. *Artificial intelligence* 27, 289–350.

*Michie, D. ed. 1979: *Expert systems in the micro electronic age*. Edinburgh: Edinburgh University Press.

Sleeman, D.H. and Brown, J.S. eds. 1981: *Intelligent tutoring systems*. New York and London: Academic Press.

Sowa, J.F. 1984: *Conceptual structures – informational processing in mind and machine*. Reading, Mass.: Addison-Wesley.

*Winston, P.H. 1984: *Artificial intelligence*. 2nd edn. Reading, Mass.: Addison-Wesley.

mathematics Originally the collective name for arithmetic (computation), geometry and algebra, however mathematics today includes so many areas of study (such as number theory, calculus, topology, analytical geometry, set theory and its derivatives) that counter-examples could be found for almost any attempt at an inclusive definition. There are, moreover, considerable differences in viewpoint. A pure mathematician might describe mathematics as the study of internally consistent formal structures, derived by specified rules from logically compatible sets of axioms. 'We then take any hypothesis that seems amusing, and deduce its consequences. If our hypothesis is about *anything*, and not about some one or more particular things, then our deductions constitute mathematics', writes Russell (1929), going on to say that one of the chief triumphs of modern mathematics consists in having discovered what mathematics really is: it is identical with formal logic.

Although this approach has contributed to the development of mathematics as a rigorous intellectual discipline, the view of mathematics which it presents is incomplete. Gödel (1931 (1962)) has shown that the consistency of a formal system cannot be proved within the system itself. Nor does it offer any way of knowing which formal systems might be more usefully studied than others, since utility does not enter into this approach to mathematics. Referring to his mathematical activities, Hardy (1940) wrote 'I have never done anything *useful*'. Utility is however an essential feature of mathematics for those such as scientists, engineers, navigators, accountants and others who find it an essential tool for understanding, predicting and sometimes controlling events in their physical environment and to a lesser degree in their social environment. This accords with the viewpoint of Bruner (1966), who sees mathematics as a tool for amplifying human ratiocinative capacity.

The view which will here be developed is that mathematics is a particularly concentrated and powerful example of the functioning of human intelligence. The product of many minds, it is a cultural inheritance which, as emphasized by PIAGET (1952) and others, has to be constructed anew by each individual in his own mind. But when it has been acquired, it can greatly increase his ability to understand and control his environment.

This environment is bound to be variable. No two experiences are exactly the same: even the same object is seen on different occasions at varying distances, angles of view, differently lit. Learning is possible only because we are able to discover common properties of experiences, and store them mentally in such a way that we can recognize them on future occasions. This mental representation of a common property is what we call a concept; and the process of "pulling out"

similarities and ignoring differences is called abstracting. Classifying is thus a basic activity in intelligent learning; and the concept of a set, which is a well-defined class, is a basic concept of contemporary mathematics.

Whenever we see or hear something in our physical environment which we recognize, a concept has been evoked. By attaching symbols to them, however, these concepts can be evoked independently of the environment. They become mental objects which can be manipulated, contemplated, organized. We can string them together to form a plan for action; and from several alternative plans, we can choose that which we think most likely to achieve our purpose. More: we can use our classifying ability at a higher level, by grouping concepts themselves together, abstracting another common property, and thereby forming a higher order concept. Having through our senses discovered regularities of the physical world, by mental activity we go on to discover regularities among these regularities, and so on to find higher and higher order regularities. This process of repeated abstraction is particularly characteristic of mathematics, resulting in concepts which in spite of their highly abstract quality have again and again proved their power in helping us to understand, and achieve our goals in, the physical world. How can this be?

Any plan of action depends for its success on having some kind of mental representation of the physical environment: or rather, of those features of the environment which matter for the success of the plan. A stereotyped plan, appropriate only to a particular category of situations, is a habit. Habits are closely tied to action, and lack adaptability. Moreover, given the variety of situations in which we find ourselves, the learning and remembering of a sufficient set of habits to deal with all these situations imposes ever-increasing cognitive strain. A much more effective way to store the necessary information is in the form of a conceptual structure, in which are embodied and interrelated regularities abstracted from a wide variety of experiences. These conceptual structures correspond to the schemata of Bartlett (1932), and the conceptual maps of Tolman (1948). (The term SCHEMA is used differently by Piaget, and is more closely tied to action.)

Within an appropriate conceptual structure, a mental model can be formed of a particular situation or class of situations, at whatever level of generality is most useful for a particular purpose. From such a model can be derived predictions of particular events, and plans to achieve particular goals. The wider the variety of actual situations which can be modeled within a particular schema, and the greater the number of possible plans which can be derived from this model, the more powerful for action is this organization of knowledge.

The abstract, general, and thereby powerful, schemata of mathematics contain possibilities for constructing models of such a wide variety as to be remarkable when we begin to consider it. Space allows no more than two examples. First, the natural numbers. Each particular number is a property abstracted from a set of sets, ignoring both the nature of the objects and their spatial configuration, and collecting together those sets whose members can be put in one-to-one correspondence. In such a way we might get the concept 4. Other collections of sets might give rise to the concepts 7, 3. We now have the beginning of a set of new concepts, alike in one way (they are the property of *any* set of sets chosen in the way described) and different in other ways. On the basis of their similarity we call all of these concepts numbers, and on the basis of their differences we can begin to organize our new set of numbers; e.g. by putting them in order, 3, 4, 7. We also see gaps to be filled; and the sequence invites extrapolation, upward and downward. Even at this level, the process of mental creativity is evoked. Still at the level of natural numbers, there is much else which space does not allow to be even touched on here. Further abstraction takes us into algebra, in which statements such as $a(p+q) = ap+aq$ represent what is common to an

infinite number of particular cases such as $7(5 + 8) = 7 \times 5 + 7 \times 8$, just as each of these represents an infinite number of possible statements about actual objects.

In combination with the concept of a unit, we now have an extensive and multi-purpose schema from which particular models can be constructed to represent almost any physical object or event. Thus, with appropriate units, $a/b = c$ can represent the relationship between distance, time and speed (so we can use it to plan a car journey or run an airline). It can represent the relationship between electrical power, electromotive force ("voltage"), and current (so we can decide whether to use a 3A or 13A fuse). It can represent the relationship between mass, volume and density (so we can decide how much buoyancy material we need for our lifejacket). The fact that we use different letters as mnemonics for what they represent should not cause us to overlook that mathematically,

$$\frac{d}{t} = s, \frac{W}{E} = I, \frac{m}{v} = d$$

are the same. By simply changing the units, we have adapted them for very different jobs; and this adaptability is a key feature both of intelligence in general, and of mathematics as a special case.

As a second example, consider $\sin\theta$. (We shall assume knowledge of this concept, and use it to illustrate the present argument further.) Some of the lower order regularities on which it is based are: sets of similar triangles; ratio and proportion; angles in general, and right angles in particular; measures of length (involving an expansion of the concept of counting number to measuring number); and a relation between the first and second of these, that for any set of similar triangles, the ratios of the lengths of pairs of corresponding sides are in the same proportion. This illustrates the concentration of conceptual information, nested within nests, which are handled by this concept. Now consider just three of the many situations for which $\sin \theta$ can act as a model. One is navigation. Here, one

155

triangle is small enough to go on a map or chart, the other (though not actually drawn) is on the earth's surface. Another is in optics. By combining this with the preceding model we get

$$\frac{\sin i}{\sin r} = \mu$$

which some will recognize as Snell's law describing a regularity in the change of direction of a ray of light as it passes from air to glass, from air to water, or between any other two transparent media. A third use of this concept gives the instantaneous value of an alternating current, in the formula $I = I_{max}\cos_{wt}$.

The reader is invited to seek for himself other examples of the multi-purpose nature of mathematical concepts; and also of their high level of abstraction, since this is one of the major stumbling blocks in the learning and teaching of mathematics (Hughes 1983).

As we have seen, one of the strengths of mathematics is the way in which it enables its users to handle a great concentration of information within a small number of highly abstract concepts. A consequence of this is that a few lines of mathematics contain as much information as perhaps a page or more of less abstract material. In teaching mathematics, it is easy to overlook this, and give out information faster than it can be taken in by the learner.

We have also seen how at every stage, the learning of new mathematical concepts is dependent on the learner having already available an appropriate conceptual structure. Learning with understanding takes place if and only if the new concepts are assimilated to this schema. If teaching is not carefully sequenced in such a way that the progressive building up of the successive levels of abstraction can take place, genuine mathematical understanding is impossible and the learner can only, at best, resort to the rote memorizing of rules without reasons.

Yet another way in which learners can go astray is in their conception of the nature of the learning task. The situation in which pupils are placed conduces to the belief that what they are supposed to be learning is a collection of methods for getting right answers to mathematical questions (see Lawler 1985). The true nature of the task, however, is threefold. First, they need to construct in their own minds mathematical schemata, i.e. conceptual structures of the abstract and hierarchical kind already described. Second, they need to learn how to derive from these schemata particular methods for particular tasks. For novel tasks, this constitutes problem-solving ability. Many mathematical tasks are however of kinds frequently encountered, so it is also desirable to build up a set of ready-to-hand methods by which routine tasks can be done with a minimum of effort. This also has the advantage, when these routine tasks occur within a context of problem-solving, of freeing attention to concentrate on the novel, which is to say the problematic, aspects of the tasks. Thirdly, it is necessary to acquire fluency and accuracy in the execution of these tasks. These three components of mathematical ability we may call knowing-that, knowing-how, and being able. In combination, they form one of the most powerful and adaptable mental tools which mankind has yet devised. RRS

Bibliography

Bartlett, F. 1932: *Remembering*. Cambridge: Cambridge University Press.

Bruner, J.S. 1966: *Towards a theory of instruction*. Cambridge, Mass.: Harvard University Press.

*Chapman, L.R. ed. 1972: *The process of learning mathematics*. Oxford and New York: Pergamon.

Ginsburg, H. ed. 1983: *The development of children's mathematical thinking*. New York and London: Academic Press.

Gödel, K. 1931 (1962): *On formal undecidable propositions*. New York: Basic Books.

Hardy, G.H. 1940: *A mathematician's apology*. Cambridge: Cambridge University Press.

Hughes, M. 1983: What is difficult about learning arithmetic? In *Early childhood development and education*, eds. M. Donaldson, R. Grieve and C. Pratt. Oxford: Blackwell.

Lawler, R.W. 1985: *Computer experience and cognitive development*. Chichester: Ellis Horwood.

*Newman, J.R. 1956: *The world of mathematics*. New York: Simon and Schuster.

Piaget, J. and Szeminska, A. 1952: *The child's conception of space*. London: Routledge and Kegan Paul.

Resnick, L.B. 1985: Constructing knowledge in school. In *Development and learning: conflict or congruence?* Eds. L. Liben and D. Feldman. Hillsdale, N.J.: Erlbaum.

Russell, B. 1929: *Mysticism and logic*. New York: Norton.

*Skemp, R.R. 1971: *The psychology of learning mathematics*. Harmondsworth: Penguin.

*——— 1979: *Intelligence, learning, and action*. New York and Chichester: Wiley.

Tolman, E.C. 1948: Cognitive maps in rats and men. *Psychological review* 55, 189–208.

menarche The onset of menstruation in adolescence. It takes place relatively late in the developmental sequence of puberty, always after the peak growth velocities have been reached. On average, it occurs at 12.9 years, 3.3 years after the onset of the ADOLESCENT GROWTH SPURT and 1.1 years after peak height velocity is attained (see Frisch and Revelle 1970). Timing is influenced by genetic factors, nutrition, illness and geographical location. There is evidence that the age of menarche has been decreasing during the last century by a few months each decade although the trend may have slowed down (see Tanner 1978). The causation of this secular trend remains controversial but it has been linked with improved nutrition, general health and standards of living. The age of onset has different psychological consequences. Early menarche associated with precocious puberty may generate a negative self-image stemming from feelings of isolation and difference from peers but generally delayed menstruation is not a source of distress. WL.IP-J

Bibliography

Frisch, R.E. and Revelle, R. 1970: Height and weight at menarche and a hypothesis of critical body weights and adolescent events. *Science* 169, 397.

Tanner, J.M. 1978: *Foetus into man*. London: Open Books; Cambridge, Mass.: Harvard University Press.

menopause The permanent cessation of menstruation occurring during the middle period of life. It is associated with the end of ovulation and with atrophy of the female reproductive organs. It is not known to occur in other mammals, and its evolutionary origin is probably associated with the prolonged period of infant care in humans.

Symptoms specific to the menopausal period include vasomotor, genital and psychological changes. Some normal aspects of aging (e.g. dryness of the skin, loss of proteins from the bones, leading to brittleness, or osteoporosis) – are exaggerated by aspects of the postmenopausal bodily state, such as lack of estrogen.

The most common and well known vasomotor symptom is the hot flush, produced by impairment of the neural mechanism controlling the blood vessels, and this may be further exaggerated by emotional factors. The principal symptoms affecting urinary and sexual functioning are dryness of the vagina and the urethra. Psychological symptoms such as irritability, depression, insomnia and feelings of nervousness, as well as general somatic symptoms such as headaches and giddiness, are also reported.

While the main physical changes (hot flushes, genital symptoms) probably result from declining estrogen levels, the cause of the psychological changes is controversial. One view is that they derive directly from a change in hormone balance, specifically from the decline in estrogen levels. Another is that they result from the physical consequences of hormonal changes, e.g. sweating or incontinence may lead to insomnia, and hence to tiredness and irritability, which produce further interpersonal conflicts and stresses, and eventually depression. A third view is that any symptoms of a decline in general health, or signs of depression or emotional problems occurring around the time of menopause will be attributed (generally incorrectly) to it. Major stresses, mostly involving the death of close friends and relatives, or children leaving home, often coincide with the time of the menopause. These stresses could be responsible for many of the general health and psychological symptoms.   JA

Bibliography

Bart, P.B. 1971: Depression in middle-aged women. In *Women in sexist society*, eds. V. Cornick and B.K. Moran. New York: Basic Books.

Newman, B.M. 1982: Mid-life development. In *Handbook of developmental psychology*, ed. R.B. Wolman. Englewood Cliffs, N.J.: Prentice-Hall.

Weideger, Paula 1975: *Menstruation and menopause*. New York: Knopf; London: Women's Press, 1978 (*Female cycles*).

mental handicap Can be defined as 'that condition where intellectual deficit is associated with social, physical or psychiatric handicap, and requires special services or treatment' (Corbett 1977). (Mental handicap is also sometimes used to describe conditions where intellectual deficit appears to be present because of social inadequacy resulting from chronic psychiatric disorder. This has led to much confusion, and the term is not used in this sense here.)

Intellectual deficit is assessed by standardized tests of intelligence, such as the Wechsler Adult Intelligence Scale (WAIS) (see WECHSLER SCALES). An INTELLIGENCE QUOTIENT of less than two standard deviations below the mean (i.e. an IQ of less than 70) is usually taken as the cut off point for legal and administrative purposes. There are two main categories of mental handicap, mild (IQ 50–70) and severe (IQ below 50). Most severe mental handicap is associated with organic brain disease.

A number of epidemiological surveys in various countries have reported the incidence of mild mental handicap to be 20–30 per 1,000 population, and the incidence of severe mental handicap between 3 and 4 per 1,000 population aged 15–19. Variations in findings are related to differences in the concepts of mental handicap used – some studies base their findings on measures of IQ alone; others use a combination of IQ and social criteria. There is a strong association between mild mental handicap and low socioeconomic status: poor housing, overcrowding, poverty, poor nutrition, inadequate stimulation and education.

The commonest genetic cause of mental retardation is DOWN'S SYNDROME (mongolism) – a chromosome abnormality accounting for 25 per cent of severely retarded hospitalized patients. Other genetic conditions include the inherited metabolic disorders (e.g. phenylketonuria); tuberose sclerosis; neural tube defects. Clinically, these disorders are recognized by the presence of various physical abnormalities with intellectual deficit. Some conditions (e.g. the chromosome abnormalities) can be diagnosed antenatally if amniocentesis is undertaken. Although genetic defects cannot be corrected, there are some genetic conditions where treatment is possible to prevent further intellectual impairment (e.g. a special diet for phenylketonuria; surgical treatment of hydrocephalus associated with spina bifida). In mild mental handicap, it is believed that polygenic inheritance plays an important part, in association with the adverse social circumstances already described. Incidentally, there is some evidence that children of mentally handicapped parents tend to have higher IQs than their parents ("regression to the mean").

The distribution of intelligence in the population means that a certain proportion of mentally handicapped people are to be expected as a result of normal variation. During pregnancy, the growth and development of the fetus's brain and nervous system can be harmed in a variety of ways: e.g. by maternal infections such as rubella (German measles); high blood pressure or toxemia which affects placental function; antenatal hemorrhage; rhesus incompatibility; drugs such as thalidomide; poisons such as coal gas; alcohol and smoking. During birth, damage may occur from birth trauma, lack of oxygen or low blood pressure. In the immediate postnatal period, the damaging factors include neonatal seizures, infection, hypoglycemia (low blood sugar), hypothermia, severe jaundice, intraventricular hemorrhage, and the other complications of prematurity, such as the respiratory distress syndrome. Trauma to the skull and underlying brain may be caused accidentally during this period, or as a result of non-accidental injury (child abuse). Brain infections (meningitis, encephalitis), prolonged hypoxia due to respiratory or cardiac arrest, poisoning by carbon monoxide or lead may all cause mental handicap in a previously normal child. Infantile spasms, a form of epilepsy which develops during the first year of life, may also be accompanied by mental handicap.

Children with severe mental handicap present early in childhood with delay in attaining their developmental milestones, together with the signs of any accompanying physical disorder (e.g. cerebral palsy). Most of these children will be recognized during their first year of life. Some, such as those with Down's syndrome, will be recognized at birth, and their parents given a prediction of the degree of mental handicap to be expected.

Mild mental handicap may go unnoticed until the child starts school, or even later if little attention is paid to educational achievement. Learning problems or behavior disturbance in the school setting will then alert the teacher to the need for psychometric assessment by a psychologist. The finding of low scores on all subtests of intelligence will confirm intellectual deficit and the child will then be placed in an appropriate educational environment, such as a special unit or school. (See EDUCATION OF HANDICAPPED CHILDREN.) Occasionally, previously unrecognized mentally handicapped adults present with behavior disturbance when faced with a life stress such as the death of their parents, or a change in management of the firm where they have been happily carrying out a simple job for years.

In addition to general intellectual deficit a full assessment of individual difficulties may then reveal handicap in any (or all) of the following areas:

Physical: defects of motor coordination and movement, hearing, vision or speech; epilepsy occurs in 30 per cent of severely retarded children.

Social: problems may range from social incompetence (inability to ask for and follow directions, handle money, use a telephone, etc.) to antisocial behavior (masturbating or urinating in public, taking other people's possessions, making overt sexual advances in public).

Psychiatric: children and adults with intellectual deficit have an increased risk of psychiatric disorder. This is accounted for by many factors, including brain malfunction, temperament, immaturity, the effects of social rejection, and institutional care. The types of psychiatric disorder seen are the same as those occurring in people of normal intelligence; i.e. conduct and emotional disorders in children; schizophrenia, affective psychoses, neuroses and personality disorders in adults. The following are more commonly associated with mental handicap: infantile AUTISM, HYPERKINETIC STATES, stereotyped repetitive movements and pica.

Prevention and treatment

It is now possible to prevent mental handicap in a number of ways such as:

GENETIC COUNSELING for prospective parents in cases where there is a high risk of the occurrence of an abnormal fetus.

Amniocentesis in pregnancy, detecting fetuses with genetic abnormalities such as Down's syndrome at a stage when termination of pregnancy can be considered.

Ultrasonic scanning in pregnancy to detect abnormalities such as spina bifida.

Careful antenatal and obstetric care.

Good neonatal care of the newborn baby, reducing brain damage caused by treatable conditions such as hypoglycemia, phenylketonuria and congenital hypothyroidism.

Rubella immunization of all schoolgirls, to prevent congenital rubella.

Enriching the child's environment in deprived areas, as was done in the Milwaukee early intervention program (see COMPENSATORY EDUCATION).

Additional social and psychiatric handicaps may be preventable by early recognition of mental handicap through developmental screening. The family can then be supported from an early stage, and helped to develop the child's skills and counter any behavior problems before they become established. Later, appropriate school and occupational placement; training in social skills; improving the quality of institutional care; and changing society's attitude toward the mentally handicapped from rejection to acceptance may all contribute to the prevention of other difficulties.

A number of research studies have now shown that mentally handicapped adults and children in longstay hospitals have fewer skills, more disturbed behavior and a lower level of functioning than those living at home or in small "family" units. This has led to a reappraisal of the role of hospitals in the care of the mentally handicapped. There is growing acceptance of the view that this should be limited to the short-term treatment of problems such as disturbed behavior, seizure control or psychiatric illness, except for the most severely mentally and physically handicapped who need continuous nursing care. Most others can be cared for much more appropriately in the community, in small group homes, foster homes, hostels, etc. Special secure facilities may be necessary for adolescents and adults whose aggressive or antisocial behavior cannot be contained in any other setting.

The mentally handicapped living in the community need education, occupation, recreation and opportunities to take part in as many everyday activities as possible. Their families need support – financial, practical and emotional – and opportunities for relief from the stresses of coping with a handicapped child or adult for shorter or longer periods. Children and their families can often attend a pediatric department or assessment center, which provides a range of assessment and treatment facilities. In some areas preschool counselors or specially trained health visitors visit at home to provide stimulation for the child and guidance for the parents. Attendance at the nursery class of a special school can start when the child is two and continue to sixteen, or even

longer in some cases. Short-term care is usually provided through foster parents or children's homes. Resources for adults are often scarce. They should include different types of living accommodation, to meet their varying levels of dependency; and provide short- and long-term care; and a range of occupational activities, e.g. Adult Training Centers, sheltered workshops or sheltered employment. Community based multidisciplinary teams of professionals (psychologists, nurses, social workers, etc.) are available in many areas to offer expert help with specific problems and support families. Voluntary organizations also form an important part of the network of community support and often provide valuable resources through fund raising activities.

The life expectancy for the mentally handicapped is now greater than ever before, and many are reaching their sixties and seventies. Where there is an underlying physical condition the severity of this, and its treatability, will affect life expectancy. The prognosis for associated behavioral and psychiatric difficulties depends on a number of factors including the family background, placement in an institutional environment, and the availability of occupation and training facilities.

GCF

Bibliography

Caldwell, B.M., Bradley, R.H. and Elardo, R. 1975. Early intervention. In *Mental retardation and developmental disabilities*, vol. 7, ed. E.J. Wortis. New York: Brunner/Mazel.

Corbett, J. 1977. Mental handicap – psychiatric aspects. In *Child psychiatry, modern approaches*, ed. M. Rutter. Oxford: Blackwell Scientific; Philadelphia: Lippincott.

Ellis, N.R. and Bray, N.W. eds. 1985: *International review of research in mental retardation*, vol. 13. New York and London: Academic Press.

Tizard, J. 1960: Residential care of mentally handicapped children. *British medical journal*, 1041–6.

meta-memory Knowledge of the processes involved in information storage and retrieval that can be used voluntarily to regulate remembering. Many developmental psychologists have noted improvements with age in meta-memory.

The child or adult who has some awareness of the workings of his or her own mind will make use of this knowledge in memorizing new materials. For example, new information will be systematically categorized before being committed to memory. This knowledge is complemented by an awareness of the nature of forgetting, so that external memory aids such as a diary or a knot in a handkerchief come to be used as reminders. In both examples, the ability to "reflect" upon the memory process enables the voluntary introduction of superordinate monitoring and control processes. Other meta-mnemonic processes include checking, planning, testing, revising and evaluation.

Meta-memory is an aspect of reflective self-awareness, the capacity to think about one's own cognitive processes. Like other forms of knowledge, children's meta-cognition undergoes systematic changes with development.   GEB

Bibliography
Brown, A.L., Bransford, J.D., Ferrara, R.A. and Campione, J.C. 1983: Learning, remembering, and understanding. In *Handbook of child psychology*. 4th edn, vol. 3, eds. J.H. Flavell and E.M. Markman. New York: Wiley.
Fabricius, W.V. and Hagen, J.W. 1984: Use of causal attributions about recall performance to assess metamemory and predict strategic memory behavior in young children. *Developmental psychology* 20, 975–87.
Flavell, J.H. and Wellman, H.M. 1977: *Metamemory*. In *Perspectives on the development of memory and cognition*, eds. R.V. Kail and J.W. Hagen. Hillsdale, N.J.: Erlbaum.

methodology *See* developmental psychology: methods of study.

mid-life crisis A term denoting any of several types of behavior in the middle years, from the private awareness of the finitude of the life span to the life style rearrangements of career change or divorce and remarriage. The term was introduced to describe phenomena which arise as a consequence of demographic changes – increased longevity and the quickening of the life cycle of the family, producing a normative expectation of an extended post-parental period. Increased scientific attention to the middle years has shown that this middle phase of life is not a plateau but a time of changes, and has given rise to the popular term "mid-life crisis". The awareness of biological decline, the irrevocability of decisions made earlier in the life cycle, possible stagnation in marriage and career, declining opportunities with advancing age: in brief, intrinsic and extrinsic causes, maturational, social and existential, contribute to change as well as to the sense of crisis in middle life. Costa et al. (1983), however, provide evidence that the experience of a crisis in mid-life is a result of a consistently neurotic personality rather than any particular stage of development.
                ND

Bibliography
Costa, P.T., McCrae, R.R. and Arenberg, D. 1983: Recent longitudinal research on personality and aggression. In *Longitudinal studies of adult psychological development*, ed. K.W. Schaie. New York and London: Guilford.
Norman, William H. and Scaramella, Thomas J. eds. 1980: *Mid-life: developmental and clinical issues*. New York: Brunner/Mazel.

mirror-phase Moment in infant development postulated by Jacques Lacan (1936), based on infant observation, animal ethology and psychoanalysis of adults. Between six and eighteen months, infants exhibit a characteristic fascination with their image in a mirror – or similar surface such as the mother's eyes – a moment of watchful jubilation, often punctuated by an inquiring look to an accompanying adult. Lacan sees in this moment the foundation of the EGO; the mirror-image is taken as the ideal ego, representing a self-sufficient unity in contrast with the child's sense of its own powerlessness and incoordination: it finds itself in this first "other", its own image. In seizing on its image as its self, this initial alienating identification is typical of the ego's primary function: misunderstanding, misrecognition and, more broadly, fantasy. Language (the Symbolic) allows the child to find a way out of the aggressive dyadic mirror-relation to the other (Imaginary), leaving as a residue the Real (that which cannot be symbolized).   JF

Bibliography

Lacan, J. 1936 (1977): The mirror stage as formative of the function of the I as revealed in psychoanalytic experience. In *Écrits: a selection*. Trans. A. Sheridan. London: Tavistock; New York: Norton.

moral development Psychologists' definition of the "moral" broadly encompasses the avoidance of anti-social action and the performance of pro-social (altruistic) action. There are several different approaches to the explanation of moral development which reflect differing assumptions about basic human nature, and about the desirable outcomes of moral development; for example, conformity to social norms versus autonomy.

We can outline three approaches to moral development by asking three questions. Firstly, how does the individual come to be a properly socialized member of the society into which he or she is born? This is about the acquisition of good habits and constraining motives, and learning how and when to conform. It implies the development of "character"; a set of virtues, enduring traits and consistency of action. Secondly, how does the individual come to be able to make moral decisions? Behind this question is the assumption that a moral act has to be *intended* in order to be deemed "moral". However, within this approach action itself is less important than how the individual comes to *understand the moral*, how he or she develops the ability to make a *reasoned moral judgment* about the behavior of self and others. Thirdly, why do otherwise apparently normal and virtuous people act cruelly or heartlessly, or allow others to perform such acts? "Bystander apathy" (failure to intervene in an emergency), obedience to "immoral" commands, and conformity to pressures which induce anti-social behavior or inhibit pro-social behavior all happen in ordinary life, and they can also be induced under laboratory conditions (Latané and Darley 1970; Milgram 1974; Zimbardo 1974). Such findings tend to undermine the conventional assumption that adequate socialization of individuals makes for predictably "moral" action. Clearly, *situational* factors and social processes are powerful agents in creating *immoral* behavior; perhaps they are also responsible for much *moral* behavior.

There are several different and conflicting assumptions behind these questions. One assumption is that most people will behave morally so long as the socialization process inculcating the right habits and motives has been adequate and successful. Another is that some people will behave more morally than others, especially under social pressure; in other words most people's morality is adequate for ordinary interpersonal encounters and for the maintenance of a reasonable level of honesty and virtue, but does not extend to the unusual or demanding situation. A third assumption is that social situations provide the main stimulus to action (or inaction), and that individual variability in socialization or level of moral development at best mediates or moderates these social processes.

Developmental explanations of morality can be broadly divided into models of acquisition and models of growth. The first imply that morality is *learnt*: through conditioning and learning individuals acquire the motives of guilt, shame (see GUILT AND SHAME) and concern for others, and these constrain and regulate their behavior. Habits, skills and values become internalized in the individual and provide a repertoire of behavior and appropriate responses. The child comes to *monitor* its own behavior. According to this model, effective moral development depends upon effective reinforcement, and the kind of relationship with adults which provides good role models and good conditions for imitation and identification. Development is a slow process of acquiring habits and motives and strengthening conscience (Aronfreed 1976).

In contrast, according to *growth* models, moral development progresses through *transformation* and *restructuring*. Development is *change*, not accumulation. This model has been applied to the study of moral reasoning. Moral reasoning reflects the way the individual makes sense of the world, how he or she conceptualizes the rules and norms which govern behavior. The individual does not acquire *more* rules or learn of more rights and duties but develops greater *understanding* of the *function* of rules and norms, and comes to take into account more factors in the situation, and more points of view on the issues. Progress and development results in more *differentiation* and greater integration of these factors and perspectives. Kohlberg has proposed six stages of moral reasoning. Each stage is a consistent system of moral reasons. Kohlberg's stages are shown in the table.

KOHLBERG'S SIX STAGES IN THE DEVELOPMENT OF MORAL JUDGMENT

Level 1 – Preconventional level

STAGE I Punishment and obedience orientation – the physical consequences of an action determine its goodness or badness. Unilateral respect for authority, law defined by the voice of authority, avoidance of punishment reason for doing right.

STAGE II Instrumental relativist orientation – right action consists of that which instrumentally satisfies one's own needs and occasionally the needs of others. Concern with "fairness" and reciprocity, in a pragmatic, quid pro quo, sense.

Level 2 – Conventional level

STAGE III Interpersonal concordance or "good-boy-nice-girl" orientation – good behavior is that which pleases or helps others and is approved by them. Conformity to stereotyped images of what is "natural" behavior. Emphasis on good intentions and being "nice", mutuality of relationships, concern for others.

STAGE IV "Law and order" orientation – importance of maintaining social order, obligations, social duties, to avoid breakdown of system. Law and constituted authority ultimate arbiters. Emphasis on doing one's duty, public and societal function of which is perceived.

Level 3 – Post-conventional level

STAGE V Social contract legalistic orientation – utilitarian overtones, concern with individual rights and the greatest good for the greatest number. Awareness of the relativism of values and the fact that laws are agreed tools of social organization, and that they can be changed by discussion if they fail to fulfill social utility.

STAGE VI Universal ethical principle – right is defined by appeal to ethical principles. These principles are abstractions. Moral and legal rules are clearly separate, and the idiosyncrasy of each situation is recognized, and each dealt with on its own merits by an appeal to the abstract principle.

The emphasis in this approach is on cognitive processes and the organization of appraisal. The researcher elicits the individual's stage of moral reasoning by presenting him or her with hypothetical moral dilemmas. These dilemmas focus upon rights and justice and the conflict between legal and moral rules and obligations. Some critics, however, have argued that this is too narrow a definition of what constitutes the "moral"; the focus on justice and rights is peculiarly restricted to certain aspects of western industrial society. Gilligan has also argued that there is an important sex difference; women are more likely to think about moral questions in terms of relationships between people, and the interdependence of people which generates mutual responsibilities (Gilligan 1982). Kohlberg's longitudinal study was with males only, and the preoccupation with rights and justice may be more of a masculine style.

Kohlberg's original subjects were ten- to sixteen-years-old, and his longitudinal data cover twenty years of their thinking. There have been other, shorter, longitudinal studies and several cross-sectional studies of adolescents and adults. From this data it is clear that under good conditions a person will progress "through" a stage in about two and a half years. Most adults, however, do not reach post-conventional reasoning; the majority studied operate with stage 3 or stage 4. What are the implications of this? Is there a connection between moral reasoning and moral action? Does moral reasoning relate to reasoning about social or political issues? The evidence is that moral stage correlates *to a degree* with behavior, but it is not a straightforward relationship (Blasi 1980). Moral stage does not, on the whole, predict the avoidance of anti-social behavior, for example, cheating. On the other hand, moral stage does predict certain forms of pro-social behavior – particularly behavior stemming from action performed in support of a principle, or in defiance of pressures to conform (Kohlberg 1984). The most extensive data on this has come from several studies of student activism. These studies demonstrate a close relationship between political action and moral stage. In a study of "bystander intervention" McNamee found that higher stage individuals were considerably more likely to intervene to help someone in distress and to disobey the instructions of an experimenter in order to do so (1978). Milgram found that only post-conventional individuals resisted pressures to inflict electric shocks on a "subject" in a learning experiment (1974).

This is evidence of some relationship between judgment and action. So it would appear that the higher the level of moral reasoning, the more "moral" the behavior to be expected. However, studies which examine the relationships between cognitive processes and morality consistently indicate the importance of *appraisal* in moral reasoning *and* in moral action. If we consider first the stages of moral reasoning, what is clear is that people at different stages perceive the situation differently. Consequently, they perceive their own responsibility and involvement in the situation in different ways. Haan, Smith and Block's (1968) study demonstrated that students of different moral stages perceived what was going on in the confrontation at Berkeley differently. McNamee's study indicates that people at different stages had different perceptions as to whether they should help the distressed drug-user and whether they were personally responsible for giving such help. So, in fact, the relationship between moral reasoning and moral action is very complex. The actor, depending on his or her moral stage, interprets differently what is going on and what action is appropriate.

There are other cognitive perspectives on moral behavior besides those concerned with stages of moral reasoning. Hoffman (1984), for example, argues that *empathic motivation* is a source of moral, particularly pro-social, behavior. The basis of his argument is that EMPATHY depends upon the child's developing understanding of role-taking, and ability to take the perspective of the other. According to Hoffman, the state of sympathetic distress promotes action, but if action does not occur, the individual feels guilty. Guilt is a state which may promote further action, but guilt may also cause the individual to *redefine* the situation in such a way that the situation no longer induces sympathetic distress.

Another approach which focuses upon cognitive processes is *equity theory*. This approach explains altruistic behavior or pro-social intervention in terms of the observer's perception of *imbalance*; the injured or distressed person is in a state of *inequity* vis-à-vis the observer. To restore equity the observer must (a) act to remove or alter the injury or distress; (b) distort the situation by diminishing its importance; (c) degrade the victim; or (d) deny responsibility. This is not a model of empathic *affect*, but essentially a social *cognitive* model.

Models of character consistency have always been undermined by the early failure of Hartshorne and May to find satisfactory intercorrelations between different areas of morality. Since then, there has been a constant tension between approaches which treated each area of morality (resistance to temptation, guilt, altruism, moral judgment, etc) as separate entities, requiring different explanations, and approaches which sought some unifying overall theme. The unifying theme has usually been some concept of "moral competence", identified with strength of motive or consistency of character – allied to "will". The cognitivist perspective, in contrast, focuses upon the individual's appraisal of the situation and perception of responsibility for action within that situation. In a comprehensive review of the field, Rest (in Kurtines and Gewirtz 1984) has proposed that it is *cognitive* competence which relates (a) the complexity of moral judgment, (b) the individual's potential for action, and (c) the individual's own personally perceived responsibility for taking action. However, though this model presents an integration of judgment and action (including habits) it only partly integrates the affective element in morality.   HW-H

Bibliography

Aronfreed, J. 1976: Moral development from the standpoint of a general psychological theory. In *Moral development and behavior*, ed. T. Lickona. New York: Holt, Rinehart and Winston.

Blasi, A. 1980: Bridging moral cognition and moral action: a critical review of the literature. *Psychological bulletin* 88, 1–45.

Colby, A. et al. 1983: A longitudinal study of moral development. *Monographs of the Society for Research in Child Development* 200.

Gilligan, C. 1982: *In a different voice*. Cambridge. Mass: Harvard University Press.

Haan, N., Smith, M.B. and Block, J. 1968: Moral reasoning of young adults. *Journal of personality and social psychology* 10, 183–201.

Hoffman, M.L. 1984: Empathy, its limitations and its role in a comprehensive moral theory. In Kurtines and Gewirtz, op. cit.

Kohlberg, L. 1984: *Essays on moral development*, vol. 2. *The psychology of moral development*. San Francisco: Harper and Row.

Kurtines, W.M. and Gewirtz, J.L. eds. 1984: *Morality, moral behavior and moral development*. New York: Wiley.

Latané, B. and Darley, J.M. 1970: *The unresponsive bystander: why doesn't he help?* New York: Appleton-Century-Croft.

McNamee, S. 1978: Moral behavior, moral development and motivation. *Journal of moral education* 7, 27–32.

Milgram, S. 1974: *Obedience to authority*. New York: Harper and Row.

Snarey, J.R. 1985: Cross-cultural universality of social-moral development: a critical review of Kohlbergian research. *Psychological bulletin* 97, 202–32.

Zimbardo, P.G. 1974: On the ethics of intervention in human psychological research: with special reference to the Stanford prison experiment. *Cognition* 2, 243–56.

N

neo-Freudian theory A term used of the approach of psychoanalytic theorists who have rejected, added to, or modified significant portions of Freud's original theory. The term is used by different writers with varying levels of specificity. In its most general sense it can apply to a wide range of psychoanalytically-orientated psychologists whose theories diverge from Freud's in greater or lesser degree: in this sense for example, Carl Jung, Erik Erikson, Otto Rank and object relations theorists could all be considered neo-Freudians, even though ERIKSON accepts the basic premises of Freudian analysis while Jung rejects many of them. Usually, however, the term neo-Freudian is reserved for a smaller group of psychoanalysts whose theories share two core features: (1) they reject Freud's "libido theory", his view that the primary motivators in personality are innate biological instincts of sexuality and aggression which are specific to childhood; and (2) they correspondingly emphasize the importance of social needs, the influence of cultural and interpersonal factors and the role of the self in personality development.

The four theorists most frequently described as neo-Freudians in this more restrictive sense are Alfred Adler, Karen Horney, Erich Fromm and Harry Stack Sullivan. The following brief discussion first describes the major contributions of these thinkers and then summarizes what their theories have in common.

ADLER was born in Vienna in 1870. He was a member of the original small group of psychoanalysts which met at Freud's house to discuss analytic theory, and was the first president of the Vienna branch of the Psychoanalytic Society. He came to reject some basic tenets of Freud's theory, however, including the notion that sexual trauma is the basis for neurosis, and resigned from the society in 1911 to form his own school which he named *individual psychology*. Adler sees the person as a united whole, indivisible, responsible for his actions, free and striving towards conscious goals. The major tenets of his theory are contained in six key concepts:

1. *fictional finalism*, the notion that people are motivated not primarily by past events, but by their images and expectations for future possibilities;
2. *striving for superiority*, the individual's innate tendency to develop his capacities to the full and to strive for perfection;
3. *inferiority feelings*, which Adler sees as the normal response to the realization of being less than perfect and which motivate all efforts towards self-actualization;
4. *social interest*, the innate tendency to be interested in other people and in the social group, manifested in cooperation, empathy, altruism and, ultimately, the desire for a perfect society;
5. *style of life*, the different unique forms in which individuals strive for perfection; and
6. the *creative self*, the active, constructive center of personality which interprets experience and chooses a response to it.

Karen Horney was born in Germany in 1885. She was associated with the Berlin Psychoanalytic Institute from 1918 to 1932, then emigrated to the USA where she founded an association and a training institute. Horney saw herself as remaining within the Freudian tradition, though she tried to correct what she saw as the limitations of Freud's approach: his biological and mechanistic orientation. She accepted Freud's notions of psychic determinism, unconscious motivation and the importance of irrational emotional experience. The root of neurosis for Horney is the childhood experience of basic anxiety and the strategies adopted in response to it. The helpless, totally dependent child encountering rejection, inconsistency or harsh treatment from its parents, feels that its safety and fundamental security are threatened. The child can adopt various strategies to cope with this, and these can become permanent features of personality and eventually take on the status of needs in their own right. Horney catalogues ten of these neurotic needs; they all mirror needs of normal people, but in an unrealistic, exaggerated and insatiable form: for example, the need for perfection, for total love, for complete control. Horney does not believe that the experience of basic anxiety is an inevitable part of development; it can be avoided if the child is treated with love, respect and consistency.

Like Horney, Erich Fromm was born in Germany and emigrated to the United States in the early 1930s. Fromm's work was influenced by the writings of Karl Marx and by existentialism as well as by psychoanalytic theory. He calls himself a "dialectical humanist". The central notion in Fromm's theory is his description of the human condition. Humans, he says, are animals and thus part of nature; however, because of their distinctively human nature they are also more than an animal and experience a separation between themselves and the natural world and between themselves and other people. This separateness from the natural order gives human beings the freedom to choose their lives; this freedom gives human life its meaning and potential, but it also gives rise to anxiety. As a result, people often try to relinquish their freedom through conformity or submission to authorities. Like Freud and Adler, Fromm believes that there is a species-specific, innate human nature which is independent of culture. However he has also emphasized the role that social context plays in determining the way in which the individual deals with basic human needs. Different societies and different groups within society create particular types of "character". Moreover Fromm judges societies on the basis of how well they meet the basic human needs of their members; he argues that no present society makes an adequate job of this task, and calls the form of society that he believes would do so "Humanistic Communitarian Socialism".

More than any of the other neo-Freudians, Harry Stack SULLIVAN moved away from Freudian theory and articulated a model of personality that is thoroughly social and interpersonal. In fact Sullivan claims that the notion of personality, conceived in terms of the single individual, is hypothetical, an illusion. Personality, he argues, consists in the relatively enduring patterns of interpersonal relations which are manifested in our lives – our relations both with real others and with the imagined others which make up the content of our thoughts, feelings and fantasies. He was strongly influenced by social psychology and anthropology, particularly by George Herbert Mead and other theorists at the Chicago School of Sociology. He was born in 1892 in New York and trained as an analyst. Sullivan described six stages in personality development, each of which represents a new interpersonal constellation. In *infancy* the child relates to the mother via its oral activity towards the nipple and develops notions of the good and bad other, and the correct and the wrong other. In *childhood* with the beginning of language, the child begins to relate to playmates and to form more cognitive representations of others. In the *juvenile* period (first school) the child learns to relate to the peer group and to authorities outside the home. In *pre-adolescence* "chum" relations with same sex peers are central for learning cooperation, mutuality, reciprocity and intimacy. The development of patterns of heterosexual relationships become the focus in *early adolescence*, as puberty brings the beginning of the lust dynamism and this becomes differentiated from companionship and intimacy. Finally, in *late adolescence*, a long period of education in varying social roles and relations brings about the transition to the complexity of adult social living and citizenship.

All four theorists share several core orientations which characterize the neo-Freudian approach. First, they all take a more positive and optimistic view of human nature than does classical psychoanalysis; they stress the striving for self-actualization, for active adaptation to the environment and for social relatedness and harmony, in contrast to Freud's emphasis on antisocial impulses of sexuality and aggression. Where Freud sees the individual as in inevitable conflict with the society which demands restriction of his impulsive acts, the neo-Freudians propose a more harmonious relationship between the individual and society. They see social life as a fulfillment of basic human nature, not a repression of it. In addition, these writers pay as much attention to the role of conscious conflicts and experiences in adolescence and adulthood as to unconscious conflicts in early childhood. Finally, they stress the effects of the social milieu in determining personality. (See also FREUD; DEVELOPMENT: PSYCHOANALYTIC THEORIES.)

SB

Bibliography

Adler, A. 1927: *The practice and theory of individual psychology*. New York: Harcourt, Brace and World.

Ansbacher, H.L. and R.R. eds. 1956: *The individual psychology of Alfred Adler*. New York: Basic Books.

Fromm, Erich 1941: *Escape from freedom*. New York: Rinehart.

—— 1947: *Man for himself*. New York: Rinehart.

—— 1955: *The sane society*. New York: Rinehart.

Hall, C.S. and Lindzey, G. 1978: *Theories of personality*. 3rd edn. New York and Chichester: John Wiley.

Horney, K. 1942: *Self-analysis*. New York: Norton

—— 1950: *Neurosis and human growth*. New York: Norton.

Munroe, R.L. 1955: *Schools of psychoanalytic thought*. New York: Dryden Press.

Sullivan, H.S. 1953: *The interpersonal theory of psychiatry*. New York: Norton.

O

object permanence Knowledge of the continued material existence of an object, even when the object itself is not accessible to direct sensory awareness. In Piaget's theory, it is argued that the concept of object permanence is a belief that is only slowly acquired in development. Piaget's evidence was that babies below approximately eight months will not search manually for a hidden object but behave as though it has ceased to exist. This led him to suppose that "out of sight was out of mind" so far as the baby was concerned. (See PIAGET.)

An alternative is that the perception of object permanence is one of the constancies (Wishart and Bower 1985). Just as the size and shape of an object are perceived as invariant under transformation, so is the existence of an object perceived as continuing despite temporary occlusion. Hood and Willatts (1986), for instance, have found that infants a few months old reach for objects in the dark after the light is switched off. This shows that the object's invisibility is not in itself enough to make the infant forget it. The primary developmental problem may not lie in acquiring the concept of object permanence, but in making use of perceptually specified information to control manual search. (See also PERCEPTUAL AND COGNITIVE ABILITIES IN INFANCY.)   GEB

Bibliography

Hood, B. and Willatts, P. 1986: Reaching in the dark to an object's remembered position: evidence for object permanence in 5-month-old infants. *British journal of developmental psychology* 4, 57–65.

Piaget, J. 1937 (1954): *The construction of reality in the child*. New York: Basic Books.

Wishart, J.G. and Bower, T.G.R. 1985: A longitudinal study of the development of the object concept. *British journal of developmental psychology* 3, 243–58.

object relations A term used frequently by contemporary psychoanalytic writers, its shades of meaning reflecting a theoretical movement away from a model of the subject as isolated and biologically (instinctually) motivated toward a view which encompasses the subject's interactions with its surroundings – its interpersonal relations. Use of the word *object* to refer to persons derives from the commitment of psychoanalysts to an instinct theory. The object through which instinctual gratification is held to be achieved is usually a person, an aspect of a person or a symbolic representation of a person toward which the subject directs its actions or desires. Technically "object relations" refers to the mental representations of the self and other (the object) which are an aspect of ego organization and not to external interpersonal relationships. (See DEVELOPMENT: PSYCHOANALYTIC THEORIES; INSTINCT: PSYCHODYNAMICS; KLEIN.)   BBL

Bibliography

Greenberg, J.R. and Mitchell, S.A. 1983: *Object relations in psychoanalytic theory*. Cambridge, Mass.: Harvard University Press.

Oedipus and Elektra complexes After the Greek legends in which, respectively, King Oedipus inadvertently killed his father, and Elektra avenged the murder of her father by assisting in the murder of her mother, these terms refer in psychoanalytic personality theory to two clusters of mainly unconscious feelings and ideas which set in at the "phallic" stage of psychosexual development. The child's attachment to the opposite-sex parent becomes sexualized, so that the child wishes to possess him or her and get rid of the other parent. The boy's rivalry with the father produces "castration anxiety", the female parallel of which is "penis envy". The child deals with the associated anxieties by eventually "identifying" with the same-sex parent and "introjecting" his or her prohibitions as a basis for the primitive superego, and his or her positive values as ego ideal (Freud 1917, ch. 21). Some non-clinical studies of dreams and projective tests do seem to support some of the constituent hypotheses of these complexes (see Kline 1981, ch. 6).   NMC

Bibliography

Freud, Sigmund 1917: *Introductory lectures*, part 3. *Standard edition of the complete psychological works of Sigmund Freud*, vol. 16. London: Hogarth Press; New York: Norton.

Kline, Paul 1981: *Fact and fiction in Freudian theory*. 2nd edn. London and New York: Methuen.

ontogenetic sequence Set of stages in any model of development in which each organ or organ system undergoes a CRITICAL PERIOD of rapid growth and differentiation at a specific time and in a particular, fixed sequence. Failure to develop during the critical period dooms the organ or organ system, and thus the organism, to developmental defects. In psychology, the theory of FREUD is of this type. He considered the psychosexual development of the individual to undergo a similar series of critical periods, or stages: the oral stage, the anal stage, the Oedipal stage, the latency period, and the genital stage. Failure or fixation at any stage endangered the subsequent stages and the individual's development. (See also below, and EPIGENETIC SEQUENCE.) ND

ordered change theory Refers to a class of developmental theories describing human action over time in terms of an orderly and reliable sequence. Such theories are most frequent within the domain of child development, but in principle could apply within any branch of psychology concerned with cross-time pattern. A prime exemplar of an ordered change theory is Piaget's ontogenetic theory of cognitive development. As PIAGET argues, during normal development the quality of the child's thought undergoes a series of orderly transitions from the primitive and concrete to the abstract and adaptive. Ordered change theories may be contrasted with other theoretical forms emphasizing either cross-time stability in pattern or non-replicable, historically contingent trajectories.   KJG

P

peer group The concept is used in two different senses: first, as a term for a small group of friends or associates who share common values, interests and activities; second, as a term for virtually all persons of the same age, a definition which reflects the fact that schools tend to be age-graded. Peer group influence can therefore be the influence that friends exercise on one another or the influence exerted by a much wider category of age-mates. The term "peer-group influence" is generally restricted to discussions of young people or adolescents, despite the fact that there is little evidence that peer group influence among adolescents is either highly distinctive or greater than among other age groupings. Using the first sense of the term, educational researchers have drawn heavily on the theory of group dynamics in social psychology. The sources and effects of influence are related to concepts such as leadership, conformity and self-concept. Using the second sense of the term, researchers have been more interested in youth SUBCULTURES within any one of which many smaller friendship groups can be contained. The differences between subcultures are usually explained with reference to the broader social class subcultures in society.

In some studies, such as Coleman's classic account (1961), the different senses of peer groups and their influences are brought together. In most studies there is a tension, as yet not adequately clarified, between two ideas: on the one hand pupils come to school already sharing subcultural values which influence attitudes to school and educational achievements; on the other hand the school itself plays an active role in the formation of subcultures and friendship groups, perhaps especially in the forma-tion of oppositional (or counter-cultural) groups who are alienated by their school experience, and these peer groups then influence educational attitudes and aspirations. A further unresolved problem is that of determining the relative power of family and peer group to influence adolescents.

The subculture varies with age-level. In childhood, when dependence on parents is high, the peer group serves as an extension of the socialization mediated by the family and peer associates are likely to be governed by parents. In adolescence its quality and functions change as orientation shifts away from the family. The adolescent peer group may be part of a subculture that is at variance with the parental culture although generally its influence is congruent with parental values. The extent to which the peer group is relied upon by the adolescent as a reference group depends on the degree of estrangement from parents, parental attitudes to the peer group and the nature of the dilemma, since adolescents perceive parents and peers as useful guides in different areas (Brittain 1968). During adolescence the peer group plays an important part in providing social support and identity, although some of its pressures e.g. for conformity and social acceptability, may generate difficulties. Its effects may be important in the development of antisocial behavior and DELINQUENCY although they are difficult to estimate.

It is now widely recognized that research has hitherto focused excessively on peer groups which are male, working-class and deviant at the expense of groups which are female or middle class or non-deviant. This bias is being corrected in current research. DHH/WLIP-J

Bibliography

Bany, M.A. and Johnson, L.V. 1964: *Classroom group behaviour*. London and New York: Collier-Macmillan.

Brake, M. 1980: *The sociology of youth culture and youth subcultures*. London and Boston: Routledge and Kegan Paul.

Brittain, C.V. 1968: An exploration of the basis of peer-compliance and parent-compliance in adolescence. *Adolescence* 2, 445–58.

Coleman, J.S. 1961: *The adolescent society*. Glencoe Ill.: Free Press.

Conger, J.J. 1977: *Adolescence and youth: psychological development in a changing world*. New York: Harper and Row.

Hartup, W. 1983: Peer relations. In *Handbook of child psychology*, vol. 4, ed. E.M. Hetherington. 4th edn. New York: Wiley.

perceptual and cognitive abilities in infancy

Those processes and capacities that give rise to sensory experience, the acquisition of knowledge and the formation of beliefs during the first eighteen months of life. Research in this branch of developmental psychology has flourished in recent years and has challenged the popular conception of the young baby as an "incompetent" organism.

A particularly interesting aspect of this research is the light it throws on our philosophical assumptions concerning the original nature of mind. The traditional empiricist hypothesis, that much of perception is learned during the earliest months of life, has gradually given way as research has progressed to a nativist position which emphasizes the presocial, preadaptive organization of human sensory systems. Thus, although the motor abilities of the newborn are limited, the baby's sensory capacities are relatively well developed. The force of much recent research has been to show that even very young infants are well equipped to obtain information about their environment. All sensory systems are functional at or soon after birth; neonates are capable of discriminating odors, they show taste preferences, and are sensitive to visual, tactile and auditory stimulation (Werner and Lipsitt 1981).

Perhaps the most interesting questions about infant perception concern the structure of early experience. It is here that traditional theories have been most influenced by philosophical preconceptions concerning the nature and origins of space perception. The empiricist philosophers explained perception of an extended, three-dimensional space and perception of substantiality by the correlation of visual with tactual-motor experience during early infancy. Developmental theories based on these assumptions, such as Piaget's (1954), were naturally led to characterize the pre-locomotor infant as deficient in space perception and as lacking intersensory coordination. Investigators did not expect, and perhaps not surprisingly, did not find evidence for space perception or for sensory coordination in the first few months of life.

In recent years, however, an information based approach to perception has won increasing favor. The informative value of sensory stimulation was particularly stressed by Gibson (1966) in his theory of direct perception. He argued that the senses have evolved as perceptual systems whose function is to "pick up" information which specifies properties of objects and events. Perception is by means of invariant information that may be common to the various modalities, as well as modality specific. The developmental implication is that prolonged learning may not be necessary to extract significant information from sensory experience or to relate information obtained in one modality to another.

Among the first people to test this theory with young infants was Bower. He showed, in many studies with pre-locomotor babies (0–6 months), that they perceive visual constancy of size and shape and that their vision can specify some of the tangible properties of things before they have learned the invariant properties of objects by correlating vision with touch. Further evidence that perception is coherently organized came from Bower's studies of perception of the continued existence of objects that disappear temporarily from view (Bower 1979; Wishart and Bower 1985). Others have shown space perception in the pre-locomotor infant and auditory-visual coordination in neonates (see Butterworth 1981a). This has led to the gradual realization that even very young babies may be capable of sophisticated feats of perception, which in turn has prompted a re-examination of the origins of cognitive development in infancy.

While there is still an important function for active tactual and motor exploration in infancy, one implication of recent research on visual and auditory perception is that the distance senses (vision and audition) may also contribute in important ways to early experience through the mechanisms of selective ATTENTION and storage of information. For example, techniques for measuring auditory discrimination have shown that newborn babies are particularly sensitive to the intonation patterns and syllabic structure of speech (Bertoncini and Mehler 1981). Further insights into language relevant perceptual mechanisms have been obtained with the discovery that neonates can imitate movements of mouth and tongue (Meltzoff and Moore 1977; Abravanel and Sigafoos 1984). Attending to the visual configuration of the adult's mouth may help the infant in articulating his or her own speech sounds.

That there is an inborn ability for imitation may also have important implications for the development of social relations and the transmission of culture. Indeed, some theorists, notably Trevarthen (1982) have stressed that the primary function of infant sensory preadaptations is to allow babies to relate to other people.

There is evidence that a new phase of development begins at about forty weeks and may depend upon acquisition of the ability spontaneously to retrieve information from memory. The child can now coordinate its activities with people and things, bringing both social and physical worlds together in play; it will search for hidden objects and shows fear of strangers. These phenomena suggest that the baby now has access to stored information. (There is evidence that the infant stores information and recognizes things from

the neonatal period onwards; this new ability is to do with recall not simply recognition.) This capacity for representation develops rapidly so that by the end of infancy the child is well able to plan activities mentally before putting them into effect.

Another ability, easily observed in the second year of life, is the capacity to make elementary inferences. The baby will infer that if an object it has seen disappear cannot be found at one point along its path of movement, it must be elsewhere. Babies will search persistently for desirable objects even if their movements are not directly visible. Piaget (1937) says that this indicates that the baby has acquired the object concept, a belief in the permanence of objects. Coupled with an ability for delayed imitation (Piaget 1946) this may mark the beginnings of symbolism, the onset of language and the end of infancy. Although research on the perceptual abilities of young infants has led to a fundamental revision of the popular stereotype of the helpless, passive infant, we still know little of how fundamental sensory processes give rise in development to higher order capacities (see Carroll and Gibson 1986). The solution of this problem stands on a firmer base, now that the sophisticated perceptual capacities of babies have been recognized. (See also ADAPTATION IN INFANTS; CROSS-MODAL DEVELOPMENT; IMITATION; OBJECT PERMANENCE; PIAGET; SENSORI-MOTOR STAGE.)

GEB

Bibliography

Abravanel, E. and Sigafoos, A.D. 1984: Exploring the presence of imitation during early infancy. *Child development* 55, 381–92.

Bertoncini, J. and Mehler, J. 1981: Syllables as units in infant speech perception. *Infant behavior and development* 4, 247–80.

Bower, T.G.R. 1979: *Human development*. San Francisco: Freeman.

Butterworth, G.E. 1981a: The origins of auditory visual perception and visual proprioception in human development. In *Intersensory perception and sensory integration*, eds. R.D. Walk and H. Pick, Jr. New York: Plenum Press, 37–70.

—— ed. 1981b: *Infancy and epistemology: an*

evaluation of Piaget's theory. Brighton: Harvester; New York: St Martin's Press (1982).

Carroll, J.J. and Gibson, E.J. 1986: Infant perception of gestural contrasts: prerequisites for the acquisition of a visually specified language. *Journal of child language* 13, 31–49.

Gibson, James J. 1966: *The senses considered as perceptual systems*. Boston: Houghton Mifflin; London: Allen and Unwin (1968).

*Hofer, M.A. 1981: *The roots of human behavior*. San Francisco: Freeman.

Meltzoff, A. and Moore, M.K. 1977: Imitation of facial and manual gestures by human infants. *Science* 198, 75–8.

Piaget, J. 1937 (1954): *The construction of reality in the child*. New York: Basic Books.

—— 1946 (1951): *Play, dreams and imitation in childhood*. London: Routledge and Kegan Paul.

Trevarthen, C. 1982: The primary motives for cooperative understanding. In *Social cognition: essays on the development of understanding*, eds. G. Butterworth and P. Light. Brighton: Harvester; Chicago: Chicago University Press.

*Walk, R.D. 1981: *Perceptual development*. California: Brooks/Cole.

Werner, J.S. and Lipsitt. L.P. 1981: The infancy of human sensory systems. In *Developmental plasticity: behavioral and biological aspects of variations in development*, ed. Eugene S. Gollin. New York and London: Academic Press.

Wishart, J.G. and Bower, T.G.R. 1985: A longitudinal study of the development of the object concept. *British journal of developmental psychology* 3, 243–58.

perceptual development Despite the fact that there are relatively few texts on the development of perceptual skills, for example Gibson (1969), Piaget (1969), Vurpillot (1976), the field is vast, ranging from tactile sensitivity to comprehension of the basis of visual metaphor. How can one disentangle what is specifically perceptual from more general mental changes?

With children, from preschool to early adolescence, the aim is to describe (a) sensory information to which they seem sensitized, (b) their perceptual knowledge (Flavell 1978) and (c) symbolic skills to which they have gained access. One can often check a psychological theory against physical laws. For example, since light does not travel round corners, the fact that children perceive that it does must be a feature of their visual environment. But only when children have built a data-base about its predictable effects can these effects become incontrovertible facts of visual experience for them. Without such perceptual knowledge, covert or overt, they can neither hide properly (head-in-the-sand syndrome) nor seek efficiently. This is not a trivial point for anyone who has had to ask a child to try again to find something on a shelf. An intimate relationship exists between possession of perceptual knowledge and preparation of appropriate action.

Yet perceptual skills are difficult to bring to the level of awareness. Take size-perception: we all have extensive visual experience of body-parts, yet few people notice that a relaxed hand will typically cover from brow to chin. That is evident in untutored drawings at all ages. The problem is often posed as arising from the existence of two types of knowledge, procedural and declarative. Much perceptual skill seems to pertain to the former, to knowing how to organize information within particular contexts, rather than to the build up of solid facts across contexts.

The straight-line law of light-projection specifies that perceptual habits must be organized to deal with parallelism, angular inclination and the like. Some clear demonstrations of perceptual skill have been based on children's sensitivity to geometrical frames of reference, But, by the same token, they have high-lighted children's problems with visual-symbolics. The ability precisely to interpret pictorial linear perspective develops late, in middle childhood, yet the basic laws of perspective are the straight-line rule and size-distance relations. Even when such simple perceptual rules are grasped, they still have to be welded into a *symbolic system*. In that sense, perceptual development is something which can continue throughout life.

Mandler (1982) questions 'whether it is possible to have a perceptually sophisticated organism without a related conceptual system integrated'. She adds, 'much of our knowledge of the world, even as adults, is organized around expectations of what we will see next or what will happen next'. The more knowledge one can deploy, the less continuous attention has to be paid, and the more advance planning can be allocated to checking expectations by categorizing perceptual input. Perceptual processing can actually be physically tiring. The development of mental labor-saving devices enables effort to be concentrated upon analyzing input efficiently. If one knows that landmarks have not only to be physically salient but distributed in a manner informative about one's route, it will be easier to avoid one's attention being distracted by attractive, non-informative things. Children can be acute at noticing things that could be landmarks, far less so in restricting attention to those which actually are.

In sum, though the senses can repeatedly be *recalibrated* with age and tuition, there is no reason to seek a unique motor of development in new sensory capacities "coming on stream". Behind the monitoring of sensations, which may be stable over development lies the assessment of the consequences of the sensations. These may be grave for short-range senses such as touch or taste. 'All novel sensations of taste and smell are actually viewed with suspicion until their consequences have been assessed' (Engen 1979). What happens if children become "hooked" on a high salt dosage, say? 'As in the case of too much sugar . . . learning must have overcome whatever innate preferences and body wisdom there might have been' (Engen 1979). The influence of cultural norms and social setting, with a new chemical sensation, can be profound (Galef 1982). For these "evolutionarily ancient" senses there is no childhood development after infancy, only the acquisition of good and bad habits, and the engagement with, or avoidance of, intelligent assessment of consequences. How we get children of different developmental status to make the assessment is quite a different matter.

PIAGET, who had an acute eye for developmental discontinuities, denied the existence of perceptual stages. Even where age-related differences are sharp, one looks to the underlying interpretative skills for a reasoned account of changes in strategic skills in the use of senses. There are two important provisos. First, counter-instances can be found. Thus, Mayer (1977) reported development in anisotropy (differential sensitivity to lines differing in orientation). Yet the theoretical basis, that such development should demonstrably be of adaptive significance in relation to the geometry of the environment, is questionable (Switkes et al. 1978). The second proviso is that, as new techniques enable researchers finely to decompose the elements of an array, future models will have to contain some very subtle developmental parameters (Dowd et al. 1980).

A case example of perceptual development is with orientation. Bodily stability requires collation of external visual cues and internal balance cues. Butterworth and Cicchetti (1978) showed that when infants manage to sit unaided, visual motion cues cause them to sway in over-compensation. This again happens when learning to stand. But motor-retarded Down's syndrome infants compensate comparatively less at the sitting stage and stagger more at standing, arguably as a result of doing less work at collation at the earlier stage. Rosinski et al. (1978) estimate that compensation is normally fully developed by age six, to about 50 per cent of what an ideal system would do. This is an impressive achievement.

If contextual sensitivity can be sharpened so early, what is left to develop are strategies for controlling it. One research tool is to manipulate the number of diagonals in the visual field, for even adults find them difficult to encode. Children find it easier to align two square targets than two diamonds, but this square-advantage vanishes if alignment has to be done under conflict: squares within diamond frames and diamonds within square frames. A simple explanation is that children distribute finite avail-

175

able encoding-resources over both target and context. The corollary is that a diagonal anywhere in the field uses up a constant amount of perceptual effort. The effects hold up to the age of seven or eight (Freeman 1980). Only after that can children reasonably be expected to focus perceptual effort on demand. That may possibly be part of a more general tendency for young children not to utilize their analysis of stimulus dimensions where an adult almost compulsively may do so (Ward 1980).

Yet this leads to a puzzle. With complex pictures, children sometimes concentrate on parts, sometimes on wholes (Vurpillot 1976). Pre-schoolers may be sensitive to both height and width yet fall back on just height for judging the "bigness" of a rectangle – so much so that five-year-olds may be worse than three-year-olds (Maratsos 1973). Strategies for gathering information depend upon development of the conceptual categories which the perceptual information is supposed to serve. Andersen (1975) reports a beautiful study of perceptual widening and narrowing between the ages of three and twelve, when searching for a cup. Children also have to learn to control the odd biases, built up during normal wide-ranging perceptual exploration, in the interests of working hard at a specific perceptual puzzle. Every case of age-related perceptual bias will have to be theorized in terms of possible normal adaptive significance. One can see how spread of resources could be triggered by cues associated with overlearned skills, such as stability, and over-selectivity in cases of puzzling out the unique referent which the adult apparently intends. Finally, children develop ideas about when it is appropriate to shut off entirely: use of gaze-aversion can only be understood by going beyond perceptual mechanisms to the child as a person in social contexts.   NHF

Bibliography

Andersen, E.S. 1975: Cups and glasses: learning that boundaries are vague. *Journal of child language* 2, 79–103.

Aslin, R.N. and Smith, L.B. 1987: Perceptual development. In *Annual review of psychology*, vol. 38, eds. M.R. Rosenzweig and L.W. Porter. Palo Alto: Annual Reviews Inc. (in press).

Butterworth, G.E. 1983: Structure of the mind in human infancy *Advances in infancy reseach* 2, 1–29.

—— and Cicchetti, D. 1978: Visual calibration of posture in normal and motor retarded Down's syndrome infants. *Perception* 7, 513–25.

Dowd, J.M. et al. 1980: Children perceive large-disparity random-dot stereograms more readily than adults. *Journal of experimental child psychology* 29, 1–11.

Engen, T. 1979: The origin of preferences in taste and smell. In *Preference behaviour and chemoreception*, ed. J. Kroeze. London: IRL.

Flavell, J.H. 1978: The development of knowledge about visual perception. In *Nebraska symposium on motivation*, vol. 25, ed. C.B. Keasey. Lincoln: University of Nebraska Press.

Freeman, N.H. 1980: *Strategies of representation in young children: analysis of spatial skills and drawing processes*. London and New York: Academic Press.

Galef, B.G. 1982: Development of flavour preference in man and animals: the role of social and nonsocial factors. In *The development of perception: psychobiological perspectives*, vol. 1, eds. R.N. Aslin, J.R. Alberts and M.R. Petersen. New York and London: Academic Press.

Gibson, J.J. 1969: *Principles of perceptual learning and development*. New York: Appleton-Century-Croft.

Mandler, J.M. 1982: Representation. In *Cognitive development*, eds. J.H. Flavell and E.M. Markman, New York: Wiley.

Maratsos, M.P. 1973: Decrease in understanding of the word "big" in preschool children. *Child development* 44, 747–52.

Mayer, M.J. 1977: Development of anisotropy in late childhood. *Vision research* 17, 703–10.

Piaget, J. 1969: *The mechanisms of perception*. London: Routledge and Kegan Paul; New York: Basic Books.

Rosinski, R.R., Degelman, D. and Mulholland, T. 1978: Intermodal relationships in children's perception. *Child development* 49, 1084–95.

Switkes, E., Mayer, M.J. and Sloan, J.A. 1978: Spatial frequency analysis of the visual environment: anisotropy and the carpentered environment hypothesis. *Vision research* 18, 1393–9.

Vurpillot, E. 1976: *The visual world of the child*. London: Allen and Unwin; New York: International Universities Press.

Ward, T.B. 1980: Separable and integral

responding by children and adults to the dimensions of length and density. *Child development* 51, 676–84.

personality development Personality is defined as those characteristics of an individual which determine the unique adjustment he makes to his environment. Development begins at birth and continues throughout the life span.

Published work on the development of personality deals mainly with children. It is useful to distinguish two main approaches to this area. One emphasizes measurement at the expense of theory. A typical study uses data from assessments of the individual's personality throughout infancy or childhood in an attempt to discover regularities and continuities in development. The other approach deals mainly with the theory of personality development and systematic observation of behavior is less important. Freud's well-known theory (Freud 1910) of psychosexual development is an excellent example of this type of theory.

FREUD believed that instinctual forces, primarily sexual in nature, were the basis of all human behavior (see DEVELOPMENT: PSYCHOANALYTIC THEORIES). He termed these forces "libido". Libido is sexual in a very broad sense, and during infancy and early childhood libidinal energy is associated with the various orifices of the body. The first stage is associated with the mouth and is known as the *oral* stage. Freud assumed that the extent to which libidinal drives are gratified or frustrated by the environment may lead to *fixation* at that stage. This means that a disproportionate amount of libidinal energy will be invested in a particular bodily zone. Those fixated at the oral stage are expected to develop personalities which make them compulsive eaters, smokers, talkers, etc.

Following the *oral* stage is the *anal*. Freud assumed that the baby derives pleasure from the process and products of his own excretions and that this pleasure is opposed by those who socialize him. If fixation occurs at this period, Freud expected that the child would develop later problems with relationships to authority and the need for self-control. The third stage is called *phallic*. Here, the child is said to engage in specifically sexual play and to show sexual curiosity. It shades into the final or *genital* stage of early psychosexual development. During this stage, the boy's feelings and fantasies toward his mother (the primary libidinal object from the beginning) assume a specifically sexual character. (See OEDIPUS AND ELEKTRA COMPLEXES.) According to Freud, this is a very important period for children of both sexes because many anxieties and conflicts have to be dealt with. Freud claimed that most of the individual's later patterns of traits and defenses are determined by the particular ways in which the genital conflicts are resolved.

Freud, therefore, saw personality as fully developed or at least determined by about the age of four years. His critics often reject this view and, in addition, point out that he overinterpreted as universal and instinctual certain aspects of human nature which were specific to the time and place in which he worked. Even modern theorists generally sympathetic to his views have almost rejected the emphasis on sexual drives and paid more attention to the social and interpersonal aspects of personality development. ERIKSON (1963) and SULLIVAN (1953) are both influential theorists of the psychoanalytic school who constantly stress interpersonal relationships across the individual's life span as determining the capacity for other personal adjustment and development. Nevertheless, four characteristics of Freud's theory have persisted and influenced modern work on personality development. Firstly, interaction with a social environment is necessary for each successive stage to unfold. Secondly, adult personality is largely a function of interactions likely to occur within a nuclear family. Thirdly, early personality development often occurs as a resolution of internal conflicts and is likely to be unobservable (and therefore difficult for the behaviorist to "understand"). Fourthly, events in early childhood determine personality to a greater extent than do later events.

Observational studies, as mentioned earlier, lay little stress on theory and seek instead to sample the activities of individuals (usually from birth) with the object of discovering regularities and continuities in personality. There is a limited range of activities engaged in by the newborn but observations have been made of the frequencies of sucking and crying and on the lengths of periods of sleep and wakefulness (Korner et al. 1981). Such observations are made of the same children at regular intervals. Results suggest that most individuals show an unstable pattern of behavior in early life (0–6 months) and only moderately stable patterns thereafter (Thomas et al. 1963). The extent to which these inconsistencies are due simply to problems of measurement is not clear. There are obviously problems both in sampling individual behavior properly and in relating behavior in infancy to later behavior (Nunally 1973). Despite these problems certain consistencies have been found. Some of the main discoveries are that (a) locomotor activity level is moderately consistent in infancy and childhood and there is a link between high activity and lack of self control in adulthood (Escalona and Heider 1959); (b) passivity and submissiveness tend to be consistent characteristics (Honzik 1964); (c) dominance is a consistent characteristic during childhood and adolescence (Bronson 1967). Other longitudinal studies (e.g. Kagan 1960) for age periods from infancy to twenty years indicate that individuals tend to have a consistent approach to social situations. At the same time, there are instances in these and other longitudinal studies which show that personality development involves large and abrupt adjustments to the environment. Many personality traits seem not to be fixed in the individual but changeable throughout the life span.

Although it is interesting simply to describe and to assess personality, it is also important to try and specify its origins and the causes of permanence and change. Efforts have been made to determine the extent to which personality characteristics are inherited. Such studies of inheritance have not met with conspicuous success either in identifying the traits most likely to be inherited or the degree to which any such traits are inherited. Research into the personalities of monozygotic and dizygotic twins (e.g. Goldsmith and Gottesman 1981) yield moderate estimates of the heritability of "extroversion", "anxiety", "persistence" and "fearfulness". However, because twin data are used, even these moderate heritabilities are likely to be overestimates. This evidence that personality traits owe little to inheritance probably goes against popular belief. Prenatal experience is another variable which is widely expected to influence personality development. Yet, here again the data are poor and no clear trends can be reported.

The best researched and most fruitful investigations into the causes of individual personality development are concerned with the impact of specific early experiences. Most work here has been done in an attempt to refine the statements of Bowlby (1951) on maternal deprivation in early infancy. In his widely quoted and influential book, BOWLBY declared that 'mother love in infancy and childhood is as important for mental health as are vitamins and proteins for physical health'. Bowlby and others offer evidence that a child deprived of proper mothering in the first two years of life will be poorly adjusted psychologically and be unable to develop close affectional ties with others (see DEPRIVATION: PARENTAL.).

Bowlby's body of evidence has been carefully dissected during the past twenty years (Rutter 1981). Bowlby (heavily influenced by Freud) appears to have exaggerated the irreversibility of deprivations in infancy and early childhood. Although infantile experiences are still held to be important, the effects of early deprivations of attachment can be reversed if opportunities for long term attachments are offered in childhood and adolescence. Furthermore, experiences at all ages can probably have a profound influence on personality development. However, there is a shortage of evidence available on adult personality development and thus it is not yet possible to evaluate this idea fully. That work which has been done certainly does not suggest that personality is ever fixed from one period to another (see, for example, Neiner and Owens 1982).

Our grasp of this area is still tentative. Nevertheless, certain basic facts are emerging. These are:

1. The organization of personality into traits probably takes place after birth: evidence for the heritability of global and organized characteristics is poor.
2. Individual differences in personality and its development are strongly influenced by the processes of caretaking and socialization.
3. Many personality characteristics develop as a result of internal psychological conflicts which are unobservable.
4. Later socialization experiences, even those in adulthood, can greatly modify earlier trends. Early experience is not as fundamental to the later course of personality development as was once thought.

RMcH

Bibliography

Bowlby, J. 1951: *Maternal care and mental health*. World Health Organisation, Geneva.

Bronson, G.W. 1967: Adult derivatives of emotional expressiveness and reactivity control: developmental continuities from childhood to adulthood. *Child development* 38, 801–18.

Clarke, A.D.B. and Clarke, A.M. 1984: Constancy and change in the growth of human characteristics. *Journal of child psychology and psychiatry* 25, 191–210.

*Clarke, A.M. and Clarke, A.D.B. 1976: *Early experience: myth and evidence*. London: Open Books.

*Erikson, E.H. 1963: *Childhood and society*. 2nd edn. New York: Norton.

Escalona, S.K. and Heider, G.M. 1959: *Prediction and outcome*. New York: Basic Books.

Freud, S. 1910: Infantile sexuality. Three contributions to the sexual theory. *Nervous and mental disease monographs*. No. 7.

Goldsmith, H.H. and Gottesman, I.I. 1981: Origins of variation in behavioral style: longitudinal study of temperament in young twins. *Child development* 52, 91–103.

Honzik, M.D. 1964: Personality consistency and change: some comments on papers by Bayley, Macfarlane, Moss, Kagan and Murphy. *Vita humana* 7, 139–42.

Kagan, J. 1960: The long term stability of selected Rorschach responses. *Journal of consultational psychology* 24, 67–73.

Korner, A.F., Hutchinson, C.A., Koperski, J.A., Kraemer, H.C. and Schneider, P.A. 1981: Stability of individual differences of neonatal motor and crying patterns. *Child development* 52, 83–90.

Neiner, A.G. and Owens, W.A. 1982: Relationships between two sets of biodata with 7 years separation. *Journal of applied psychology* 67, 146–50.

Nunally, J.M. 1973: Research strategies and measurement methods for investigating human development. In *Life-span developmental psychology: methodological issues*, eds. J.R. Nesselroade and H.W. Reese. New York: Academic Press.

Parke, R.D. and Asher, S.R. 1983: Social and personality development. *Annual review of psychology* 34, 465–509.

*Rutter, M. 1981: *Maternal deprivation reassessed*. 2nd edn. Harmondsworth and New York: Penguin.

Sullivan, W.S. 1953: *The interpersonal theory of psychiatry*. New York: Norton.

Thomas, A. et al. 1963: *Behavioral individuality in early childhood*. New York: New York University Press.

Piaget, Jean A Swiss biologist who began his work on the nature of children's intellectual development during the 1920s and continued it until his death in 1980 at the age of eighty-three. During that long time he produced a massive body of research and developed a theory about childhood which is the single biggest influence on child psychology today. The central idea in this theory is that children at first lack the capacity either to understand their environment or to reason about it coherently, and that they gradually acquire these abilities through the informal experiences with the world around them. Piaget was concerned not only with the extent of children's intellectual capacities at different ages but also with the kind of experiences which lead to intellectual growth; it was mainly because of this latter interest that Piaget's ideas have played so large a part in recent debates about education.

From the beginning his main interest in child development centered around logic. It was Piaget more than anyone else who promoted the idea that logical reasoning cannot be taken for granted in humans and is to a large extent out of the range of young children's capacities. This idea seems to have come to him during his first systematic experience of research with children while on a visit to Simon's laboratory in Paris. Simon, an erstwhile colleague of Alfred Binet, suggested that Piaget should try out some intelligence tests which involved syllogisms. Piaget did so and was so struck with the difficulty which children as old as eight and nine years had with these apparently simple logical tasks that he decided to explore the possibility that children originally lack certain logical capacities and that much that is important in child development is the result of the gradual but inexorable growth of logic during childhood.

Piaget's first studies, reported in *Language and thought of the child* (1923) and in *Judgement and reasoning in the child* (1924), concentrated on the young child's knowledge of his physical and social environment. This early work suggested that young children are egocentric, in the sense that they do not realize when they talk to others that these other people have different viewpoints from theirs and know different things. (See EGOCENTRISM.) It also suggested that young children's thoughts are "animistic" – a term which Piaget used to describe a failure to distinguish animate from inanimate things – and are also characterized by "artificialism", which meant that children often do not seem to be able to distinguish between man-made and naturally formed objects in their environment.

Nearly all this early work was based on conversations between Piaget and young children or on conversations between children which were overheard by him. Soon however Piaget's work acquired a more experimental and a less conversational bent. The change came about in two ways. The first was that Piaget turned

much of his attention to very young children in their first two years of life who could not converse. The second was that he decided to tackle the problem of logical abilities more directly by giving older children a series of problems which involved more experimental manipulations and less interrogation on the part of Piaget and his colleagues.

The work on the first two years of life which Piaget calls "the sensori-motor period" (see SENSORI-MOTOR STAGE) was based on observations of his own three children and various experiments with them. It is described in two books *The child's construction of reality* (1937) and *The origin of intelligence in the child* (1936) which still exert a powerful influence on current research on infancy. Piaget tried to show that children are born with a few built in behavior patterns such as sucking, grasping with the hand and looking at moving objects, which he called reflexes. Apart from these basic activities infants are incapable of understanding their environment or of coping with it in any way. But these reflexes provide the experiences which lead the child by the end of the two years to have a reasonable idea of the world around him, and to understand in a simple way space, time and causality. Much of this development is due to the eventual coordination of the different reflexes. For example Piaget claimed that for the first four months of life the baby does not have a proper idea of its own physical existence because its reflexes are not coordinated. The child moves his arm and feels it moving. He also sees it moving, but these two perceptions are quite unconnected. To him his own arm has exactly the same status as any other passing object. He does not know that it is his own, and only makes the connection when at four to five months of age he begins to be able to reach for things which he sees. This coordination and others allow him by the age of six months or so to have a reasonable idea of himself as a separate physical entity. But according to Piaget there is still a lot for the baby to learn, and his next major development must be to discover more about the properties of the objects around him. The major discovery which the child has to make is that these are not evanescent: they are durable and have an independent existence quite regardless of whether the baby is perceiving them at the time or not. Piaget claimed that babies at first do not understand that objects still exist when they are no longer visible, on the basis of some observations which he made that up to the age of about eight months they lose interest in a toy which they see placed under covers even though they could in principle perfectly easily retrieve it. Even when they begin to recover these hidden objects their performance remains very shaky. One of Piaget's best known and most provocative observations was of the so called A not B error. Babies between about eight and twelve months manage to retrieve a toy hidden in place (A) but then when they see it hidden somewhere else (B) they often wrongly look for it in its original hiding place. Piaget's explanation for this phenomenon was that it showed that the child could not separate the object's existence from his own actions: he actually thinks that his original action of reaching to place A somehow recreated the object. If Piaget is right it is not until the child gets over this sort of curious mistake that he really understands that the existence of the objects around him is by and large independent of his own actions. By the age of two years, however, the child has achieved what Piaget called a "practical" understanding of this and of other basic concepts, such as causality and space and time. But there is still a long way for the child to go. He still has, according to Piaget, to find out how to solve logical problems and to use logic to solve everyday problems, and this takes to the end of what Piaget called "the concrete operations period".

The concrete operations period lasts, in Piaget's theory, until roughly thirteen years of age. During this time the child's major underlying intellectual achievement is to free himself from the domination of his immediate perception, a liberation which allows him to be logical and which indeed explains logical development. Sup-

pose for example that an experimenter has three sticks of varying size, so that $A > B > C$. Suppose too that the child is shown them in two pairs: $A > B$ and $B > C$. In Piaget's theory these two presentations, because they represent two separate perceptions would so far as the child of five, or six, or even seven or eight is concerned remain separate. While he is perceptually dominated he cannot combine the two and this means that he cannot make the logical deduction that $A > C$. Perceptual domination thus prevents logic, and this is the theme which unites the many, varied experiments which Piaget carried out on children between the ages of three and thirteen years. There is for example the well known conservation experiment, described in such books as *The child's conception of number* (1941) and *The child's construction of quantities* (1941). The child is shown two identical quantities – say two identical glasses containing the same amounts of liquid. He compares them and judges them to be equal. The liquid from one is then poured into a thinner container which means that its level is now higher than that of the liquid which was left as it was. The child is then asked to say whether or not the two containers contain the same amount of liquid, and his usual answer is that they do not. The one with the higher level is usually said to have more than the other by children up to the age of eight years or so. Piaget's explanation for this striking error was that the perceptually dominated child has to treat a perceptual change as a real one, and as a consequence does not understand the principle of invariance. Both the explanation and the conclusion about the young child's incapacity have always been controversial, but the experiment itself is without doubt one of the most important and one of the best known in psychology. But Piaget's list of the things which a child of below about eight years cannot do did not stop there. He cannot, Piaget added, understand the logical inclusion of classes; he cannot understand Euclidean spatial relationships; he cannot even understand that someone sitting opposite him has a different viewpoint from his own. All these difficulties he documented in ingenious, but some would say flawed, experiments. Certainly his pessimism about the child's rank inability is under strong dispute at the moment, even though there is universal admiration both for the elegance of the actual theory and the ingenuity of the simple tests which Piaget and his colleagues devised.

The last developmental period in Piaget's theory was the formal operations period. It lasts roughly the length of adolescence. Of the three major periods which made up Piaget's theory this one is the Cinderella. Piaget himself did not write very much about it, and very few people have tried to repeat his experiments on children of this age range. Broadly speaking Piaget argued that this was the time when scientific thought, or at any rate the possibility of it, developed. In his view this demanded not just logic, but also the ability to isolate first the variables which are relevant to the logical argument. His major evidence for this idea came from experiments in which adolescent children were basically asked to design experiments to isolate causes – such as the cause of the extent of the swing of a pendulum. The question was whether they could manage to look at one variable at a time, holding all others constant, This was something which seemed quite out of the range of the young adolescent, though many managed later on. They managed it, Piaget claimed, because they began to reflect on their own thought processes, a quality which Piaget thought of as the quintessence of development at this time and indeed the crowning glory of intellectual development. It was a summit which later on he was ruefully to agree always eluded many children and adults too.

With this one exception Piaget concentrated on development which he regarded as inevitable and indeed universal. Although the child depended on his informal experiences with the environment to lead him from one intellectual stage to the next, this experience led him along the same path as everyone else. The mechanisms which Piaget thought caused intellec-

tual change are to be found in his theory of equilibrium. Piaget thought that children, and adults too, are content with their own intellectual experiences provided that these give a satisfactory and above all a consistent explanation of what happens around them. If they do the child is said to be in a state of equilibrium. But inevitably, according to Piaget, the child will find that he has two quite contradictory explanations of the same event, and his failure to reconcile them throws him into conflict. The conflict causes disequilibrium, and the child is forced to reorganize his intellectual processes to rid himself of the conflict which is causing all the trouble; hence the consequent intellectual change. These ideas are most forcefully described in two of Piaget's last books, *Experiments in contradiction* (1974) and *The development of thought* (1975). It must be said that there is little direct evidence for the causal side of Piaget's theory, and yet, with its stress on the importance of informal experiences and of the child making his own discoveries, it is the part of Piaget's work which has had the strongest effect on educators.

His interest in universal developmental changes was obviously guided by his enduring involvement with biology and his consistent wish to link that subject and philosophy. He became a psychologist almost by default. He simply wanted a scientific, biological explanation of the growth of knowledge. No one has done more to achieve that than he did himself.

(See also EMOTION: PIAGETIAN VIEW). PEB

Bibliography
Boden, M.A. 1979: *Piaget*. Brighton: Harvester; New York: Viking Press (1980).

Gruber, H.E. and Voneche, J.J. 1977: *The essential Piaget*. London: Routledge and Kegan Paul; New York: Basic Books.

Piaget, Jean 1923 (1959): *Language and thought of the child*. 3rd edn. London: Routledge and Kegan Paul; New York: Humanities.

–––––– 1924 (1962): *Judgement and reasoning in the child*. London: Routledge and Kegan Paul; New York: Humanities.

–––––– 1936 (1953): *The origin of intelligence in the child*. London: Routledge & Kegan Paul; New York: International Universities Press (1966), *The origins of intelligence in children*.

—— 1937 (1955): *The child's construction of reality*. London: Routledge and Kegan Paul; New York: Basic Books (1954), *The construction of reality in the child*.

—— 1941 (1952): *The child's conception of number*. London: Routledge and Kegan Paul; New York: Norton (1965).

—— 1967 (1971): *Biology and knowledge*. Edinburgh: Edinburgh University Press; Chicago: University of Chicago Press.

—— 1974: *Experiments in contradiction*. London: Routledge and Kegan Paul; New York: Norton.

—— 1977: *The development of thought*. London: Routledge and Kegan Paul. New York: Viking Press.

—— 1983: Piaget's theory. In *Handbook of child psychology*. 4th edn, vol. 1, ed. W. Kessen. New York: Wiley.

—— and Inhelder, Barbel 1941 (1974): *The child's construction of quantities*. London: Routledge and Kegan Paul; New York: Basic Books.

pivot class The term "pivot class" along with "open class" was introduced by Braine (1963) to distinguish the types of words found in two-word utterances in early FIRST LANGUAGE ACQUISITION.

Pivot words are statistically much more frequently used than open class words. In the utterance *this good, this come, this doggie, this red*, "this" is the pivot word, whereas all the other lexical items belong to the open class.

Pivot words can only be described with reference to the child's own grammar and not in terms of adult categories, such as functional words.

The following objections have been raised against the notion of "pivot class":
1. Statistical considerations should not enter the description of linguistic competence;
2. The distinction between the two classes is gradual particularly when seen from a developmental point of view;
3. There are significant inter-individual differences as regards membership of lexical items in pivot and open class.   PM

Bibliography

Braine, M.D.S. 1963: The ontogeny of English phrase structure: the first phase. *Language* 39, 1–13.

pivot-open grammar The terms "pivot" and "open" were introduced by Braine (1963) following a distributional analysis of child speech during the two-word phase. Children were found to distinguish between two syntactic word-classes: a relatively closed pivot class and a constantly growing open class. Pivot words express the grammatical relations of modification (allgone, big) and predication (there, come, want).

The grammatical reality of the pivot-open distinction is derived from the observation that only combinations of the type P + O, O + P and O + O (not P + P) are encountered.

The principal limitation of this distinction is its being restricted to surface sequences rather than to deeper semantic relations. (See FIRST LANGUAGE ACQUISITION.)   PM

Bibliography

Bowerman, Melissa 1973: *Early syntactic development*. Cambridge and New York: Cambridge University Press.

Braine, M.D.S. 1963: The ontogeny of English phrase structure. *Language* 39, 1–13.

McNeill, D. 1970: *The acquisition of language*. New York and London: Harper and Row.

plasticity Has two distinct meanings in general psychology which, although overlapping, possess very different implications. First, theorists such as Hollis use the term in referring to the view of the human as environmentally determined. To invoke this plasticity argument is to hold that individual action is principally a product of external rather than innate forces. Much weaker versions of this concept of plasticity are also found among those who believe that behavior and capabilities are principally determined by genes, but that development is influenced by the environment, at least during certain CRITICAL PERIODS. In contrast, the concept of plasticity is used by others in arguing that human life trajectories are not frozen or fixed by early life experiences. Plasticity in this case refers to the capacity of the organism to undergo transformation at any time during the life course.   KJG

Bibliography

Clarke, A.D.B. and Clarke, A.M. 1984: Constancy and change in the growth of human characteristics. *Journal of child psychology and psychiatry* 25, 191–210.

Hollis, M. 1977: *Models of man*. Cambridge and New York: Cambridge University Press.

plasticity: physiological concept

Plasticity refers to the capacity of neurons in the central nervous system to grow beyond their normal developmental period, or to regenerate or reorganize after injury or environmental change. Although the term is sometimes used to refer to any reorganization of neural connections observed after an experimental manipulation, its use is most appropriate when referring to changes that have functional significance for the organism. At the level of the neuron, or nerve cell, the structural changes that subserve plasticity involve the growth of axons and dendrites, which are fibers that extend from the cell body of the neuron, and are involved in the transmission of neural impulses, as well as the formation of new synapses, which are the interconnections between neurons (see DEVELOPMENT OF THE NERVOUS SYSTEM). Such structural changes are most prominent during early development, but may be possible throughout adulthood in fish and amphibians. In mammals, a significant capacity for plasticity appears to be limited to a period early in post-natal development, which has been called the "sensitive" or "critical" period (see CRITICAL PERIOD). In addition to referring to the structural changes that can be observed in axons, dendrites and synapses the term plasticity is used to refer to functional changes that are not accompanied by observable alterations in structure. The functional changes to which the term is applied may occur at the neuronal level, where the function of pre-existing synapses may change, or at the behavioral level, where the recovery of some behaviour after neurological damage may occur without evidence of neural growth.

In humans there is some indication that the brain remains plastic for language during a critical period in development. In most adults language functions are lateralized to the left cerebral hemisphere. For the right-handed population, the incidence of left hemisphere language is well above 90 per cent. Most left-handed individuals also have left hemisphere language, but as a group, there is a higher incidence of language being represented in either the right hemisphere, or both hemispheres. One of the consequences of language lateralization is that for right-handed people, damage to the left hemisphere due to stroke, tumor or trauma will frequently produce a language dysfunction. However, comparable damage to the right hemisphere in right handed adults rarely produces problems with language. The prognosis for recovery of language function after left hemisphere damage depends on the extent of the damage and the type of language dysfunction present. Although the physiological basis for recovery of function in adults is not well understood, it is generally acknowledged that the observed improvement is not due to the plastic changes seen during the early development of the central nervous system.

In very young children, on the other hand, there tends to be a much greater recovery of function following lateralized brain injury than is observed in adults. Young children who have suffered extensive damage to, or even surgical removal of the left hemisphere lose the language function they have developed just as adults do after left hemisphere injury. If the left hemisphere of a young child is damaged prior to the acquisition of language, however, language may develop in the intact right hemisphere. In the developing human, then, there appears to be some plasticity for language function in so far as the hemisphere not normally involved in language may acquire this runction in response to severe damage to the language hemisphere. Such plasticity in language development is found only in childhood, and although there is no general agreement as to the length of the critical period, it appears that plasticity in language function sharply declines after the initial acquisition of language.   JJS

Bibliography

Blakemore, C. and Cooper, G. 1970: Development of the brain depends on the visual environment. *Nature* 228, 477–8.

Gazzaniga, M.S., Steen, D. and Volpe, B.T. 1979: *Functional neuroscience.* New York and London: Harper and Row.

Jacobson, M. 1978: *Developmental neurobiology.* New York and London: Plenum Press.

Marx, J.L. 1980: Regeneration in the central nervous system. *Science* 209, 378–80.

Woods, B.T. and Carey, S. 1979: Language deficits after apparent clinical recovery from childhood aphasia. *Annals of neurology* 6, 405–9.

—— and Teuber, H-L. 1978: Changing patterns of childhood aphasia. *Annals of neurology* 3, 273–80.

play Despite innumerable attempts to define play they have failed to achieve universal acceptance. The difficulty of defining play is not, in fact, accidental. It stems directly from our main method of categorizing behavior by its outcome or function. It is precisely the hallmark of play that the relation between the activities and their outcome or apparent goal looks paradoxical (Millar 1968). Friendly AGGRESSION, exploring the apparently familiar, pretense that is not intended to deceive are typical examples.

The criteria we use to classify behavior are, to a large extent, arbitrary. But attempts to classify play by mood or emotion have not proved successful. It is difficult to score emotion objectively. More importantly, the level of excitement varies considerably for different types of play. Similarly, there is no single or prototypical activity by which play could be defined. Almost any voluntary activity could be performed playfully, or in a play context. Here again typical aggressive, sexual or feeding activities take their significance from obvious endstates or outcomes. Uncertainties over classifying sometimes occur also with marginal instances of aggression or sex. But the uncertainty is whether the instance belongs to one or other agreed category. There is no doubt over the goal or function once the behavior is classified. With play, by contrast, the observer may be fairly certain that a child dressing a doll, or foxcubs tumbling over one another are instances of play. But he can only guess at the goal of the individual or the function for the species in either case. Such guesses are more in the nature of hypotheses that require testing rather than criteria by which the activities can be defined.

Play is more easily recognized than defined (see Smith and Vollstedt 1985). Recognition is not infallible but a number of characteristics are typical. The most important of these are firstly that the behavior is *voluntary*: – reflex actions and acts to which the individual is constrained by others or by necessity do not count as "play". The second is the *paradoxical or peculiar nature of the relation between activities and their outcomes*. The paradox is in the eye of the beholder because the function is not obvious. An object which is being endlessly manipulated may still hold novel features for the child. Friendly fights may be necessary because they yield practice in safe conditions. But activities that lead to obvious goals are not called "play". Two further characteristics that are observed very frequently are *repetition* and *repetition with variations*. Specific activities or sequences of activities are repeated over and over again in games such as "mothers and fathers" by human children, or "king of the castle" games that seem to be equally popular with monkeys. Repetition with variations, called, "diversive exploration" by Berlyne (1960), is apparently directed more to what can be done with an object or a skill than to novel features. It occurs more in species with complex brains and behavior. Word repetition with variations of intonation and stress patterns is common when infants first learn to speak. Another characteristic that has been observed in play of animals below primates is that play bouts tend to consist of *parts of* behavior that belong to quite *different behavioral categories*, following each other in rapid succession. *Incomplete behavior* which is arrested before the endstate or goal is achieved (e.g. "toying" with prey by satiated animals) has also sometimes been listed. *Exaggerated movements* are common.

Many species have special signals which signify that the animal is about to play. Among the most common is the relaxed open mouthed "play-face" that occurs both in monkeys and human children. Particular chirping sounds (Altmann 1962), exaggerated "galumphing" gaits (Loisos 1966), special tones of voice in children (Garvey 1977) are used as signals for play. Looking at your partner through your legs, used by the rhesus monkeys, and young baboons of both sexes "presenting" to the play partner, are invitations to play. Play signals typically occur prior to, and also during *social* play. But the same sort of signs are also sometimes found in solitary play. It is not quite clear as yet under what conditions they occur in solitary play.

Theories of play center on the "useful/useless" dichotomy of behavior which derives from our preference for defining behavior by its functions. This is not only arbitrary, but the fact that we do not know what functions given types of behaviors have does not entitle us to assume that they have no function. However, most theories of play consist either of attempts to explain the apparent uselessness of play, or to supply and argue for a particular function.

Spencer in the mid-nineteenth century embodied a surplus energy theory of play in his theory of evolution. Animals with more complex brains and behavior play because not all their time has been taken up with food getting. A link with creative art was implied. Overspill from instincts, or a pre-run of parts of these before they are properly sequenced, was a later version by ethologists. The analogy with hydraulic systems served as the main model of behavior also for behaviorists until the mid-twentieth century. Berlyne (1960) proposed a use for play as diversive exploration which restores the organism's arousal to an optimal level when external stimulation is too low to maintain this.

Specifically developmental theories started with HALL's recapitulation hypothesis, at the turn of the century. Development of the individual was supposed to be a re-run of development of the species. Freudian psychoanalysis assigned a cathartic function to play at various stages of emotional development. For PIAGET (1951) play and imitation were pure forms of assimilation and accommodation respectively, which he assumed to be the two main biological forces responsible for *cognitive* development. The child assimilates new information by applying to it the action schemas he has developed so far. Manipulative play, symbolic play and play with rules follow a sequential course with innately set ceilings. VYGOTSKY (1933) also assumed that play had a function in cognitive development.

A separate, unitary instinct "to practice other instincts" was proposed by Groos at the turn of the century. It was intended to account for human creative art also. Very similar assumptions are made by a number of current theories; some stressing the *practice*, and some the *innovative* element in play (Bruner, Jolly and Sylva 1976). Current models use analogies with computer systems, and some embody ideas from sociobiology (Fagen 1981).

Evolutionary theory makes it likely that behavior that occurs in many different species is not fortuitous, but has definite biological advantages. But it is not necessary to assume that all the activities we label "play" because their functions are not obvious have the *same* function. Millar (1968, 1981) argued that different types of play relate to different behavioral systems, and belong to *establishing control mechanisms* which regulate these, particularly although not solely, during development and acquisition. "Superfluous" gross motor activity such as frisking and gambolling may be homoestatic controls, ensuring stimulation that is necessary for growth, and for toning up after short periods of confinement. Practice or repetitive sensori-motor play could belong to the establishment of motor programs by incorporating feedback information and automatic subroutines. Object manipulation and diversive exploration which were distinguished by Hutt (1966) from specific exploration, would provide information not merely about the object, but about new uses for it or for the activity in question. Sylva (see Bruner, Jolly and Sylva 1976), has provided some evidence that responses are more divergent after play than after more structured activity. Pretend, FANTASY or imagination play (e.g. Singer 1973) is likely to relate to the organization of symbolic activities rather than to "feints" that are sometimes useful in aggressive bouts. Rehearsal and reorganization of information is needed for its later flexible use. Pretend play could be an overt form of this. Social play is probably concerned with the regulation of social relations within species. But the functions even of "play-fighting" could vary from establishing dominance hierarchies before the eruption of canine teeth makes biting lethal in species such as the polecat, to group cohesion in species such as monkeys and man where the older, heavier animals handicap themselves when play-fighting with younger ones. But we need to know a great deal more about the conditions which elicit specific types of play before any guesses at functions can be formulated sufficiently precisely for adequate testing.

The assumption that play activities belong to the control systems of a number of different behavioral functions explains the difficulty of finding a prototypical activity by which play could be defined. It also suggests that answers to questions "why" should wait on answers to questions "how" in studies of play. SMi

Bibliography

Altmann, S.A. 1962: Social behavior of anthropoid primates: analysis of recent concepts. In *Roots of behavior*, ed. E.L. Bliss. New York: Harper.

Berlyne, D.E. 1960: *Conflict arousal and curiosity*. New York: McGraw-Hill.

Bruner, J.S., Jolly, A. and Sylva, K. 1976: *Play: its role in development and evolution*. New York: Basic Books; London: Penguin.

Fagen, R. 1981: *Animal play behavior*. Oxford and New York: Oxford University Press.

Garvey, C. 1977: *Play*. London: Fontana.

Hutt, C. 1966: Exploration and play in children. *Symposium of the Zoological Society of London* 18, 23–44.

Loisos, C. 1966: Play in mammals. *Symposium of the Zoological Society of London*.

Millar, S. 1968: *The psychology of play*. London: Penguin.

—— 1981: Play. In *The Oxford companion to animal behaviour*, ed. D. McFarland. Oxford and New York: Oxford University Press.

Piaget, J. 1951: *Play, dreams and imitation in childhood*. Boston: Routledge and Kegan Paul.

Singer, J.L. 1973: *The child's world of make-believe*. New York: Academic Press.

Smith, P.K. ed. 1984: *Play in animals and humans*. Oxford: Blackwell.

—— and Vollstedt, R. 1985: On defining play: an empirical study of the relationship between play and various play criteria. *Child development* 56, 1042–50.

Vygotsky, L.S. 1933: Play and its role in the mental development of the child. *Soviet psychology* 3, no. 5.

prenatal development Is of interest to development psychologists mainly from two aspects: first in relation to the maturation of sensory and motor capacities that occurs during prenatal life, and second on account of the influence of factors affecting prenatal development on the later behavior of the infant. In relation to the latter, research interest has been focused on: the maternal diet (which can affect brain maturation); drugs, alcohol and smoking during pregnancy; irradiation; fetal anoxia; maternal emotional state. These influences have been investigated in both human clinical studies and animal experiments. With the exception of irradiation, the various agents effect the fetus indirectly, via changes in the maternal blood supply, since a wide variety of pharmacological, hormonal and nutritional agents can pass through the placenta. JA

Bibliography

Kopp, C.B. 1983: Risk factors in development. In *Handbook of child psychology*. 4th edn, vol. 2, eds. M.M. Haith and J.J. Campos. New York: Wiley.

—— and Parmalee, A.H. 1979: Prenatal and perinatal influences on infant behavior. In *Handbook of infant development*, ed. J.D. Osofsky. New York: Wiley.

programmed instruction Structured teaching material designed for individual student use with little, or no, teacher interaction. Early material was in programmed texts with linear presentation in a form easy to assimilate, or in a branching presentation dependent on student responses. Later developments mechanically or electronically automated the presentation and the branching. In recent years computers have been used to allow increasingly detailed analysis of student responses and patterns of response.

One of the major attractions of programmed instruction has been the provision of individualized education (Suppes 1967). The shift in emphasis from simple automation to improved education can be seen in Lumsdaine and Glaser's collection (1960) of a sequence of key historic papers on teaching machines and programmed learning covering the period 1924 to 1959, and in Galanter's symposium (1959) on automatic teaching at the end of that period. Lumsdaine and Glaser begin with Pressey's original teaching machines of 1924 and quote (p.47) his discussion of 'the coming "industrial revolution" in education' which will result in 'freeing the teacher from the drudgeries of her work'. Thirty-five years later Galanter (1959, p.4) is looking for a machine that will 'be able to make plans for itself, and also able to diagnose the plans and ideas that the student has formed'.

As programmed instruction became COMPUTER-AIDED INSTRUCTION or learning (CAI, CAL) individualization became more attainable, though it proved difficult to develop systems that would model the learner, his plans and ideas (Mitchell 1981). These considerations led to Bunderson's development (1974) of learner managed instruction in which the user rather than the computer controlled the individualization. Recent research on knowledge representation in studies of

personal construct systems (Pope and Shaw 1981; Pope and Keen 1981) and artificial intelligence (see MACHINE LEARNING) has led to a far greater understanding of the processes necessary to represent knowledge structures.

During the past few years reductions in the cost of micro electronics have made it feasible to introduce microcomputers into schools and use them throughout the curriculum (Tagg 1980). Some applications involve forms of programmed instruction but this is only one component of the wider uses of the computer for simulation, information retrieval and the provision of a variety of learning environments (Papert 1980).

In conclusion it should be noted that the effectiveness of programmed instruction is crucially dependent on the quality of the teaching material used, both in terms of the content and the method of presentation, regardless of the sophistication of the technology.   MLGS

Bibliography

Bunderson, C.V. 1974: The design and production of learner-controlled courseware for the TICCIT system: a progress report. *International journal man-machine studies* 6(4), 479–91.

Galanter, E. 1959: The ideal teacher. In *Automatic teaching: the state of the art*, ed. E. Galanter. New York: John Wiley, 1–11.

*Lumsdaine, A.A. and Glaser, R. eds. 1960: *Teaching machines and programmed learning*. Washington: National Education Association of the United States.

Mitchell, P.D. 1981: Representation of knowledge in CAL courseware. In *Computer assisted learning*, ed. P.R. Smith. New York and Oxford: Pergamon Press.

Papert, S. 1980: *Mindstorms: children, computers and powerful ideas*. Brighton: Harvester Press; New York: Basic Books.

Pope, M.L. and Keen, T.R. 1981: *Personal construct psychology and education*. New York and London: Academic Press.

—— and Shaw, M.L.G. 1981: Personal construct psychology in education and learning. In *Recent advances in personal construct technology*, ed. M.L.G. Shaw. New York and London: Academic Press.

Suppes, P. 1967: On using computers to individualize instruction. In *The computer in*

American education, eds. D.D. Bushnell and D.W. Allen. New York: John Wiley.

*Tagg, E.D., ed. 1980: *Microcomputers in secondary education.* Amsterdam: North-Holland/ Elsevier.

psychological assessment in education *See* education: psychological assessment.

psycholinguistics A sub-discipline of linguistics dealing with the psychological mechanisms underlying language acquisition, language processing, and language use. Psycholinguistics may be viewed either as the continuation of earlier traditions of research into language learning and the cognitive basis of language (see LANGUAGE AND COGNITION) or as a relatively new area of research focusing on the issue of the psychological reality of the rules and units postulated by modern linguistic theory. The relation between linguistics and psycholinguistics has often been clouded by the imprecise status assigned to the linguist's notion of the grammar of a language. Consequently, the question whether linguistic analyses can be proved or disproved by psychological tests remains open. Similar imprecisions affect the relations between psycholinguistics and neurolinguistics.

Early research that may be classified as psycholinguistic concerned the documentation of the stages of FIRST LANGUAGE ACQUISITION. This tradition continued into the twentieth century and still remains strong, owing to the stimulus given to language acquisition research by the nativist theories of generative grammar. Another important tradition is the gestaltist approach to language. Wundt, for example, objected to the physicalism of neo-grammarian accounts of language change and stressed general perceptual and creative principles. He distinguished two levels of linguistic performance: the holistic or sensori-motor as opposed to that of the higher, more abstract cognitive structures. Gestaltist views on language have been recuperated by those generative psycholinguists who view the sentence, not as a sequence of linear transitions from one stimulus to the next, but as a formal whole, structured hierarchically.

One of the most important schools of psycholinguistics has been behaviorism, with its intellectual roots in American Pragmatism and in the work of Watson and Pavlov. Behavioral psycholinguists see language learning as a particular application of general learning abilities. New sentences are held to be produced and understood as the result of the development of associative links (stimulus-response) between surface forms. Concepts such as introspection and consciousness are mistrusted in behaviorist psycholinguistics, and the study of behavior is limited to the observation of "objective" regularities or habits. Watson's word association theory claimed that speakers learn to associate sounds and their referents, and in learning sentences they learn the relations between the component words. Hull (1943) was not committed to the idea that all learning takes place by reinforcement and introduced the notion of a mediated response. Mediated responses include classes of segments such as phoneme, morpheme, verb. The most noted behaviorist psycholinguist, Skinner, postulated that speakers learn structural frames or patterns as a basis for sentence composition. He took operant rather than classical conditioning to be the psychological process behind language learning. The operant is pictured as the basic unit of verbal response and conditioning takes place by a post hoc reinforcement. The result is that the organism learns to predict and control response probabilities. Other neo-behaviorist linguists are Mowrer (1960) and Osgood (1957). Mowrer concentrated on the way in which word-referent associations are established and modified the S-R learning model to include mediated responses. As with other behaviorists, reward and punishment are held to be the impulses for learning. Osgood is noted for his study of how words acquire connotative meaning and of how this can be scientifically measured. He denied the simplistic equation between (a) behavior in response to a sign and (b) behavior in response to the corresponding object. The former was held to be only a small part of the latter.

Behaviorist learning theory and structural linguistics came under attack in the late 1950s in the influential writings of CHOMSKY, who criticized Skinner's behaviorist account of language learning. Chomsky argued that language is free of stimulus control and that absence of stimulus does not limit the frequency of use of a word. He also claimed that the behaviorist notion of reinforcement and many other notions from learning theory were inapplicable to linguistic analysis. Most importantly, behaviorist psycholinguistics was held to be incapable of explaining how native language users could produce and understand sentences they had never before encountered. Chomsky denied the behaviorist claim that linguistic ability could arise as the result of generalizations from experience and pointed instead to the child's frequent exposure to deviant and ungrammatical utterances. Nevertheless, Chomsky argued, in spite of such misleading input, the child still succeeds in constructing the correct grammar of the language. An innate mechanism (the LANGUAGE ACQUISITION DEVICE) was postulated to account for this achievement, and the psycholinguist was urged to focus his attention on the discovery of the principles regulating that mechanism.

Equally significant for the development of psycholinguistics was Chomsky's distinction (1965) between linguistic *competence* and *performance* as well as his claim that linguistics is a branch of cognitive psychology. The motivation behind much of contemporary psycholinguistic research stems in large part from these early principles of Chomsky's work. Owing to Chomsky's influence, language universals became an important topic of discussion in linguistics and psycholinguistics. It was assumed that, by studying what was universal to all languages, the linguist could discover the details of the child's innate language-learning mechanism. In recent years, however, there has been a renewed interest in studies of the mother's input to

the child's acquisition of language as well as a greater awareness of the interactional context of language learning (see BABY TALK).

The question of the psychological reality of grammatical structures has been explored in a number of ways. Steinberg (1982) holds that the study of the speech encoding process cannot be based on Chomsky's syntax-based grammar but must accept a meaning-based grammar such as that proposed by generative semantics. Other researchers have focused on speech errors as evidence of encoding mechanisms (Fromkin 1968). The issues in this domain are clouded by Chomsky's shifting attitude toward the question whether language performance should be taken as a reflection, direct or indirect, of underlying competence (Fodor, Bever and Garrat 1974).

The study of speech perception and decoding processes has been equally contentious. Fodor and Bever (1965) sought to demonstrate the psychological reality of constituent and clause boundaries by examining the way subjects "mishear" clicks superimposed on input utterances. Other studies have related transformational and derivational complexity to decoding ease (i.e. processing time) and have attempted to decide between alternative grammatical models on the basis of processing plausibility.

The diversity of psycholinguistic studies increased during the 1970s. Many psycholinguists have begun to question some of the linguistic principles on which Chomsky based his early attacks on behaviorism. Nevertheless, generative grammar remains the dominant linguistic model. Some psycholinguists claim that the topic of native speaker intuitions belongs to the study of linguistic performance and that these do not directly reflect competence as Chomsky had argued. Others argue that if the notion of linguistic competence cannot be linked to psychological mechanisms it should be abandoned. Indeed, some child language theorists are now returning to imitation and association, topics neglected during the anti-behaviorist revolution.   CMH/TJT

Bibliography

*Cambell, R. and Wales, R. 1970: The study of language acquisition. In *New horizons in linguistics*, ed. J. Lyons. Harmondsworth: Penguin.

Chomsky, N. 1965: *Aspects of the theory of syntax.* Cambridge, Mass.: MIT Press.

*Fodor, J. and Bever, T. 1965: The psychological reality of linguistic segments. *Journal of verbal learning and verbal behavior*, 420.

—— and Garrat M. 1974: *The psychology of language: an introduction to psycholinguistics.* New York; McGraw-Hill.

Foss, D.J. 1987: Psycholinguistics. In *Annual review of psychology*, vol. 38, eds. M.R. Rosenzweig and L.W. Porter. Palo Alto: Annual Reviews Inc. (in prep.).

Fromkin, V. 1968: Speculations on performance models. *Journal of linguistics* 4, 1–152.

*Greene, J. 1972: *Psycholinguists.* Harmondsworth and Baltimore: Penguin.

Harris, M. and Coltheart, M. 1986: *Language processing in children and adults.* London and Boston: Routledge and Kegan Paul.

Hull, C. 1943: *Principles of behavior.* New York: Appleton-Century-Crofts.

Mowrer, O. 1960: *Learning theory and symbolic processes.* New York: Wiley.

Osgood, C., Suci, G. and Tannenbaum, P. 1957: *The measurement of meaning.* Urbana, Ill.: University of Illinois Press.

*Steinberg, D. 1982: *Psycholinguistics, language, mind and world.* London and New York: Longman.

Watson, J. 1924: *Behaviorism.* New York: Norton.

puberty The process of sexual maturation and other physical changes marking the transition from childhood to adult maturity. It is accompanied by the development of secondary sexual characteristics and culminates in the capacity for reproduction. Various psychological changes, e.g. cognitive development, also take place (see ADOLESCENCE).

Puberty is initiated and controlled by changes in hypothalamic and anterior pituitary function. Changes in the reproductive system occur over two to three years and are related to the ADOLESCENT GROWTH SPURT. Puberty occurs approximately eighteen to twenty-four months later in boys than in girls and the growth spurt takes place at an earlier point in the pubertal sequence in girls than in boys. The sequence of outward signs in boys is, accelerated growth of the testes and scrotum with the appearance of pubic hair; penile growth, coinciding with the onset of the growth spurt; the first seminal discharge; deepening of the voice. In girls the process begins with the appearance of breast buds and of pubic hair. Menstruation begins near the completion of the sequence, after the peak velocity of the growth spurt (see MENARCHE). Tanner (1962) has described stages in breast growth in girls and genital development in boys.

There is wide individual variation in the age of onset and rate of progress, with different psychological correlates. Late maturation in boys, for example, may be followed by difficulties in personal adjustment. WLIP-J

Bibliography

Brook, C.G.D. 1982: *Growth assessment in childhood and adolescence.* Oxford: Blackwell Scientific Publications.

Tanner, James M. 1962: *Growth at adolescence.* Oxford: Blackwell Scientific; Springfield, Ill.: C.C. Thomas.

punishment If the performance of a particular response results in an aversive consequence the response is being punished. Punishment was little studied by earlier learning theorists, and when it was they questioned its effectiveness. There can, however, be no question but that immediate, consistent and severe punishment of a particular action will effectively stop that action being performed. But there do remain legitimate doubts. Punishment may cause people to refrain from performing the punished action only when they believe that they will be punished again: the child smacked by his parent for performing some undesirable action may simply go and do it elsewhere far from the parent's view. Punishment may have undesirable side effects: painful or harmful consequences may generate a state of fear or stress, and the punished child may become very anxious. Subsequently, a punished child may turn out to be more aggressive (Huesmann et al. 1984). This is usually interpreted as an example of imitative social learning – doing what the parent does rather than what he says. It may, of course, be that the cycle of punitive aggression is the result of a genetic constitution shared by parent and offspring (see Eysenck and Eysenck 1985). Finally, it is always important to ask whether the infliction of pain on another person or on an animal is morally justified.

NJM

Bibliography

Eysenck, H.J. and Eysenck, M.W. 1985: *Personality and individual differences*. New York: Plenum.

Huesmann, L.R., Eron, L.D., Lefkowitz, M.M. and Walder, L.O. 1984: Stability of aggression over time and generations. *Developmental psychology* 20, 1120–34.

R

reaching The development of skilled reaching undergoes a transition from visually elicited, swiping movements of the arm (which can be observed in the neonate) to visually guided movements of the hand at around five to six weeks. Visually elicited can be distinguished from visually guided reaching because the former is pre-programmed, or ballistic and cannot be corrected in the course of the action, whereas the latter is under continuous voluntary control. It can be corrected should an error occur in the trajectory of the hand to the object. It was thought that the acquisition of voluntary control may depend on feedback from the sight of the hand but evidence of normal development of reaching in blind babies now suggests that this may not be necessary.   GEB

Bibliography

Bower, T.G.R. 1982: *Development in infancy*. 2nd edn. San Francisco: Freeman.

von Hofsten, C. 1984: Developmental changes in the organization of prereaching movements. *Developmental psychology* 20, 378–88.

reading: cognitive skills Reading may be defined as the extraction of information from text; the process by which we get meaning from a printed message. In recent years cognitive psychologists have devoted a considerable amount of effort to trying to understand the processes involved in this complex skill.

Research on reading is generally conducted within a human information processing framework. The processes by which people read are explicitly fragmented into separate stages and the processes operating at these stages are systematically investigated in experiments. There are several sub-processes which are often distinguished in discussions of reading.

To begin with the reader must perceive the visual patterns of the words on a page. An average rate of reading for normal adults is somewhere in the region of 250–300 words per minute. A widely held belief, which accords with our subjective experience, is that as we read our eyes sweep smoothly along the printed line. This impression is, in fact, quite false, as first shown by Javal (1879) (see Huey 1908, p. 16). Our eyes move along a line of print in a series of small rapid jerks, which are called saccades. These saccades are punctuated by short periods when the eyes are still, called fixations. On average fixations last around 1/5th to 1/3rd of a second, and the saccades happen much more quickly, taking around 1/50th of a second. The perception of the printed material occurs only during fixations; during the saccades no clear vision is possible. In most situations about 94 per cent of reading time is devoted to fixations.

During the reading of a line of print the eyes sometimes move backwards towards the beginning of the line to re-read some of the material. These backward movements are known as regressions. Regressions are related to the difficulty of the material being read. When the material is difficult more regressions occur. When one line of print has been read the eyes make a long return saccade to fixate the beginning of the next line.

The mechanisms responsible for the pattern of eye movements observed during reading are the subject of a good deal of research. So called structural factors, such as the fact that visual acuity is highest at the fovea of the eye and falls off rapidly towards the periphery, and limitations on the rate at which people can understand material presented to them, will certainly place constraints on the pattern of eye movements observed. Recently, some ingenious experiments in which changes are made to a text which subjects are reading while their eyes are moving, have revealed a great deal about how eye movements are controlled (Rayner 1975).

On the basis of the visual information picked up by the eye, the reader must decode the meanings of the individual words present. This process involves going from a visual representation of a word to some stored representation of that word's meaning. According to current theories of this process the meanings of words which the reader knows are stored in a kind of internal dictionary or "lexicon". The problem is to specify the processes by which the stored information in the lexicon is accessed.

A major issue here is the type of visual perceptual information which is used in order to recognize a word. A straightforward approach to this question is to assume that a word is recognized by recognizing each of its component letters. Given that the letters within each word are recognized at the same time as each other (in parallel) and that readers utilize knowledge about the predictability of letter sequences within words to reduce the perceptual word load, it is possible to produce models which can explain much of what we know about how people recognize words (e.g. McClelland and Rumelhart 1981).

It has also often been suggested, however, that the recognition of a word may not simply be the result of recognizing its component letters. Rather, in addition to information about letters in the word, the reader may extract information about what have been called supra-letter features. The most common idea is that the reader uses information about the overall shape of the word. Processing the shape of the whole word would be an even quicker process than identifying each letter separately.

It seems likely that both these sorts of processes complement each other in skilled word recognition. Logically it is obvious that information about the component letters in a word will be important for its identification, but the putative role of supra-letter features such as word-shape is a far less obvious matter. Some recent evidence, however, does indicate a possible role for word shape information as a cue for recognition. For example, if subjects are asked to read a passage and detect misspelt words, misspellings which alter the overall shape of a word are found to be easier to detect than those which preserve word shape.

It has often been remarked that reading, historically and developmentally, is secondary to speech. It seems quite plausible to suppose, therefore, that at some stage reading will engage processes previously developed for the understanding of speech.

When recognizing individual words it is possible that we translate the letters in the printed word into a representation of the word's pronunciation (see Bradley and Bryant 1983). Understanding the word might then depend on the operation of the same mechanisms responsible for recognizing spoken words. The evidence for this view remains inconclusive at present. It appears that some impairments of reading observed in people with brain damage (dyslexias) can be explained in terms of such a process and its disorders (Coltheart, Patterson and Marshall 1980; Campbell and Butterworth 1983) but considerable controversy surrounds the possible importance of this process in normal skilled readers (for example, Parkin 1982).

This discussion of how we recognize words has given no consideration, so far, to the context provided by other words. This is undoubtedly artificial since it is well established that such context can facilitate recognition. Having previously seen "bread" leads us to respond more quickly to a related word such as "butter" (Meyer and Schvaneveldt 1971). Although processes like these, and others such as constraints imposed by grammatical structure, are probably important, it seems reasonable to suppose, in the absence of evidence to the contrary, that their effect is one of general facilitation, not a radical departure from the processes outlined so far.

Having identified the meanings of the individual words in a sentence, the reader must undertake a syntactic analysis. That is, he must relate the meanings of the individual words in a sentence according to the rules of the grammar of his language. The meaning of a sentence will depend not only upon the individual words present, but also upon the way in which they are combined. It appears that in order to perform the syntactic analysis of written messages readers hold the string of words in the form of internal speech. Using speech may be a very good way of remembering the order of words, which is clearly crucial in understanding sentences, and when our ability to do this is impaired comprehension suffers (Kleiman 1975; Baddeley, Eldridge and Lewis 1981).

Finally, the meaning of individual sentences within a passage must be related to each other to reach an understanding of the passage as a whole. Much of the work of psychologists who have been grappling with these complex questions has been reviewed by Sanford and Garrod (1981). It seems clear that in these later stages of the reading process, models of written sentence and text comprehension will merge with theories of language comprehension in general. The reader is in a sense, performing a kind of problem solving exercise. The ease of understanding a text will not only depend upon the characteristics of the passage such as its grammatical form but also upon the reader's past experience, his familiarity with the concepts involved and the previous knowledge he brings to bear.

This undeniable complexity of the reading process is nicely captured in the following quotation from Huey (1908, p. 6), one of the fathers of modern research into reading. 'And so to completely analyze what we do when we read would almost be the acme of a psychologist's achievements, for it would be to describe very many of the most intricate workings of the human mind, as well as to unravel the tangled story of the most remarkable

specific performance that civilization has learned in all its history.' It is clear that we are a long way from achieving a complete analysis of the reading process, but it seems certain that the challenge this poses will continue to engage the efforts of psychologists and those in related disciplines for many years to come.

(See also DYSLEXIC CHILDREN; READING: ORIGINS AND LEARNING; REMEDIAL READING; SPELLING.)   ChasH

Bibliography

Baddeley, A., Eldridge, M. and Lewis, V. 1981: The role of subvocalization in reading. *Quarterly journal of experimental psychology* 33A, 439–54.

Bradley, L. and Bryant, P.B. 1983: Categorising sounds and learning to read: a causal connection. *Nature* 301, 419–21.

Campbell, R. and Butterworth, B. 1985: Phonological dyslexia and dysgraphia in a highly literate subject. *Quarterly journal of experimental psychology* 37A, 435–75.

Coltheart, M., Patterson, K., and Marshall, J.C. eds. 1980: *Deep dyslexia*. London and Boston: Routledge and Kegan Paul.

*Gibson, E.J. and Levin, H. 1975: *The psychology of reading*. Cambridge, Mass.: MIT Press.

Huey, E.B. 1908 (1968): *The psychology and pedagogy of reading*. Cambridge, Mass.: MIT Press.

Kleiman, G.M. 1975: Speech recoding in reading. *Journal of verbal learning and verbal behavior* 14, 323–39.

McClelland, J.L. and Rumelhart, D. 1981: An interactive activation model of context effects in letter perception: Part 1. An account of basic findings. *Psychological review* 88, 357–407.

Meyer, D.E. and Schvaneveldt 1971: Facilitation in recognizing pairs of words: evidence for a dependence between retrieval operations. *Journal of experimental psychology* 90, 227–34.

Parkin, A.J. 1982: Phonological recoding in lexical decision: effects of spelling-to-sound regularity depend on how regularity is defined. *Memory and cognition* 10, 45–53.

Patterson, K.E., Marshall, J.C. and Coltheart, M. eds. 1985: *Surface dyslexia: cognitive and neurophysiological studies of phonological reading*. London: Erlbaum.

Rayner, K. 1975: The perceptual span and peripheral cues in reading. *Cognitive psychology* 7, 65–81.

Sanford, A.J. and Garrod, S.C. 1981: *Understanding written language: explorations in comprehension beyond the sentence*. New York and Chichester: John Wiley.
*Smith, F. 1982: *Understanding reading*. New York: CBS College Publishing.

reading: origins and learning The processes involved in responding to language in its written form: these processes include the perception and recognition of individual letters, the recognition of significant letter combinations, their association with relevant sounds and meanings and the interpretation of meaning relationships in written language. The term "reading" can be used to refer to any or all of the processes mentioned in the above definition.

In its origins, reading can be thought of as a natural development of earlier modes of communication. For example, in the gesture language of early man it was necessary to "read" meanings conveyed by hand signals. Symbolic meanings were also encapsulated in pictures drawn on bark or stone.

The use of sequences of pictures, each representing a single idea, brought reading as we know it a stage nearer. These pictures became more and more conventional in form in the course of time. Writing systems based on such "ideographs" are still used in some countries today, notably in China, where successive attempts to introduce the western alphabet have had little success.

In such a system it is necessary to learn some thousands of symbols or characters. Hence, over a period of time, symbols came to be used in some writing systems to represent the sounds in words, rather than their meanings, so that eventually a fairly small number of symbols could be used in different sequences and combinations to represent all the words in the language.

Symbols were used to represent syllables in the Mycenaean script (the earliest written records of Greek) although this script also included some pictorial characters. The ancient Semitic writing systems used by the Phoenicians and the Hebrews were syllabaries, and these persist in modified form in modern Hebrew writing and the Arabic script used in the Middle East. The Japanese continue to use a mixture of pictorial characters (the kanji), derived from Chinese, and syllabic script (the kana).

In ancient Greece the Mycenaean syllabary gave way to a system in which each consonant and vowel, that is, each segmental phoneme, had its own symbol, and this writing system was the forerunner of our present European alphabets.

As the Greek alphabet was taken up first by the Romans, and subsequently in other countries, the relationship between each sound and its unique letter tended in some cases to become rather tenuous. In Italian, Spanish, and Finnish, there is still a fairly close relationship between spelling and pronunciation. In English, however, there are only twenty-six letters available to represent a spoken language which uses some forty-five different phonemes and the spelling conventions represent a diverse mixture of imports and adaptations. Added to this, pronunciations have changed over the centuries but spellings have tended to be conservative, becoming more so with the invention of print.

The difficulties this presents both for learning to read and learning to spell have led to various attempts to simplify English spelling conventions since the introduction of print. These are well documented by Pitman and St John (1969). Such attempts have been rather more successful in other countries, notably Norway and Holland, where official spelling reforms have been made. As an alternative to spelling reform, some educators have introduced diacritics – marks added to letters to signal pronunciation, e.g. mat; mate — as a means of simplifying the learning task. Other schemes use colored letters or colored backgrounds for letters to provide cues to pronunciation. Another approach is the selection of words with very simple spellings in designing materials for the early stages of learning to read, e.g. "A man is in a tan van", with more complex spellings being introduced in the later stages at a controlled rate.

Another widespread alternative is the initial use of a very small vocabulary, irrespective of spelling, so that children do not have to learn to recognize too many words at once.

In the late 1950s there was an experiment in the use of an initial teaching alphabet (i.t.a.) of forty-four characters for use in the early stages of learning to read, with transfer to the traditional spelling system once the child could read with a reasonable degree of fluency. Many educators, however, have insisted that children can learn to cope quite adequately with our spelling system if we make full use of their own language patterns in early reading materials. This concept has informed the design of a number of modern reading schemes. The principle is more closely followed, however, when children read what they, and other children, have written with the help and guidance of the teacher – the "language-experience" approach (Stauffer 1970).

With the coming of universal education, the complexities of written English brought the problems of teaching reading to the fore in all English-speaking countries. This led to a vast amount of reading research and, in the United States particularly, to the growth of many very powerful publishing firms producing material for all stages of reading development. The teacher is now faced with a bewildering choice of materials and suggested methods for teaching reading.

The "Great Debate" in this field (Challe 1967) centered for many years on the question of whether children learn best if they start with the parts of words and learn to build them up to make meaningful "wholes" or start with the "wholes" and analyse them as and when the need arises. One school of thought emphasizes the teaching of letters and sounds, and how they go together to make up words, e.g., "ku-a-tu" says "cat" – the "phonic" approach. The other school emphasizes the importance of words of greater interest to children, e.g. words such as "elephant" or "aeroplane", and insist that these can be recognized by their overall shape – much as we learn to recognize most other things in everyday life. This is referred to as the "whole word" approach (see READING: COGNITIVE SKILLS).

It was evident even at the beginning of this century (Huey 1908), that such arguments took too narrow a view of the nature of the reading process and the demands on the adult reader. Nevertheless, it is only since the early 1960s that research has led to the development of more sophisticated models of the reading process (reviewed in Singer and Ruddell 1976), a more realistic appraisal of the reading demands of the adult world (Murphy 1973) and research into the teaching implications (Guthrie 1981; Mandl et al. 1984).

Information science has shown how much of the information in spoken and written communication is technically redundant (Smith 1978) and linguistic research has indicated many of the factors contributing to this redundancy (Shuy 1977). This evidence has provided substantial support for Huey's early insistence on the importance of context cues. Thus, presented with the following:

The glenks strove drortibly to lift it, encouraged by the elders of the tribe

the reader pronounces the unfamiliar "words" without hesitation, because of his familiarity with a wide range of letter-sound associations and sequences, and attributes a great deal of meaning to them as a result of responding to the various meaning relationships within the sentence. Had one of the "words" not been encountered previously in print, but was nevertheless in the reader's spoken vocabulary, then even if the spelling was also largely unfamiliar the fluent reader would have little difficulty in pronouncing it by analogy, the reader has little difficulty with, e.g., "He climbed into the laught" (loft).

The vast majority of letter-sound associations to which a child learns to respond, and the "whole words" he learns to recognize, are not in fact taught, but are learned inductively in this way. Current emphases in the teaching of reading take advantage of the insights provided by this type of observation, insisting on a primary

197

attack on context and meaning rather than attending first to letters and sounds (see Carr 1985).

Studies of reading comprehension have tended to focus on a logical analysis of what is involved in analyzing a text, the underlying intellectual abilities, and, more recently, the relationships between text content and the existing knowledge of the reader. The first type of study has led to the production of lists of skills, often hierarchically organized, and tests purporting to measure them. These might include tests of the ability to identify facts and main ideas, to make inferences, to note similarities and differences, to reorganize information, and so on. Studies of underlying intellectual abilities have drawn heavily on the factor analytic techniques used in studies of human intelligence – with broadly similar results. Studies which focus on conceptual structures and knowledge structures lie in the main stream of current research in cognitive psychology and artificial intelligence.

Text analysis now provides a substantial contribution to studies of reading at all levels. It covers such aspects as legibility and lay-out, grammatical structure, conceptual structure, and attitudinal features. Another important area, not yet as extensively researched, is what might be termed, "the ethnography of reading" – who reads what, when, why, and to what effect (Murphy 1973). This area is likely to become more important as society becomes more dependent on access to relevant information from an ever increasing data base. All of this has many implications for education.

The teaching of reading includes the provision of any practical experiences that the teacher may think necessary for the child's understanding and appreciation of what is read and opportunities for developing oral language relating to these experiences. Within this context the teacher seeks to develop a growing awareness of what print is, and does, as a prelude to teaching specific reading skills, that is to say, all that is involved in the effective achievement of the reading task – or in simply enjoying reading. This can include clarifying reading purposes, locating and selecting reading materials likely to be suitable for achieving these purposes, strategies for dealing with different kinds of text for different kinds of purpose and ways of evaluating both the particular reading outcome and the processes involved in achieving the outcome, with such evaluation leading to decisions about how best to bring about further self-improvement. Thus, the teaching of reading can now be viewed within the more general context of information science and the growing technology relating to information storage and retrieval, as well as being part of the teaching of English generally. Although the actual definition of reading may continue to be restricted as indicated above, the practicalities of teaching reading inevitably relate to this much broader setting (Pearson 1984). JEM

Bibliography

Carr, T. 1985: The development of reading skills. *New directions in child development*, vol. 27. San Fancisco: Jossey Bass.

Challe, Jeanne 1967: *Learning to read: the great debate*. New York: McGraw-Hill.

Guthrie, J.T. ed. 1981: *Comprehension and teaching: research reviews*. Newark, Delaware: International Reading Association.

Huey, E.B. 1908 (1968): *The psychology and pedagogy of reading*. Cambridge, Mass.: MIT Press.

Mandl, H., Stein, N. and Trabasso, T. eds. 1984: *Learning and comprehension of texts*. Hillsdale, N.J.: Erlbaum.

Murphy, R.T. 1973: *Adult functional reading study: final report*. Princeton, N.J.: Educational Testing Service.

Pearson, D. ed. 1984: *Handbook of reading research*. New York: Longman.

Pitman, Sir J. and St John, J. 1969: *Alphabets and reading: the initial teaching alphabet*. London: Pitman.

Shuy, R.W. ed. 1977: *Linguistic theory: what can it say about reading?* Newark, Delaware: International Reading Association.

Singer, H. and Ruddell, B. eds. 1976: *Theoretical models and processes of reading*. 2nd edn. Newark, Delaware: International Reading Association.

Smith, F. 1978: *Understanding reading: a psycholinguistic analysis of reading and learning to read*.

2nd edn. London and New York: Holt, Rinehart and Winston.

Stauffer, R.G. 1970: *The language-experience approach to the teaching of reading*. New York: Harper and Row.

reasoning Drawing conclusions from premises expressed in argument or represented in thought. In psychology Piaget's theory has been most influential in describing qualitative changes in reasoning that occur with development although it is not universally accepted. He describes the reasoning of the pre-operational child aged between approximately two and eight years as transductive. That is, it is neither inductive nor deductive but proceeds by haphazard connections between elements that may not actually be related. Only with the acquisition of concrete operations between eight and eleven years does the child become capable of systematic deductions with respect to objects in the real world. With adolescence and the acquisition of formal operations the child becomes able to engage in hypothetico-deductive reasoning with respect to abstract propositions. (See also LOGICAL THINKING; PIAGET.)   GEB

Bibliography

Piaget, J. 1983: Piaget's theory. In *Handbook of child psychology*. 4th edn, vol. 1, ed. W. Kessen. New York: Wiley.

Siegel, L.S. and Brainerd, C.J. 1978: *Alternatives to Piaget*. New York: Academic Press.

regression In common use, the appearance of behavior appropriate to an earlier life stage, triggered by stress. Examples include the adolescent who "regresses" to whining or tantrums when parental demands are imposed; the young child who "regresses" to bedwetting or thumbsucking with the birth of a younger sibling. The term derives from FREUD's ontogenetic model of development, in which the individual passes through a series of developmental stages. Ideally, progress requires a balance of gratification and frustration; either excessive frustration or excessive gratification leads to fixation. In reality, normal development inevitably entails a less than perfect balance, and earlier stages leave residues in the form of minor fixations. Regression represents a return to an earlier stage, commonly a stage at which gratification was experienced.   ND

Bibliography

Freud, S. (1916–17) 1963: *Introductory lectures on psychoanalysis*. Part 3. Trans. J. Strachey. London: Hogarth.

regression, in statistics is used in two distinct ways. In regression analysis values of a dependent variable are predicted from a linear function: $y = bx + a$, where y is the value of the dependent variable, b is a constant by which values of the independent variable x are multiplied, and a is a constant which is added in every case. We are therefore able to predict how much increase or decrease in the value of the independent variable x will produce a stated increase or decrease in the value of the dependent variable y. In multiple regression the values of the dependent variable y are predicted from the values of several independent variables $x_1 \ldots x_j$ rather than one.

The other use of the word "regression" is in the phrase "regression to the mean". This was a phenomenon noted by Galton, who found that the children of two tall parents tend to be shorter than their parents, although still taller than average. This seemed to imply that the population was continuously getting closer to the mean. But this was clearly not happening. The solution to this conundrum lies in the fact that in a normally distributed population the majority of members have heights (or weights, or abilities) which are close to the mean. The probability of any individual deviating far from the mean is therefore very small. Hence it is very unlikely that any child of two extremely tall parents would also be extremely tall.   RL

Bibliography

Winer, B.J. 1962: *Statistical principles in experimental design*. New York: Holt, Rinehart and Winston.

releasers Are social stimuli which are especially effective in producing a response by another individual. The term also implies that both the stimulus features and the responsiveness have become mutually adapted during the course of their evolution. The term was originally used in early ethological writings. In developmental psychology the concept is most readily applied to the infant's ATTACHMENT responses to its caregiver, such as SMILING and CRYING, which are regarded as resulting from selective pressures favoring proximity-seeking signals. JA

Bibliography

R.A. Hinde 1982: *Ethology*. New York and Oxford: Oxford University Press.

remedial mathematics Although arithmetic disability is seldom encountered apart from reading disability, the literature in remedial education is predominantly concerned with reading. Reference to remedial mathematics is minimal.

There is widespread uncertainty among teachers about both content and methods of teaching mathematics to slow learners, and there has been a lack of consensus about the proper emphasis in mathematics instruction: computational and conceptual approaches maintain an uneasy balance.

Although efforts to reform the mathematics curriculum aim at introducing basic concepts of the discipline as early as possible, computational skills form a major part of children's experience in primary school mathematics. Speed and accuracy for computation appear to improve with practice, hence drill has been used as a justifiable means of building arithmetic skills. But various arguments, particularly the objection that drill cannot develop mathematical thinking, have been put forward against using it as the main method of instruction. Proponents of instruction in the concepts which underlie computations have claimed that understanding these concepts enhances children's ability to apply their knowledge in novel situations. (See MATHEMATICS.)

COMPUTER-AIDED INSTRUCTION programs use the computer as a basis for providing individual practice on computational skills and giving continuing feedback. The importance of feedback is not as reinforcement, but as a way of providing information to enable the pupil to correct errors. Scope for adjustments in problem presentation and difficulty level mean that children do not have to work on problems that are too easy or too difficult, and represents a deliberate attempt to enhance motivation.

Those who make much of the distinction between simple computational skills and an awareness of mathematical concepts often believe that efforts should be made to teach the fundamental structures of mathematics in ways that take into account children's intellectual capabilities. The use of structure oriented materials such as Diene's blocks and Cuisenaire rods is intended to help children to discover and refine concepts as they engage in manipulations of the materials which embody the mathematical properties. The structure oriented methods and materials raise questions about the nature of mathematical understanding and about the sorts of structures they actually teach.

Little is known about children's mathematical learning, and teaching methods have not been adequately evaluated. Most children routinely carry out computations and demonstrate a basic understanding of number concepts and quantity. Being mathematically competent involves more than knowing a range of concepts and mastering computation. The importance of problem solving with the use of particular heuristic strategies is widely recognized in mathematics teaching. Suggestions for remedial work in this area stem more from a commonsense approach to mathematics instruction than from any clear understanding of mathematics problem solving processes. Setting up problems of the real world in which actual mathematical problems are encountered, simplifying the text in which the problem is formulated, and establishing a strategy for what is known and what must be found out are the guidelines given to teachers in their efforts at remedial work. SDS

Bibliography

Bell, A.W. et al. 1980: *A review of research in mathematical education. Section A: research on learning and teaching.* University of Nottingham: Technical Report, Shell Centre for Mathematical Education.

Ginsburg, H. 1977: *Children's arithmetic.* New York: Van Nostrand.

Kintsch, W. and Greens, J. 1985: Understanding and solving word arithmetic problems. *Psychological review* 92, 109–29.

Resnick, L.B. and Ford, W.W. 1981: *The psychology of mathematics instruction.* Hillsdale, N.J.: Lawrence Erlbaum.

Romberg, T. and Carpenter, T. 1986: Research on teaching and learning mathematics: two disciplines of scientific enquiry. In *The handbook of research on teaching.* 3rd edn, ed. M. Wittrock. New York: Macmillan.

remedial reading Teaching methods for reading acquisition may broadly be classified under one of two groups, one with its emphasis on decoding written language, the other on extracting meaning from text. The different methods are generally not dramatically opposed to one another, except that each tends to focus on a particular aspect of the total reading process. Individual schools in the UK have considerable freedom in the choice of method, and materials used for the teaching of reading. Although the popularity of particular methods varies from time to time, different methods and ideas concerning the teaching of reading may co-exist depending on their appropriateness for use with children who vary in reading ability.

Over the past decade there has been a sudden increase in the publication of materials which represent attempts to fulfill the needs expressed by teachers who are helping pupils who have difficulty learning to read in the regular classroom. Apart from the accent on drill and continual revision the bulk of this material is not distinguishable from materials available for use with beginning readers. With a few exceptions the majority of remedial methods do not provide a theoretical rationale for their effectiveness in meeting specific needs. Some have grown out of experience and have been developed on a pragmatic basis. This is hardly surprising in view of the fact that the preponderance of research on reading difficulty is devoted to diagnosis. The long term effect of specific remedial methods receives hardly any attention.

Several remedial methods are designed for use with children having moderate to severe reading problems. Remedial techniques focusing on decoding skills include the diacritical marking system, i.e. color coding of either letters or words, and other techniques which aim to establish sound–symbol associations leading on to the development of word recognition. (See READING: ORIGINS AND LEARNING.) Multisensory methods are based on the premise that some children learn best when content is presented in several modalities. Kinesthetic and tactile stimulation are frequently used along with the visual and auditory modalities. Some research supports the use of the multi-sensory method with retarded readers. Instructions for the use of these methods despite their emphasis on decoding skills reflect the important principle that the learning activities should always be meaningful and interesting.

The Method of Repeated or Simultaneous Reading also called the Impress Method in the United States literature is a technique with theoretical and empirical support currently in use in remedial work. The focus is on deriving meaning from what is heard and what is read. Claims for its effectiveness are not only for remedial purposes but for developing fluent reading in beginners. The method relies crucially on the pupil reading while simultaneously hearing the text read aloud by a competent reader. Both accuracy and speed are said to improve. This suggests that although not complete in itself the method improves reading fluency and has a positive effect on pupils' confidence in their ability to read. The rationale for the success of this method is based on its potential to facilitate comprehension by the chunking of information or reducing the attentional burden of slow decoding. The technique possibly assists the child in the process of exploiting its ability to cope with spoken language and so derive meaning from written language.

On a higher level several techniques are encouraged for use in remedial work to develop reading comprehension and effective study skills. These include an introduction to the passage to serve as an advance organizer, pictures appropriate to the text, activities which involve sequencing and organizing scrambled text, setting a purpose for reading a passage, prediction of events when reading fictional material, and producing such things as graphs, tables and diagrams from text. Most of these methods are inspired by the recent theoretical analysis produced by Frank Smith (1971) and Kenneth Goodman (1982) which stresses the importance of children's desire to extract meaning from passages which they read and of the rather complex and sophisticated hypotheses which they use to do this.   SDS

Bibliography

Goodman, K.S. 1982: *Language and literacy*, vols. 1 and 2. London: Routledge and Kegan Paul.

Naidoo, S. 1981: Teaching methods and their rationale. In *Dyslexia research and its applications to education*, eds. G. Th. Pavlidis and T.R. Miles. New York: John Wiley.

Pearson, D. ed. 1984: *Handbook of reading research*. New York: Longman.

Samuels, S.J. 1978: *What research has to say about reading inclination*. Newark, Delaware: International Reading Association.

Smith, F. 1971: *Understanding reading: a psycholinguistic analysis*. New York: Holt, Rinehart and Winston.

Strang, R. 1975: *Reading diagnosis and remediation*. Newark, Delaware: International Reading Association.

reversibility In Piaget's theory of intellectual development, that property of a system of mental operations that enables return to a particular point of departure. Two kinds of reversible operation are acquired during the concrete operational period (see CONCRETE THINKING) and allow a new flexibility of thought. These are (1) Inversion (negation). Any mental operation that can be carried out in one direction can be carried out mentally in the opposite direction. The child who understands that $2 + 4 = 6$ should also understand that $6 - 2 = 4$. (2) Compensation (or reciprocity). For any mental operation there exists another that will compensate or nullify its effects within a total system of transformations. For example in the conservation of liquid-volume task (see PIAGET) the child who has entered the concrete operational period can, according to Piaget, mentally compensate for an observed change in the height of liquid by noting the change in width. This helps the child to comprehend that the volume stayed constant despite a change in its appearance.   GEB

Bibliography

Brainerd, C.J. 1978: *Piaget's theory of intelligence*. Englewood Cliffs, N.J.: Prentice-Hall.

S

schema Body of knowledge that provides a framework within which to locate new items of knowledge (plural *schemata* or *schemas*). Bartlett (1932) suggested that the schema is the active, organized setting within which new experiences are influenced by those previous reactions and experiences that are connected by some common aspect. In recent years interest in the schema has again become prominent in cognitive psychology and its role has been explored in, for example, the comprehension of text. This research has been influenced by work in artificial intelligence which emphasizes the importance of large schema-like data structures that have been termed *frames* or *scripts*. The development of different types of schema in children has been described by Piaget. Children, in his description, develop simple, sensori-motor action schemata, such as the "sucking schema". They apply such patterns of behavior to a growing number of objects, and thereby *assimilate* more of the environment to their established schemata. In so doing, however, they adapt the schemata to new circumstances, a process Piaget calls accommodation. The initial schemata may therefore be hereditary. Their expansion into new domains and the changes in them which this expansion brings are the basis of cognitive growth (see ACCOMMODATION; ASSIMILATION). As the child grows its schemata develop from simple grasp of a particular relationships such as the causal one embodied in "pulling a string in order to shake a hanging rattle" to secondary, more abstract schemata which are "fit for new coordinations of cause and effect". Further abstraction towards *formal operations* and schemata of highly abstract relationships, such as those of algebra, carry the child to mature, adult intellectual functioning (see PIAGET; MATHEMATICS).   GVJ/RL

Bibliography

Anderson, John H. 1984: *Cognitive psychology and its implications.* 2nd edn. San Francisco: W.H. Freeman.

Bartlett, Frederic C. 1932: *Remembering: a study in experimental and social psychology.* London and New York: Cambridge University Press.

Piaget, J. 1954: *The construction of reality in the child.* New York: Basic Books.

school as a social organization This is a general concept which embraces a range of theoretical and methodological perspectives on the school as a complex social system which has a *structure* (a formal and informal organization, a system of management and administration, an allocation of roles with rights and duties etc.) and a *culture* (one or more systems of values, norms and sanctions among its members). From a psychological point of view these perspectives consider the impact of the school on the attitudes and achievements of individual teachers and pupils and on the interactions between individuals or groups of individuals.

The classic account of the school as a social system is that by Waller (1932), who pioneered many of the themes developed in later theory and research on the school – the distinctive culture of the school, the characteristics and social relations of the teachers, the transactions and conflicts between teachers and pupils, pupil subcultures, and the relations between the school and its local community. Waller skillfully combined functionalist, conflict and symbolic interactionist perspectives, showing that each was essential to an adequate account of the school as a social system.

Subsequent work lacks the coherence and range of Waller's book mainly because it treats in greater depth areas which

Waller covered at a relatively superficial level. Later work, especially in the United States, initially specialized in the application of organization theory to the study of the school as a social system, drawing upon a large literature on other complex institutions such as hospitals and factories and on a burgeoning literature on bureaucracies in modern societies. This tradition continues, especially in North America, with a strong emphasis on functionalist theory and on quantification. Certainly this field is now highly fragmented, but it continues to yield applications for the management and administration of schools (see Davies 1982).

In Britain, by contrast, the dominant, but far from exclusive, preference has been for more ethnographic approaches (see Hammersley 1980) in which, under the influence of anthropology and symbolic interactionism, social psychological and microsociological concerns coalesce. Typically in ethnographic studies a single school, or one or more segments within a school, are closely examined, commonly with some attention to social class factors, in the spirit of Hollingshead's pioneering American investigation (1949). Of the smaller segments within the school as a social system, relations between the school principal and the teachers, and between the teachers and their colleagues, have until recent times been relatively neglected by ethnographers, whose primary focus has been TEACHER-PUPIL INTERACTIONS, pupil-pupil interactions and PEER GROUP influences. Usually ethnographic studies of the school rely heavily on naturalistic observation and qualitative evidence. Hargreaves (1967) examined the impact of streaming or tracking on teacher-pupil and pupil-pupil relations, with special reference to delinquency prone youth and DISRUPTIVE PUPILS, and making use of subcultural theory, group dynamics research and sociometric techniques. This approach to pupil differentiation has been consolidated by Ball (1981) in his study of a comprehensive school which introduced the organization of "mixed-ability" teaching. He offers a careful assessment of its impact on subject choice and pupil identity. In the United States, Jackson (1968) used ethnographic methods to elucidate the powerful impact of schools as social institutions on pupils, their feelings towards school and their consequent involvement or withdrawal. Because Jackson carefully related his analysis to more conventional psychological studies of pupils, his work exercised a profound influence on the psychology of education (see EDUCATION: PSYCHOLOGY OF), in part through the novel methodology and in part because it set psychological studies of pupils within a more adequate social psychological framework. Smith and Geoffrey (1968) used ethnographic methods for the more intensive study of classroom processes, paying special attention to teacher strategies and TEACHING TECHNIQUES. By 1979 in Britain Woods was able to offer a sophisticated account of pupil adaptations to school which greatly advanced the earlier and more simple division of pupils into "conformists" and "deviants", and to counterbalance this by an investigation of the ways in which a variety of teachers' adaptations to their situations are constrained by the social organization of the school.

In recent work, such as that by Sharp and Green (1975), the responses of teachers and pupils are set within a neo-marxist theoretical perspective, strengthening the links with macrosociology but weakening the value for educational psychology. Complementing this, however, there has been a massive growth of classroom research which is essentially social psychological in character.

It is evident that the concept of the school as a social organization is now a vague, umbrella term under which an extremely wide range of theories, methodologies and substantive studies can be subsumed. In principle the school as a social organization could be a useful bridging concept between the sociological and psychological studies of schooling. Although there are notable continuities of theme pursued by these diverse studies, there has been little consistent theoretical development, and the absence of a cumulative set of empirical findings is striking: the different paths of both theory and empirical research seem to be diverging rather than converging. Since sociological work does not always overtly acknowledge the social psychological nature of its subject, educational psychologists have sometimes remained uninfluenced by research which carries a sociological label. These disciplinary boundaries are currently weakening and educational psychology is taking greater account of the vast literature on the school as a social organization. Rutter et al. (1979) in their study of school effectiveness, SCHOOL DIFFERENCES and EDUCATIONAL ATTAINMENT provide a good example of an influential psychological investigation which is likely to stimulate the interest of educational psychologists in the school as a social organization.   DHH

Bibliography

Ball, S.J. 1981: *Beachside comprehensive*. Cambridge: Cambridge University Press.

*Davies, B. 1982: Organisational theory and schools. In *The social sciences in educational studies*, ed. A. Hartnett. London and Boston: Heinemann.

*Hammersley, M. 1980: Classroom ethnography. *Educational analysis* 2(2), 47–74.

Hargreaves, D.H. 1967: *Social relations in a secondary school*. London and Boston: Routledge and Kegan Paul.

Hollingshead, A.B. 1949: *Elmstown's youth*. London and New York: Wiley.

Jackson, P.W. 1968: *Life in classrooms*. London and New York: Holt, Rinehart and Winston.

Rutter, M. et al. 1979: *Fifteen thousand hours*. London: Open Books; Cambridge, Mass.: Harvard University Press.

Sarason, S.B. and Klaber, M. 1985: The school as a social situation. *Annual review of psychology* 36, 115–40.

Sharp, R. and Green, A. 1975: *Education and social control*. London and Boston: Routledge and Kegan Paul.

Smith, L. and Geoffrey, W. 1968: *The complexities of an urban classroom*. London and New York: Holt, Rinehart and Winston.

Waller, W. 1932: *The sociology of teaching*. New York: Wiley.

Woods, P. 1979: *The divided school*. London and Boston: Routledge and Kegan Paul.

school differences Many parents go to considerable lengths to place their children in particular schools thus demonstrating that they believe in the existence of school differences. Social researchers however have not always shared this belief, but rather have argued that apparent differences may result from variation in the social background and ability of pupils.

Large-scale American studies (e.g. Jencks 1973) failed to identify any school-related variables to account for differences in life chances. In comparison to individual characteristics and family background, they argued, school influence was trivial. (According to Jencks, school influence was less important than "luck".)

By their nature, however, these large scale studies focused only on relatively conspicuous school variables such as style of buildings, levels of resourcing and pupil-teacher ratios. They did not attempt to collect information on attitudes, values and styles of the teachers. Furthermore because they lacked information on pupil characteristics prior to secondary school entrance, they were unable to measure any increment in achievement which could be attributed to differences in effectiveness. Finally their findings are limited because of the use of verbal reasoning scores rather than measures of learning in subjects actually taught by schools. More recent research in America and in the United Kingdom has re-opened the debate by demonstrating school differences in examination results (Brimer et al. 1978), delinquency (Power et al. 1972 and Gath et al. 1977) and attendance. The complex statistical study by Summers and Wolfe (1977) actually posed the question "Do schools make a difference?". After a series of analyses that utilized pupil-specific data gathered over several years of schooling they concluded that, even after allowing for a whole series of other influences, schools could make a difference.

The contribution to the debate by Rutter et al. (1979) is important for it attempted to control for intake variation to the schools. Having allowed for this, the researchers still found differences in outcome measures of attendance, behavior, delinquency and attainment between pupils from twelve inner-city schools. The need for such control is clear because Rutter et al. demonstrated substantial differences between the pupil intake to the schools studied. However, other researchers (Heath et al. 1980) have criticized the methodology and have argued that more careful control might have reduced the variation in the outcome measures. Replications of similar studies are needed to resolve the matter.

School differences in process – atmosphere, organization and style of teaching – have also been investigated both in the United States (Brookover et al. 1976) and in Britain (Rutter et al. 1979). The researchers have all argued that those differences are of crucial importance and are likely to have a direct effect on pupils' achievements. Further studies are needed to clarify these issues and to document the ways in which schools that are shown to be effective have created and sustained their pupils' achievements.   PJM

Bibliography

Brimer, M.A. et al. 1978: *Sources of difference in school achievement.* Slough, Bucks: National Foundation for Educational Research.

Brookover, W.B. et al. 1976: *Elementary school climate and school achievement.* East Lansing: Michigan State University, College of Urban Development.

Doyle, W. 1986: Classroom organization and management. In *The handbook of research on teaching.* ed. M. Wittrock. New York: Macmillan.

Gath, D. et al. 1977: *Child guidance and delinquency in a London borough.* Maudsley monographs no. 24. Oxford: Oxford University Press.

Heath, A. et al. 1980: The seventy thousand hours that Rutter left out. *Oxford review of education* 6, 3–19.

Jencks, C. et al. 1973: *Inequality.* London and New York: Allen Lane.

Power, M.J. et al. 1972: Neighbourhood, school and juveniles before the courts. *British journal of criminology* 12, 111–32.

Rutter, M. et al. 1979: *Fifteen thousand hours: secondary schools and their effects on children.* London: Open Books; Cambridge, Mass.: Harvard University Press.

Summers, A.A. and Wolfe, B.L. 1977: Do schools make a difference? *American economic review.*

school failure Cannot be identified without some reference to the aims and objectives of education. However these are diverse, and their specification will vary considerably between individuals, social groups, cultures and countries. Furthermore many essential facets of education are not open to precise definition, measurement or evaluation. Much research on school failure has therefore had to use limited indices of education, such as competence in reading and computation or performance in public examinations. These indices have a measure of objectivity and are pertinent to education but cannot be equated with it. Other aspects of education, concerned with social behavior, knowledge of the world, self-sufficiency, independence of outlook and maintenance of mental health are arguably no less important but they are more difficult to define, objectify and assess.

In practice it is the broad spectrum of cognitive skills and knowledge that receives most attention in education. Children whose performance in such activities falls below the norm for their age group are considered as "failing", with those markedly below such a standard being identified as requiring special attention. Fully reliable methods of identifying school failure, even in these terms, do not exist, nor are there general prescriptions guaranteed to rectify it (see EDUCATIONAL ATTAINMENT; REMEDIAL READING; REMEDIAL MATHEMATICS). It is also difficult to specify the size of the problem. In the United Kingdom it has been estimated that some 20 per cent of the school population need some form of additional specialist attention during their school career but this estimate does not include children who meet the expected standard for their age but are capable of achieving very much more.

The possible reasons for less than

optimal performance in school are numerous and varied and complex in their interactions, with the incidence, however defined, much more prevalent in boys than girls. In developing countries, where education is not freely or easily available, "school failure" as such is likely to be far less prevalent and more closely linked to physical health and nutrition.

In western developed countries it is estimated that about 2 per cent of the school population have moderate or severe LEARNING DIFFICULTIES attributable to their genetic endowment. However, it is being increasingly realized that such children can learn more and to greater effect if the teaching and learning experiences offered are appropriately structured in relation to existing skills and feasible objectives. The importance of early identification and appropriate action, to include increased involvement with parents, now receives much wider recognition. Regrettably, many educational systems still make insufficient provision for the continuing education of such children beyond their school years.

Other children are identified as failing in school because they lack the necessary component skills essential, for example, to be competent in reading (see REMEDIAL READING; READING: COGNITIVE SKILLS). Specific sensory and neurological deficits may contribute to such problems and in extreme cases perhaps cause them (see BLIND, THE: PSYCHOLOGY AND EDUCATION; HEARING IMPAIRED AND DEAF THE: PSYCHOLOGY AND EDUCATION; DYSLEXIC CHILDREN; LEARNING DIFFICULTIES). Some children who have had a learning disability nevertheless appear able to develop their own alternative strategies which enable them to achieve success.

Emotional stress and conflict, whether arising from organic factors, from family tensions or from poor relations with peers or teachers, may also contribute to school failure. Many normal children can experience difficulties with school work of course, but these often prove transient and remit spontaneously over time. The resilience of some children exposed to stress, or their ability to cope with it without any apparent disadvantage, require more investigation.

Many more children exist who appear normal in every respect except for their poor school performance. A disproportionate number of them come from low socioeconomic group families living in the poorer city areas. This fact in itself provides no explanation, of course, and many exceptions are found that counter this general trend. Nonetheless the poor educational responses of such children have long caused concern to educationists and in recent years to central governments (see COMPENSATORY EDUCATION; EDUCATIONAL ATTAINMENT AND SOCIAL CLASS). Parental interest and involvement, particularly at the preschool stage, has been emphasized as important to later progress. Personality and temperamental characteristics are also relevant. Introverted children generally perform better than extroverts, at least at the secondary stage of their schooling. However, this could be partly a function of teaching style and the demands of an academic curriculum at this stage. The expectations of teachers as well as pupils have also been implicated (see EDUCATIONAL ATTAINMENT AND EXPECTATIONS). Other research has emphasized the importance of the child's orientation to learning (see EDUCATIONAL ATTAINMENT AND LOCUS OF CONTROL). Children who play truant from school or who are delinquent usually fail in school but they also tend to come from the most disadvantaged sectors of the community (see ABSENCE FROM SCHOOL AND TRUANCY; DELINQUENCY). The effects of allergies, artificial additives in food and lead pollution from traffic fumes have recently been identified as other possible contributors to poor school performance and behavior. Simple explanations of school failure are therefore precluded by the number and complexity of interacting factors.

Learning has generally been found to be more efficient and better retained when it is based on intrinsic motivation – when the learning task elicits the natural curiosity and interests of the child. Extrinsic motivation is dependent on the use of external rewards or punishments and tends to be less effective. However, extrinsic motivation may provide the only basis or strategy that will induce learning some tasks, particularly in the early stages of development or at later stages when the task set may appear quite unrelated to any previous experience of the child (see COGNITIVE DEVELOPMENT: NON-PIAGETIAN THEORIES; PIAGET).

Schools and educational services may fail as well as pupils. The relevance of the school curriculum and the manner of its presentation obviously have crucial importance. Some countries and some schools seem more successful than others in providing valued alternatives to the prevalent academic emphasis. School organization and the management of pupils by their teachers is also being increasingly recognized as needing much closer examination (see SCHOOL DIFFERENCES; SCHOOL AS A SOCIAL ORGANIZATION).

Research on teaching, which may be considered the obverse of learning, remains inconclusive in offering solutions to the problem of school failure, because of the complexity of the interactions between teacher and pupil and the broader social context to learning (Entwistle, 1981). However, focusing on teaching rather than learning, by way of conclusion, may serve to highlight some of the more difficult issues that confront all parents, teachers and educational administrators concerned with reducing school failure and maximizing educational attainment. These may be summarized as follows:

(1) Children vary enormously in the rate and the manner in which they learn. Any educational provision to reduce school failure must take this into account.
(2) The requirement to teach groups in the classroom and to foster the development of individual children places extremely high demands on educational resources, particularly in relation to the personal qualities and skills of the teaching profession.
(3) Identifying children who are failing or who are likely to fail in school is a necessary first stage requirement but in itself resolves no problems.

(4) A more rigorous monitoring of the curriculum and its effectiveness in demonstrating relevance to the child and at least meeting basic employment demands in terms of literacy and numeracy, seem highly desirable.
(5) The acquisition of cognitive skills needed to reduce and prevent school failure cannot be divorced from their social context. However, it is often not possible to change this radically or quickly even when it appears patently desirable to do so. In such circumstances the only feasible alternative is to attempt to devise, experimentally and pragmatically, learning programs tailored to the individual child that have some effect. Such an approach, which has already had some success in helping severely retarded children, requires not only competence in terms of the subject matter to be acquired but also specialized knowledge of the basic psychological processes involved, such as perception, learning, memory and reasoning.   RM/AKW

Bibliography
Como, L. and Snow, R.E. 1986: Adapting teaching to individual differences among learners. In *The handbook of research on teaching*. ed. M. Wittrock. New York: Macmillan.

Entwistle, Noel J. 1981: *Styles of learning and teaching*. Chichester and New York: John Wiley.

Holt, J. 1981: *Teach your own*. Brightlingsea, Essex: Lighthouse Books; New York: Delacorte Press, Seymour Lawrence.

Rutter, M. et al. 1979: *Fifteen thousand hours: secondary schools and their effects on children*. London: Open Books; Cambridge, Mass.: Harvard University Press.

school learning, evaluation The evaluation of effectiveness of school learning involves the attempt to judge the success and value of pupils' learning against specified criteria. In order to evaluate effectiveness, aims and objectives are needed against which pupils' performance is judged. This usually takes the form of specifying formal curricula and assessing pupils' knowledge or understanding of it, although there is also a "hidden" or informal curriculum which it is more difficult to evaluate. Techniques ranging from objective, quantitative measurement to more informal or qualitative description have been used for this purpose.

Until the 1970s, educational success in England was measured largely by national examinations, in particular the now defunct 11+ examination and the now threatened national GCE (General Certificate of Education) and CSE (Certificate of Secondary Education) examinations at 16+. In 1974 the Bullock committee made as the first of its principal recommendations the need for a system of monitoring, and the Assessment of Performance Unit (APU) was set up in 1975 as a unit within the Department of Education and Science (DES) to promote 'the development of methods of assessing and monitoring the achievement of children at school'. The APU is different from public examinations because its aim is to monitor national standards rather than assess individual learning. Using "light sampling" (i.e. testing about 2 per cent of all children) and an "item bank" of questions, the APU monitors national attainments in mathematics, language, science, aesthetics, and physical, personal and social development.

Whereas the centralized educational system of Britain is amenable to monitoring and public tests, the de-centralized, highly local system in the US makes national monitoring difficult. The National Assessment of Educational Progress (NAEP) was set up by the federal government in 1967 to evaluate educational outcomes nationally for use in determining policy.

Although national monitoring is an important part of educational evaluation, most evaluation of school learning aims at assessing individuals rather than large groups. The various methods employed for such evaluation include:

National tests: The most widely-used and well-known technique of evaluating pupils' learning is still examinations, culminating in Britain at the end of the school career in the national public examinations (GCE and CSE) which attempt to measure the outcome of the educational pro-

cess through a series of objective tests (NORMATIVE- AND CRITERION-REFERENCED TESTS). This is a national assessment, administered through different local examination boards, which caters for pupils considered to be sufficiently able to attempt courses leading to the national examination, normally about 60 per cent of the age cohort. Public examinations provide a summative or terminal assessment of the learned material, and claim high objectivity and validity (see TESTS, INTELLIGENCE). The criterion of validity they use is known as content validity, and involves describing a given body of knowledge and measuring the pupils' mastery of it, i.e. what they have learned (see TESTS, VALIDITY OF). In the USA, there are no public tests administered to the majority of pupils but a variety of norm-referenced tests of academic skills are administered by local school boards and used for comparative purposes.

Local tests: Many schools use their own internal examinations to assess pupils' learning; these tests may take place once a year or more frequently as part of continuous assessment and are set and marked by teachers. Objective tests (whether administered nationally through the examination boards or the DES in Britain, or locally through the school boards in the USA) for monitoring progress and evaluating the effectiveness of learning aim at high validity, objectivity, and reliability. Tests however tend to evaluate the "product" of learning rather than the "process", thereby missing out on an important aspect of education.

Examination results are only a small part of what are generally considered to be desirable outcomes. Bloom's taxonomy of educational objectives includes the cognitive, affective and psychomotor domains, but very few formal tests attempt to assess more than the cognitive "product". Research has shown (Raven 1977) that the vast majority of teachers, pupils and parents 'want schools to foster such qualities as ... independence, the ability to make their own observations and learn without instruction, the ability to apply facts and techniques to new problems, to

209

develop their characters and personality'. Yet the fact that the product of learning is so much easier to define and evaluate than the process has led to a concentration on the cognitive areas of assessment.

Behavioral observations: Partly for this reason, observational methods are sometimes used to evaluate learning, particularly with children under the age of eleven. Some "process" objectives refer to *specific activities* on the part of pupils rather than an increase in knowledge. For example the teacher may wish pupils to work collaboratively with one another. One direct way to assess whether such an objective is achieved is to observe and record children's classroom behavior. Galton and Croll (1980) used this method to study the effect of different kinds of teaching strategies in the primary school. Individual "target pupils" were observed for short periods to see whether they were working alone, with others, attending to or interacting with the teacher, or socializing among themselves. They found that pupils in a large sample of classrooms spent no more than 5 per cent of lesson time in group-work, despite exhortations of the Plowden Committee (1967) about the effectiveness of this form of learning.

Sylva, Roy and Painter (1980) used direct behavioral observation to assess the effectiveness of different kinds of preschool curriculum. They observed target children in a variety of preschools and found that those attending "structured" programs engaged in more imaginative pretend and problem solving play. In most observational studies classroom process is assessed and not the performance of individuals.

Informal school-based assessments: Teachers often devise less formal methods of measuring progress, although still striving for objectivity, when they assess course work and make pupil profiles. The teacher specifies the nature and amount of coursework to be assessed (and sometimes graded) and completes a profile on each pupil as part of a formative (as opposed to summative) assessment. 'Formative assessment . . . is an aid to teaching and learning, it takes account of work at

present by looking back over the past in order to look forward to future development . . . summative assessment tends to freeze time, to isolate performance and competence from their developmental context and, because it can be imagined to deal in absolute, objective values, lends itself to being thought of as a means of conclusively classifying people' (in Burgess and Adams 1980). Informal methods have the advantage of providing continuous feedback as part of the evaluation, and of including all the pupils and not just those who are college-bound. As well as assessing pupils' learning in this way, teachers are increasingly using self evaluation systems (Simons 1980) to evaluate the effectiveness of the whole curriculum and different teaching methods.

Pupil self-assessment: In Britain Burgess and Adams (1980) describe an ambitious scheme whereby pupils are involved both in the planning (objectives) of the content of the curriculum and in the recording of outcomes (evaluation) of their education; 'at the heart of our proposals is a statement which every sixteen-year-old will have on leaving school, showing his experience, competence, interests and purposes, which he can show to parents and employers alike'. They propose that this system of evaluation should be nationally validated and accredited so that it carries the same validity and objectivity (and therefore status, particularly to those outside the education system) as the present public examinations. Developments along these lines provide evaluation of the effectiveness of the learning process as well as the product.

School inspections and investigations: Inspections are a means of evaluating the effectiveness of individual schools and often include examination of the results of the four methods listed above. In Britain a team of Her Majesty's Inspectors (HMI) or local advisers, visits a school for a few days to inspect different records, observe teaching and learning, interview staff and sometimes pupils, look at test results, and then publish a full report for the school and the Local Education Authority. In the

US similar investigations into one or more schools may be undertaken by the School Board to evaluate effectiveness.

The means of evaluation will vary according to its purpose, which in turn depends on the role of those carrying it out. While evaluation of learning takes place throughout the school career, it is at 16–18 years that the issue becomes crucial. National evaluation, carried out in Britain by the Assessment of Performance Unit or by the examination boards and in the US by the National Assessment of Educational Progress, allows national monitoring of standards or objective assessment of individuals for purposes of selection. The cost of objectivity, validity and quantifiable outcome is the neglect of areas of unquestionable educational validity, such as Bloom's affective area, the exclusion of the less able school-leaver in Britain, and the neglect of a qualitative description of the process of education. Intrinsic evaluation, carried out by the school or by teachers in conjunction with pupils provides continuous feedback which may be used for diagnosis and guidance about the learning process, but may be vulnerable to the biases of subjectivity.

While evaluation implies judgment, though this may be self-judgment, accountability refers to the obligation to describe one's activities to anyone who has a legitimate interest in them and to meet certain obligations in the fulfillment of duty. In schools three levels of accountability can be distinguished – (i) moral accountability (to the clients); (ii) professional accountability (to oneself and colleagues); and (iii) contractual accountability (to the employers). This raises important questions as to what teachers are to be held accountable for. Is it possible to show that a teacher has succeeded or failed in stated objectives? Although the clarity of the objectives determines the efficiency of the evaluation, the educational process is sufficiently complex to make it difficult to assign responsibility when objectives are not achieved. For example, there has been at least one case in the United States of America in which a school-leaver has sued the State Department of Education for failure to instil basic competencies in him (the criterion of minimum competencies for school leavers is fairly widespread in USA). Although accountability depends on the evaluation of educational outcome, clearly accountability procedures must be concerned with factors which are under the control of teachers and are stated as objectives by the schools themselves.

Psychology has made its greatest contribution to education in constructing methods of evaluation. While psychology can contribute greatly to measuring the success of pupils' learning, it cannot determine the value; this is a moral and political decision.

(See also SCHOOL FAILURE.) KS/IL

Bibliography

Bloom, B. ed. 1956: *The taxonomy of educational objectives*. London: Longman.

*Burgess, T. and Adams, E. 1980: *Outcomes of education*. London: Macmillan.

Galton, M. and Croll, P. 1980: Pupil progress in basic skills. In *Progress and performance in the primary classroom*, eds. M. Galton and B. Simon. London: Routledge and Kegan Paul.

Haney, W. 1984: Testing, reasoning and reasoning about testing. *Review of educational research* 54, 597–654.

Holt, M. 1982: *Evaluating the evaluators*. London: Hodder and Stoughton.

Messick, S. 1983: Assessment of children. In *Handbook of child psychology*. 4th edn, vol. 1, ed. W. Kessen. New York: Wiley.

Plake, B. ed. 1984 *Social and technical issues in testing: implications for test construction and usage*. Hillsdale, N.J.: Erlbaum.

Raven, J. 1977: *Education, values and society*. London: Lewis; New York: Psychological Corp.

Simons, H. 1980: Process evaluation in schools. In *Accountability and education*, eds. C. Lacey and D. Lawton. London and New York: Methuen.

Sylva, K., Roy, C., Painter, M. 1980: *Childwatching in playgroup and nursery school*. London: Grant McIntyre.

school phobia (Sometimes known as school refusal.) The principal manifestation of a neurotic disorder, characterized by severe reluctance to attend school.

Reports of prevalence among children attending child guidance clinics in the United Kingdom range from 1 per cent to 8 per cent; there is no authoritative account of the overall prevalence within the country. Disturbed family relationships are reported in many cases. Hersov (1977) cites possible causes of school refusal, and emphasizes that it should be seen as occurring against a background of a variety of psychiatric disorders. The problem can occur at any age, though acute onset is seen most often in younger children. Common precipitating factors are a change of school or class, death or disturbance in the family, and illness. Clinicians have differed on the frequency of separation anxiety. The prognosis is good, irrespective of type of treatment, provided that the child is pre-adolescent, and is referred soon after onset, and that the school refusal is not associated with serious social problems. (See also ABSENCE FROM SCHOOL AND TRUANCY.) DMG

Bibliography

Hersov, L. 1977: School refusal. In *Child psychiatry: modern approaches*, eds. M. Rutter and L. Hersov. Oxford: Blackwell Scientific; Philadelphia: Lippincott.

school psychological services: general The scope, nature and organization of school psychological services vary so greatly throughout the world that no pattern or list of services is typical. Factors influencing services include the industrial level of the country, the proportion of school-age children attending schools, the extent to which individual human services are encouraged by a country's values and whether schools are located in urban or rural areas. In many countries it is difficult to determine what services should be called psychological because of overlap among the services offered by psychologists, social workers, counselors and special educators.

Among countries offering comprehensive services, including screening, assessment, counseling and consultation on pupil learning and adjustment, some tend to offer services through child guidance or specialized clinics; for example, Finland, Iceland, Israel, New Zealand and the United Kingdom. In Denmark, Norway and Sweden psychologists work directly in schools. In the United States and Canada services vary from nonexistent to sophisticated. Urban areas tend to have centralized district-wide arrangements. Moderately sized school districts mostly assign psychologists directly to a limited number of schools. Rural areas have cooperative service centers for a number of districts.

In countries offering services limited mainly to general guidance and assessment for special education, the clinic model is most often used as by Australia, Belgium, Japan, Panama and Turkey (but only in the two largest cities). No clear patterns exist in Austria, France, West Germany, South Africa or Switzerland. Services of an even more limited kind appear to be offered in Poland and Mexico. JIB

Bibliography

Catteral, C.D. 1982: International school psychology: problems and promise. In *The handbook of school psychology*, eds. C.R. Reynolds and T.B. Gutkin. New York and Chichester: John Wiley.

school psychological services: in North America School psychological services have expanded greatly in North America during the last decade. This has come about because of public pressure and subsequent legislative mandate for in-school psychological services for children with special educational problems and needs. Virtually all larger school districts and most school districts in North America now employ school psychologists who possess at least a master's degree. School districts vary from providing extensive school psychological services to providing services at minimal levels and referring most cases to general agencies. The responsibilities of these professionals include administering a variety of diagnostic tests, supervising the conduct of large scale standardized tests, the counseling of teachers and parents on the values and limitations of psychological assessments and interventions, the counseling of students about available psychological services, delivering psychological interventions for minor psychological disturbances (e.g. acting out) and advising school administrations about how psychological principles can be used in schools. School psychologists often play a prominent role in special education units, such as classes for teaching disabled students. Training in school psychology usually includes work in psychological assessment, clinical psychology, developmental psychology, education and special education. Field work is almost always a part of the training. The number of training programs in school psychology (especially doctoral programs) is increasing in the United States and Canada, although the absolute number of such programs is small relative to the number of clinical and experimental programs. MP

school psychological services: in the UK Their central functions are the identification, assessment and treatment of individual children with special educational needs and emotional or behavioral problems. They offer a service of advice and consultation to schools and other agencies on these matters. They are also frequently involved in counseling parents, in-service training of teachers, advice on children to social services departments and systems intervention in institutions providing for children.

Schools' Psychological Services have an assured support role in educational administration but many educational psychologists are dissatisfied with this limited role and consider that psychology has a great deal more to offer in the field of education. TIC

Bibliography

Department of Education and Science, 1980: *Special needs in education*. London: Her Majesty's Stationery Office.

Williams, P. 1974: The growth and scope of the schools' psychological service. In *The practice of educational psychology*, ed. M. Chazam et al. London: Longman.

second language acquisition A study closely associated with applied psycholinguistics (Slama-Cazacu 1976, Rieber 1979) and, in the case of untargeted second language acquisition, the development of pidgin and creole languages. For most of its history the study of second language acquisition has been dependent on prevailing psychological and linguistic theories, as well as on the requirements of foreign language teachers.

During the second half of the nineteenth century the development of second language skills was seen, under the impact of faculty psychology, to be a form of mind training which could promote concentration, reasoning and remembering. Both classical and modern languages were taught according to the grammar-translation method, involving the memorization of grammatical rules, inflectional paradigms and vocabulary lists. Errors were regarded as signs of insufficient training. Grammatical correctness was the principal aim and language learning was not seen as involving the acquisition of wider communicative skills.

Around the turn of the century there was a growing body of opinion that second language acquisition was basically the same as first language acquisition and should therefore be taught accordingly. An application of this view is the direct method of second language teaching. Teaching is carried out entirely in the foreign language with no memorization of rules or learning of vocabulary via translation. Critics have pointed out that this method encourages inaccurate fluency in a second language.

Whereas both the faculty view and the view that first and second language acquisition are basically identical were founded on extremely limited experimental evidence, behaviorist psycholinguists began systematically to investigate second language acquisition during the 1950s. The central assumption of the behaviorists was that language is a system of verbal habits learnt by a process of building associations between concepts and sound structures. Learning was

213

viewed as a mechanical process of making the right connections between a stimulus and the desired response.

As the second language learner already possessed well established native speech habits, transfer from L_1 (the mother tongue) to L_2 (the second language) could be expected in the form of either facilitation or interference. By carefully avoiding areas of contrastive difficulties it was hoped that errors in second language acquisition could be reduced to a minimum.

The behaviorist view of second language acquisition has been very influential, particularly in the derived audio-lingual method of second language teaching, which has four main characteristics.

(1) Speaking rather than writing is taken as the primary manifestation of language. In the ideal classroom teaching proceeds along the natural hierarchy of listening, speaking, reading and writing.
(2) Second language acquisition differs from first language acquisition. Constructions may not be acquired in the same order.
(3) New linguistic habits are acquired by mimicry-memorization and pattern drilling, preferably in a language laboratory.
(4) Languages are invariant systems of habits such as described in a structuralist grammar, context-determined variation being regarded as non-significant and hence not part of the acquisition process.

The behaviorist view of language acquisition came under attack during the 1960s in the wake of Chomsky's contributions to psycholinguistics (see Chomsky 1959). Chomsky argued that behaviorist explanations could not account for the most basic aspect of human language, its creativity. The transformational cognitive criticisms of behaviorist accounts of language acquisition include:

(1) Language is stimulus free and innovative; an S-R model cannot capture the processes underlying acquisition.
(2) Speakers internalize highly abstract grammars without having been given explicit rules.

(3) Individual languages are not unique and randomly different but manifestations of more abstract universal principles of language; second language learners have (at least partial) access to such universal knowledge.
(4) Competence underlies performance. Students must know the rules of a language before they can perform in it.

No full cognitive account of second language acquisition has been developed, and the overall impact of transformational-generative grammar on second language teaching was accordingly minor.

By the late 1970s it had become clear that second language skills consisted of more than abstract competence. Instead communicative competence was made a central concept, with some important consequences for second language research:

(1) Interest developed in the systematic aspects of learners' errors (cf. error analysis, interlanguage).
(2) The relationship between linguistic variability and language external factors was investigated.
(3) Large-scale longitudinal studies were undertaken.

In spite of some progress, a considerable amount of pre-theoretical work remains to be carried out. At present, research is somewhat compartmentalized. The questions which have received most attention include: (1) The differences between first and second language acquisition; (2) the question of a "universal syllabus"; (3) the role of motivation and related factors.

The differences between first and second language acquisition are related to differences in the critical learning age as well as the linguistic functions of the target language. Madden et al. (1974) have found significant differences between child first and second language acquisition, but no great distinction between adult and child second language acquisition. Thus, it appears that the variable of learning age cannot explain differences in acquisition (see also GENIE).

A possible alternative explanation, however, which is in need of further substantiation is that differences between L_1 and L_2 acquisition are related to the *functions of language*. HALLIDAY (1974) has suggested that the functional development in first language acquisition proceeds as follows:

instrumental (function)
directive
phatic
expressive
heuristic
metalinguistic
poetic
referential (cognitive)

(Note that the names used to denote these functions differ from Halliday's original ones). Mühlhäusler (1980, p. 47) suggests a very different hierarchy for natural second language acquisition, and the development of untargeted pidgin languages:

referential (cognitive) function
directive
heuristic
expressive
phatic
metalinguistic
poetic

Should structural development turn out to be dependent on functional development this could explain many of the differences between first and second language acquisition.

The close similarity between child and adult second language learning suggests that there may be an inbuilt "syllabus" which is activated in this situation and much recent research into pidginization and *inter-language* phenomena is designed to determine its nature. Research (see Corder and Roulet 1977) suggests that:

(1) The order in which new L_2 constructions are acquired is independent of the structures of L_1 and L_2.
(2) L_2 learners make errors even where contrastive analysis would suggest facilitation.
(3) The nature of L_1 and L_2 can account for differences in the speed of learning.

Whereas such findings support the view that L_2 acquisition is a creative and universally determined process, there are some important restrictions:

(1) A distinction needs to be made between second language acquisition as a natural subconscious process and second language learning, i.e. the result of overt instruction. The extent to which the mastery of a second language involves "acquisition" and "learning" depends on such factors as motivation, age of the learner, relatedness between L_1 and L_2 and various others.
(2) In the absence of a formal learning context, L_2 learners will end up with a fossilized pidgin rather than a fully elaborated version of the target language.

The very complexity of the innate syllabus means that only descriptions of small parts are available at present. As the interrelationship between the various developing parts of *grammar* becomes better known valuable suggestions can be given to applied linguistics.

Second language acquisition does not take place in a social vacuum. Much recent research has concentrated on the relationship between the learner as a social being and the learning or acquisition process. It appears that the two principal factors involved are individual differences between learners and differences in the learning context.

Individual differences said to influence second language acquisition include general learning ability, phonetic coding ability, grammatical sensitivity, inductive learning ability and associative memory (see Ingram 1975). It is not clear whether such factors affect the implicational order postulated as underlying the universal syllabus or merely the speed with which learning proceeds. This also applies to motivation, a factor which has received considerable attention, in particular Lambert's distinction (1967) between instrumental and integrative motivation. Instrumental motivation refers to the learner's desire to better him or herself materially by means of acquiring a new additional language, whereas integrative motivation refers to the desire to get to know and to become friendly with the speakers of another language. According to Lambert, an integrative motivation is more likely to lead to successful second language acquisition, though McNamara (1973) adduces a number of counter-examples, e.g. the fact that language shift such as that from Irish to English has often been accompanied by unfavorable attitudes towards the conquering peoples and their language (see also Gardner 1985).

Factors external to the learner include hours spent in the classroom, size of class, teaching method, personality of instructor and others (cf. Fatham 1976).

It is impossible at this point to present a view of second language acquisition which integrates the various findings outlined here. However, with the shift in emphasis towards the description of actual speech rather than idealized abstract constructs in psycholinguistics and renewed interest in the speaker's performance, it may not be long before such an integrated view emerges. For recent reviews see Ellis (1985) and Klein (1986).

(See also FIRST LANGUAGE ACQUISITION.) PM

Bibliography

*Chastain, Kenneth 1971: *The development of modern language skills*. Chicago: Rand McNally.

Chomsky, Noam 1959: Review of B.F. Skinner's *"Verbal behavior"*. *Language* 35, 26–58.

*Corder, S. P. and Roulet, E. eds. 1977: *The notions of simplification, interlanguages, and pidgins and their relation to second language pedagogy*. Geneva: Librairie Droz.

Ellis, R. 1985: *Understanding second language acquisition*. Oxford and New York: Oxford University Press.

Fathman, Ann K. 1976: Variables affecting the successful learning of English as a second language. *Tesol Quarterly* 10, 433–49.

Gardner, R.C. 1985: *Social psychology and second language acquisition*. London: Arnold.

Halliday, Michael A.K. 1974: *Explorations in the functions of language*. London: Edward Arnold.

Ingram, Elisabeth 1975: Psychology and language, learning. In *The Edinburgh course in applied linguistics*, vol. 2, eds. J.P.B. Allen and S.P. Corder. Oxford: Oxford University Press.

Klein, W. 1986: *Second language acquisition*. Cambridge and New York: Cambridge University Press.

Lambert, Wallace E. 1967: A social psychology of bilingualism. *Journal of Social Issues* 23, 91–109.

Madden, C., Bailey, N. and Krashen, S. 1974: Acquisition of function words by adult learners of English as a second language. In *Papers from the Fifth Annual Meeting of the North Eastern Linguistic Society*, Harvard University Press, 234–24.

McNamara, John 1973: Attitudes and learning a second language. In *Language attitudes*, eds. R.W. Fasold and R.W. Shuy. Washington D.C.: Georgetown University Press.

*Mowrer O. Hobart 1979: *Psychology of language and learning*. New York: Plenum.

Mühlhäusler, Peter 1980: Structural expansion and the notion of creolization. In *Theoretical orientations in Creole studies*, eds. Albert Valdman and Arnold Highfield, New York and London: Academic Press, 19–56.

Rieber, R.W. ed. 1979: *Applied psycholinguistics and mental health*. New York: Plenum.

*Rivers, Wilga M. 1964: *The psychologist and the foreign language teacher*. Chicago: University of Chicago Press.

Slama-Cazacu, Tatiana 1976: Applied psycholinguistics: its objects and goal. In *Proceedings of the Fourth International Congress of Applied Linguistics*, 27–64, ed. G. Nickel. Stuttgart: Hochschulverlag.

self-esteem 'The evaluation that the individual makes and customarily maintains with regard to himself; it expresses an attitude of approval or disapproval and indicates the extent to which the individual believes himself to be capable, significant, successful and worthy' (Coopersmith 1967). Rosenberg (1965) more succinctly defined it as 'a positive or negative attitude towards . . . the Self'.

James's brief (but vague) 'self esteem = success divided by pretensions' (1890) draws attention to possible causes: one will be satisfied with oneself if one perceives one's achievements to measure up to one's aspirations. A similar idea has been crucial in Rogers' theorizing about the self-concept and ideal self. "Self-concept discrepancy theory" (Higgins et al. 1985) proposes that disparities between one's beliefs about what one is, and what one ought to be, or what one would ideally like to be, are associated with agitation and dejection. James suggested that one could increase one's self-esteem by increasing achievement *or* reducing aspiration, but Higgins et al. found that individuals with low self-esteem were less inclined than those with high self-esteem to believe that they set 'personal goals and standards as high as possible'. This might imply that the people with high self-esteem are as satisfied with their standards as with their success in living up to them.

The relation between self-esteem and beliefs or thought processes has found a (foster) home in work on the possible causal connection between depression (typically associated with very low self-esteem) and cognition (e.g. Peterson and Seligman 1984). The literature on self-esteem, however, is the majority of the empirical work on the self, and much of it is concerned with the manifest external causes and effects of self-esteem. Rogers (1951) suggested that high self-esteem comes from an upbringing in a family which does not make love conditional on one's obedience or success. Coopersmith (1967), in a study of 1700 boys (10–12 years old), found that the parents of those with high self-esteem showed warmth and interest, set high standards, but were fair though firm in enforcing them, and used rewards rather than punishments as an incentive. Boys with low self-esteem had permissive parents who showed comparatively little interest in their children, but could sometimes be punitive and unfair. The parents of the boys with high self-esteem had high self-esteem themselves, and wanted their children to be self-confident and independent. Rosenberg (1965), studying 5000 adolescents, found that high self-esteem was associated with a closer, warmer relationship with parents. Two assumptions are often made about these findings:
(1) that the family relationship causes the high or low self-esteem;
(2) that the self-esteem is something one acquires in one's upbringing and is then stuck with.

It is obviously possible that neither of these assumptions is true.

Experimental studies have shown that self-esteem can be manipulated. This supports the idea that the cause of self-esteem lies in experience, but it does not support the idea that self-esteem is stable. Videbeck (1960), for example, found that people who were rated by an "expert" changed their beliefs about the rated ability and other aspects of their ability. Other studies with different designs also suggest that self-ratings can be raised or lowered by another person's responses to one's claims (Gergen 1965), or that a job-applicant's self-ratings can be affected by sharing a waiting room with a more unlikely or more likely candidate for the job (Gergen and Morse 1967). In addition, Rosenberg (1979) concluded that his evidence showed that self-esteem declines during ADOLESCENCE until some improvement begins in one's late teens.

There are, however, other studies which show that it is not always easy to change self-esteem. If plenty of people agree with one's own estimate of oneself, one is less likely to respond to attempts to change it (Backman et al. 1963). Shrauger and Lund (1975) found that if high self-esteem subjects were negatively evaluated, they were inclined to say they doubted the evaluator's competence. These results imply that a failure or criticism will not affect someone's high self-esteem. This tallies with Coopersmith's finding that high self-esteem boys were independent and not sensitive to criticism. Such reactions may, of course, be seen as defensive (Schneider and Turkat 1975), and possibly not expressions of belief.

It is not surprising that people play down evidence which might undermine their self-esteem (or the good impression they make on others). Various writers have held that people have a 'basic need for self-regard' (Rogers 1959), and therefore a need to enhance their self-esteem or protect it from damage (Allport 1937). Unsurprisingly, low self-esteem subjects often, but not always, prefer positive evaluation and praise to derogation and criticism (see Jones 1973). But finding praise pleasant (and praisers more attractive than derogators, as in Jones et al. 1962) does not make one believe the praise. A glance at the work on depression shows that it is difficult to get people with a genuine, chronic lack of self-esteem to re-evaluate themselves more positively. Again, contrary to Rosenberg's claims, Savin-Williams and Demo (1984) found that adolescents' self-esteem was remarkably stable over a three year period.

If one's level of self-esteem is related to one's beliefs about one's effectiveness and competence, it will also be reflected in one's actions and one's interpretations of events. Many educational psychologists consider this to be related to major problems of motivation in schools. People with high self-esteem persevere longer on difficult tasks (Shrauger and Sormon 1977). This parallels the findings in attribution theory that belief that one can secure success through effort leads to one making more effort and hence, perhaps, succeeding (Weiner 1980; cf. Bandura 1982). This process could be due to a mechanism suggested by Covington (1983). If, as Covington believes, people want to perceive themselves as able and competent, they will make an effort to obtain success and thereby a basis for their self-esteem. But making an effort and failing seems to reveal lack of ability. Effort followed by failure is therefore a worse blow to one's self-esteem than failure which follows no effort. Those who are diffident may choose not to risk their effort. Those who have a higher opinion of themselves will have no such hesitation. Furthermore, if a depressed or low self-esteem person thinks he or she cannot succeed by effort or ability, a success may be attributed to luck, or the ease of the task, and such successes will therefore do little to modify the self-concept or self-esteem, while failures will simply confirm the beliefs (see Peterson and Seligman 1984). One's self-esteem will obviously be difficult to change if the beliefs associated with it affect the evidence available and the way in which one interprets that evidence.

Self-esteem is also believed to have effects on aspirations, creativity and relationships with others (see Coopersmith 1967; Rogers 1959). Manipulating self-esteem can certainly affect social judgments and social behavior. In a study in 1970, Kiesler and Baral took male students one at a time. The student's self-esteem was raised or lowered. Then he was introduced to a girl and left alone with her. If her dress and make-up were attractive, the men with raised self-esteem were very sociable. If her dress and make-up were unattractive, the men with lowered self-esteem were the sociable ones. Need for approval may be involved here, but expectation is clearly playing a crucial role. The low self-esteem students probably expect success with the plain girl rather than the attractive one. The high self-esteem students may expect success with both, or they may be prepared to take a risk. Either way they seem only to be tempted by the greater prize (another example of the higher aspirations of those with high self-esteem).

One thing wrong with many of these studies, or at least their interpretation, has been the apparent assumption that "self-esteem" is a global favorable or unfavorable attitude to oneself. Dissatisfaction with one aspect of oneself need not generalize to other aspects, although it may lead to compensatory efforts in other activities. Another problem is that different measures of self-esteem do not intercorrelate with each other. Wylie (1974) stated that: 'Factor-analytic studies of instruments purporting to measure "overall" self-esteem ... lead one to believe that either there is no such measurable dimension ... or at least that some of the scales ... are doing a poor job'. Wells and Marwell (1976) also concluded that 'orthodox verbal self-ratings' of self-esteem are inadequate. Demo (1985) found that self-ratings and observer-ratings fall on two distinct factors, which he labeled "experienced" and "presented" self-esteem. Given these empirical problems, and the underlying difficulties which they reveal, it is hard not to accept Demo's conclusion that, 'At present ... we lack a sufficiently clear ... conceptual framework for understanding self-conception, or even self-esteem'.   RL

Bibliography

Bandura, A. 1982: Self-efficacy mechanism in human agency. *American psychologist* 37, 122–47.

Burns, R.B. 1979: *The self-concept*. London and New York: Longman.

Covington, M.V. 1983: Motivated cognitions. In *Learning and motivation in the classroom*, eds. S. Paris, G. Olson and M. Stevenson. Hillsdale, N.J.: Erlbaum.

Demo, D.H. 1985: The measurement of self-esteem: refining our methods. *Journal of personality and social psychology* 48, 1490–1502.

Gergen, K.J. and Morse, S.J. 1967: Self-consistency: measurement and validation. *Proceedings of the American Psychological Association*, 207–8.

Higgins, E.T., Klein, R. and Strauman, T. 1985: Self-concept discrepancy theory: a psychological model for distinguishing among different aspects of depression and anxiety. *Social cognition* 3, 51–76.

Peterson, C. and Seligman, M.E.P. 1984: Causal explanations as a risk factor in depression: theory and evidence. *Psychological review* 91, 347–74.

Rosenberg, M. 1979: *Conceiving the self*. New York: Basic Books.

Savin-Williams, R.C. and Demo, D.H. 1984: Developmental change and stability in adolescent self-concept. *Developmental psychology* 20, 1100–10.

Weiner, B. 1980: *Human motivation*. New York: Holt, Rinehart and Winston.

Wells, L.E. and Marwell, G. 1976: *Self-esteem: its conceptualization and measurement*. Beverley Hills: Sage.

Wylie, R.C. 1974, 1979: *The self-concept*. 2 vols. Lincoln: University of Nebraska Press.

All other references may be found in Burns (1979) and Wylie (1974, 1979).

sensori-motor stage In Piagetian theory, the first stage of development from birth to approximately eighteen months. It is so called because the connection between infant and environment consists in particular motor responses to classes of sensory stimuli. Development begins with reflexive responses to a strictly limited range of sensory events and proceeds through the coordination and elaboration of motor responses to more complex combinations of eliciting stimuli. Throughout the sensori-motor period actions are controlled by direct sensory stimulation. The end of this stage is marked by the development of representation (the ability to retrieve information from memory) and the regulation of action by stored knowledge. During the sensori-motor stage, the infant develops concepts of space, time, causes and objects, expressed in the control of motor activities.

(See PIAGET.)   GEB

Bibliography

Butterworth, G.E. 1983: Structure of the mind in human infancy. *Advances in infancy research* 2, 1–29.

Piaget, Jean 1936 (1953): *The origin of intelligence in the child*. London: Routledge and Kegan Paul; New York: International Universities Press (1966).

separation A term derived from psychoanalytic theory to describe the anxiety held to be generated by the absence of a person believed necessary for survival (prototypically the mother) and to denote a major developmental process – separation-individuation (Mahler, Pine and Bergman 1975). Mahler and her co-workers described sub-phases of differentiation, practicing and rapprochement to account for development from a symbiotic phase in the middle of the first year when the infant and mother are still primarily a unit, to the autonomy or separation of the three-year-old from its mother. (See in DEVELOPMENT: PSYCHO-ANALYTIC THEORIES.) More widely known are the three phases – protest, despair and detachment – described by Bowlby as the young child's response to separation from its primary caregiver and his hypothesis relating maternal loss or deprivation and psychiatric illness. Research in the past thirty years has supported and clarified this proposed relationship but also shown the need to distinguish between bonding failure and bond disruption, between qualitative differences in care and their effects on intellectual, social and emotional factors, between long- and short-term effects and the influence of individual differences on outcomes (Rutter 1981). (See also ATTACHMENT; DEPRIVATION.) BBL

Bibliography

Mahler, M.S., Pine, F. and Bergman, A. 1975: *The psychological birth of the human infant*. London: Hutchinson; New York: Basic Books.

Rutter, M. 1981: *Maternal deprivation reassessed*. 2nd edn. Harmondsworth and New York: Penguin.

sex differences in development A field of study concerned with the measurement and explanation of differences in the behavior of males and females as they appear throughout the life span. These differences embrace aspects of intellectual functioning, temperament and interests relating to work and leisure. The psychological study of differences is not directly concerned with primary sexual characteristics such as those involving hormones and reproduction or such secondary characteristics as size and bone structure. Psychological differences are often uncovered incidentally when experimenters compare the performance of males and females before combining scores for the two groups. The lack of systematic study is reflected in the variety of reported differences. Not surprisingly controversy surrounds the conclusions which have been drawn from the empirical evidence and conflicting theoretical accounts are offered to explain alleged differences.

Maccoby and Jacklin's landmark survey (1974) of over 1,600 studies reported reliable differences in only four areas and challenged many stereotypic beliefs. They concluded that the evidence supported the belief that females have greater verbal skills although it was unclear whether these are present in early childhood or emerge shortly before puberty. Males were found to have higher visual-spatial and mathematical abilities; these appear reliably in adolescence. In addition boys

displayed more aggression, both physical and verbal; differences could be observed in the play of toddlers. On the other hand Maccoby and Jacklin concluded that the evidence failed to support beliefs that girls are more sociable or suggestible, that girls are better at simple tasks and rote memory while boys are better able to deal with complex intellectual tasks or those requiring analytical thinking, that girls lack achievement motivation and self esteem, that boys are visually orientated while girls are auditorially orientated, or that boys are more responsive to environmental factors while girls' development is more influenced by heredity. They noted that the evidence was inconclusive concerning sex differences in tactile sensitivity, anxiety and fear, activity level, competitiveness, dominance, compliance and nurturance.

Although Maccoby and Jacklin have provided a starting point for much further study their survey has been attacked both for the limited nature of its conclusions and for its lack of stringency (Block 1976; Fairweather 1976; Hyde 1981).

Block argues that the fortuitous reporting of differences in studies which were not designed to reveal them and the reliance on subjects from a restricted age range (over three-quarters of the studies reviewed by Maccoby and Jacklin were of children below the age of thirteen years) challenges the conclusions which are drawn. In addition she questions Maccoby and Jacklin's decision procedures, for example giving equal weight to statistically weak and powerful studies, omitting some significant reports and failing to achieve conceptual clarity in their own analysis. Block believes that the evidence can just as well support many of the differences which Maccoby and Jacklin reported as unproven and is often clearer than they indicated. In contrast Fairweather, examining studies of intellectual ability, challenged the evidence for differences in verbal and mathematical skills although he supported the view that males and females differ in their visual-spatial abilities.

This lack of consensus has not deterred psychologists from seeking and providing explanations for the differences they believe they have found. These explanations are generally not derived directly from psychological theory but are as wide-ranging and controversial as the evidence they attempt to explain.

Common-sense accounts of sex differences link psychological traits to biological differences of form and reproductive function. Psychological explanations often reveal their origins in naive accounts. So pervasive has the common-sense view been that Victorian scholars sought women's alleged intellectual inferiority in their smaller absolute brain size. This belief has been discredited; when comparisons of intelligence are made across species the ratio of the mass of the brain to the total mass of the individual is employed. Even this alleged relationship is doubtful.

The contemporary and competing naive explanation of differences in terms of social conditioning has gained impetus from the women's movement. It emphasizes that the differences which we are trying to trace reflect the roles which men and women in our society are expected to fulfill – the preparation of girls for motherhood and undemanding low-status work and of boys for achievement and competition for society's most prestigious positions. These expectations and aspirations are believed to be differentially inculcated by conditioning, a term which owes little to Pavlov but is used in everyday speech to explain the learning of social values.

Psychologists acknowledge the influence of both biological and environmental factors in development but many emphasize the former at the expense of the latter. Typically, volumes reviewing theories and evidence of sex differences in intellectual ability devote one section to social factors but one each to the effects of genes, hormones and the brain (Wittig and Petersen 1979).

In discussing genes, spatial ability has been linked to a recessive gene on the X chromosome. The evidence for such an inheritance pattern is not strong nor is that for the variability hypothesis which suggests that male heterozygosity (X and Y chromosomes) results in greater extremes in the male on a variety of traits. Hormones which have been shown to affect reproductive behavior in rats are often implicated in explaining temperamental differences as well as intellectual ability. Varying effects of greater lateralization of the right or the left hemisphere of the brain have been used to account for differences in verbal and spatial abilities. None of these explanations has gone unchallenged.

The superior performance of males in educational and occupational domains involving mathematical and visual-spatial abilities has enlivened the debate. There is fairly wide consensus concerning the contribution of biological factors to differences in spatial ability (McGee 1979) and the relation of these to mathematical achievement (Sherman 1978).

However, psychologists such as Sherman argue for including the impact of sex-role factors in any account of differential performance in mathematics. She has measured children's beliefs about their chances of being successful in mathematics, about the usefulness of it in their lives and about their parents' evaluations of their achievement and shown that they influence performance as much as visual-spatial ability. Sherman's explanation is interactive in that mathematical achievement is shown to reflect biological and social processes. Although interactional explanations of many varieties are widely considered they are still challenged. A recent study of almost 10,000 adolescents of superior mathematical ability in the United States demonstrated a male superiority and its authors ascribed this difference to inherent factors which distinguished males and females (Benbow and Stanley 1980, 1983).

The vehemence of the controversy focuses attention on the nature of the differences being explained. Primary sex characteristics such as genital structure yield categorical differentiations: males and females show no overlap; while psychological traits are distributed along a continuum, most average differences are small and there is much overlap. The magnitude of difference in visual-spatial abilities is medium to large yet 25 per cent of females perform better than the male average.

Categorical differentiation based upon genitals may be important in subtle ways. Maccoby and Jacklin reported few differences in the socialization of boys and girls but by the time children begin to speak they correctly label themselves. Both SOCIAL LEARNING THEORY and cognitive-developmental theory offer explanations: the former in terms of rewards and punishment as well as imitation and learning through observation and the latter according to the child's developing understanding of the social world and its place in the sex role system (Mischel 1970, Kohlberg 1966; Bussey and Bandura 1984).

Undoubtedly the processes described by social learning theorists contribute to the acquisition of differences in behavior. A particular advantage of the cognitive-developmental approach is its emphasis on the child's active participation in constructing its own identity. A new approach to sex differences, which derives from ethnomethodology, begins by attacking the term "sex" and by noting that the processes through which individuals are categorized as male or female are social and problematic in their precise operation (Kessler and McKenna 1978). To mark the social construction of the categories "man" and "woman" the term "gender" is being used increasingly to designate psychological differences and sex is reserved for reference to biological distinctions. The introduction of the term "gender" provides no explanation in itself but accentuates the need for caution before accepting exclusively biological accounts of psychological differences. In addition it stresses that the very situations in which differences are recorded, be they surveys or experiments, are social situations differently interpreted by men and women. The explanation of psychological differences observed in them will require understanding of these situations as well as of biological and intrapsychic phenomena (Deaux 1976; 1985). BBL

Bibliography

*Archer, J. and Lloyd, B. 1982: *Sex and gender in society*. Harmondsworth: Penguin.

Benbow, C.P. and Stanley, J.C. 1980: Sex differences in mathematical ability: fact or artifact? *Science* 210, 1262–4.

—— 1983: Sex differences in mathematical reasoning: more facts. *Science* 222, 1029–31.

Block, J.H. 1976: Issues, problems and pitfalls in assessing sex differences: a critical review of "The psychology of sex differences". *Merrill-Palmer quarterly* 22, 283–308.

Bussey, K. and Bandura, A. 1984: Influence of gender constancy and social power on sex-linked modeling. *Journal of personality and social psychology* 47, 1292–1302.

Deaux, K. 1976: *The behavior of men and women*. Belmont, Calif.: Wadsworth Publishing Company.

—— 1985: Sex and gender. In *Annual review of psychology*, vol. 36, eds. M.R. Rosenzweig and L.W. Porter. Palo Alto: Annual Reviews Inc.

Fairweather, H. 1976: Sex differences in cognition. *Cognition* 4, 231–80.

Hyde, J.S. 1981: How large are cognitive gender differences? *American psychologist* 36, 892–901.

Kessler, S.J. and McKenna, W. 1978: *Gender: an ethnomethodological approach*. New York: Wiley.

Kohlberg, L. 1966: A cognitive-developmental analysis of children's sex role concepts and attitudes. In *The development of sex differences*, ed. E.E. Maccoby. Stanford, Calif.: Stanford University Press; London: Tavistock Publications (1967).

Maccoby, E.E. and Jacklin, C.N. 1974: *The psychology of sex differences*. Stanford, Calif.: Stanford University Press; Oxford: Oxford University Press (1975).

McGee, M.G. 1979: Human spatial abilities: psychometric studies and environmental, genetic, hormonal and neurological influences. *Psychological bulletin* 86, 889–918.

Mischel, W. 1970: Sex-typing and socialization. In *Carmichael's manual of child psychology*, ed. P.H. Mussen, vol. 3. 3rd edn. New York: Wiley.

*Sherman, J.A. 1978: *Sex related cognitive differences: an essay on theory and evidence*. Springfield, Ill.: C.C.Thomas.

Shields, S.A. 1975: Functionalism, Darwinism, and the psychology of women: a study in social myth. *American psychologist* 30, 739–54.

Wittig, M.A. and Petersen, A.C. 1979: *Sex-related differences in cognitive functioning: developmental issues*. New York and London: Academic Press.

sex roles A repertoire of attitudes, behaviors, perceptions and affective reactions which are more commonly associated with one sex than the other. Over the last fifteen years, social scientists have documented the content of sex roles and considered their implications for the treatment of men and women by various social institutions such as education, mental health, criminal justice and the labor force.

Ancillary but separate from the study of sex roles is the investigation of sex differences (or gender differences) in human performance. Empirical studies suggest that the most reliable sex differences are to be found in IQ tests (with males performing on average higher on spatial-mathematical subscales, females higher on verbal subscales; see previous entry) and aggressive behavior (males on average displaying spontaneously higher levels). The interaction of sex differences and sex roles has been variously explained by different disciplines. Some anthropologists (e.g. Tiger 1970) have argued that originally small morphological and neuroanatomical differences between the sexes were augmented by early bifurcation of social responsibilities; men's hunting behavior leading to increases in aggression and spatial discriminations, and women's child-rearing resulting in increased verbal ability and decreased aggression. Neuroendocrine bases of sex differences have been documented by Gray and Buffery (1971) and related to evolutionary processes. Other anthropologists and sociologists have stressed the mutability of sex roles, noting cultures in which men perform "women's" work (Mead 1935), and the way in which economic and social changes have altered the prevailing notions of appropriately "feminine" activities.

Developmental psychologists have pursued three major approaches to sex role acquisition in children. The psychoanalytic school directs attention to the OEDIPUS COMPLEX and its successful resolution as crucial for appropriate identification, while at the same time positing the passive and active nature of women and men respectively as relatively fixed (Strachey and Richards 1973). Social learning theorists (see SOCIAL LEARNING THEORY) believe that behavior appropriate to sex role results from differential positive reinforcement and imitation (Mischel 1970; Bussey and Bandura 1984). Cognitive developmentalists suggest that only after the acquisition of the concept of permanence can the child understand the immutability of gender which is a prerequisite for sex role learning (Kohlberg 1966). A number of studies suggest that the *father's* rather than the mother's sex-typed personality is the dominant influence on young children's sex-role identities (Weinraub et al. 1984).

Studies of sexually anomalous babies by Money and Erhardt (1972) have shed more light on the plasticity of sex role learning. One of two male identical twins had his penis amputated as a result of a surgical accident. The child received plastic surgery and endocrine treatment resulting in an appearance of femininity although remaining genetically male. While exhibiting heightened levels of rough-and-tumble play more characteristic of a male, the child's behavior by the age of four-and-a-half years was significantly different from the brother's, and virtually indistinguishable from other females. This indicates the importance of socialization in sex role development. Critics of such an interpretation would point to animal experiments in which opposite-sex behavior is produced by administration of the appropriate hormones soon after birth (Edwards 1968; Levine and Mullins 1966). The critics' case might also be supported by Baucom et al. (1985), who found that self-report sex role among women was related to testosterone levels in saliva, less "feminine" women having higher levels of this male hormone.

Most recent theorists agree that human behavior is malleable even when they argue for biological causation in sex differences (Daly and Wilson 1983). Many psychologists now dislike the term "sex role", and prefer to restrict the use of the word "sex" to biological functions and differences. The preferred term is "gender role".   AC

Bibliography

Baucom, D.H., Besch, P.K. and Callahan, S. 1985: Relation between testosterone concentration, sex role identity and personality among females. *Journal of personality and social psychology* 48, 1218–26.

Bussey K. and Bandura, A. 1984: Influence of gender constancy on sex-linked modeling. *Journal of personality and social psychology* 47, 1292–1302.

Daly, M. and Wilson, M. 1983: *Sex, evolution and behavior*. Boston: Grant Press.

Edwards, D.A. 1968: Mice: fighting by neonatally androgenized females. *Science* 161, 1028.

Gray, J.A. and Buffery, A.W.H. 1971: Sex differences in emotional and cognitive behaviour in mammals including man; adaptive and neural bases. *Acta psychologica* 35, 89–111.

Kohlberg, L. 1966: A cognitive developmental analysis of children's sex role concepts and attitudes. In *The development of sex differences*, ed. E.E. Maccoby. Stanford, Calif.: Stanford University Press.

Levine, S. and Mullins, R.F. 1966: Hormonal influences on brain organization in infant rats. *Sciences* 152, 1585–92.

Maccoby, E. and Jacklin, C.N. 1974: *The psychology of sex differences*. Stanford, Calif.: Stanford University Press.

Mead, M. 1935: *Sex and temperament in three primitive societies*. New York: Morrow.

Mischel, W. 1970: Sex typing and socialization. In *Carmichael's manual of child psychology*, vol. 1, ed. P.H. Mussen. New York: Wiley.

Money, J. and Erhardt, A.A. 1972: *Man and woman, boy and girl*. Baltimore, Maryland: Johns Hopkins University Press.

Strachey, J. and Richards, A. eds. 1973: *New introductory lectures on psychoanalysis*. Harmondsworth: Penguin. (Lectures by Freud 1925 and 1931.)

Tiger, L. 1970: *Men in groups*. New York: Random House.

Weinraub, M. et al. 1984: The development of sex role stereotypes in the third year. *Child development* 55, 1493–1503.

shame *See* guilt and shame.

sibling relationships The study of the nature of the relationship itself and the variables affecting the bond between children in the same family (usually genetically related). It is a branch of the study of relationships which has evolved from social psychology and ethology (see Hinde 1979). Researchers are just beginning to investigate how to describe relationships, but many aspects of the sibling relationship have been studied; for instance the nature of their interactions and perceptions of each other or how other family members feel about them.

The sibling relationship is special and unlike any other. Siblings might be friends, enemies, companions, playmates, teachers, and, in some cultures, caretakers. Rutter (1981) says that siblings of any age have been found to be effective in reducing SEPARATION anxiety and attributes this to their familiarity with one another and the strength of the sibling bond.

Siblings are important to one another's social and cognitive development. Studies which have examined sibling status, sibling sex, and sibling age differences have demonstrated that these variables alone cannot account for the magnitude of the siblings' individual differences in behavior, personality and cognition. Rowe and Plomin (1981) argue that non-shared environmental differences like the effects of sibling interaction upon each participant and differential parental treatment can explain the individual differences and they advocate research within families.

Finding out how preschool children feel about their siblings has presented special difficulties. Two particular concerns are the young child's supposed inability to express complex feelings or to understand the perspectives of others. (See EGOCENTRISM.) In studying siblings' behavior and, in particular, how very young children empathize with, tease, and irritate their siblings, Dunn (1984) has overcome many of these problems and found that children as young as 16 months are extremely sophisticated in their understanding of one another.

It would be a mistake to represent the

study of sibling relationships in isolation because each relationship within a family affects all the others. For example, Corter et al. (1983) have examined the role of the mother in sibling interaction and have shown that not only did her presence reduce the frequency of sibling interactions but also the siblings were more aggressive to one another when she was present. Dunn and Kendrick (1981) found that where the mother and firstborn girl had intense, non-prohibitive interactions before the baby was born, there was little positive interaction between siblings when the youngest was 14 months old.

Although the research presented here represents work with young children, siblings have a lifelong relationship which will probably outlast that of most parent-child and peer relationships (see Bank and Kahn 1982). Furthermore, it must be emphasized that relationships are developmental and what happens between siblings at any time may be influenced by the relationship at a previous time. Thus, relationships should be studied both in the context of other relationships and longitudinally.   JBa

Bibliography

Bank, S. and Kahn, M. 1982: *The sibling bond.* New York: Basic Books.

Corter, C., Abramovitch, R. and Pepler, D. 1983: The role of the mother in sibling interaction. *Child development* 54, 1599–1605.

Dunn, J. 1983: Sibling relationships in early childhood. *Child development* 54, 787–811.

—— 1984: *Sisters and brothers.* London: Fontana.

—— and Kendrick, C. 1981: Interaction between young siblings: association with the interaction between mother and firstborn child. *Developmental psychology* 17(3), 336–43.

—— and Kendrick, C. 1982: *Siblings: love, envy and understanding.* Cambridge, Mass.: Harvard University Press.

Hinde, R. 1979: *Towards understanding relationships.* New York and London: Academic Press.

Rowe, D. and Plomin, R. 1981: The importance of nonshared (E1) environmental influences in behavioural development. *Developmental psychology* 17(5), 517–31.

Rutter, M. 1981: *Maternal deprivation reassessed.* 2nd edn. London: Penguin.

skills Capabilities to perform particular tasks or to achieve particular goals. Many skills can be acquired, sometimes after a long period of training and practice. The essence of a skill is its effectiveness, so it does not necessarily have to be learnt, but can develop largely as a result of the normal maturation process and be hardly at all dependent on a specific training program. The sequence of maturing skills in infants and toddlers is well established. Such taken-for-granted "milestones" are sitting and REACHING (6 months), crawling (9 months), and walking (18 months). After that the child starts to develop the bases of activities which are more obviously "skilled", such as throwing a ball. Fine control, however, cannot be developed until the myelinization of the nerve fibers is complete at four or later (Janner 1978).

"Skill" covers a wide range of acts and behavior. Some skills, such as playing tennis, are easily observed. Others, such as mental skills, are so structured that the underlying skill has to be inferred. It is useful to define three major categories of skill: (1) perceptual skills which depend mainly on the mechanisms which underlie perception, particularly of complex patterns; (2) perceptual-motor skills which emphasize the coordinated contribution of both perceptual (input) and motor (output) processes and mechanisms; and (3) mental skills such as reasoning. Thinking and reasoning, though logically inseparable from other kinds of skill, have been studied separately. It is not clear whether the ultimate analysis of different categories of skill will reveal a common set of underlying processes, or whether different contents will demand different underlying mechanisms (see, for example, Shapiro and Schmidt 1982).

To date the bulk of psychological research on skill has been concentrated on the nature and acquisition of perceptual-motor skills with considerable emphasis being placed on those with easily observable dynamic variations in input and output. While ball-games offer an interesting source of information it has been found convenient to invent new tasks in controlled (laboratory) situations with which to investigate the processes which underlie skilled performance. Tasks have been devised which make differential demands on hypothetical underlying processes including, for example, speed of decision, spatial and temporal accuracy of response and the capacity to share attention among a number of more or less simultaneous demands (Legge and Barber 1976).

The defining attributes of skill are effectiveness and flexibility. Effectiveness means that the act in question can be achieved quickly and accurately, and with economy which confers stamina. At a lower level of performance, in contrast, even if the right thing is done, it may have taken a long time to determine, it may be done clumsily and it may be done with less than the desired (or required) degree of accuracy. Furthermore, the actor/operator will probably appear harassed by the situation instead of seeming to have time in hand.

The flexibility which epitomizes skill is, however, the more important and less obvious characteristic. In real life, the same problem hardly ever occurs twice. When receiving service at tennis, badminton or squash, it is very unlikely that the same problem will be presented in terms of speed, position and trajectory of the flight of the ball. Skilled players can accommodate vast ranges of services, including those they have never seen before, and still produce effective return shots. They have a flexible skill which can deal with widely varying circumstances. A very simple (and untrained) example of this is the way in which relatively small boys can throw stones which vary quite widely in weight without the accuracy of the throw being significantly affected. An automatic allowance is made for the mass of the stone and the signals sent to the throwing muscles are adjusted accordingly. (See also DEVELOPMENT OF MOTOR SKILLS).

Underlying mechanisms

The flexibility which characterizes skill also points to the sorts of processes and mechanisms which must underlie it. It places skill in stark contrast with, for example, habit. When stimulus-response (S-R) conceptualizations held sway it was postulated that all behavior could be analyzed into a series of S-R connections, each S being a sufficient condition for the occurrence of its associated R. This behaviorist scheme was initiated by Watson and continues in the work of Skinner and his students. Unfortunately the S-R framework does not offer a rich enough theoretical structure to accommodate the flexibility which characterizes skill. A different level of analysis is needed which incorporates a more complex building block than the S-R link. This was provided by the growing interest of engineers in control theory and the self-stabilizing feature of the negative feedback circuit in which the output of the system is fed back and matched against a demand signal which defines the state that should be achieved.

A negative-feedback controlled system such as a thermostatically controlled refrigerator is stable in the sense that it always strives to produce the demand state even though there are factors in the system's environment that tend to disturb its output. The thermostat will produce an appropriate response regardless of whether it has "experienced" the specific environmental condition before. It operates according to a principle rather than producing a specific associative response.

Open-loop and closed-loop operation

Although feedback systems offer attractive models of the processes underlying human skills there is considerable debate about the extent to which skills actually operate as feedback systems. In an open-loop system the response is not connected back to the stimulus, while a closed-loop system is one in which, by feedback, the system can respond to its own output. If a performance is closed-looped, cutting the loop should cause a marked deterioration in performance. For example, when a car windscreen shatters at speed the driver has only his residual memory of the road and his position on it, and he will crash unless he manages to stop first. However, it can be shown that there are many skillful movements, such as aiming, playing a keyboard instrument, etc. that are unaffected by blocking the feedback and thereby cutting the loop. These quick responses are completed too fast for any feedback from them to influence their execution. These responses are called ballistic (Legge and Barber 1976).

Analysis of skilled performance indicates that the key to high levels of skill is to be found in open-loop operation. For while a number of skills such as car-driving clearly have a closed-loop aspect, it is equally clear that the individual movements that make up the sequence of control adjustments are themselves selected and executed in an open-loop mode. For example it is the antithesis of skillful driving to make a random series of alterations to the setting of the front wheels of the car. The essential question is about how the skilled driver finds the right steering-wheel movement and then programs his motor system to produce that movement with virtually no further supervision.

A stimulus-response theory would argue that responses that fit a particular situation are learned and as skill increases a larger and larger repertoire of responses is compiled. As this bank of responses grows the chances of meeting a situation for which no at least approximately suitable response is available decrease. This theory offers a credible account but it also provokes a number of problems. First it would seem to require that all skills be learned since it is almost inconceivable that a person could inherit the specific patterns necessary to respond to particular stimuli, except in the gross sense of, say, turning to look at a source of noise. Secondly, it implies that the selection of an appropriate response would have to be a remarkable process carried out extremely rapidly. Otherwise the larger the repertoire the slower would be the selection of each response. Experimental studies of the time it takes people to choose one from among varying numbers of alternatives indicate that choice or selection time increases quite steeply as the number of alternatives increases. Although this relationship is logarithmic rather than linear (that is the gradient of the increase becomes less and less steep as the number of alternatives expands) it is clear that a process that depended upon sorting through and choosing from a very large repertoire would still be very time consuming (Welford 1976). It would be inconceivable that such a time-consuming process could produce the very rapid precise responses demanded by fast ball games such as tennis.

It is necessary, therefore, in all but the simplest choice problems (where the repertoire of responses is really very small, probably less than about fifteen) for a different principle to operate. Instead of selecting from among pre-programmed, learned responses it would be necessary for the responding mechanism to have a way of building an appropriate response from basic units using a set of design principles that have been acquired from training and practice. In this scheme what has been learned is not specific responses associated with specific stimuli but a set of algorithms or operational rules for building a program that will, when executed, produce a response. The skill of the performer will then be determined by the efficiency of those algorithms.

Since the majority of skilled actions take place in a dynamic context an important component of skill is anticipation. Some mechanism or process must operate to predict the state of affairs in the future, at the time when the movement which is being planned will actually take place.

Tennis players need to aim at where the ball will be when the racquet gets there, not where the ball is when they are preparing their shot. An essential feature of increasing skill is the increasing precision of the prediction processes which make major contributions to the spatio-temporal coordination of movements allowing the right movements to be made at the right times.

Skill acquisition

There is an important distinction between practice and training: in training a deliberate scheme to assist learning is defined and followed by the trainee. In many cases this scheme involves a trainer who both guides the trainee towards making more satisfactory movements and attending to more appropriate feedback and gives the trainee encouragement and an evaluation of progress. Practice may simply involve using the skills that have been acquired, sometimes imperfectly. There will be a fuzzy area between training and practice in which the benefits are greater than those which arise from simple repetition, but the guidance and feedback is considerably less precise than would be provided in a properly managed training program.

Psychologists have been much exercised by the nature of learning, probably because many have taken the view that the adult is very largely a product of the countless learning experiences that characterize development. However, a relatively small proportion of the effort that has been devoted to studying learning in general has been dedicated to the question of how skills are acquired.

Clear recommendations about how to promote skill acquisition have been very well covered by Holding (1965).

(1) Guidance (verbal or physical) which helps the learner to produce approximately the right sort of responses. for example, special contraptions have been made to ensure that a golf-club is swung only in the near-ideal arc, giving the beginning golfer a chance to feel what the swing should be like.

(2) Feedback informs the learner how close he or she is to producing the desired performance. Some kinds of feedback are knowledge of results. Feedback may involve a trainer or special equipment but often the situation produces a considerable amount without further enhancement, for example, failing to connect with an on-coming tennis-ball or the dart failing to hit its target.

An important landmark in the development of skill is when sufficient progress has been made for further improvement to follow simply from further practice. This could not be provided by a simple stimulus-response model of learning, but one that entails the learning of algorithms could accommodate it.

Perhaps one of the most remarkable ways of improving a skill is by "immobile" practice. The trainee goes through the activity mentally but makes no movements at all. Although probably much less effective than actual practice, this kind of mental rehearsal can help maintain a skill when circumstances prevent full-scale practice. DL

Bibliography

Annett, J. 1969: *Feedback and behaviour.* London: Penguin.

Fitts, P.M. and Posner, M.I. 1967: *Human performance.* Belmont, Calif.: Brooks/Cole.

Holding, D.H. 1965: *Principles of training.* Oxford and New York: Pergamon.

—— 1969: *Experimental psychology in industry.* London: Penguin.

—— ed. 1981: *Human skills.* New York and Chichester: Wiley.

Legge, D. ed. 1970: *Skills.* London: Penguin.

—— and Barber, P.J. 1976: *Information and skill.* London and New York: Methuen.

Mackenzie, C.L. and Marteniuk, R.G. 1985: Motor skill. *Canadian journal of psychology.*

Schmidt, R.A. 1975: *Motor skills.* New York: Harper and Row.

Shapiro, D.C. and Schmidt, R.A. 1982: The schema theory: recent evidence and developmental implications. In *The development of motor control and coordination,* eds. J. Kelso and J. Clark. New York: Wiley.

Stammers, R. and Patrick J. 1975: *The psychology of training.* London: Methuen.

Stelmach, G.E. ed. 1976: *Motor control: issues and trends.* New York and London: Academic Press.

Tanner, J.M. 1978: *Fetus into man: physical growth from conception to maturity.* Cambridge, Mass.: Harvard University Press.

Welford, A.T. 1968: *Fundamentals of skill.* London: Methuen.

—— 1976: *Skilled performance: perceptual and motor skills.* Glenview, Ill.: Scott Foreman.

sleep: psychological features A

state of temporary loss of consciousness

and of unresponsiveness to external stimuli. Its nature and functions are not clearly understood. Using an electro-encephalograph to monitor the electrical activity of a sleeping brain reveals five discernible stages of sleep which occur in cycles of about ninety minutes. Stages 1 ("light sleep") to 4 ("deep sleep") are characterized by an absence of, or only slow, eye movements, and are conventionally referred to as non-rapid eye movement or non-REM sleep. (Stages 3 and 4 are often combined and called "delta sleep".) The fifth stage is associated with rapid eye movements and known as REM or "dreaming" sleep. Delta sleep occurs mainly in the first third of the night, REM sleep in the latter third. The sleep cycle shows wide individual variations whose significance is unknown.

During the onset of sleep individuals are easily awakened and often report dreamlike fantasies. Waking thresholds are higher during stage 2, with mental content more thoughtlike and fragmentary, and recall is sparse and less reliable. Waking thresholds in delta sleep are generally high, with poor dream recall. There is mixed evidence on waking thresholds from REM sleep in humans, though they are low compared to delta sleep. Dream recall after REM awakenings is characteristically abundant and detailed.

Both the total time spent asleep and the distribution of particular sleep stages are closely related to age. In general, total sleep time is greatest in infancy. During the first year of life a reduction in the amount of sleep is accompanied by a change in its pattern towards a combination of one long sleep at night and daytime naps. Through the early years sleep totals continue to decline towards the pattern of young adulthood, with its average of between seven-and-a-half and eight hours concentrated into a single period at night. Old age sees a recurrence of napping and more frequent awakening during the night. The proportion of REM sleep is highest in infancy and childhood, amounting to half or more of total sleep time in the newly born. Both males and females show a marked decrease in the proportion of REM sleep from infancy to puberty, followed by a more gradual drop until the late twenties, when it levels off at between a fifth and a quarter of total sleep time until late adulthood. In men the proportion of REM sleep drops again in old age. Women, however, show no further decline after their twenties.

Variations in the amount of time preceding sleep ("prior wakefulness") affect both the length of time taken to go to sleep ("sleep latency") and the length of time spent asleep. Generally speaking, the longer an individual has been awake the stronger the urge to sleep and the shorter sleep latency, though there is only a weak relationship between prior wakefulness and sleep length. Sleep latency is strongly influenced by when in the day an attempt to sleep occurs. This is the case even when the length of prior wakefulness is held constant, and helps to explain why jet travelers and workers on irregular shifts often experience difficulties in falling and staying asleep. Sleep during the day, or what an individual's "biological clock" tells him is daytime, differs in a number of ways from regular night sleep. The timing of sleep stages is radically altered, and day sleep is more likely to be broken or curtailed.

There are wide differences between individuals in the length, depth and quality of their sleep. We simply do not know why people should differ in their need for sleep. There is disagreement, for example, about variations in the waking personalities of naturally short and long sleepers. These individual differences should not be confused with "sleep disorders" such as insomnia and narcolepsy. Dissatisfaction with the brevity and poor quality of sleep, or insomnia, is most common in women and the elderly. Difficulty in getting to sleep is related to waking anxiety; difficulty in staying asleep or waking too early to depression. The use of hypnotic drugs to induce sleep rarely provides a "normal" night of sleep: REM is usually reduced, with consequent withdrawal from the drug often leading to REM rebound, nightmares and further insomnia. In contrast, narcolepsy is excessive or irresistible sleepiness, often involving periods of involuntary sleep during the day which may prove acutely socially embarrassing. RPE

Bibliography

Cartwright, R.D. 1975: *A primer on sleep and dreaming*. Reading, Mass. and London: Addison-Wesley.

Cohen, D.B. 1979: *Sleep and dreaming: origins, nature and functions*. Oxford and New York: Pergamon.

Oswald, I. 1980: *Sleep*. 4th edn. Harmondsworth and New York: Penguin.

Webb, W.B. 1975: *Sleep, the gentle tyrant*. Englewood Cliffs, N.J.: Prentice-Hall.

smiling: developmental can be minimally defined as a facial expression which involves the corners of the mouth turning up, but there are many variations on this even in infancy. The conditions which elicit smiling at this time are equally varied.

Smiling may occur in neonates without external stimulation, but during the first month after birth is likely to be elicited by sounds, including voices, and in the second month by visual stimulation which is usually human faces, but which (in experiments) can be reduced two-dimensional configurations such as eye-like dots.

The appearance of the smile is not dependent on visual experience, for it emerges at the same age since conception rather than at the same chronological age since birth, and at similar ages in blind and sighted children.

Nevertheless the frequency of smiling has been shown to be different for children reared in institutions and at home, and can be increased almost immediately by the experience of contingent responses of smiling, talking and touching from a social partner. Furthermore, smiling tends to become restricted to familiar people after about six months of age.

Darwin pointed out that the infant's early smiles have survival value, as they help to establish and maintain the relationship between the mother and her child. As development continues, smiling, like other facial expressions, comes under voluntary control. This is mediated by different cerebral mechanisms from those which control spontaneous emotional expressions (Rinn 1984). Developmental changes in smiling therefore rest initially on growing discrimination among stimuli, and subsequently on learning to follow rules about when to smile and when not to. (See also EMOTIONAL DEVELOPMENT; EMOTIONAL EXPRESSION IN INFANCY.) AW/RL

Bibliography

Rinn, W.E. 1984: The neuropsychology of facial expression. *Psychological bulletin* 95, 52–77.

Sroufe, L.A. and Waters, E. 1976: The ontogenesis of smiling and laughter: a perspective on the organisation of development in infancy. *Psychological review* 83, 173–89.

social disadvantage The concepts of social disadvantage and cultural deprivation were invoked to explain the disproportionately high rate of SCHOOL FAILURE found among children from lower-class families. The concepts were derived from studies of animal behavior which found that deprivation of sensory input in early life resulted in organisms with impaired intellectual and affective functioning (Hebb and Thompson 1954). Similar detrimental effects were found in human infants reared in the atypical and under-stimulating environment of orphanages and institutions (Hunt 1961). Based on results such as these, the idea of sensory deprivation was extended to apply to the home environments of the poor – hence the terms social disadvantage and cultural deprivation (Deutsch 1967). The school failure of children from these groups was then seen as the inevitable consequence of this hypothesized deprivation, and educational efforts were made to overcome the children's deficiencies (see COMPENSATORY EDUCATION). In recent years the concepts of social or cultural deprivation have been challenged. The claim has been made that while child-rearing practices of various subgroups are different from those of the dominant group, they are not deficient (Labov 1970). The controversy has caused these terms to fall increasingly into disuse. However, the social and educational problems of the children have not abated. (See also EDUCATIONAL ATTAINMENT AND SOCIAL CLASS.) MB/JM

Bibliography

Hebb, D.O. and Thompson, W.R. 1954: The social significance of animal studies. In *Handbook of social psychology*, ed. G. Lindzey. Reading, Mass.: Addison-Wesley.

Hunt, J.M. 1961: *Intelligence and experience*. New York: Ronald Press.

Deutsch, M. et al. 1967: *The disadvantaged child: studies of the social environment and the learning process*. New York and London: Basic Books.

Labov, W. 1970: The logic of nonstandard English. In *Language and poverty*, ed. F. Williams. Chicago: Markham.

Ramey, C.T., Yeates, K.O. and Short, E.J. 1984: The plasticity of intellectual development: insights from preventive intervention. *Child development* 55, 1913–25.

Schooler, C. 1984: Psychological effects of complex environments during the life span: a review and theory. *Intelligence* 8, 259–81.

social learning theory An attempt to explain various examples of human behavior and aspects of personality by reference to principles derived from experiments on learning. The first systematic effort in this direction was that of a group of Yale psychologists, in particular John Dollard and Neal Miller. Much of their effort was spent on trying to explain phenomena pinpointed by FREUD as the products of mechanisms suggested by Hull. They believed that there are innate *primary drives*, such as sex, hunger or pain. A drive is a stimulus which is strong enough to lead to action. Behavior is a means of reducing drives. They also believed that there are acquired *secondary drives*. These are conditional stimuli whose drive-force is the result of their association with primary drives. An important example of a secondary drive is anxiety (or fear) learnt from the experience of the primary drive, pain. These associative mechanisms, and the supposed force of secondary drives are the building blocks of complex behavior and motivation.

As in other behavioral theories reinforcement (reward and punishment) plays a major role. This acts as the equivalent of the "pleasure principle" in Freud's theories since animals, including humans, presumably pursue pleasure and avoid pain. Animals learn "instrumental responses", such as turning a wheel to avoid shock, because these are associated with the increase of pleasure or reduction of pain. In this way complex behavioral repertoires are gradually built up. Such behavior may be normal or abnormal, since the contingencies of reinforcement will lead to the repetition of behavior associated with reward, and thereby establish habits which may as easily be bad as good. Neurotic or deviant behavior is therefore thought to develop through exactly the same learning processes as normal, socially acceptable behavior.

Dollard and Miller paid some attention to imitation (1941) which they saw as a factor in socialization. They explained it by the reinforcements a person (or animal) gains from the successful achievement of an outcome after imitating someone else. They also made important contributions to theorizing about conflict, AGGRESSION and psychotherapy. Miller (1944) worked out the concept of *approach-avoidance conflict* in which the same object is desired and feared. As one approaches the object the tendency to approach increases, but so does the tendency to avoid, and the latter increases faster. One is therefore baulked at some distance from the goal, driven both to go on and to go back (see Brown 1948).

They claimed that aggression was caused by frustration i.e. interruption of a sequence of goal-directed behavior. The amount of aggression was taken to depend on the amount of frustration, which in turn depended on the strength of the drive to make the frustrated response, and the amount and scope of the interference. The psychotherapeutic ideas centered on the role of conflict and anxiety in psychopathology, and the possibility of the patient learning new responses or to discriminate threatening from non-threatening situations.

The second phase of social learning theory is associated with the work of BANDURA and his colleagues from the late 1950s to the present. They too have used ideas derived from laboratory studies of learning, but have proceeded in a more piecemeal fashion, not basing their approach on a particular theory such as Hull's. In fact the primary idea behind much of their work seems to have been the rejection of either Freudian or behaviorist conceptions of human behavior. As Bandura (1977) put it, 'People are neither driven by inner forces nor buffeted by environmental stimuli. Rather, psychological functioning is explained in terms of a continuous reciprocal interaction of personal and environmental determinants. Within this approach, symbolic, vicarious, and self-regulatory processes assume a prominent role'.

Bandura, Walters and other colleagues conducted a famous series of experiments on aggression in children (see Bandura 1973). Their interest was in observational learning (which they called "modeling"). They found that frustration was unnecessary for aggressive behavior, since a child would imitate an adult's aggression in free play without any preliminary upset or frustration. Furthermore, contrary to the views of Dollard and Miller, such imitation occurred without any incentive or reinforcement. Bandura believed that observational learning must be a basic process in human development. As he said (1977), 'One does not teach children to swim . . . and novice medical students to perform surgery by having them discover the appropriate behavior through the consequences of their successes and failures . . . Apart from the question of survival, it is difficult to imagine a social transmission process in which the language, lifestyles, and institutional practices of a culture are taught to each new member by selective reinforcement of fortuitous behaviors . . .'. They showed that such observational learning took place even when the actions of the adult model were punished. Children who had seen this, but were subse-quently offered an incentive, proved just as ready and able to produce an accurate imitation as children who had seen an aggressive model rewarded (Bandura 1965). The children therefore *learn* regardless of the reinforcement contingencies. Whether they act on their learning is influenced by reinforcement. Bandura distinguished observational learning from imitation because people do not simply ape others' behavior. They extract general rules about how to affect their environment, and put these into effect when they expect them to produce a desirable outcome. Modeling has also been offered as an explanation of children's development of SEX ROLES (or gender roles), and it proved useful in the treatment of anxiety and phobia (Bussey and Bandura 1984; Bandura 1969).

The role of expectations of success and failure has been a major consideration for Bandura and other social learning theorists. Bandura (1982) has been interested in "self-efficacy" beliefs (i.e. beliefs about whether one can act effectively to achieve what one wants) especially, but not solely, as they affect patients in psychotherapy or recovering from physical illness such as heart disease. Mischel (1973) has attempted to build a model of personality based on the assumption that people's behavior is determined by the cognitive processes illustrated in Bandura's experiments. Mischel argues that 'behavior is controlled to a considerable extent by externally administered consequences', but that people also control their own behavior 'by self-imposed goals (standards) and self-produced consequences . . . The essence of self-regulatory systems is the subject's adoption of *contingency rules* that guide his behavior in the absence of, and sometimes in spite of, immediate external situational pressures'.

The latter-day social learning theorists differ from Dollard and Miller in playing down the importance of motivational (drive) factors such as frustration and in playing up the importance of cognitive factors. States of anxiety are explained in terms of beliefs about self-efficacy rather than as conditioned secondary drives.

Above all, reinforcement is seen as neither necessary nor sufficient to explain learning or even behavior. Learning by observation without reward or punishment is taken to be the central process of human SOCIALIZATION. Because this involves the abstraction of rules which are stored for future as well as immediate guidance, observation and curiosity allow people to set themselves practical and moral standards. Naturally, as the passages above show, these writers do not deny the effects of reward and punishment, nor do they suppose that learning is not frequently a result of explicit instruction.   RL

Bibliography

Bandura, A. 1965: Influence of models' reinforcement contingencies on the acquisition of imitative responses. *Journal of personality and social psychology* 1, 589–95.

—— 1969: *Principles of behavior modification.* New York: Holt, Rinehart and Winston.

—— 1973: *Aggression: a social learning analysis.* Englewood Cliffs, N.J.: Prentice-Hall.

—— 1977: *Social learning theory.* Englewood Cliffs, N.J.: Prentice-Hall.

—— 1982: Self-efficacy mechanism in human agency. *American psychologist* 37, 122–47.

Brown, J.S. 1948: Gradients of approach and avoidance responses and their relation to level of motivation. *Journal of comparative and physiological psychology* 41, 450–65.

Bussey, K. and Bandura, A. 1984: Influence of gender constancy and social power on sex-linked modeling. *Journal of personality and social psychology* 47, 1292–1302.

Dollard, J., Doob, L., Miller, N.E., Mowrer, O.H. and Sears, R.R. 1939: *Frustration and aggression.* New Haven: Yale University Press.

—— and Miller, N.E. 1950: *Personality and psychotherapy.* New York: McGraw-Hill.

Miller, N.E. 1944: Experimental studies of conflict. In *Personality and the behavior disorders*, vol. 1, ed. J.M. Hunt. New York: Ronald Press.

—— and Dollard, J. 1941: *Social learning and imitation.* New Haven: Yale University Press.

Mischel, W. 1973: Toward a cognitive social learning reconceptualization of personality. *Psychological review* 80, 252–83.

socialization A technical term which gained currency in anthropology, psychology and sociology during the late 1930s to describe the processes through which an individual becomes a competent member of society. Interest in the experiences which influence the young and their participation in the community is as old as the Bible and readily found in the writings of philosophers and diarists as well as the founding fathers of modern social science such as Durkheim and FREUD. Emphases differ within disciplines; anthropologists stress cultural transmission or enculturation, personality psychologists focus on impulse control, while sociologists concentrate on role learning. In each field the term has a unique history and meaning but its popularity coincided with the rise of positivism in the social sciences, with efforts to deal with social policy issues such as education in a scientific, value-free manner, and with a model of the child as a passive recipient of social experiences which transforms a biological organism into a human being.

According to Whiting (1968) the term "socialization" was first used formally in anthropology in 1935 but it was Freud's *Totem and Taboo*, published in 1913, which launched the study of childhood, not as a cataloging of rituals and their cultural diffusion, but as the period in which culture had its most profound impact on the individual. Within anthropology the study of socialization is associated with the particularly American speciality known as Personality and Culture. Among its hallmarks is reliance on psychoanalytic theory. Prototypical of this approach is the collaborative work of Kardiner, a psychoanalyst, and Linton and Dubois, anthropologists. The merging of their disciplinary interests is seen in concepts such as "basic personality structure" (Kardiner 1945). The term reflects both the concern of depth psychologists with that which is enduring, central or genotypic rather than merely surface or phenotypic and of anthropologists with that which is common or modal across individuals in a society. "Basic personality structures" were assumed to differ as a function of culturally specific socialization experiences. Learning theory, particularly Hul-

233

lian theory with its emphasis on drive reduction as the central mechanism of reinforcement and compatible with psychoanalytic instinct theory, was later added to Culture and Personality formulations. Disenchantment with grand theories, global concepts and deductive systems in the 1960s produced a new anthropology of childhood characterized by interest in cognitive development and concerned with precise observations of behavior typical of ethological research. (British social anthropologists have not espoused the Culture and Personality approach and have generally eschewed psychological explanations.)

A variety of conceptual and methodological perspectives are included in reviews of psychological studies of socialization (Danziger 1971, Zigler and Child 1973). This diversity reflects the different theoretical orientations and research strategies employed by psychologists to explain the influences of the social world on individual development. Initially psychoanalysis provided impetus for psychological studies of socialization and its influences are found even in Piaget's early work. The term "socialization" is, however, most often linked in psychology as in anthropology with general behavior theory – the positivist amalgam of psychoanalysis and Hullian learning theory developed at Yale University by an interdisciplinary group of psychologists, anthropologists and sociologists. Complex processes such as IMITATION and IDENTIFICATION were explained within this behaviorist learning framework (Miller and Dollard 1941; see SOCIAL LEARNING THEORY). It had a major influence in the 1940s, 1950s and early 1960s both on psychological studies of socialization and in Personality and Culture (Whiting and Child 1953). In socialization studies the dominant strategy was to measure, in adults or older children, molar traits held to be enduring, such as aggression, dependence or conscience, and to relate these measures to early childhood experiences. The complex character descriptions of psychoanalysis became the quantified traits or consequent variables which

were linked to a host of child rearing or antecedent variables by a variety of learning mechanisms such as generalization and avoidance learning.

Patterns of child rearing (Sears, Maccoby and Levin 1957) is typical of the general behavior theory approach to socialization. It is the report of almost 400 interviews with mothers of five-year-olds and contains quantified data on antecedent dimensions such as feeding and the training of aggression and obedience. As a scientific study it was considered an authoritative source of information about American socialization practices for many years. Methodologically it was flawed by reliance on mothers' reports both for information on child rearing and for assessment of consequent variables such as strength of a child's conscience. Criticisms of the approach have come from many quarters. Learning theorists questioned Hullian assumptions about reinforcement and in developmental psychology, the observational learning theory of BANDURA provided a more fruitful model with which to explain the influence of parents, peers and others.

Dissatisfaction with the dominant socialization approach extended well beyond learning theorists. In the attacks upon behaviorism in the 1960s Bandura's neo-behaviorist model was a target as well as the passive view of the infant as a lump of clay needing to be shaped by social forces. The unidirectional influence of adults or experienced members of society upon the young and inexperienced was questioned and a need to recognize individual differences among infants stressed. The unique and fundamental importance of early experience was queried. So pervasive were the negative attitudes attached to the term "socialization" that Richards offered a detailed explanation for rejecting the word as part of the main title of a volume on early development even though he and other contributors were writing about processes which in a general sense would be described as socialization (Richards 1974). Crucial to their position and that of many contemporary investigators is a view of the human infant as an active participant in the socialization process and of the interaction as based upon reciprocity.

Attention to biological factors was reintroduced in studying socialization, and the infant's biological potential became a focus alongside any effects of culture. The rediscovery of biology has engendered new controversies. The extent of the innate social propensities of the infant is contentious. Some psychologists describe the newborn as presocial, a highly developed biological organism ready to learn to live in society (Schaffer 1979); yet other theorists maintain that at birth the human infant has rudimentary social skills (Trevarthen 1980). Nonetheless, most psychologists now take care not to underestimate the contribution of the infant to its socialization.

The sociological study of socialization has undergone a similar reassessment of theoretical and research priorities. The Parsonian position, influential during the 1950s, viewed socialization as the psychological process through which the role-differentiated nuclear family ensured that children developed human personalities, e.g., systems of socially appropriate action (Parsons and Bales 1955). These personality systems were held to reflect the social structures which the individual had experienced. Parsons was criticized for presenting an over-socialized view which left little scope for individual differences or innovation in society (Wrong 1961). In a spirit akin to that of psychologists, sociologists rejected the passive and malleable child model which had suited the positivist, determinist orientation of the social sciences in the mid-twentieth century. In search of a model which recognized the child's view of his social world, sociologists returned to the writings of G. H. Mead (White 1977). Crucial elements in Mead's work are its emphases on a reflexive self and on symbols. In order to construct and to understand the language or primary symbol system of society the child needs to interact with others. Mastery of language equips the child to understand itself and others (see Cox 1986).

Depth and detail were sacrificed in order to consider socialization from anthropological and sociological as well as psychological perspectives. This strategy has led to recognition of wider epistemological issues such as the nature of the explanatory theory employed and the model of the child which was its object, but it has resulted in a neglect of many other dimensions and changes. There has also been a marked shift in emphasis from the study of personality and motivation to concern with intellectual abilities and social understanding. Childhood is no longer the sole focus of interest and processes of socialization are investigated in adolescence, adulthood and old age. Socialization is generally viewed as an interactive process and no longer the passive receipt of expertise by a novice (see Maccoby and Martin 1983). Along with a diversity in content psychological research also presents a variety of theoretical positions. Social psychological studies drawing inspiration from the symbolic interactionist theory of Mead take their place alongside Piagetian (see PIAGET) explorations of the social world and Vygotskian (see VYGOTSKY) analyses of the internalization of socially constructed tools of thought (see Maccoby 1984).   BBL

Bibliography

Cox, M.V. 1986: *The child's point of view*. Brighton: Harvester.

Danziger, K. 1971: *Socialization*. Harmondsworth: Penguin.

Kardiner, A. 1945: The concept of basic personality structure as an operational tool in the social sciences. In *The science of man in the world crisis*, ed. R. Linton. New York: Columbia University Press.

Maccoby, E.E. 1984: Socialization and developmental change. *Child development* 55, 317–28.

—— and Martin, J.A. 1983: Socialization in the context of the family: parent-child interaction. In *Handbook of child psychology*. 4th edn, vol. 4, ed. E.M. Hetherington. New York: Wiley.

Miller, N.E. and Dollard, J. 1941: *Social learning and imitation*. New Haven: Yale University Press; London: Greenwood Press (1979).

Parsons, T. and Bales, R.F. 1955: *Family, socialization and interaction process*. Glencoe, Ill.: Free Press; London: Routledge and Kegan Paul (1956).

Richards, M.P.M. ed. 1974: *The integration of a child into a social world*. Cambridge and New York: Cambridge University Press.

Schaffer, H.R. 1979: Acquiring the concept of dialogue. In *Psychological development from infancy: image to intention*, eds. M. Bornstein and W. Kesson. Hillsdale, N J : Erlbaum; London: Halstead (1979).

Sears, R.R., Maccoby, E.E. and Levin, H. 1957: *Patterns of child rearing*. Evanston, Ill.: Row, Peterson.

Trevarthen, C. 1980: Neurological developmental and the growth of psychological functions. In *Developmental psychology and society*, ed. J. Sants. London: Macmillan; New York: St. Martin's.

White, G. 1977: *Socialization*. London and New York: Longman.

Whiting, J.W.M. 1968: Socialization: anthropological aspects. In *International Encyclopedia of the social sciences*, vol 14, ed. D.L. Sills. New York: Macmillan and Free Press.

—— and Child, I.L. 1953: *Child training and personality*. New Haven: Yale University Press.

Wrong, D. 1961: The over-socialized conception of man in modern society. *American sociological review* 26, 184–93.

Zigler, E.F. and Child, I.L. eds. 1973: *Socialization and personality development*. Reading, Mass.: Addison-Wesley.

sociobiology: human The scope and definition of work of human ethologists, especially those who considered themselves to be working in the wider framework of evolutionary biology and the adaptiveness of human behavior, shifted markedly in the 1970s with the growing influence of sociobiology. The adaptive value of behavior was seen no longer in terms of species survival, but in terms of individual and inclusive fitness. Observational and traditional ethological methods became only one of many ways of studying this. The sociobiological assumption of genetic influences on behavior, applied to the human case, has led to vigorous attacks and controversy. It has been stressed by those objecting to this assumption that many of the fundamental processes of human interaction are based on the expectations of individuals about each other which in turn are based on rights and duties embodied in human institutions. These are held to be man-made, and not subject to genetic influence. Such objections are directed against what may be called naive (genetic) sociobiology. For a balanced review see Ruse (1979).

General expositions of human sociobiology include Wilson (1978) and Alexander (1980). Among numerous areas of human behavior approached from a sociobiological perspective are the following: marriage systems: the rareness of polyandry, and the relation of monogamy/polygyny to resource ecology and parental care, sexuality and sexual dimorphism, different reproductive strategies of males and females; kinship terminologies and unilineal and bilineal descent: their relationship to sexual strategies and to paternity and certainty; choice of marriage or mating partners: for example the effects of early co-socialization on later incest avoidance; altruism, reciprocity and exchange: their relationship to kinship; territoriality and aggression: for example circumstances predicting human tribal warfare; parental care and investment: for example the occurrence of preferential female infanticide in highly stratified societies, and adoption of kin and non-kin.

Human sociobiology, even more than human ethology, has the potential to bring together a variety of disciplines other than psychology – notably anthropology, sociology, politics, economics and history (Chagnon and Irons 1979), as well as population genetics and demography. However, in so doing it is likely to be transformed into a wider theory of gene-culture evolution and the interaction of both genetic and cultural factors in human behavior. Recent attempts to consider such interaction are typified by Lumsden and Wilson (1981). In general such approaches lead to the conclusion that human behavior will not always be adaptive in the way that naive human sociobiology would predict, not only because the human environment has changed so much from that of our hominid ancestors, but also because culture itself can be considered an evolutionary process, embodying selection, variation and retention, which may co-evolve with but can also conflict with the pressures of biological evolution.

PKS

Bibliography

Alexander, R.D. 1980: *Darwinism and human affairs*. London: Pitman; Seattle: University of Washington Press.

Blurton Jones, N.G. ed. 1972: *Ethological studies of child behaviour*. Cambridge and New York: Cambridge University Press.

Bowlby, John 1969: *Attachment and loss*, vol. 1. *Attachment*. London: Hogarth Press; New York: Basic Books.

Chagnon, N.A. and Irons, W. 1979: *Evolutionary biology and human social behavior: an anthropological perspective*. Massachusetts: Duxbury Press.

Eibl-Eibesfeldt, I. 1979: Human ethology: concepts and implications for the sciences of man. *Behavioral and brain sciences* 2, 1–57.

Ekman, P. and Friesen, W.V. 1976: Measuring facial movement. *Environmental psychology and nonverbal behavior* 1, 56–75.

Lumsden, Charles J. and Wilson, Edward O. 1981: *Genes, minds and culture*. Cambridge, Mass.: Harvard University Press.

McGrew, W.C. 1972: *An ethological study of children's behaviour*. London and New York: Academic Press.

Ruse, M. 1979: *Sociobiology: sense or nonsense?* Dordrecht, Holland: D. Reidel.

Smith, P.K. 1983: Human sociobiology. In *Psychology Survey IV*, eds. B.M. Foss and J. Nicholson. Leicester: British Psychological Society.

—— and Connolly, K.J. 1980: *The ecology of preschool behaviour*. British Psychological Society. Cambridge and New York: Cambridge University Press.

Wilson, E.O. 1978: *On human nature*. Cambridge, Mass.: Harvard University Press.

Spearman, Charles Edward Born in London in 1863, as a young man Spearman was a regular army officer. After leaving the army he studied in Germany. In 1904 he took his doctorate at Leipzig where he studied under Wundt. In an article which Spearman published that year he put forward the two factor theory of intelligence. According to this, performance on any mental task depends on two distinct factors. Firstly there is a *general factor* (*g*), which is the common basis of INTELLIGENCE. Secondly there is a *specific factor* (*s*). These specific factors are abilities which are verbal, arithmetical, musical etc. and contribute to performance on particular kinds of task. This idea of a general factor has been a central topic in the debates about intelligence and is still very much alive today (see Jensen 1979). As a necessary adjunct to his theory Spearman developed the statistical technique of FACTOR ANALYSIS. He also produced the Spearman rank-correlation coefficient which allows for the correlation of two variables by ranks (e.g. position in the 100 yards and position in the long jump) rather than measurements of performance (e.g. each contestant's time and distance). Spearman taught at University College, London from 1906 until 1931. He died in London in 1945.

LM/RL

Bibliography

Jensen, A.R. 1979: *g*: outmoded theory or unconquered frontier? *Creative science technology* 2, 16–29.

Spearman, C.E. 1904: General intelligence objectively determined and measured. *American journal of psychology* 15, 201–93.

—— 1927: *The abilities of man*. London and New York: Macmillan.

speech: telegraphic The term "telegraphic speech" was introduced by Brown (1970) to describe the short incomplete utterances produced by children after the two-word stage of FIRST LANGUAGE ACQUISITION. The use of telegraphic speech reflects a constraint on the length of utterance children are able to produce. This limitation grows less restrictive with age.

Forms most likely to appear in telegraphic speech are nouns, verbs and adjectives, in that order. Forms likely to be omitted (when compared with adult speech) are inflections, the COPULA, auxiliary verbs, articles and conjunctions. As the telegraphic speech stage progresses such function words are gradually added.

The appearance of telegraphic speech rather than a three-word stage after the two-word stage is still in need of explanation. It may be a reflection of the fact that most syntactic and semantic relations are binary rather than ternary.

A possible objection to the term "telegraphic speech" is that it may misleadingly imply that a child's utterances are merely reductions of adult models and not novel creations. PM

Bibliography

Brown, Roger 1970: *Psycholinguistics*. New York and London: Macmillan.

Wanner, E. and Gleitman, L.R. eds. 1983: *Language acquisition: the state of the art*. Cambridge and New York: Cambridge University Press.

spelling This term refers to two different psychologically interesting areas: first the letter-by-letter structure of words, and second the letter-by-letter production of words. Spelling in the sense of letter-by-letter structure of words (orthography) applies only to alphabetic writing systems. The basic principle of these systems is that continuous speech sound can be represented by discrete letters. However, the relationship between units of speech sound (phonemes) and units of the visible word (graphemes) is fraught with problems (Gleitman and Rozin 1977).

In many languages spelling deviates from the sound of the spoken word. Deviations are the more marked the older the history of the orthography. Pronunciation changes over time, and successive spelling reforms have their effect. English orthography is especially complex as different languages with different orthographic systems have contributed to its form, the main ones being Germanic and Romance (Scragg 1974). The origin of many English words is still preserved in their spelling even if the sound has changed considerably (e.g. psychology, preserving the Greek *ps* and *ch*, which are sounded *s* and *k*).

Spelling can convey information about words on a number of important linguistic levels: not only the sound of a word, but often also a previous pronunciation (the *b* in lamb was once pronounced), a word's language origin, sometimes its syntactic form (*-ed* ending for past tense in English, capital letters for nouns in German), relationships between words that belong together (sign-signature), and distinctions between words that do not belong together even though they sound the same (to, two, too). These factors all contribute to spelling which means that spelling knowledge is not a trivial accomplishment (Haas 1970). This knowledge is not usually conscious but it can be demonstrated that people use it in rapid word recognition (see READING: COGNITIVE SKILLS) and word production. Languages with very recent spelling reforms based solely on representing speech sound by spelling (Finnish, Serbo-Croat, or Turkish) have as a result much less orthographic complexity and script is considered phonetically accurate.

A description of letter-to-sound correspondences in English is provided by Venezky (1970) who classifies words according to the degree of predictability of spelling from the sound in context. If letter position is taken into account, as well as morphological units, regularity of spelling is much greater than is usually thought. Besides regularity or predictability, frequency of occurrence and length of a word influence how well its spelling is perceived and remembered. Morton (1979) provides a truly remarkable model that succeeds in taking into account the many processes involved in word recognition and yet simplifies their overwhelming complexity. The influence of linguistic factors on spelling is less clear than that of cognitive ones since a systematic linguistically based analysis of English orthography is not available.

Orthography not only determines letter-by-letter structure of words, but also whether small or capital letters are to be used and rules of punctuation. There are also conventions about abbreviation and hyphenation or separation of words. All these aspects of written language are subject to continual change. Spelling conventions are greatly influenced by social and political factors (Venezky 1980).

The *production* of words, either when writing, typing or orally naming the constituent letters, is the other meaning of spelling. This process of production or reproduction can be contrasted with the process of recognition. Clearly, one is not the inverse of the other. Dissociations can occur, so that a person can be an excellent reader but an atrocious speller, or that a child may be able to spell a particular word but may not be able to recognize it, and vice versa (Bryant and Bradley 1980).

Spelling skill is acquired during the early school years and according to the orthographic complexity of the language, may take a long time to become automatic and may loom large in LEARNING DIFFICULTIES. Despite the artificial nature of spelling skill and its dependence on learning, young pre-readers with bare knowledge of the letters of the alphabet can be observed to invent their own spellings. Read (1971) has analyzed linguistically these early productions and has been able to relate them to the child's own conceptions of phonology. Children at this stage write as they speak, or rather as they consciously analyze their own speech. They are usually not able to read back what they have written.

Much of the early stages of learning to spell is taken up by learning to segment words into those sound units that often arbitrarily correspond to letters, or letter strings (e.g. the sound ʃ is *sh* in English, *ch* in French, *sch* in German, *sci* in Italian, *s* in Portuguese).

One particular problem for conscious segmentation is such consonant clusters as in h*int* or pu*mp* (Marcel 1980). Many beginners tend to reduce these clusters, so that *n* or *m* are omitted. This exactly parallels what happens in normal early speech development and is therefore particularly fascinating. It occurs consistently in certain cases of severe spelling disability, as are found with dyslexia (see DYSLEXIC CHILDREN). It is by no means clear whether phonological segmentation skills are a prerequisite or a consequence of being able to spell: both processes are normally acquired at the same time by young children. Illiterate adults in a peasant community have been shown to have poorer awareness of speech as a sequence of phonemes than those who had learned to read (Morais et al. 1979).

Later stages of learning to spell require two main strategies: one has to do with the application of general spelling rules, the other with the memorizing of specific word spellings. Both strategies are needed and instructional techniques have been devised to promote these skills. The aim is a fully automatic production process: a skilled speller can write a word effortlessly and correctly. Automatic sequences are presumably governed by internal programs that precede specific motor programs. The speller is equally able to write, type, print or orally spell the word correctly. The nature of the internal representation is not accessible to introspective awareness. Many good spellers believe that they rely on visual images of spellings. However, these visual images are more likely to be a later and optional manifestation of the internal program. Seymour and Porpodas (1980) have found a directional quality to these programs from left to right in the letter string, in experiments where people had to produce either the preceding or following letter in a string. Also there are clear relationships between the position of a letter in sequence and error probability. Initial letters are almost always correctly produced, middle positions, and especially vowels, least well (Wing and Baddeley 1980).

Level of spelling skill is assessed by educational attainment tests. These tests usually consist of dictation of word lists. Mostly they are of little use in diagnosing particular spelling problems. The quality of a spelling mistake can potentially pinpoint the source of spelling difficulty. For instance, errors that involve the type of cluster reduction mentioned above can be diagnostically useful. They point to problems with phonological analysis and/or awareness. A tendency to such errors can best be revealed with nonsense words. The spelling of real familiar words can of course be learned by various means and thus this problem may be hidden. In general, serious non-phonetic errors are likely to betray difficulties with phonological analysis. Minor non-phonetic errors, that is, those that still preserve the syllable structure of the word, often mean that the child does not yet know the sound-to-letter rules very well. This error would be especially noticed in very regular or predictable words. Remedial teaching needs to distinguish this type of non-phonetic error from the more serious one mentioned above. Minor errors can also simply be slips of the pen.

Phonetically plausible errors account for a large proportion of misspellings in English. They are of course a very rational way of representing spoken words that have not been encountered before or that one cannot remember in letter-by-letter detail. They imply good phonological analysis and good knowledge of sound-to-letter rules. Nevertheless, neither of these important steps in spelling progress are sufficient. In many orthographies (especially English, French or German) the exact letter-by-letter structure needs to be known for many unpredictable or irregular words and those word pairs that sound alike but have otherwise little to do with each other. At the highest level of spelling skill, it is this aspect that discriminates most between individuals. This may well be a matter of learning specific words by rote. Interestingly, some people have life-long difficulties specifically with this stage in spelling. One possible cause might be their disinclination to take in the full letter-by-letter detail of words, when reading (Frith 1980). Such a strategy works perfectly well in reading but for spelling the full detail is essential. This again serves to demonstrate that reading and spelling strategies are relatively independent and each deserves to be looked at in its own right.   UF

Bibliography

*Frith, U. ed. 1980: *Cognitive processes in spelling*. London and New York: Academic Press. (Contains articles cited in text by Baker; Bryant and Bradley; Frith; Marcel; Morton; Seymour and Porpodar; Venezky (1980); and Wing and Baddeley.)

—— 1984: Specific spelling problems. In

Dyslexia: a global issue, eds. R.N. Malatesha and H.A. Whitaker. The Hague: Martinus Nijhoff.

Gleitman, L. and Rozin, P. 1977: The structure and acquisition of reading, 1: Relations between orthographies and the structure of language. In *Toward a psychology of reading*, eds. A.S. Reber and D.L. Scarborough. Hillsdale, N.J.: Erlbaum.

Haas, W. 1970: *Phonographic translation*. Manchester: Manchester University Press.

*Kavanagh, J.F. and Venezky, R.L. eds. 1980: *Orthography, reading and dyslexia*. Baltimore: University Park Press.

Morais, J., Cary, L., Alegria, J. and Bertelson, P. 1977: Does awareness of speech as a sequence of phones arise spontaneously? *Cognition* 7, 323–31.

Morton, J. 1979: Word recognition. In *Structures and processes*, eds. J. Morton and J. C. Marshall. Psycholinguistics series 2. London: Paul Elek.

Read, C. 1971: Preschool children's knowledge of English phonology. *Harvard educational review* 41, 1–34.

Scragg, D.G. 1974: *A history of English spelling*. Manchester: Manchester University Press.

Venezky, R.L. 1970: *The structure of English orthography*. The Hague: Mouton.

statistical methods Procedures for the planning of data collection in experiments and surveys together with techniques for describing and summarizing sample data so that inferences may be made about populations from which the samples were taken. They offer a rigorously based approach to the design and analysis aspects of investigations. Methods for analysis are usually pre-determined by the particular experimental or survey design employed and its implementation. Knowledge of (a) the design and its characteristics, (b) the methods of analysis which may be associated with the design, (c) the amount of precision required for estimation and (d) the variation in the population may be used to determine the sample sizes which will be necessary for a satisfactory investigation.

Following the collection of statistical data the first requirement is usually a description. In the light of the nature of the variables, whether they are nominal, ordinal, interval or ratio in character, appropriate graphical methods are used for presentation. For the first two types of variable a bar chart, pie chart or pictogram is normally used whereas for the last two a histogram or a frequency diagram suffices. Certain probability distributions may be confirmed by plotting sample frequencies on special graph paper. Multivariate data is treated by plotting scatter diagrams or frequency contours for two variables at a time. Graphical methods are used for exploratory data analysis and residual analysis which allow the validity of assumptions made by classical methods to be examined and appropriate action taken.

Following graphical descriptions, statistical measures are calculated from the observations to provide estimates of population characteristics. These may be quantities which describe the distribution of the values of a variable in the population in terms of its location (e.g. mean, median, mode, mid-range) or its dispersion (e.g. standard deviation, mean deviation, range, semi-interquartile range) or its shape (e.g. skewness, kurtosis). Where single values are calculated to represent these population characteristics, the estimates are called "point estimates". More useful are "interval estimates" which consist of two values between which the true value of the population parameter in question will be expected to lie with some stated probability. Such intervals are known as "confidence intervals".

Whereas it is possible to proceed to make inferences about hypotheses involving population parameters using confidence intervals, it is more common to compute "test statistics" for this purpose. These are quantities calculated from samples which are standardized so that their distributions over repeated samples can be derived theoretically and "critical values" obtained and tabulated for use in statistical tests.

Statistical tests are said to be "parametric" if they refer to the form of the underlying distribution of the observations and "non-parametric" or "distribution-free" if they do not. Parametric tests are concerned with hypotheses which mention

the population values of parameters of this underlying distribution. The most common parametric tests are based on the sample mean and test a hypothesis regarding the population mean (e.g. normal z-test, Student's t-test) whereas non-parametric tests often use the ranked sample values for testing a hypothesis about the population median (e.g. Mann-Whitney U-test, Wilcoxon test, sign test). The advantage of the latter is that the specific test used will be more valid over a wide range of underlying distributions and the main disadvantage, where both may apply, will be a loss of power. Parametric tests often assume that the sample values follow a normal distribution, or at least that the sample mean is approximately normally distributed and this is true in practice unless the sample sizes are very small because of the Central Limit Theorem.

Non-parametric tests are used for testing the goodness-of-fit of an observed distribution to a theoretical one or may compare two observed distributions. The chi-square (χ^2) test and the Kolmogorov-Smirnov tests are both suitable for these purposes with the latter being more sensitive to the largest deviation between two distributions. Where individuals are classified into categories by two attributes the resulting contingency table may be analyzed using a chi-square test for association between the attributes. Fisher's exact test is used in this situation for small frequencies. Where the samples are correlated, another non-parametric test, McNemar's, is used to test for a difference between the proportions in the categories.

Tests of means for a single population or for two populations are based on the standard normal z- or the t-distribution according as the variance in the population sampled is known or unknown. Tests for proportions use a test statistic which is taken to be approximately normal for large samples. Where there are more than two populations, an analysis of variance is applied using an F-statistic for difference between means or a chi-square statistic for a difference between proportions.

As well as providing for the testing of

means of several samples, the analysis of variance, due to R.A. Fisher, is used to test for the effects of several factors which are varied in a systematic way in the same experiment. Such uses of the analysis of variance are examples of linear models which describe the measured response in terms of a sum of effects due to the factors and the interactions between them. For a single factor the simplest design is known as the "completely randomized" design in which the levels of the factor (or treatments) are applied randomly to the experimental units. Where these units are arranged in groups or "blocks" and complete sets of treatments are applied in each block the design is known as a "randomized block design". This very commonly used design allows for independent testing of treatment and block effects by means of an analysis of variance.

Whereas the randomized block design may be seen to exploit the heterogeneity of experimental units in one dimension, an extension of the design known as the "Latin Square" design caters for two dimensions. If the two dimensions are thought of as "rows" and "columns" then the rows constitute blocks within which all treatments appear and the columns likewise. This balanced but restricted design allows for independent tests of the "rows", "columns" and treatments factors. Extensions of the randomized block design provide for additional treatment factors and for incomplete blocks containing subsets of the available treatments. The latter include confounded designs in which main effects are estimated with full precision and only those interactions which are of interest are deliberately estimated in the analysis. In balanced incomplete designs, some of the interactions may be estimated with lower precision than main effects. This is also achieved by "split-plot" designs in which less important factors are applied at the level of plots within blocks and more important factors are applied to sub-plots which are formed by splitting main plots. Whereas factorial designs in which all levels of all factors appear in every possible combination are known as "crossed" designs, the split-plot design is

an example of a "hierarchical" or "nested" design.

The analysis of variance F-tests are based upon underlying assumptions that the observations are normally distributed and have equal variance within groups. When these assumptions are untenable recourse is made either to transformation of the variable to restore the desired properties or to ranking and a non-parametric test. In the single factor experiment the Kruskal-Wallis test is used and for several factors, Friedman's test for matched samples is applied for each factor separately.

Where the factors may be expressed in the form of quantitative variables, the analysis of variance may be used to test the significance of the trend or response function. The levels of a factor may be equally spaced on an appropriate scale and it is then convenient to consider the response function by fitting orthogonal polynomials. For a factor with two levels, a linear component is tested, with three levels, a quadratic component, etc. If there are several factors of this type operating simultaneously, interactions between these components are investigated also.

As well as the response variable, a concomitant variable is sometimes measured. Adjustment for the effect of this concomitant variable is by an analysis of covariance. This procedure is able to deal with several concomitant variables.

Regression and correlation methods are applied to investigate the relationships between two or more variables. In the case of simple regression, one variable which is statistically varying is seen to depend upon another mathematical variable which is not subject to statistical variation. There are applications, however, where both variables involved are statistical but the "dependent" variable is subject to more variation than the "independent" one. The form of the relationship is most often linear but can also be a higher degree polynomial or exponential or any other mathematical continuous function. Correlation refers more generally to the relationship or interdependence between two variables and therefore applies to situations where regression may be inappropriate. Measures of correlation include the "product-moment correlation coefficient" which measures the degree of linear correlation between two continuous variables and, for ranked variables, Kendall's "tau" and Spearman's "rho".

Multiple linear regression is a method for fitting a relationship in which the "dependent" variable is a linear function of several "independent" variables. Multiple correlation refers to the degree of interdependency between variables in a group and is often calculated as a coefficient in the multiple regression context where it represents the measured correlation between observed values of the dependent variable and the values predicted by the multiple regression equation.

Factor analysis and associated techniques in multivariate analysis seek to explain the relations between the variables in a set, using the correlation matrix for the set. Principal component analysis establishes a set of uncorrelated combinations of the original variables which explain in decreasing order of magnitude the variation in the sample. Ideally, most of the variation is accounted for by the first few components and the remainder may be discarded. Where the set of original variables is structured with two subsets, one "regressor", the other "independent", canonical analysis is relevant. Discriminant analysis deals with the problem of a single set of variables which have different mean values but identical correlations in two or more populations. A discriminant function is estimated using individuals from known populations and then used to classify unknown individuals. Other techniques such as multi-dimensional scaling and cluster analysis are employed to explore the structural relationships between individuals for whom multiple observations are available.

Finally, it should be remarked that some research workers prefer to incorporate "prior" information with experimental evidence in a formal way when making inferences. Bayesian inference, which originates from a theorem of Thomas Bayes on inverse probability, provides for this by requiring a specification of the prior distribution of parameters. This can involve some complicated mathematics and non-Bayesians are concerned by the difficult and arbitrary choice of this prior distribution. The arguments for Bayesian analysis are that this generalizes the inferential procedure so that nothing of the conventional approach is lost, that it encourages the formulation of prior knowledge and that it provides a decision-theoretic approach which is relevant to many situations. Bayesians and non-Bayesians all use prior information and mostly arrive at the same conclusions despite the differences in approach.   RWH

Bibliography

Fisher, R.A. 1935: *The design and analysis of experiments*. Edinburgh: Oliver and Boyd.

Guilford, J.P. and Fruchter, B. 1956: *Fundamental statistics in psychology and education*. New York: McGraw-Hill.

Marriott, F.H.C. 1974: *The interpretation of multiple observations*. London: Academic Press.

Siegel, S. 1956: *Non-parametric statistics for the behavioral sciences*. New York: McGraw-Hill.

Winer, B.J. 1962: *Statistical principles in experimental design*. New York: Holt, Rinehart and Winston.

subculture A subdivision of the culture of the whole population or a major section of it at a particular period, consisting of persons who share special concepts and mores whilst adhering to the dominant characteristics of the wider culture. Significant subcultures are determined by social class, racial and religious affiliations. Their emergence is explicable in terms of mutual facilitation and support in groups facing common problems that cannot be solved by traditional methods (Cohen 1955). By sharing beliefs, objectives and ways of behaving, a sense of corporate identity is created, distinctive perspectives about values are provided and role strain, caused by conflict between ideology and role expectations, is reduced. The protective effect of subculture variation on early socialization is especially important. This is mediated initially through the family, then the PEER GROUP.

Deviant subcultures have been related to the occurrence of DELINQUENCY in certain geographical areas, although it is more adequately understood in the context of intrafamilial and small group processes.

WLIP-J

Bibliography

Cohen, A.K. 1955: *Delinquent boys: the culture of the gang.* Chicago: The Free Press of Glencoe, Ill.

McClelland, K.A. 1982: Adolescent subculture in the schools. In *Review of human development,* eds. T.M. Field et al. New York: Wiley.

Sullivan, Harry Stack (1892–1949) American psychoanalyst who was one of the main figures in producing a more social, interpersonal version of FREUD's theories (see also NEO-FREUDIAN THEORY). Sullivan was influenced by symbolic interactionist ideas about the growth of the child's sense of itself based on the treatment it receives from (significant) other people. He placed great emphasis on the role of the early relationship between the infant and the mother in the development of the infant's anxiety and sense of him- or herself.

Sullivan believed in two primary types of human behavior: the pursuit of security and the pursuit of satisfaction. The latter is a pursuit of the fulfillment of instinctive drives. The former category is cultural. The child learns by EMPATHY and the deliberate attempts made to teach him or her what is good and bad. Empathy refers to the child's sensitivity to the mother's, or other caregiver's, suppressed attitudes and feelings which show through in tension and various nonverbal cues. The child is therefore picking up clues to the mother's acceptance or disapproval even though she may be making no conscious effort to teach or shape behavior. Gaining satisfaction in culturally and parentally approved ways makes the child feel good, while failure to find such satisfaction leads to feeling bad. This is a state of anxiety, and is clearly similar to *approach-avoidance conflict* (see SOCIAL LEARNING THEORY). Sullivan played down the energizing,

dynamic aspects of the unconscious, regarding it as a matter of selective inattention to aspects of the self which are associated with anxiety. He believed that the self-system attempts to maintain itself in a sense of its goodness (the good me).

Sullivan regarded the juvenile and adolescent periods as very important in the growth of the self (cf. ERIKSON). Peers and teachers then begin to play a major role in socializing the child. In pre-adolescence, friendship with a same-sex "chum" becomes an important source of SELF-ESTEEM, and a potential source of anxiety. The same is true of heterosexual relationships which develop in adolescence, although the adolescent is frequently more egocentric and anxious in these relationships than in the earlier same-sex friendships. If *intimacy* is successfully achieved, however, the adolescent matures with self-respect and respect for others.

RL

Bibliography

Munroe, R.L. 1955: *Schools of psychoanalytic thought.* New York: Dryden; London: Hutchinson (1957).

Sullivan, H.S. 1953: *The interpersonal theory of psychiatry.* New York: Norton.

superego In psychoanalytic personality theory that part of the mind from which emanate evaluative and moralistic prohibitions or recommendations about actions and mental life. These directives have been internalized from childhood experience of (or perhaps rather fantasy about) parental controls. It cannot be equated with CONSCIENCE because its activity is often unconscious, and because these continuing pressures may actually be at odds with the person's conscious values. The severity of those pressures also reflects the strength of the person's own aggressive impulses, and therefore does not reflect the actual severity of parents. In Freudian theory the superego develops out of the EGO as a result of the OEDIPUS AND ELEKTRA COMPLEXES, and is especially apparent in obsessional neuroses.

Although FREUD places such development in the fourth-fifth years of life

Kleinian theory (Segal 1979; see KLEIN) puts it earlier. Since the superego's pressures are essentially non-rational, and at least partly unconscious (hence totems and taboos), psychoanalytic treatment aims at bringing them more under ego-control. (See also EGO IDEAL.)   NMC

Bibliography

Freud, S. 1923: The ego and the id. *Standard edition of the complete psychological works of Sigmund Freud*, vol. 19. London: Hogarth Press; New York: Norton.

Segal, H. 1979: *Klein*. London: Fontana.

T

teacher-pupil interactions It is generally agreed that the encounter between teachers and pupils is at the heart of the process of schooling, so teacher-pupil interactions have been a major research topic in educational psychology. All theories of learning and cognitive development have their implications for teacher strategies and TEACHING TECHNIQUES, especially with reference to the work of PIAGET and Bruner, though it must be conceded that psychologists have paid far less attention to theories of instruction than to theories of learning. The pedagogical aspects of teacher-pupil interactions have been the subject of more sustained research when the pupils experience LEARNING DIFFICULTIES, require remedial help of various kinds, or are considered to be DISRUPTIVE PUPILS (see also BEHAVIOR CHANGE IN THE CLASSROOM). Various research methodologies have been used to investigate the nature and effects, especially on educational attainment, of teacher-pupil interactions. The oldest and most popular method is that of *systematic observation* in which, on the basis of time-sampling, each observed teacher and pupil behavior is assigned to one of a set of pre-determined categories which comprise the observation schedule. The earliest schedules concentrated almost entirely on the teacher's verbal behavior, but later schedules greatly expanded the categories of pupil talk and of non-verbal behavior. Systematic observation is considered to provide not only a technique for the quantification of teacher-pupil interactions, but also a means of evaluating classroom innovations and of training teachers. Very few generalizable research findings have been generated by the use of systematic observation schedules. More recently ethnographic methods of observation (see SCHOOL AS A SOCIAL ORGANIZATION) have become a second method for investigating teacher-pupil interactions. Naturalistic observation combined with the use of lesson transcripts and of interviews for the elicitation of participants' accounts have proved to be powerful tools for uncovering important aspects of teacher-pupil interactions neglected by systematic observation, though the two approaches should be seen as complementary. Both have, for example, made a significant contribution to the study of the self-fulfilling prophecy in classrooms, a topic which brings together the substantial research on teachers' and pupils' perceptions of one another and their effects on interaction, and then the consequences of this interaction. A third approach to teacher-pupil interactions derives from sociolinguistics (and sometimes ethnomethodology and conversational analysis). These studies have yielded significant insights into the structure of classroom interactions and the ways in which teachers, through their talk, control meanings and maintain their authority over pupils.

(See also EDUCATION: PSYCHOLOGY OF.)

DHH

Bibliography

Brophy, J.E. and Good, T.L. 1974: *Teacher-student relationships: causes and consequences.* New York and London: Holt, Rinehart and Winston.

—— 1986: Teacher behavior and student achievement. In *The handbook of research on teaching.* 3rd edn, ed. M. Wittrock. New York: Wiley.

Brophy. J.E., Rohrkemper, M., Rashid, H. and Goldberger, M. 1983: Relationships between teachers' presentations of classroom tasks and students' engagement in those tasks. *Journal of educational psychology* 75, 544–52.

Edwards, A.D. and Furlong, V.J. 1978: *The language of teaching.* London: Heinemann.

McIntyre, D.I. 1980: Systematic observation of classroom activities, *Educational analysis* 2(2), 3–30.

Rogers, C. 1982: *A social psychology of schooling*. London and Boston: Routledge and Kegan Paul.

teacher training Schoolteachers are required to undergo a period of training – either a three or four year BEd, or a one year post-graduate certificate – before teaching in state schools, and it is in such courses that the body of knowledge called the psychology of education (see EDUCATION: PSYCHOLOGY OF) has traditionally been given a major emphasis. Recently however the questions *why* psychology should be taught to such students, *what* exactly should be covered and *how* it should be taught have been the subject of serious debate. The soul-searching amongst psychologists of education concerning their contributions to courses of teacher training has arisen as a result of a number of factors. One is the persistent dissatisfaction of students with "educational studies", of which psychology forms a considerable part. Another is the doubt whether such courses actually enhance teaching competence. A third is the increasing recognition, as a general psychological issue of some importance, of the frequent failure of intellectual *knowledge* to affect cognitive, perceptual or behavioral *processes*.

Thus the successes and failures of psychology in teacher training throw up in sharp relief some of the most important issues which it, *qua* content, attempts to treat. Students' concerns are overridingly practical, especially at the start of a course, and psychology, whilst having extolled the evident (and research-based) virtues of "starting where the learner is" has been somewhat lax in following its own advice, and in developing soundly-based psychological dicta that can be formed into an effective pedagogy for meeting students' felt needs. There is a general consensus that didactic methods of academic presentation are relatively ineffective, and many institutions are now conducting promising experiments with discussion-based, problem-solving or experiential forms of learning.

(See also TEACHING TECHNIQUES.) GCI

Bibliography
Francis, H. ed. 1985: *Learning to teach: psychology in teacher training*. Brighton: Falmer Press.

teaching techniques

Points of origin
Some teaching techniques follow from psychological theories. For instance, programmed instruction was developed from classical learning theory (Skinner 1961) and cognitive conflict techniques for presenting social studies materials are based on Piagetian-cognitive developmental models of cognitive growth (Johnson and Johnson 1979; see PIAGET). At the other extreme many instructional techniques are based just 'on what someone feels ought to work'.

Focus of application
Some instructional/teaching techniques involve changing what teachers do, and others involve modifying the activities of children. For instance, in direct instruction the focus is on changing what teachers do. Direct instruction approaches to classroom organization (as contrasted to open classroom techniques) involve 'academically focused, teacher-directed classrooms' (Rosenshine 1979; Rosenshine and Stevens 1986) with clear goals for students, many low-level questions from teachers, strict monitoring of student performance, and immediate, academically-focused feedback from the teacher to the student (Peterson 1979, Rosenshine and Stevens 1986). In contrast, other instructional approaches rely on changing the ways children teach each other. A great deal of attention has been paid to having children serve as tutors in classrooms with particular interest in cross-age tutoring (e.g. Allen 1976). Also, the major instructional content of the cognitive conflict models of education referred to above are the differing views of different children about difficult social problems.

Degree of curriculum materials modification

Many instructional techniques involve changing the format of materials that are presented to learners. Instructional television, programmed instruction, pictorial presentation of materials, and the addition of questions to text are but a few of the format changes that have been researched in recent years (see LEARNING STRATEGIES). In contrast, other instructional variations require no change in materials, merely a change in the way in which materials are presented. For example in personalized systems of instruction (Johnson and Ruskin 1977) traditional texts are typically used, but the text is broken down into smaller units with the student required to pass quizzes on each of these units. Particularly striking format changes involve the application of recent developments in electronic technology into classroom settings (e.g. computer and hand-held calculators).

Effectiveness

The available data do not show whether any particular instructional technique is "the best". The research on many of the instructional techniques referenced in this article has been conducted in only a limited number of situations. For example most of the research on direct instruction versus open classrooms has been conducted in primary schools with most of the interpretable data emanating from studies of reading and mathematics achievement (Rosenshine 1979). Also, many instructional strategies are suited only to particular purposes and particular populations. Instructional techniques have been specifically devised for teaching such diverse subjects as mathematics, psychomotor skills, creativity, clinical medical skills and foreign languages. There are also population-specific instructional strategies for children of all ages and abilities.

A third constraint on establishing a best strategy is that it has long been believed that some children are going to benefit more than others from some instructional techniques. In recent years the study of such potential aptitude/treatment interactions (ATI henceforth) has been formal-ized with the development of sophisticated methodology for evaluating whether or not an ATI exists (Cronbach and Snow 1977; Snow and Lohman 1984). The various types of instruction that can be given to children in school can be thought of as treatments and any dimension of an individual 'that predicts response to instruction' (Snow 1976) can be regarded as an aptitude. There are occasions when a treatment will affect one group of learners and have no effect on another group. When this occurs, the interaction is said to be ordinal. If the treatment causes harm to some people and has no effect on others it is obvious that it should be dropped. If the treatment is helpful to some and has no effect on others, administering the treatment on an across-the-board basis can be defended, unless it is expensive in terms of time or money. In that case, it is difficult to defend giving it to the people who do not need it. In addition to the ordinal interactions there are also cases in which a given treatment helps one population and harms another group relative to an alternative instruction. It would be difficult to make a case for all-or-none adoption when this type of disordinal interaction exists (see also Clark 1982).

Although it is not possible to decide on a "best" instructional technique, there is a growing awareness that the "best" way to evaluate instructional treatments is through the use of true experiments. Experimental psychologists have made great strides in specifying how the experimental method can be applied in real-world settings (Riechen and Boruch 1974; Brophy and Good 1986), and it has been possible for educational psychologists to devise tests of a number of large-scale instructional treatments. Because of this increasing methodological sophistication, researchers in the area have become aware of errors of the past. For example in many studies in the literature classroom 1 with teacher X was asked to use instructional treatment A, while classroom 2 with teacher Y used treatment B. The performance of pupils in classroom 1 was then compared with the performance of those in classroom 2, and an inference was made about the relative efficacy of treatments A and B. Researchers are now aware that such a design confounds a number of factors, most obviously teacher and treatment. There is a growing realization that when the unit of instructional treatment is the classroom, the unit of analysis should be the classroom, and not the individual learner within the classroom, as has been the case in the past (Riechen and Boruch 1974; Rosenshine 1979). A large number of instructional treatments have been proposed but much more research is needed to establish the conditions for effectiveness of each of these instructional/ teaching techniques.   MP

Bibliography

Allen, V.A. ed. 1976: *Children as teachers: theory and research on tutoring*. New York, San Francisco and London: Academic Press.

Brophy, J.E. and Good, T. 1986: Teacher behavior and student achievement. In *The handbook of research on teaching*. 3rd edn, ed. M. Wittrock. New York: Macmillan.

Clark, R.E. 1982: Antagonism between achievement and enjoyment in ATI studies. *Educational psychology*.

Cronbach, L.J., and Snow, R.E. 1977: *Aptitudes and instructional methods: a handbook for research on interactions*. New York: Irvington.

Johnson, D.W. and Johnson, R.T. 1979: Conflict in the classroom: controversy and learning. *Review of educational research* 49, 51–70.

Johnson, K.R. and Ruskin, R.S. 1977: *Behavioral instruction: an evaluative review*. Washington, D.C.: American Psychological Association.

Peterson, P.L. 1979: Direct instruction reconsidered. In *Research on teaching: concepts, findings, and implications*, eds. P.L. Peterson and J. Walberg. Berkeley, California: McCutchan.

Riechen, H.W. and Boruch, R.F. 1974: *Social experimentation: a method for planning and evaluating social intervention*. New York, San Francisco and London: Academic Press.

Rosenshine, B.V. 1979: Content, time, and direct instruction. In *Research on teaching: concepts, findings and implications*, eds. P.L. Peterson and J. Walberg. Berkeley, California: McCutchan.

—— and Stevens, R. 1986: Teaching functions. In *The handbook of research on teaching*. 3rd edn, ed. M. Wittrock: New York: Macmillan.

Skinner, B.F. 1961: *The technology of teaching*. New York: Appleton-Century-Crofts.

Snow, R.E. 1976: Aptitude-treatment interactions and individualized alternatives in higher education. In *Individuality and learning*, eds. Samuel Messick et al. San Francisco, Washington and London: Jossey-Bass.

—— and Lohman, D.F. 1984: Toward a theory of cognitive aptitude for learning from instruction. *Journal of educational psychology* 76, 347–76.

tests: educational attainment (USA – achievement)

Systematic procedures devised to sample and measure educationally relevant knowledge or skills. Reading, spelling and number (mathematics) attainment tests are the ones most commonly used by teachers and psychologists, but tests are available to cover many other areas of the school curriculum. The same principles of "measurement" are used as for intelligence tests (see also TESTS: NORMATIVE- AND CRITERION-REFERENCED). The main difference being that the content of attainment tests is more circumscribed, the individual being required to read a standard list of words, or several prose passages, or solve mathematical problems. The number of correct answers or solutions is converted to an index of educational attainment in the particular subject. This may take the form of a reading (or number) quotient (see INTELLIGENCE QUOTIENT) or an "age" score. A child with a "reading age" of ten years, in effect reads correctly the same number of words as did a reference group of children with a chronological age of ten years.   MBe

Bibliography

Levy, P. and Goldstein, H. eds. 1984: *Tests in education: a book of critical reviews*. London: Academic Press.

Sweetland, R.C. and Keyser, D.J. eds. 1983: *Tests*. Kansas City: Test Corporation of America.

tests: intelligence

One or more sets of tasks or problems, the solution of which is assumed to be a function of "intelligence". INTELLIGENCE is a hypothetical construction, an assumed property or capacity of the individual introduced *post hoc* to account for individual differences in certain classes of performance, for example, academic accomplishment or an ability to solve complex problems. The selection of tasks for a test reflects the test constructor's theory of "intelligence". There is some consensus as to the sorts of tasks which expose the operation of "intelligence". However, as there is no generally accepted theory or definition of intelligence, the tasks which comprise a particular test will usually reflect the theoretical orientation of the test's author as well as the intended use of the test. For instance, tests designed for use with children will contain items which differ from those in tests for adults.

The more widely used tests usually require the definition of words, answering general knowledge and reasoning questions and the completion of jigsaw-like puzzles. Tests are available for different age ranges, for individual or group administration and for testing people with certain handicaps. When devised for administration to children below about two years of age, they are called developmental tests but they are less reliable. Performance on each task is scored and the total score is transformed to an INTELLIGENCE QUOTIENT (IQ).

IQs, for a variety of possible reasons, have some predictive power in terms of both current and future performance in a range of activities. However, prediction is by no means perfect and large changes in IQ over time for some individuals are well documented.

Partly because of doubts about traditional paper and pencil tests and the theoretical (or atheoretical) assumptions which underlie their interpretation (see Gardner 1986), attempts have been made to develop tests based on reaction times (see INTELLIGENCE). There is, however, a good deal of dispute about whether various measures of reaction time do correlate with the supposed general cognitive ability which is intelligence (see Longstreth 1984; Jensen 1986). On a more straightforwardly practical level, there have also been recent attempts to use interactive computing as a medium for the administration of intelligence tests (Hunt and Pellegrino 1985). (See also WECHSLER SCALES.)

MBe

Bibliography

Gardner, H. 1986: The waning of intelligence tests. In *What is intelligence?* eds. R.J. Sternberg and D.K. Detterman. Norwood: Ablex.

Hunt, E. and Pellegrino, J. 1985: Using interactive computing to expand intelligence testing. *Intelligence* 9, 207–36.

Jensen, A.R. 1986: Intelligence: definition, measurement and future research. In *What is intelligence?*, eds. R.J. Sternberg and D.K. Detterman. Norwood, N.J.: Ablex.

Longstreth, L.E. 1984: Jensen's reaction-time investigations of intelligence: a critique. *Intelligence* 8, 139–60.

Sweetland, R.C. and Keyser, D.V. eds. 1983: *Tests*. Kansas City: Test Corporation of America.

tests: normative- and criterion-referenced

Norm-referenced tests utilize the performance of some reference group as a standard against which the performance of an individual can be compared. An "above average IQ" is an abbreviated description for a score obtained by an individual which is above the average of the scores obtained by comparable individuals on the same test.

Criterion-referenced tests use as their basis for comparison or reference a specified set of performances or actions, the criteria. The purpose of the test is to quantify or describe in some standard systematic way, the extent to which the individual has achieved or possesses the criterion behavior. The immediate aim of the test is to describe an individual's behavior or competence rather than to draw a comparison with some reference group. Such a test might for instance be developed to index knowledge of basic arithmetic skills, or self-sufficiency among handicapped people. Self-sufficiency, for example, would be defined in terms of a number of components (able to cope with eating, or dressing unaided) which would then be broken down further into a hierarchy of unitary subskills, such as holding a fork or doing up buttons. Criterion-referenced testing would then involve ascertaining which of the component skills were present, and thereby the extent to which the individual had achieved the criterion of self-sufficiency.

It should be noted that "errors" of measurement can be identified fairly precisely in normative- but not in criterion-referenced tests, where the tester's own notional standards are used.   MBe

Bibliography

Anastasi, A. 1982: *Psychological testing*. 5th edn. New York: Macmillan.

tests: reliability of The extent to which a measure is free from random error. An observed score on any measure (including, of course, psychological tests) consists of two parts, one of them random (chance events) and the other systematic. A reliability estimate shows the relative size of these two parts. Methods for estimating the reliability of scores involve studying their consistency on a single occasion or their stability over two of more occasions.

The most straightforward way of testing reliability is to correlate the scores of the same people on the same test on two occasions (test-retest reliability). The more reliable the test, the higher will be the correlations (although clearly the length of time between the occasions is likely to affect the strength of the correlation).

Another method is to use two different forms of a test (alternate-form reliability) and correlate the same people's scores on the two. Alternate-form reliability also requires a time-interval between one testing and the next.

A third method of assessing reliability is to correlate scores on one half of a test with scores on the other (split-half or internal reliability). The whole test is done at once, so this method does not require a time-interval. It therefore has the advantage that random factors associated with differences between two occasions cannot intrude. A common way of dividing the test in half is to compare odd items with even items. This eliminates effects of warm-up and fatigue.

Two final methods of estimating reliability use the standard deviations of total scores, and either the number of people who "pass" or "fail" each item (Kuder-Richardson) or the sum of the variances of each item (Cronbach's alpha). The latter can be used on tests with a Likert (several point) scale answer format whereas the Kuder-Richardson is designed for tests with a pass/fail or yes/no marking.

Different methods might give different estimates, depending on which components of the score are regarded as random and which are regarded as systematic. The systematic portion of the score may be composed of a single component or of several independent effects which are added together in a composite. For example, if a mathematics examination is given to a group of people on two occasions, some portion of the score on the second occasion will consist of the examinee's memory of answers to the questions on the first occasion. The memory component would be a systematic effect, and from the researcher's viewpoint it may or may not be desirable. In any event it is not random, so it increases the systematic or reliable portion of the score.

(See also STATISTICAL METHODS.)
          MDH/RL

Bibliography

Anastasi, A. 1982: *Psychological testing*. 5th edn. New York: Macmillan.

Campbell, J.P. 1976: Psychometric theory. In *Handbook of industrial and organizational psychology*, ed. M.D. Dunnette. Chicago: Rand McNally.

Cronbach, L.J. 1951: Coefficient alpha and the internal structure of tests. *Psychometrika* 16, 297–334.

Kuder, G.F. and Richardson, M.W. 1937: The theory of estimation of test reliability. *Psychometrika* 2, 151–60.

tests: validity of The extent to which scores on tests or other measures are justified or supported by evidence. Validity refers to the relationship between a test and what it is purported to measure or predict. Researchers gather evidence for the validity of a measure from three different angles: content, criterion, and construct.

A test has content validity when it contains relevant items. For example, an exam must have questions which test all relevant knowledge and skills. There are obvious problems of adequate coverage and due weight being given to different skills and topics. Content validity must not be confused with "face validity". A test has face validity when it *appears* to cover a domain. In test-construction items are often included because they seem likely to measure what one is interested in. But they may have to be discarded if they turn out not to. Such items have face validity only.

Criterion validity is the most clear-cut. A test has criterion (or experimental) validity if it relates appropriately to an external standard. For example, IQ scores should be positively correlated with academic achievement, and questionnaire measures of introversion/extraversion should relate to introverted and extraverted social behavior. Criterion validity may be concurrent, as with a diagnostic test supposed to reveal the present state of affairs, or predictive, as with selection tests for courses or jobs. The validity coefficient is the correlation between a test and its criterion.

Construct validity (Cronbach and Meehl 1955) is a more complicated concept. It is not always possible to establish a criterion against which to rate a test. But a test may be useful in confirming relationships derived from a theory. For example Eysenck's arousal theory of introversion-extraversion leads to a range of predictions about concentration, conditionability, wakefulness and fatigue on motor tasks, as well as predictions about sexual preferences and probable social behavior. If a test proves useful in picking up a distinction predicted by the theory and correlates with other tests and observations, it has construct validity. A complex theory comes to be accepted through a gradual accumulation of data

from different sources. New tests may have higher construct validity than established ones because they make finer or richer distinctions, or more accurately distinguish between groups the theory predicts will be distinct.

Campbell and Fiske (1959) discuss methods of ensuring that a test has both convergent validity and discriminant validity, i.e. that it correlates with variables which the theory predicts it will, and does *not* correlate with variables which the theory predicts it will not. Until recently it has been believed that validity evidence is specific to the research setting in which it was gathered. However, Schmidt and Hunter (1977) and many others have reported investigations showing that under some circumstances validity evidence may be generalized to new settings.

(See also STATISTICAL METHODS.)

MDH/RL

Bibliography

Anastasi, A. 1982: *Psychological testing*. 5th edn. New York: Macmillan.

—— 1986: Evolving concepts of test validation. In *Annual review of psychology*, vol. 37, eds. M.R. Rosenzweig and L.W. Porter. Palo Alto: Annual Reviews Inc.

Campbell, D.T. and Fiske, D.W. 1959: Convergent and discriminant validation by the multitrait-mulimethod matrix. *Psychological bulletin* 56, 81–105.

*Cascio, W.F. 1982: *Applied psychology in personnel management*. 2nd edn. Reston, Virginia: Reston Publishing Company.

Cronbach, L.J. and Meehl, P.E. 1955: Construct validity in psychological tests. *Psychological bulletin* 52, 281–302.

Schmidt, F.L. and Hunter, J.E. 1977: Development of a general solution to the problem of validity generalization. *Journal of applied psychology* 62, 529–40.

truancy *See* absence from school and truancy.

twin studies The comparison of genetically identical with genetically similar humans, with a view to establishing the interaction between biological and environmental factors that give rise to behavior.

The usual method involves comparisons between monozygotic (identical) twins and dizygotic (fraternal) twins. Where both sets have been reared in similar environments, the lesser variability of behavior between identical twins is taken to reflect their greater genetic similarity for that trait. Various measures of heritability (some controversial) for different traits have been derived. Heritability is the proportion of variance in behavior due to genetic factors that appeared over generations, when environmental factors were held to be constant. The best known example concerns the INTELLIGENCE QUOTIENT for which heritability estimates vary between 0.4 and 0.8.

Other methods compare identical twins reared together with those reared apart, to establish more precisely the role of the environment in behavioral development. It is generally found that adopted monozygotic twins reared apart are nevertheless more similar to each other (and to their biological parents) than to their adoptive siblings (or adoptive parents). Although this does not rule out a general contribution of a common human environment to development, it suggests that specific effects of the environment as in the development of particular interests or aspects of personality, may occur only in relation to genetic predispositions shared by parent and child.

Another method has been to compare identical twins who are dissimilar (discordant) for a particular trait. This has proved very useful in establishing that environmental factors are crucial to the etiology of schizophrenia.   GEB

Bibliography

McGue, M., Bouchard, T.J., Lykken, D.T. and Feuer, D. 1984: Information processing abilities in twins reared apart. *Intelligence* 8, 239–58.

Mittler, P. 1971: *The study of twins*. Harmondsworth: Penguin.

Stevenson, J. and Fielding, J. 1985: Ratings of temperament in families of young twins. *British journal of developmental psychology* 3, 143–52.

V

visual discrimination Selective attention of an object or event in the visual modality. Discrimination is usually inferred from an attentional preference, or some selective response such as a directional eye movement, which suggests that the perceiver has differentiated a target attribute from others in the field of view.

Visual discrimination techniques have been useful in the study of perceptual development. Robert Fantz (1965) pioneered a method in which the baby is presented with pairs of dissimilar stimuli for comparison. Attentional preferences for one of the stimuli show that discrimination of color, movement and some aspects of form are innate. Other types of visual discrimination, especially those requiring fine distinctions within a category of objects, continue to develop throughout the life span. GEB

Bibliography

Fantz, R.L. 1965: Visual perception from birth as shown by pattern selectivity. *Annals of the New York Academy of Sciences* 118, 793–814.

Slater, A., Morison, V., Town, C. and Rose, D. 1985: Movement perception and identity constancy in the new-born baby. *British journal of developmental psychology* 3, 211–20.

vocational choice Generally used by laymen to mean either: the choice of a type of occupation, or the choice of a career, or both. Although the two terms are often used as synonyms, even by psychologists and sociologists, they have more precise meanings the use of which is favored by many specialists. An *occupation* is a group of similar jobs in which people perform essentially the same tasks, drawing on the same body of knowledge and using the same basic skills; the occupation exists independently of the person pursuing it. A *career* is the sequence of positions, jobs or occupations which a person has filled during the course of his or her life; these may differ considerably or they may all be in the same field with or without vertical movement. The term *vocation*, in the literature of the behavioral sciences, is used both to denote an occupation, and to characterize an occupation which has some of the personal meaning of career: it borrows from religious usage, signifying being called by something or someone greater than oneself to perform a given kind of work, but denotes a personal conviction that the occupation in question is most appropriate for oneself.

Historical perspective. Although studies of vocational choice and services designed to help young people and adults in the making of such choices are now taken for granted, interest in these matters did not become institutionalized until just before the first world war when large numbers of young people were entering the workforce, and in some countries large numbers of immigrants needed to be assimilated. This led to the establishment of employment bureaux and vocational counseling services, with the emphasis on occupational and job choice, on the present and the immediate future – careers, the long term, were not the issue.

Approaches and theories. This approach to vocational *choice* led to the first scientific work on what has since come to be seen as just one phase of vocational or career development (Super 1957). The rapid development of psychological tests for occupational selection and vocational guidance that resulted from their use during the first world war put assessment instruments and data for their interpretation in the hands of vocational counselors, who during the 1920s and 1930s became increasingly familiar with vocational psychology and, in countries such as France and the United States, trained in at least the most directly relevant aspects of psychology, sociology and economics.

This first scientific approach has become known as *Trait-and-factor theory* and is exemplified by books on aptitude and interest testing (e.g. Super and Crites 1962). It is also known as matching theory, for it consists of matching the abilities and interests of the client with those known to be typical of men and women in the occupations which are, or might be, of interest. This development of information concerning occupations led, when combined with older methods, to improved job descriptions, making possible such important manuals as the American *Dictionary of occupational titles* and *Occupational outlook handbook*, both revised periodically by the US Department of Labor and emulated in a number of other countries. The methods and materials of matching people and jobs proved very useful in the manpower shifts caused by the second world war and later in the return of military personnel and war-industry employees to civilian life.

But, with developments in the psychology of personality and of adulthood, a approach, a new type of theory, came into being. Differential psychology, useful though it had proved as a theoretical basis for vocational choice, was found not to be enough. Ginzberg (1951) and Super (1953, 1957) studied the work of a group of Austrian psychologists who for the first time collected and organized data on the unfolding of careers, the emergence and changing of vocational choices, throughout the life span. Ginzberg entitled his book *Occupational choice* and focused on development only until entry into the labor force; he and his colleagues viewed choice as the outcome of a developmental process beginning in early childhood. Super and his associates went further, considering the entire life span and viewing choices as evolving constantly with personal and social changes. This work led to many studies of the processes and outcomes of vocational or career development and to the emergence of a new body of theory (Hall 1976; Levinson

1978; Lowenthal 1975; Watts, Super and Kidd 1981).

Developmental theory recognizes that, although much of a child's thinking about occupations and career is fantasy, it is based on personal needs such as that to explore, to be powerful and to be loved, and furthermore it leads to and results from identification with key persons who serve as role models. This is the basis for adolescent interest in occupations with preferences changing with experiences of success and failure, of praise and ridicule, and of acceptance or rejection by adult role models.

The tools of developmental theory have, in the nature of things, been neither so accessible, nor so practical as those of differential theory. The understanding of a person's development and of the kinds of continuities that may be seen in it, is obtained by means of time-consuming interviews, projective techniques and autobiographical essays, the interpretation of which is much more subjective, and therefore unreliable, than is that of standardized tests and inventories. Understanding the nature of possible future development is even more difficult, for not only is the client developing, but so is the society in which he or she functions.

It is these complexities, and their focus on society rather than on the person, that have led many sociologists, particularly in Great Britain, to develop *structural theories* of vocational choice. Impressed by the limits imposed upon choice by the accident of birth into a particular social class, by the relationship between the socioeconomic status of a child's parents on the one hand, and the amount and type of education, the employment opportunities, and the friends available to the child on the other, these sociologists tend to view the child and youth as placed at an early age on a conveyor belt which takes him or her inevitably toward an occupation like that of the parents. Roberts states that vocational counseling should aim, not at helping the individual to implement a conception of himself or herself as a worker, nor at helping a person to find an occupation really suited to his or her abilities and interests, but at assisting the individual to fit into the socially assigned niche.

The views of "opportunity structuralists" have been examined, and in the eyes of many vocational counselors and psychologists, refuted by writers such as Daws (in Watts, Super and Kidd 1981). Others such as Cherry (in Watts, Super and Kidd 1981) have adduced new and better data which show that individual differences are important, and that a significant number of young people do, by the time they are young adults, escape from the Procrustean bed of the structuralists and find their way into more "self-actualizing" occupations. Career development, we now know, is a long process and one in which both psychological and socioeconomic variables play a part.

Life span and life space. Central to the theory of career development are the concepts of life stages and developmental tasks, and those of life space and the roles that fill it. The model brings together notions of life stage theory as formulated by a number of the developmentalists cited, and includes the major life stages of growth, exploration, establishment, maintenance and decline, together with their sub-stages and their role and personality characteristics, with the approximate ages of each stage and transition from one stage to the next. It is too often assumed that because the developmental tasks of exploration, establishment, etc. can be assigned approximate ages and because they follow in a sequence throughout the life cycle, the ages are biologically fixed and the stages must succeed each other in orderly and inevitable sequence. But most life stage theorists do not now take this point of view, for it has been shown that there are important individual differences in development, some maturing early and others late; and it has been shown that people recycle through the several stages of growth, exploration, establishment, maintenance and decline (there are minicycles within the maxicycle) as they make transitions from one stage or sub-stage to another. Each new situation calls for exploration of its characteristics, which

may lead to growth, which may in turn lead to a new establishment. Furthermore it is evident that the normal sequence of stages in the maxicycle is not inevitable, for some people virtually skip exploration as a result of what sometimes proves to be premature fixation or closure, and some keep on innovating, i.e. establishing, until well into what should chronologically be decline and skip that stage by dying at the peak or on the high plateau of their careers, well beyond the normal retirement age.

The concept of life space recognizes that the life course is made up of a number of roles, some played in sequence, others played simultaneously (Super 1980). A youth may be a child, a student, a pursuer of leisure activities and a citizen active in the community all at the same time. It is obvious that, when too many roles are engaged in, with time and emotional demands which may be excessive, role conflict results: each role has impact on the others. But the impact may also be positive, the role of part-time student enriching the worker role or the homemaking role, etc. One of the objectives of sound vocational guidance, or well-rounded career education, is to help people to view their roles as a changing constellation, some of which provide outlets for some abilities and values and meet some needs, while others are better suited to other abilities, interests, and needs.

Vocational guidance and counseling. Helping young people and adults to make vocational choices has long been a function of educational institutions, social service agencies and employment services. Although the location and nature of the services, and the training of the personnel performing them, varies somewhat from country to country it is to those institutions and ministries that the public should turn for information and counseling. Universities often offer courses taking one or two years, sometimes four, to complete: in Great Britain they are called counseling or careers advisory courses (for school counselors or careers officers); in the USA and Canada they are usually called either counseling or counseling psychology courses. Sources of information are the British Association for Counselling, the British Psychological Society, the American Personnel and Guidance Association, the American Psychological Association, the Canadian Association for Guidance and Counselling, the Canadian Psychological Society, and similar associations in other countries. (See also LIFE-SPAN PSYCHOLOGY.)   DES

Bibliography

Ginzberg, E. et al. 1951: *Occupational choice*. New York: Columbia University Press.

Hall, D.T. 1976: *Careers in organizations*. Pacific Palisades, Calif.: Goodyear Publishing Co.

Holland, J.L. 1985: *Making vocational choices*. 2nd edn. Englewood Cliffs, N.J.: Prentice-Hall.

Levinson, D.J. 1975: *The seasons of a man's life*. New York: Ballantine.

Lowenthal, M.F. 1975: *Four stages of life*. San Francisco: Jossey-Bass.

Super, U.F. 1953: A theory of vocational development. *American psychologist* 5, 155–90.

—— 1957: *The psychology of careers*. New York: Harper.

—— 1980: A life-span, life-space approach to career development. *Journal of vocational behavior* 13, 252–95.

—— and Crites, J.O. 1962: *Appraising vocational fitness*. New York: Harper.

Watts, A.G., Super, D.E. and Kidd, J.M. 1981: *Career development in Britain*. Cambridge: Hobson's Press.

Vygotsky, L.S. Vygotsky was born in Orsha, Belorussia on 17 November 1896. He attended the Gymnasium in Gomel, going on to Moscow University from which he graduated in 1917, the year of the revolution. He returned to Gomel as a teacher of literature and psychology until 1923. During this period he was already working in the borderlands between literature, drama and psychology, and it is clear that his life-long interest in the mediation of thought by language and other *public* symbolic activities must have been formed at this time. Indeed his first substantial publication of 1925 was on the psychology of art. However by 1924 he had moved to Moscow. Luria recounts the astonishing effect that this relatively

unknown provincial had had on the meeting of the psychoneurological conference in Leningrad that year, from which the invitation to move to Moscow had come.

Almost immediately Vygotsky's energy, originality and breadth of vision sparked off the long series of fundamental researches that filled the ten years to 1934. With Leontiev and Luria (the "troika") he laid down the main outlines of a remarkable psychology, whose influence is only now beginning to be properly appreciated as many of its main themes are being rediscovered. Psychology was to be reconstructed as a social science, and it is in the working out of this basic idea, inspired in part by the philosophical theories of consciousness of Marx, that Vygotsky's contributions appeared.

The main theme of Vygotsky's theoretical and methodological reflections (*Thought and language*, 1934) was the social construction of mind. The now famous statement of this theme (quoted by Wertsch, 1985) runs as follows: 'Any function in the child's cultural development appears twice, or on two planes. First it appears on the social plane, and then on the psychological plane'. This forms the basis of Vygotsky's theory of the genesis of the forms of consciousness. The main mediating activity through which what is social shapes what is mental is the use of language. But it is not the only mediating activity. There is also the active use of tools in the shaping of the material environment. It is in the light of this idea that Vygotsky's profound criticism of Piaget's idea of egocentricity (see EGO-CENTRISM) is to be understood. A child's abandonment of massively self-reflexive speech is not a consequence of a sudden grasp that there are others with their own points of view, but rather the manifestation of an ability to think (with the tools of language) sotto voce. The "I" of human speech is not a mark of egocentricity but, as we would now say, an indexical marking of the thought as the speaker's.

It was in thinking about the problem of how individual activity is detached from communal practice that Vygotsky introduced another of his bold conceptions, that of the "zone of proximal development", a rather clumsy phrase for the psychological phenomenon rediscovered recently as "psychological symbiosis" (called "scaffolding" by J.S. Bruner). Most human activities begin as communal practices. Problems are first solved by children with the help of an adult, filling in for those parts of the performance where infant competence is lacking. And this applies as much to problems of self-expression as to the more obviously physical activities such as feeding and pointing.

Three main ideas run together to create the Vygotskian point of view. There is Marx's idea that the forms of individual consciousness have their genesis in the appropriation of the forms of collective activity. Then there is the idea that it is in activity, not in the passive reception of stimuli that mind is shaped. And finally there is the idea of the communal, collaborative basis of much that is properly psychological. The astonishing thing to a modern reader of the Vygotskian corpus,

as it gradually becomes available to us (e.g. the recent publication of *Mind in society*) is the extent to which the independently and painfully established social constructionism of the contemporary attempt to create a genuine science of psychology had largely been anticipated by Vygotsky.

The enormous energy with which he animated his colleagues and students seems to have provided a kind of momentum, so that despite his early death on 11 June 1934 of tuberculosis, the development of his ideas by Leontiev and Luria has continued almost until the present moment.

(See also COGNITIVE DEVELOPMENT, NON-PIAGETIAN STUDIES.) RHa

Bibliography

Vygotsky, L.S. 1934: *Thought and language.* Cambridge, Mass.: MIT Press (1962).

———— 1978: *Mind in society*, eds. M. Cole et al. Cambridge, Mass.: Harvard University Press.

Wertsch, J.V. ed. 1985: *Culture, communication and cognition: Vygotskian perspectives.* Cambridge and New York: Cambridge University Press.

W

Wechsler scales Tests of general intelligence devised by David Wechsler for individual assessment. There are three scales: the Wechsler Adult Intelligence Scale – Revised (WAIS–R) for use with people aged 16 to 74 years; the Wechsler Intelligence Scale for Children – Revised (WISC–R), age range 6 to 16 years 11 months; and the Wechsler Preschool and Primary School Scale of Intelligence (WPPSI), age range 4 to 6 years 6 months.

The basic element of each scale is an item, a question or task, such as "who invented the jet engine?", "what important part is missing in the picture?", "put this jig-saw together as quickly as you can". Each item is scored as correct or incorrect. For some items, extra points are added according to the degree of generality of the answer and the speed with which a correct solution is provided.

Items sampling a particular area of intelligence, such as numerical skills, word knowledge, reasoning, are grouped into a sub-test (collection of homogeneous items), and presented in ascending order of difficulty. Administration of the sub-test is discontinued after a predetermined number of failures. Several sub-tests are grouped together to form a *sub-scale*. This is done partly for theoretical reasons and in part because of empirical evidence that, despite their specific characteristics and the special information or skill required for correct solution, they also appear to tap a higher level of organization of intellect. The Wechsler Scales have two sub-scales, the Verbal and the Performance. The former indexes the more general verbal ability of the testee (the ability to record, manipulate and reproduce language-related information), indexed by the Verbal Scale IQ. The Performance Scale 10 provides a measure of the ability to manipulate visual-spatial relationships.

Although the sub-scales provide separate IQs, the abilities which contribute to each overlap.

The WAIS-R has six sub-tests in the Verbal Scale, five of which are used to compute the IQ. The Performance Scale has five sub-tests. The WISC-R has six sub-tests in each sub-scale, five from each being used to compute the respective IQs. The WPPSI has 10 sub-tests, five for each sub-scale, and two supplementary sub-tests.

All the Wechsler Scales enable the computation of the Full Scale IQ, a measure of general intelligence. Like all tests of intelligence, the choice of items, their organization within the scale and their scoring reflect the test originator's underlying model of the organization of human abilities (see TESTS, INTELLIGENCE; INTELLIGENCE QUOTIENT).

Specific items in the sub-tests reflect the age group for which the particular scale is intended, with some overlap of content to enable continuous coverage of the age-spectrum. Each scale has the same basic structure, and most of the sub-tests have common titles across the three scales. All three are standardized tests, with norms derived from the USA population. None of the current versions have UK norms but the test manuals have been modified to take account of cultural differences between the two countries.

Score levels on single sub-tests, or differences between scores on several sub-tests, or between the Verbal and Performance Scale IQs are sometimes used for differential diagnosis of cognitive dysfunctions or psychological disturbance. This is a complex task for reasons to do with intricacies of the theory and practice of psychological measurement. Conclusions from such exercises in diagnostic testing are more often than not of dubious validity. See Kaufman (1979) and Sattler (1974) for more detailed discussion of the WPPSI and WISC-R and their use in assessment of intelligence, and Anastasi (1982) for a more detailed description of the three scales. MBe

Bibliography

Anastasi, A. 1982: *Psychological testing*. 5th edn. New York: Macmillan.

Kaufman, A.S. 1979: *Intelligence testing with the WISC-R*. New York: John Wiley.

Sattler, J.M. 1974: *Assessment of children's intelligence*. Philadelphia: W.B. Saunders.

Whorf, Benjamin Lee (1897–1941) Studied chemistry at the Massachusetts Institute of Technology and worked in the chemical and insurance industries for most of his life. Whorf became a student of the famous anthropologist and linguist Edward Sapir, and lecturer in anthropology at Yale University in 1937.

Whorf is best known for his views on the relationship between language and thought. According to the Sapir-Whorf hypothesis of linguistic relativity, people are not led to the same picture of reality unless their language backgrounds are the same. This view was acceptable in the structuralist period of linguistics but is in direct conflict with universalist views, such as those held by Chomsky (see CHOMSKY; LANGUAGE ACQUISITION DEVICE).

Evidence which could either confirm or disconfirm Whorf's claims is still very limited. Tests carried out by Carrol and Casagrande (1958) indicate that grammar can influence behavior under certain conditions. Recent developments in Whorfian linguistics are discussed in Pinxten (1976) and Kay and Kempton (1984). Whorf's theory about the limitations imposed by language has come under severe attack, especially in studies which show little effect of color-language on color-perception (e.g. Heider 1972). Some studies, however, have shown that language can affect some aspects of color matching (see Kay and Kempton 1984). PM

Bibliography

Carrol, John B. and Casagrande, Joseph B. 1958: The function of language classification in behavior. In *Readings in social psychology*, eds. E.E. Maccoby et al. New York: Holt, Rinehart and Winston.

Heider, E.R. 1972: Universals in color naming and memory. *Journal of experimental psychology* 93, 10–20.

Kay, P. and Kempton, W. 1984: What is the Sapir-Whorf hypothesis? *American anthropologist* 86, 65–79.

Pinxten, Rik ed. 1976: *Universalism versus relativism in language and thought*. The Hague and Paris: Mouton.

Whorf, Benjamin L. 1956: *Language, thought and reality*. Cambridge, Mass.: MIT Press.

Index

The figures in **bold** index the main article on that subject. Columns (designated a & b) are only differentiated where the subject is restricted to one column on any page.